HISTORIC RAILS
AND
FORGOTTEN TRAILS
OF EARLY GEORGIA

By R. Olin Jackson III
B.A., M.Ed.

Published by Whippoorwill Publications, LLC
Woodstock, GA 30189

ISBNs: 979-8-9900211-7-4 (pbk); 979-8-9900211-6-7 (hc); 979-8-9900211-5-0 (jkt)
Library of Congress Control Number 2024924266

Publisher's Cataloging-in-Publication Data
provided by Five Rainbows Cataloging Services
Names: : Jackson, R. Olin, III, 1951- author.
Title: Historic rails and Forgotten trails of early Georgia : subtitle / R. Olin Jackson, III.
Description: Woodstock, GA : Whippoorwill Publications, 2025. | Includes index.
Identifiers: LCCN 2024924266 (print) | ISBN 979-8-9900211-5-0 (hardcover : dust jacket) |
    ISBN 979-8-9900211-6-7 (hardcover : laminated) | ISBN 979-8-9900211-7-4 (paperback)
Subjects: LCSH: Georgia—History. | Alabama—History. | Roads—Georgia. | Names,
    Geographical—Georgia. | Indians of North America—History. | BISAC: HISTORY /
    United States / State & Local / South (AL, AR, FL, GA, KY, LA, MS, NC, SC, TN, VA, WV) |
    HISTORY / Indigenous / General.
Classification: LCC F289 .J33 2025 (print) | DDC 975.8/02—dc23.

*Pictured on the cover is a period locomotive on the now historic and long-departed Tallulah
Falls (TF) Railroad just south of the Clayton depot in northeast Georgia. In 1955, Walt Disney
Productions was using this engine - which had been transported all the way from Hollywood,
California - on the TF in the filming of the major motion picture "The Great Locomotive Chase."
One of the primary reasons for the ultimate failure of this fabled rail line was the exorbitant cost
associated with the constant maintenance of its many trestles.*

*Copies of Whippoorwill Publications, LLC books are available online at Amazon.com,
BarnesandNoble.com, IngramSpark.com, and other fine booksellers.*

For more information please visit www.georgiahistorytraveler.com

Author of:

A North Georgia Journal of History, Volumes I – IV
Georgia Backroads Traveler
Moonshine, Murder, & Mayhem in Georgia
Mystery & History in Georgia, Volumes I & II
Some Genealogy Keys to Some Georgia Family Trees
Memories of Army Life and MPs of the 529th
John Henry "Doc" Holliday: A Simple Matter of Survival
Gunmen, Lawmen, & Wild Men of Early Georgia
After All That We've Been Through

Table of Contents

Hall County

Lumpkin County

Monroe County

North Georgia

Paulding County

Polk County

Rabun County

Spalding County

Stephens County

Union County

Walker County

White County

Whitfield County

Historic Rails & Forgotten Trails of Early Georgia

Modern travelers moving across the state of Georgia today often encounter street and road signs for an avenue called *"Old Alabama Road"* in Gwinnett, Fulton, Bartow and numerous others counties. Other travelers in White, Union and adjacent counties in those areas occasionally pass by road signage for historic routes called *"the Unicoi Turnpike"* and *"the Logan Turnpike."* Still others passing across Hall, Forsyth, and counties in that realm often come across a pike called *"Old Federal Road."* Unbeknownst to most all of these "modern" travelers, these *"Turnpikes"* and *"Old Roads"* were the original routes used by pioneer settlers as they moved across the virgin forests and untamed wilderness which was fast becoming the state of Georgia. Remnants of these original westward trails can still be witnessed and experienced in numerous localities if one wishes to seek them out.

There likewise are numerous forgotten and abandoned rail lines throughout the state of Georgia dating as far back as pioneer days. Remnants of these historic holdovers can also still be seen, as can portions of their rolling stock and aged forgotten depots. Entertainment abounds for one who is willing to take the time to search out these historic vestiges of yesteryear. A few examples include the *Western & Atlantic Railroad*, which dates to Civil War days and still exists from Atlanta to Chattanooga, owned today by the state of Georgia; the *Western & Macon Railroad*, remnants of which also still exist and on which such famed individuals as Georgia native John Henry "Doc" Holliday and others once traveled; and the list goes on and on.

Today's modern travelers who venture to various destinations in the continental United States or elsewhere in the world do so via comfortable dependable air-conditioned automobiles, rail, or modern air transportation, safe from wildlife, blazing heat, freezing coldness, rain, snow, sleet and storms – pretty much anything which might be considered "uncomfortable" or "dangerous." These travelers overnight worry-free in care-free accommodations with delicious food instantly prepared for them, basically existing in a cocoon of safety, pleasure and well-being. In this

> *Remnants of these original westward trails can still be witnessed and experienced in numerous localities if one wishes to seek them out.*

and other respects, modern man has no concept of the great fortune he or she enjoys – but 200 or 300 years from today's date, still more "modern" men and women no doubt will be making the same claim about today's travelers.

Nevertheless, in the 18th and 19th centuries, immigrants from Europe and elsewhere trekked across what today is the United States on foot, by covered wagon, stagecoach, and the railroad, in all manner of good and inclement weather. Those on foot or in covered wagons had no option for food or drink other than that which could be obtained, killed, cooked and eaten along the trail, fighting off or avoiding, in the process, hostile Native Americans, vicious wildlife, disease, and countless other hazards of that day.

Modern ground-travelers also have benefit of an excellent highway system and/or rail transportation with constant directional signage and all the conveniences and comforts one might imagine along the way. Pioneer settlers fought their way through an almost impenetrable wilderness with nothing to guide them except the sun and other "natural" signs by day and the stars by night. They had no professionally-built roads, highways or interstates, and certainly no signage to keep them headed in the correct direction unless they were fortunate enough to be traveling by rail

to the few destinations reachable by rail in pioneer days.

In the earliest days, these hardy pioneer adventurers many times simply followed Native American or wild game trails in their westward migrations, knowing not the specific destination until they reached it, basically seeking a new home and life which would allow them to escape their previously-unacceptable circumstances in a previously-unacceptable land. Their primary goals were "free land," "freedom from oppressors and excess 'taxation without representation,'" and, in general, merely a "fresh start."

Early cloven-hoofed animals such as elk, bison, deer, antelope and the like traveled seasonally to new forage opportunities, and in their migrations, they invariably followed the routes of least resistance around the endless hills and through passes in the mountainsides, and across the countless streams, creeks and rivers they encountered. Native Americans later adopted many of these same game trails for their own use and improved upon them directionally, traveling more horizontally or vertically across great distances to trade with and wage war against other aboriginals.

When first they arrived on the continent of what later became "America," European and other immigrants settled primarily in the coastal regions of the American continent. As the years passed and their numbers increased, pioneer Americans gradually began venturing inland. As they did, they too adopted the game and Native American trails, widening them into rough horse and cart trails.

The earliest of the pioneer immigrants were initially confronted with the great barrier of the Appalachian Mountain Range, and were forced to migrate southward down the continental eastern seaboard of what later became the states of Pennsylvania, Maryland, Virginia, North Carolina and South Carolina before reaching Georgia, where they were finally able to turn westward – having circumvented the huge Appalachian obstacle – and travel inland. These inland routes began, as described, as the game and Native American trails but eventually assumed other identities – more often than not known as "the Alabama Roads," or "the Unicoi Turnpike," or "the Logan Turnpike," or "the Federal Road," and numerous other names.

All along these early routes, toll roads, inns and ferries eventually were established, first by enterprising upwardly-mobile Cherokee Indians determined to "assimilate" with the White hoards invading their country, and later by pioneers, who eventually took the land from the Cherokees. Throughout the

length of these travel routes, "life" – with all of its adventures, successes, failures, joys and tragedies – occurred with a vengeance.

The immigrants who settled this country or the Native Americans who were the original claimants, carved out a life in the virgin forests comprising this previously-untouched frontier. The stories which follow document the early pioneer trails and the subsequent ribbons of rail which were eventually developed across this trackless wilderness to facilitate travel to what for the pioneers would be free land and a life unburdened by the religious and social shackles of their oppressors in Europe and elsewhere.

These accounts take the reader down these early travel routes – from the easternmost portions of Georgia and on across the state – to describe the life which existed all along the way. These roads ultimately were used for everything from the death and destruction of the U.S. Civil War to the joy and happiness of wonderful getaway resorts in the north Georgia mountains. The 37 captivating articles with abundant period photographs on the pages which follow provide vivid accounts of these trails and rails and the people who experienced them. This then is the story of the *Historic Rails & Forgotten Trails of Early Georgia.*

The immigrants who settled this country or the Native Americans who were the original claimants, carved out a life in the virgin forests comprising this previously-untouched frontier.

Western & Atlantic Railroad Vital To Both Union and Confederacy

It is often missed as a travel destination by those seeking historic U.S. Civil War battle sites, and Allatoona Pass on the historic Western & Atlantic Railroad near present-day Cartersville was one of the bloodiest of the war. This battlefield, on a historically-preserved section of the old grade of the Western & Atlantic Railroad, offers not only a scenic hiking trail today, but a unique glimpse of a battlefield where the Blue and Gray fought not once, but several times in the struggle to control this strategic rail line.

Visitors to Allatoona Pass today are immediately struck by the immenseness of the bluffs on each side of the road-bed where the trains of the Western & Atlantic Railroad once sped back and forth through this unusual break in the mountains. And following a visit to the site, it is also very easy to understand why it was so important, and why the Confederate Army – though severely outnumbered by this point, starving, and bereft of munitions – was so willing to fight for it not once, but several times.

On a "hazy drowsy Indian summer day" of October 5, 1864, two huge armies met in fierce engagement over the battlements which once made up Allatoona Pass. Though the "steel ribbons" of rail are gone today, the 100-foot long 65-foot-deep dug-out gulch still bisects the Allatoona Mountain Range.

It is quiet today, but approximately 160 years ago (as of 2025), it was a strategic spot at which a railroad could descend from the uplands of northwest Georgia down into the flatter country southward toward Atlanta. It was a strategic site deemed worthy of pursuit – time and again – in battle, because it was the only such railroad from the north into Georgia at that time, and as such, it was the sole method of re-supplying the weary troops engaged in battle to the south.

This once-vital link through the pass is little more than a dirt trail today, and it is difficult to even imagine how manual labor was able to dig such a gap to allow trains to navigate this pass. The silence and peacefulness of this site today belie its bloody history.

Most all of the casualties in the battles here were eventually removed to burial sites in Marietta, but for years after the war, bodies were still being found. Some were buried along the railroad. Some were buried around the one or two homes near the pass that survived the battle. The Union armies often enjoyed what they apparently felt was the diminishment of homes in the South by excavating the yards in front and to the rear to bury the war dead.

One such historic edifice – the Clayton House – has been owned by several generations of the Mooney family in more recent years. It is a two-story clapboard residence across Old Allatoona Road from the pass. John Clayton, one of the original Bartow County settlers, is believed to have been a wealthy miner.

Mr. Clayton built this home in the 1830s, at a time when most local dwellers could afford little more than rustic log cabins. The Cherokee Indians still resided in the region and it was as yet a wild and untamed wilderness. After surviving those hard times, Mr. Clayton died one month after the battle, reportedly at least partly as a result of the shock of the incident.

Battle Scars

From May through October of 1864, the Clayton House served as a headquarters for the Union Army in this vicinity, but during the battle, the house at one time or another, served both sides as a hospital, such was the fierceness of combat and shifting nature of this battlefield.

Today, bullet holes are still visible in the upstairs walls, as is a dark blotch on one floor that is believed to be blood which soaked into the porous pine as a result of the many surgeries which took place in the home. In earlier days, new owners of such a home would have repaired and covered-over such blemishes, but today, ironically, they actually add value to a home. The Mooneys, however, preserve them solely in the memory of those who died.

A white marble marker in the front yard of the home commemorates the battle and the men who died here. With the help of a U.S. Army Corps of Engineers

The Mooney family, owners of the Clayton-Mooney home at Allatoona Pass were photographed in 1994. The graves of 21 unknown soldiers who died at the *Battle of Allatoona Pass* were buried in the yard to the rear of the historic home (pictured). (Photo by R. Olin Jackson)

archaeologist, the Mooneys have located the graves of 21 unknown soldiers buried in their backyard.

In addition to the importance of the railroad through this pass in 1864, a dusty trail through the mountains which passed by the Mooney home also represented the rustic byway for foot and cart traffic from Kingston to Marietta and then on to Atlanta, so it was vital as well.

On his zig-zag march southward in early June of that year, Gen. William T. Sherman sought a depot where supplies could be safely stockpiled for the remainder of the Atlanta campaign. He selected Allatoona Pass and ordered that forts be built on either side of the pass to protect these supplies.

Log stockades with abatis (obstacles formed of trees – their tips cut into a point – felled toward the enemy), thickly-laced

3

Photographed shortly after the initial battle at *Allatoona Pass*, this view shows one of the forts at the north end of the pass. Battlements were built above the pass on both sides. The individuals pictured are unknown. (Photo by George N. Bernard, Photographic Images of Sherman's Campaign)

with telegraph wire, and outer rows of trenches, protected the forts. Even with overwhelming troop numbers in their favor (which was a rarity for the Confederate army) in this engagement, still the men in gray struggled on this day to gain control of the strategic site.

In the fall of 1864, the village (which took its identity from nearby Allatoona Creek named by the Cherokee Indians which once had resided in the area) located at the south end of the cut included eight merchant shops, eight homes, a railroad depot, and several large new warehouses for the storage of large quantities of rations of hardtack stockpiled by Sherman.

Interestingly, 9,000 head of cattle also grazed nearby beside the Etowah River near Emerson. Today, very little remains of the former community of Allatoona Pass, the railroad station long gone, and the dirt road having been long ago circumvented by a more direct and finer U.S. Highway 41 – and still later by the large new and more modern

Interstate 75 which overtook the usefulness of Highway 41.

The Battle Begins

In 1864, after Atlanta had fallen, federal supply troops returned to Allatoona Pass to retrieve the stores of hardtack which would be needed to feed the hungry soldiers continuing on the remainder of Sherman's *"March to the Sea."* The railroad from Atlanta, southward, had been destroyed at several places – again, by both the Union and Confederate forces at differing times, depending upon who controlled the area at what time. The Confederate Army obviously wanted to eliminate – or at least delay – any Federal re-supply of their troops, since any army "travels on its stomach."

To eliminate the railroad supply line, Confederate Lt. Gen. John G. Hood sent Maj. Gen. S.G. French with approximately 2,500 men to capture Allatoona Pass and "to fill up the deep cut at Allatoona with logs, brush, dirt, and debris, etc." to forbid access by trains.

Photographed several weeks after the *Battle of Allatoona Pass*, the forts atop the pass are faintly visible in the distance. The Allatoona Depot (center) and the Clayton House (left) are pictured. The Clayton House is the only structure from this time-period still standing today. (Photo by George N. Bernard, Photographic Images of Sherman's Campaign)

Hood obviously hoped to deny Sherman the use of this portion of the Western & Atlantic Railroad.

In the midst of an autumn downpour, Gen. French and his men left Big Shanty (present-day Kennesaw, GA) and trudged up the railroad through Acworth and across Allatoona Creek. It is important to understand that, despite all the myriad and multiple roads, highways, and even pig-trails which exist today in north Georgia, in 1864, there were virtually none whatsoever, so the army which controlled the one or two roads – and the railroad – controlled the war in Georgia.

At 7:00 a.m., French's artillery commenced firing upon the federal guns at Allatoona which returned the fire.

French then sent in a courier with the following message for Gen. John M. Corse (who had recently hurried down from Rome with 1,054 men to reinforce the already strong garrison at Allatoona Pass): *"I have placed the forces under my command in such positions that you are surrounded, and to avoid a needless effusion of blood, I call on you to surrender your forces at once."*

Corse reportedly replied: *"Your communication demanding surrender of my command I acknowledge receipt of, and respectfully reply that we are prepared for the 'needless effusion of blood' whenever it is agreeable with you."*

French later claimed he never received the reply, and the fighting resumed. With bloodcurdling screams, Confederates leaped from the forest surrounding the fort and charged forward. Corse later wrote that *"a solid mass of gray advanced from the woods and started up the hill, with artillery support from the rear."*

Men were killed steadily in hand-to-hand combat, using bayonets and swords to stab and slash, and rifles and even rocks to club and crush. The federals fired their repeating rifles so rapidly that they became too hot to hold.

Bloody Engagement – Major-General S.G. French was the commander in charge of Confederate forces at the *Battle of Allatoona Pass*. Despite the fact that his losses were considerably less than were those of the Union troops defending the Pass, French later declared that the assault was so sanguinary (bloody) that the attack should not have been made.

In the end, French realized he would be unable to accomplish his mission – that of interrupting and damaging the rail line at Allatoona Pass. Midway through the afternoon, French reluctantly ordered his troops to retire – the intense abatis and other defensive measures around the Pass coupled with the Federals' repeating arms simply too much for the war-weary Confederates with single-shot muskets to overcome.

In seven hours of fighting, 1,505 men – nearly one-third of the 5,000 engaged – were killed or wounded. French reportedly lost 700 men, but the up-hill fighting Confederates were still able to bring a greater number of casualties to Corse. Nevertheless, records seem to indicate it was unsuccessful French who was the most regretful.

"History will record the Battle of Allatoona Pass as one of the most sanguinary of the war," he wrote in a communique. In his postwar book, **Two Wars**, French bitterly recalled Allatoona as a mistake. *"It was Hood's ignorance of the enemy's position that caused the battle; it should never have been made."*

Both Sides Now

As suggested above, Allatoona Pass had been strategically contested by both Union and Confederate forces at various times of the war. It was through this same Allatoona Pass that James J. Andrews, a contraband merchant and spy, and his coterie of raiders sped on April 12, 1862, having just hijacked the *General*, Engine #3 from Big Shanty Station in Kennesaw.

"With a full head of steam, the locomotive, tender and three boxcars raced from Big Shanty, beginning what is often said to have been the most daring American railroad adventure ever attempted," wrote Joe F. Head in the March, 1994 issue of the **Etowah Valley Historical Society**'s newsletter – a rather flowery description of Andrews' abortive effort.

Andrews' objective, ironically enough, was to burn bridges and destroy as much of the railroad as possible – but this time, it was being done so that *Confederate* troops wouldn't be able to use the line for supplies. The destruction would have more quickly enabled Union troops to advance upon Chattanooga, and would have prevented Confederate troops in Atlanta from moving northward to defend against the invading Yankees, but it essentially was a fruitless effort.

After speeding past Hugo – a wood and water stop in Bartow County – the train with Andrews and his raiders went past the Clayton House and hurtled

Harper's Weekly magazine depicted the assault of the strategic *Allatoona Pass on the Western & Atlantic Railroad (W&A)* north of Marietta, Georgia, by Major-General S.G. French's Confederate forces in 1864. The pass was controlled by both Federal and Confederate troops at varying points in 1864 and the *W&A* was vital as the only supply route available through Georgia for Gen. William Sherman's Union forces as they wrought destruction across the state that year.

onward into Allatoona Pass. Not too far behind, William A. Fuller, conductor of the *General*, and fellow Confederates, pursued hotly. When the engine ran low on fuel in Ringgold near the Tennessee state line, Andrews abandoned it, and he and most of his men were captured shortly thereafter, and many of them shot as spies – including Andrews himself.

Unknown Grave(s)

As would be expected with a battle-field of this nature, there ultimately were numerous burials on the spot as bodies – which began decaying quickly in the summer heat – could not be removed in time for burial in established cemeteries. As such, it was not uncommon for the dead to be buried near where they fell.

Today, approximately one-half mile south of the entrance to Allatoona Pass, the body of an unknown soldier was buried – shortly after the battle – in quiet repose beside the railroad bed. Over the years, more than one explanation has gained traction to explain sites such as this.

One story maintains the remains in this grave are those of a young man whose lifeless body was being shipped home by rail in a box labeled simply as "Allatoona, Georgia." The container – which by that point had been traveling on the rails for several days – was understandably very ripe. It reportedly showed no origin of the body, nor identification.

As the story goes – and to their credit if true – six young women took over a job normally reserved for the men,

7

Posing shamelessly for the photographer, Gen. William T. Sherman, commander of the Union forces marching upon Atlanta, needed the supply of hardtack stored at the depot at *Allatoona Pass* - no matter how rotted and spoiled it might be - to feed the Union troops. Though his men were far better armed, much more numerous, better equipped and better fed, they failed repeatedly to penetrate the Confederate lines, and suffered far worse losses than did the Confederate forces defending Atlanta. In order to achieve the Atlanta objective, he was forced time and again to perform flanking actions around the Confederate forces who, since they were a smaller force, had no choice but to fall back time and time again toward Atlanta.

who by that point in the war were in short supply.

In what could only be interpreted as an attempt to ascertain identity, the women bravely pried off the lid of the box with a crowbar. Inside, they reportedly found only a young man dressed in Confederate grey. With him lay a

rolled-up, broad-brimmed black hat, but nothing else.

The women reportedly reattached the top to the box – with several if not all of them no doubt retching in the process – then collected themselves and dug a grave, placing a crude marker upon it to mark it for posterity.

In the 1940s, when Allatoona Dam was being constructed, the gravesite would have been buried beneath the waters of the lake rising behind the dam. As a result, the body reportedly was exhumed and then reburied a short distance from the original site, reportedly so that the gravesite could be respectfully maintained by the railroad's maintenance crew.

Even that effort, however, proved to be in vain, since the railroad line itself was also relocated sometime later to accommodate the lake construction, leaving the lonely grave in an abandoned field – known only to God. In 1980, a group of surveyors reportedly erected a gravestone at the site.

Some people today disagree with the above story of the origin of the body in the grave – including Acworth resident Don Armstrong. He maintains that his grandfather – John Armstrong – who was a carpenter, came from North Carolina after the war and built the aged brick building – which once was a general store – just south of the Clayton House in Allatoona. Armstrong says he grew up listening to old soldiers talking around a pot-bellied stove in the old store, and from their comments, he believes that a more accurate explanation would be that workers – no doubt clearing the line of debris, etc. to reactivate the line – found the body of a soldier along the tracks and simply buried it where they found it – end of story.

Yet another explanation for the

An artist's rendering in **Harper's Weekly** magazine of a Union Army cavalry detachment probing methods of attacking and re-taking the strategic Allatoona Pass on the *Western & Atlantic Railroad* outside Marietta, Georgia, in 1864.

identity of the body in the gravesite has been offered by Robert White, former stationmaster of the Cartersville, Georgia Depot, and the late Colonel Thomas Spencer, a journalist and historian. According to these two men, there are <u>two</u> unknown graves at Allatoona Pass, not merely one, and the bodies were originally buried on opposite sides of the former track bed.

According to Etowah Valley Historical Society member Joe Head who researched the information from these two gentlemen, *"the lesser-known grave site lies within the pass on the east side of the original track bed and has no marker. It is assumed that this Confederate soldier was buried a few days after the battle* (quite possibly the same burial as the one associated above with the women of Allatoona)."

The Abernathy family (relatives of Head) of Cartersville is credited by Head with this lesser-known burial. Unfortunately, the location of this grave is virtually unknown today, because it has not been maintained by the railroad and the vicinity of the grave was repeatedly disturbed by relic hunters prior to the establishment and protection of a park at the site.

Head says the second and more visible grave (near the northern entrance of the pass and a few feet west of the tracks) was dug for *another* soldier who died in the battle.

"Local historians believe this is the grave site of Private Andrew Jackson Houston of the 135th Mississippi Regiment who fell during the Battle of Allatoona," he recorded. *"In 1950, the railroad relocated and marked this grave approximately one-half mile south of the pass and a few yards west of the existing tracks."* This grave is maintained today by area residents, and is the best-known of a number of unknown solder graves in the area.

Finally, in his publication entitled *The Western & Atlantic Railroad / Marietta: The Gem City Of Georgia*, former Georgia Governor Joseph Emerson Brown, an ardent student of history – and

Revisiting the Battlefield – Several years after the conclusion of the U.S. Civil War, Gen. John M. Corse (in white top-hat) returned to Allatoona Pass with *Western & Atlantic Railroad* officials to revisit the site of the battle described as one of the bloodiest of the war.

in particular the history of the Western & Atlantic Railroad – wrote a description of this soldier's gravesite in 1887.

"The most characteristic memorial of this bloody and famous struggle which now salutes the eye of the tourist, as the train darts through the deep, fern-lined (Allatoona) pass, is a lone grave at its northwestern end, immediately by the track, on the west side. This is the resting-place of a Confederate soldier, who was buried on the spot where he fell. For years past, the trackhands of the Western & Atlantic Railroad have held this grave under their special charge... A neat marble headstone has been placed there on which is the following inscription: An Unknown Hero. He Died For The Cause He Thought Was Right."

To Reach Allatoona Pass

Allatoona Pass is one hour north of Atlanta off Interstate 75. Just before reaching the Cartersville, Georgia exit, take the Emerson-Allatoona Road exit and head east, continuing for one and one-half miles. Signs direct visitors to the pass which is bordered by Lake Allatoona.

At the time of this writing, energetic sight-seers could still climb to the top of the pass to gain a first-hand look at the old forts which are still partially discernable at the site. The U.S. Army Corps of Engineers has opened the pass as a historical hiking trail, with paths, parking and signage.

Those who would disturb this site seeking relics, however, are strongly warned in advance. With federal park designation, anyone caught violating the site or using it for purposes other than that for which it is intended will be chancing a very serious fine, if not worse.

Living and Dying by the Railroad at Kingston

It began as a stagecoach stop at a refreshing mountain spring. Later, when the new Western & Atlantic Railroad was routed through the site, the town of "Kingston" sprang up – named for the railroad's founder. For many years, it blossomed as a vital mercantile center – until the U.S. Civil War reached its doorstep. Today, it barely survives as little more than a ghost-town.

One would not know it today, but the tiny burg of Kingston, Georgia, was once a thriving up-and-coming community with at least 40 commercial businesses, four substantial hotels, and commerce growing by the day. Its earliest days were characterized by travelers on a pioneer stage route to what then was considered a summer resort at a sparkling mountain spring, but its real growth occurred when the newly-chartered Western & Atlantic Railroad (W&A) was routed through the site. It even gained its name from the rail line's original president and financier – John Pendleton King.

Construction of the W&A had begun in March of 1838, and by 1845, it had reached Kingston. Since it was routed well beyond the confines of the important community of Rome, yet another rail development – the Rome Railroad – was constructed between Kingston and that city in order that its important commerce not be inhibited.

There sadly are no historic railroad buildings still extant in Kingston today. A fellow by the name of Sherman made certain of that. However, the remains of the former depot and the former rail yard's right-of-way can still be seen as of this writing (2025).

Among other commodities, it was the iron ore deposits and the sea of white cotton which ultimately provided the impetus for much of the growth of Kingston... and grow it did. Hotels and businesses seemingly sprang up overnight.

Kingston is perhaps most famous for its role in the April 12, 1862 *"Great Locomotive Chase,"* when Union Army spies and raiders organized by James J. Andrews were stranded in the yard for 64 minutes waiting for southbound freights to pass during the U.S. Civil War. If not for the lengthy delay suffered at this site which allowed the party pursuing the raiders to dramatically close the gap separating them on the line, the incident with Andrews and his men might have turned out quite differently – possibly even with

KINGSTON, GEORGIA.

Strategic Rails – Both Confederate and Union forces controlled Kingston at different times during the U.S. Civil War. The community was considered a strategic site on the *Western & Atlantic (W&A) Railroad*. The sketch above, showing the branching Rome Railroad off the W&A, was published in **Harper's Weekly** magazine on July 2, 1864.

the complete destruction of numerous bridges and trestles along the Western & Atlantic – not that it really made any difference in the final analysis. A fellow named Sherman made certain of that too.

Today, the former rail yard is still noticeable and a majority of the area is a public park. Two historical markers recognize the Rome Railroad and the city's role in the Andrews Raid.

Kingston's commerce was altered dramatically in 1943, when the Rome Railroad ceased its passenger service and the tracks were abandoned. Passenger service on the Western & Atlantic Railroad continued to decline in the 1950s, and ultimately ceased completely – leased by that time by the Louisville & Nashville Railroad.

Despite the decline, the significance of the railroad to post-Civil War Kingston had been significant. Prior to that time, trains would stop at the downtown railyard and passengers and crews alike would pause to conduct commerce in the numerous shops and businesses.

Churches in the community were also an important segment of life. Fame came to some of the ministers of these churches ... Church-goers from as far away as Atlanta would often take an excursion train to Kingston just to hear some of these men of God speak.

Today, CSX operates trains along the tracks and through Kingston. Dozens of trains still pass through town, but none of them stop – or even pause – any longer, speeding on through to more important destinations.

At the time of this writing in 2025, trees literally were growing through the deteriorating roofs that once sheltered some of the businesses in the old downtown area. The brick walls of some of the buildings are crumbling, and the only things that now thrive there are the honeysuckle and morning glories.

Mrs. Mary Lee Harper witnessed the tide turning. In 1930, she came to Kingston from Rome as a bride when she "married a Kingston boy."

"I remember when Kingston was hot – people coming and going all the time," she explained in an interview in 1992, with sadness in her voice. *"It's dead now though – pitiful really.*

"Used to be we'd come to town about every day to see the trains and to be seen," she smiled. *"Things gradually changed*

Kingston was born as a site on the *Western & Atlantic Railroad*, and as rail passenger service diminished, so also did the commerce of the community. The historic town, however, includes some 18 buildings and sites listed on the ***National Register of Historic Places.***

though, and now there's no reason even to go downtown."

Indeed, Railroad Street in the sparsely-populated community appears almost totally abandoned as of this writing. No one seeks a seat in the local barber's chair, nor a room in a hotel, nor a ticket on the next train out of town. No newspaper for the town even exists any longer – the former editors having long-since departed for more commercial climes.

Preserving The Past

There would probably be nothing left of the old downtown district at all were it not for the efforts of a few preservation-minded individuals who have clung stubbornly to the community.

The century-old Desoto Hotel – one of the few original downtown businesses still somewhat intact, is far from the showplace it once represented. Owners have come and gone over

the years. The late Charles Vernon Ayers, a former resident, was successful in steering through the listing of the Desoto in the *National Register of Historic Places.*

When he was mayor of Kingston in the early 1980s, Ayers also designated Railroad Street as a historic district.

He was a railroad and history enthusiast, and once stated the Desoto was built in 1890. It survived a disastrous town fire in 1911, and was well-known for its food in the early part of the century before it was closed in 1947.

Mr. Ayers, sadly, passed away in 2010 at the age of 82, after a short stay at the Cartersville Heights Nursing and Rehab Center.

Born in 1928 in Blue Ridge, Georgia, Ayers was a long-time resident of Bartow County, where he was a former editor of the old ***Bartow Herald***. After moving to Kingston with preservation

Kingston Inn – Photographed in 1900, Railroad Street in Kingston was a muddy thoroughfare. The Kingston Inn (far left) which burned in March of 1911, stood on the site occupied today by the Ranson Mercantile building.

in mind, he was instrumental in prolonging the life of numerous aspects of the faded community while assisting his wife, Helen S. Ayers, in operating a fine antiques shop there for many years.

Today, the abandoned downtown suggests that Kingston is home to many secrets, and no doubt many untold stories. Twelve historic markers are scattered over the town, a testament to the outstanding moments which have transcended the history of this north Georgia community, and no doubt even helped shape the future of a nation. Some 18 buildings and sites in the town are listed in the *National Register of Historic Places* today.

Even before the state of Georgia authorized the building of the W&A Railroad in 1836, businessmen and travelers had journeyed by horseback and stagecoach to Kingston to trade there at the newly-formed cotton market, drink from its delicious freshwater spring and escape the heat and mosquitoes of the state's southern plains.

The U.S. Civil War

Ironically, Kingston's fate was sealed on the day its real growth began – in November of 1849, when the W&A Railroad was completed in Georgia, hailing the state's entrance into the national railroad transportation system connecting the Mississippi River with the Atlantic Ocean. It's location on the rail line made it a natural target for the destruction of the later U.S. Civil War.

The Chattanooga-Atlanta trains regularly stopped in Kingston to take on water, fuel and passengers. With the completion of the Memphis branch railroad from Kingston to Rome in 1850, Kingston became an important distribution point on the W&A, connecting it with the riverboat transportation on the Coosa River. When the terrible war reached the interior of Georgia, Kingston could not be allowed to survive as a town.

Because of this strategic location on the railroad, Kingston became a busy supply and hospital center during the war. In the fall of 1861, so many soldiers in need of care were coming through the town on the railroad that the women of the town established temporary quarters for them in churches, vacant stores and private homes. Several of these homes still exist in good condition today, most notably the Reynolds House, built in 1846 by Benjamin Reynolds, and the home built in 1854 by the author and inventor of the sewing machine - Dr. Francis Robert Goulding.

On two occasions, Kingston took center stage in the unfolding drama of the war, both times sharing the spotlight with famous Civil War generals.

In April of 1862, the aforementioned Andrews Raiders seized the locomotive *General* at Big Shanty (present-day Kennesaw, Georgia) with the intention of taking it to Chattanooga and destroying all the bridges along the length of the route, thus crippling the W&A and the Confederate Army's ability to move soldiers, ammunition and

Railroad Street in Kingston was photographed here in 1991. The corner of the old Masonic Hall is visible (far left). The DeSoto Hotel is visible in the center, and the structure in the distance with the corner entranceway is the former Ranson Mercantile building.

supplies. James Andrews and his men, however, suffered a set-back when they rolled into the busy hub of Kingston on the *General*.

According to James C. Bogle, a leading authority on the *"Great Locomotive Chase"* as historians have dubbed it, Andrews and his men spent a very long and frustrating hour and five minutes in Kingston before they were able to pull out. As explained, the community by this time was a busy commercial center, and delays in access to switch-tracks and supplies were commonplace. It is the consensus of historians that the delay in Kingston caused the raiders' mission to fail.

Another famous general in the Civil War, William T. Sherman of the Union Army, is also forever linked with Kingston. Sherman was headquartered at the Thomas Van Buren Hargis home in Kingston May 19-23, 1864, and returned in November to plan his now-infamous *"March To The Sea."* There were eight separate skirmishes in Kingston during this time, and it was here that Sherman received permission from General Ulysses S. Grant to carry out his fateful destructive march through Atlanta and onward to Savannah.

According to the late Mr. Ayers, the Hargis home burned in 1947, but the field desk that Sherman used while in Kingston survived. It was in Mr. Ayers' possession for many years. Its location today is unknown. "I was aware of its existence for many years," Ayers once stated, "and when the opportunity came to acquire it, I couldn't resist."

As described, Sherman's troops destroyed much of Kingston. The only church remaining after he departed was the Kingston Methodist Church. It opened its doors to all denominations and was also used as a schoolhouse.

When the war ended in 1865, the last remnant of the Confederate Army east of the Mississippi was paroled in

The Desoto (New Kingston) Hotel is pictured here circa 1918. In an effort to "freshen" the image of the DeSoto following World War I, it was renamed the New Kingston Hotel. Then-owner Tom Bryant stands in front.

Kingston. Brig. Gen. William T. Wofford arranged with Brig. Gen. Henry M. Judah, U.S.A. for the surrender of some 3,000 to 4,000 Confederate soldiers, mostly Georgians not paroled in Virginia, North Carolina and elsewhere.

While the Federals and Confederates gathered in Kingston for the surrender, the people of Kingston observed the first Confederate Memorial Day in the nation.

The Ladies Of Kingston

Local folklore maintains that in the spring of 1865, the ladies of the town wanted to use the "profusion of spring flowers" to decorate the soldiers' graves. As outrageous as it may seem today, in order to achieve this humble task these ladies were first required to seek the consent of the Union Army commandant of the area. The identity of this officer is unknown today, but he reportedly assented to this request with one stipulation - that the ladies decorate all graves, Southern and Federal alike.

At that time, there were more than 275 Confederates and many Federals buried in the Kingston cemetery, but some have since been removed. Today, there are 249 unknown Confederate graves, one known Confederate, and two unknown Federals buried at the spot.

The tradition of honoring the men who died in and around Kingston during the Civil War continues today. Each spring, Kingston residents have staunchly observed *Confederate Memorial Day*, due largely to the Woman's History Club there, but their numbers unfortunately have steadily declined.

Founded in 1900 the club began as a monthly afternoon tea, designed primarily for the entertainment of members. They, ironically, have become almost as much a part of the history of Kingston as the history they originally set out to document and preserve.

Old South Beauty – One of the remarkable antebellum homes built in Kingston. This one was constructed by Benjamin Reynolds in 1846.

According to one of the elder members of the organization, the club has provided many services to the town and the state of Georgia over the years, including the maintenance and observance of the Memorial Day celebrations each year without a single lapse.

The Woman's History Club is also responsible for establishing and maintaining the Confederate Memorial Museum of Kingston. Opened in 1971, the museum houses a substantial collection of Confederate artifacts, including swords, bayonets, cannon balls and civil war script money, and is open to the public on special occasions. Other items in the museum include a case of Indian artifacts; the bulletin board, a desk and bench from the Kingston Depot; exhibits on cotton, saltpeter mines, and various other natural resources found in Bartow County.

Remnants Of The Past

Scrap books and photographs attesting to Kingston's prosperity at the turn of the century are also on display. Pages from the *Kingston Times*, a newspaper circulated around 1915, reveal a prospering community with 40 businesses, several banks and hotels. There are also stories about the massive fire of 1911 in the town, and the subsequent rebuilding of the downtown area.

The *Kingston Times* was short-lived, as were Kingston's good times. The community lived – and died – by the railroad, subsequently being stranded and strangled as passenger and even freight service dwindled and died.

Many photographs of the old downtown Railroad Street in Kingston have been meticulously preserved in the museum, and, ironically, many of these same actual downtown buildings still exist, but have been largely neglected. By the 1950s they were on the decline, headed toward abandonment, and an era had ended.

In the more than 72 years (as of 2024) since the town ceased to function as a scheduled stop on the railroad, little has changed in Kingston. Attempts

Unknown Dead – Hallowed graves are honored and decorated each year in Kingston as *Confederate Memorial Day* is observed. There are 249 unknown Confederate graves, two unknown Federal graves, and one known Confederate grave.

to attract industry have failed, and dissension among the community's leaders stymied other efforts for progress. There are still a couple of gas stations and a store or two, but Mr. Ayers and his one-time contemporaries who were once so vital to the preservation efforts are now a part of that history themselves.

In more modern times, Interstate 75 to the east and U.S. Highway 411 to the south both bypassed Kingston. As stated, the rail line is still in active use, but not in a functionary freight or passenger service capacity for the withering town.

Kingston's future

Kingston's future is uncertain at best.

is uncertain at best. The town's fate has been so closely linked with the railroad, it is doubtful it will ever again prosper without the revival of passenger train service.

Perhaps with the resurrection of travel destinations such as nearby Barnsley Gardens (five miles away), and the completion of the new Anheuser-Busch Brewery east of the city, Kingston will obtain some "bleed-off" from travelers to those sites, but locals aren't holding their collective breath.

Whatever the destiny of Kingston, its success or failure may hinge once again upon the railroad.

"Railroaded" At a Community Called "Etowah"

The remnants of a pre-Civil War industrial community which was vital to the development of railroads in the Confederacy, lie wasted and forgotten in the mud of Lake Allatoona. Along the way, several fortunes were made and lost at this site.

The waters of Lake Allatoona near the dam at Georgia Highway 294 North are relatively calm today, as are the forests and woods nearby. There was a time, however – prior to the construction of the lake – when this spot was occupied by a unique achievement in Georgia history. . . .

Resting on the lake bottom are the ruins of a town that, for a brief span of time, was responsible for a remarkable accomplishment in industrial development, particularly for this area of Georgia in the two decades prior to the U.S. Civil War. The town was called "Etowah," an aboriginal place-name of the region, and the railroad played an important role in the development of this town.

At its peak, Etowah was a small community with an impressive 2,000 to 4,000 inhabitants. It was equally impressive as a production center for iron, flour, lumber and iron manufactured goods, all in a self-contained town that even had its own railroad. No other such town had existed in Georgia prior to the Civil War. Today, this community has, for all intents and purposes, been forgotten by historians due to its present-day lake-bottom location.

The story of Etowah is especially unusual because the town was not the

Entrepreneurial Spirit – Mark Anthony Cooper was a major developer of the mills and community of Etowah, Georgia. He eventually sold his holdings there for several hundred thousand dollars - more than enough upon which to retire. However, following the sale, he unfortunately invested heavily in the Confederate States of America, and at war's end, found himself destitute.

product of some far-fetched manufacturing tycoon. The opportunities for mining and manufacturing in this area prior to Etowah's development had been well-known, even before the native Indians were forced from their north Georgia homeland. However, the state of Georgia, coasting along on an agrarian

Etowah, Georgia – The township of Etowah had grown into a vibrant industrial village by the mid-1800s. As a result, a number of commercial enterprises had taken up business in the town. Among them were a bank, a hotel, a four-story flour mill, and a brewery. This picture-postcard from the early 1900s shows the ruins of the bank at Etowah which was burned in 1864 by contingents of federal troops. Due to the production at Etowah of rails and spikes for the South's railroads, it was a major target for destruction by Gen. William T. Sherman and his Union Army. By war's end, the town had been completely destroyed. (Photo courtesy of the GA Dept. of Archives & History, Atlanta)

economic system, did little to develop the region's abundant resources of water-power, iron, gold, copper, talc, coal, marble and slate. The manufacturing realm of the young United States belonged to the factories and commercial enterprises of New England and the businessmen north of the Mason-Dixon Line.

Even in the early years of the South, however, there were maverick commercial pioneers. One such gambler was Jacob Stroup, (1771-1846) who had built iron furnaces in the Carolinas prior to starting another in Habersham County, Georgia, in 1832.

In 1836, Stroup expanded, building the first furnace in what today is Bartow County, Georgia. This small factory for purification of the local iron ore into the

pig iron used in more refined manufacturing endeavors, was adjoined by a sawmill, gristmill, and 1,300 acres of timber and mineral-rich land which formed the nucleus for the thriving township known as Etowah.

In 1842, Jacob sold out to his son Moses, who that same year, sold a half interest in the property to one Mark Anthony Cooper (1800-1885) who would shortly prove to be the brain trust behind the eventual expanded development of Etowah.

Cooper had lived through a litany of successful careers, only to be thwarted each time from reaping the true rewards of his hard work. He built one of Georgia's early cotton factories and had been a banker in Columbus, Georgia; a major in the fledgling United States Army fighting in the Seminole War of 1836; and a Georgia congressman. After a narrow defeat in a race for the Georgia governorship in 1843, he retired to the peace of a Murray County, Georgia farm.

While campaigning for the gubernatorial race in north Georgia however, Cooper had met the Stroups, and took a fancy to the production of iron. Unable to resist the lure of yet another business opportunity, he decided to give his professional talents yet another chance, and entered into a partnership with Stroup.

Almost immediately, Cooper realized his new-found endeavor faced some serious problems. The iron they were producing cost too much to compete with the iron manufacturers in the North, mainly due to extremely-unfair federal tariffs which eliminated the possibility of trade with Europe and other overseas clients. And in agricultural Georgia, there was practically no demand for the pig-iron because there were no refining facilities for the finished production of iron products.

A Chase for the Ages – The Confederate locomotive **"General"** (pictured), was a participant in what came to be known in history as *"the great locomotive chase."* It was pursued by the **"Yonah,"** which was owned at the time by Mark David Cooper and his *Etowah Railroad.*

Cooper and Stroup soon began developing new uses for the materials and water power at Etowah. In 1844, they abandoned their old furnace entirely, and erected a larger more efficient one capable of making hollowware such as skillets, which, interestingly, *did have a local market* in the South where they were highly desired by the populace and could be sold in abundance.

Two years later, the two men had put a rolling mill into production which was producing much-in-demand railroad tracks and bar-iron. This mill was in operation by 1849, as was their large flour mill which was able to produce up to 300 barrels of flour a day.

By 1859, Etowah also had carpentry shops, a nail and spike factory, a barrel factory, a corn mill, gold and copper mines,

Cooper and Stroup soon began developing new uses for the materials and water power at Etowah.

and 12,000 acres of land in four counties. In that day and time, it was one of the most unlikely enterprises ever undertaken in the north Georgia backwoods, and yet it grew in spite of its logistical drawbacks, simply because its owners had a knack for the production of items which the *local* population would purchase in quantity.

The number of people needed to run these operations grew proportionately. At its peak, the community at Etowah had an international work-force of between 500 and 600 laborers, including some 100 blacks. The employees included miners, furnace workers, mill operators, carpenters, timber cutters, charcoal manufacturers and others.

The thriving little town had a combination school and church; a boarding house, a bank,

Moses and Aaron Stroup settled in Bartow County in the 1830s, and shortly thereafter built furnaces for the extraction of pig iron from ore. The furnace pictured here was built circa 1836 by Jacob Stroup, and was one of the first iron ore furnaces built in Georgia. It was purchased and enlarged circa 1840s by industrialist Mark Anthony Cooper. Its meticulously-laid stone blocks are a beauty in their own right. Workers for Cooper's substantial early industrial complex lived in the adjacent town of Etowah which included approximately 1,200 residents at its height. Cooper's foundry at Etowah manufactured railroad rails and spikes from the pig iron smelted in the furnaces, causing the site to become a primary target of Gen. W.T. Sherman when he invaded Georgia in 1864, but by that point, Cooper had sold his Etowah enterprises to another investor. Etowah also boasted a corn mill, a flour (grist) mill, its own post office, a church, stores, warehouses, and a school house. Today, remnants of Cooper's enterprises – including the immense furnace – at Etowah are maintained as a state park. The remainder of the community lies at the bottom of Lake Allatoona near the lake's dam.

a post office, a brewery, a company store, log houses for the workers and their families – and even a bordello to service the needs of the unmarried men of the community, in order to maintain a peaceful and productive environment. However, despite the fact that it was productive and growing, Etowah, amazingly, was still not a success financially.

Cooper would later claim that the flour mill was profitable, driving all but Georgia-produced flour from the state, but critics claimed he undercut his local competition by selling flour *at cost*. Even more surprisingly, Cooper's iron sales were described as: *"most disastrous, owing to a depression in the trade."*

By most all accounts, despite the successful nature of the overall enterprises in Etowah, the town's industries were steadily losing money.

To finance continued expansion and stave off economic collapse, Cooper and Stroup added a Mr. L. M. Wiley as a partner in the operation. Cooper eventually loaned Stroup money for his share of the extra funds needed for additional expansion, and when Stroup was unable to repay the loan, Cooper assumed Stroup's share of ownership of the business – and the debt.

In 1852, the company's creditors finally forced the commercial endeavor into foreclosure. The two remaining

JS

Civil War-Era Bridge - This photo was, in all likelihood, snapped prior to 1864. The historic *Western & Atlantic Railroad (W&A)* trestle across the Etowah River in Bartow County was a crucial north-south transportation route coveted - and controlled - by both Union and Confederate forces at varying times during the U.S. Civil War. The rails on this trestle were also destroyed and rebuilt by both forces several times as control of the site was traded back and forth. In 1864, in Georgia, there were virtually no roads, and the few rough paths which did exist passed through a trackless wilderness of virgin forests and immense impenetrable undergrowth, so a railroad was an extremely valuable commodity at this time. In earlier times (1840s-1850s) the *Western & Atlantic Railroad* was a vital cog as well in the industrial operations of Mark Anthony Cooper at Etowah. The stone piers of this trestle are still visible in the river today.

partners ultimately bought back the company, but by 1857, Wiley wanted out, and insisted that Cooper buy him out. With money borrowed from friends, Cooper did just that.

Prior to the recovery of his businesses at Etowah, Cooper's life was in a very depressed and deplorable state. Had it not been for the funds lent to him by his friends, the entire endeavor undoubtedly would have simply folded up and gone out of business. For this reason, when his commercial enterprises at Etowah did eventually recover and he was able to repay his friends for the loans they had made to him, he erected a monument in front of his bank to honor those who had stood by him in his hard times.

In 1856, Cooper had formally incorporated the Etowah Manufacturing and Mining Company, and after publishing a map and an illustrated prospectus of the company, he took on another partner by the name of A. Hicks. The operations at Etowah, however, continued to struggle, and Cooper would later claim in his memoirs that the enterprise failed and recovered on three separate occasions.

The new owners of Etowah however, stridently sought an answer to their financial woes through stringent cost-cutting procedures. Cooper therefore acquired coal mines in nearby Dade County, Georgia, to fuel his iron furnaces.

As a politician, Cooper had been instrumental in the creation of the

Civil War Bridge Remnants – These immense stone piers which once supported the tracks of the Western & Atlantic Railroad (photographed here in 1999) still stand in the riverbed of the Etowah River a short distance from the ruins of Mark Cooper's former factories at Etowah. This strategic 620-foot-long span, destroyed by the retreating Confederates in May of 1864, was rebuilt by Union Army engineers in just six days, and then, after its usefulness had expired, was destroyed yet again – this time by Union troops - following Gen. William T. Sherman's departure from Atlanta for Savannah on his infamous *"March To The Sea."* In 1858-'59, Mark Cooper financed a spur line from Etowah to the *Western & Atlantic Railroad*, allowing him to transport his Etowah-produced pig-iron products to market, and to ship in coal to his Etowah mills from his mines in Dade County. (Photo by Dan Roper)

state-owned *Western & Atlantic Railroad* that passed within a few miles of Etowah, and he sought to cut transportation costs at his iron works by bringing the railroad to it. However, in 1857 the state legislature surprisingly rejected his offer of railroad iron made at Etowah's rolling mill in exchange for the state financing of a simple spur track to Etowah.

Undeterred, Cooper financed his own railroad in 1858-1859 – a short line which led directly to the *Western & Atlantic.* He had already incorporated his own railroad company in 1847, and was now well on his way to overcoming the obstacles to success once again.

Interestingly, it was Cooper's locomotive – *"Yonah"* – which was later involved in what came to be known as *"the Great Locomotive Chase"* during the Civil War. Had it not been for the interruption and capture of the spies involved in that raid, the Western & Atlantic might have suffered greatly from the loss of trestles and rolling stock. Due to the assistance provided by the *Yonah*, there ultimately was little to no damage on the line.

Despite all his best efforts however, the nationwide *"Panic of 1857"* severely depressed Cooper's markets, strangling his production efforts once again. By 1860, Etowah was clearly in decline, and Cooper, no doubt *"seeing the handwriting on the wall,"* published a new pamphlet about his Etowah property, probably hoping to sell out.

Interestingly, the onset of the U. S. Civil War soon brought a number of buyers to his doorstep, and in 1862, William T. Quinby and William A. Robinson bought Etowah for a reported $450,000.00 – a tremendous sum at that time (equivalent to approximately $16.8 million in 2024). Quinby and Robinson had been major arms manufacturing dealers before Union forces captured Memphis, Tennessee, taking over their plant there. They saw their investment in Etowah as their ticket back into the war products industry. It was an early example of what would later become known in the world as *"the military-industrial complex."*

After paying his debts, Cooper still had $200,000.00 (the equivalent of approximately $8 million in 2024), which was more than enough to make him wealthy for the rest of his life. As in his other endeavors, however, *"Lady Luck"* simply did not favor Mark Anthony Cooper. He unfortunately invested heavily in the Confederacy, and by the war's end, he, amazingly, had lost his entire fortune.

Since the Etowah mills, town, and furnaces were heavily connected to the production of iron rails for the burgeoning system of railroads in Georgia and the Southeast, they were totally destroyed by Union forces in 1864 by orders of firebrand Gen. William T. Sherman. After the Civil War, the devastated remains of the community were forgotten and overrun by undergrowth and forests. Except for one furnace, the entire site which once represented the town of Etowah now rests undisturbed beneath the murky waters of Lake Allatoona.

Mark Anthony Cooper took credit in his memoirs for a number of firsts in north Georgia, but he apparently never understood the true scope of his achievements at Etowah. Not only did he pioneer industrialization in a state dominated by agriculture ("King Cotton") and monopolistic Northern industrialists, he created an interrelated system of mining, manufacturing and transportation unique in Georgia history.

Cooper's coal mines in northwest Georgia's Dade County provided fuel which was transported on the *Western & Atlantic Railroad* (which he had helped create) to his own railroad for shipment to Etowah. At Etowah, iron was produced from the coal and charcoal, then processed in his water-powered rolling mill, and shipped to the Atlanta Rolling

> *He was also a trustee for Mercer University and the University of Georgia.*

Mill, for further milling and use in the refurbishing of the worn rails of the *Western & Atlantic Railroad.* Interestingly, despite that railroad's early rejection of Cooper's solicitations, he eventually became vital to its continued survival.

Mark Anthony Cooper was also a founder of the South Central Agricultural Society, which encouraged the Georgia manufacture of products for farmers. He joined the state's other leading manufacturers as a trustee for the state's first proposed school of mechanical engineering. He was also a trustee for Mercer University and the University of Georgia.

The career of Mark Anthony Cooper, his industrial community of Etowah, and his acclaim as Georgia's most important early industrialist are all the more fascinating considering the almost happenstance development of his industrial community at Etowah in Bartow County which now lies forgotten at the bottom of a lake.

As with his other careers in banking, the military and politics, Cooper seemed to just "try on" each new profession, to "see if it fit him." More often than not, he accomplished a great deal in the process, and then quietly receded into history.

*[Author's Note: For biographical data on Cooper, see the sketch by James Dorsey in **Dictionary of Georgia Biography**, (1983). Published sources on Etowah and its people include Gregory Jeane's **An Archival and Field Survey . . . Allatoona Lake, Georgia** (1986), and Lucy J. Cunyus' **The History of Bartow County** (1933).]*

The O.D. Anderson Family:

"We Lived In A Railroad Boxcar During The U.S. Civil War"

O.D. Anderson and his family were fated to not only live during the dark days of the U.S. Civil War, but also to be caught in the vortex of the terrible onslaught of General William Tecumseh Sherman's infamous "March to the Sea" through Georgia in 1864. Like many Georgians of that day, they were made of strong stock, and managed to find a way not only to survive, but to persevere in those unbelievably difficult times. One method they used was to live in a railroad boxcar during the darkest days of the war.

The name "Anderson" translates to "son of Andrew." Variant forms of the name include "Anders" and "MacAndrews." The family line originates from Ireland, and usually is of immigrant origin, having been introduced into Ulster Province by settlers and traders who arrived from Scotland and England, especially during the 17th Century, and then later into burgeoning colonial America. The name is particularly common of Scots-Irish settlers in the Pennsylvania and Virginia sections of the 18th Century.

According to records, the line of Andersons from which Oliver Davis Anderson descends – as far back as can be traced by this writer – did in fact originate in Scotland, and prior to that quite likely from an ancient Celtic tribe in pre-history. Beyond the above-quoted possible sources, the O.D. Anderson family ancestors undoubtedly – as did multitudes of early American settlers – simply sought a better life in the New World.

Isaac Anderson was born in 1668, and married *Martha Bell*, born in Ireland in 1703. From them descended *James* (b. 1720, Ireland); James' son, *Robert* (b. 1763, York, PA); Robert's son, *Isaac (the younger)* (b. 1795, Rockbridge Co., VA); and then Isaac's son, *Oliver Davis "O.D."* (b. 04/05/1824 in Maryville, Blount Co., TN). As is obvious, these Andersons "moved around."

Early Life

Isaac Anderson (the younger) moved his family from Tennessee to what soon would become Cassville and Cass County (later incorporated into Bartow County), Georgia, in 1834, when O.D. was still a small boy. Growing up in what then was the American frontier, the Andersons lived among the native Indians (most probably Muscogee or Cherokees) who still claimed ownership of that land and would continue to reside in this vicinity until 1838 when they were forcibly removed in the tragic "Trail of Tears."

O.D., possessing very blond hair, apparently was one of the first – if not the first – fair-haired child witnessed by the native Cherokees there. In later life, after having reached an elder age, O.D. would tell his grandchildren how the Indians had picked him up and carried him about exuberantly upon their shoulders, continuously frightening his mother.

Upon reaching maturity, O.D. married *Amelia Gaines* in 1845, moving to Adairsville to operate a hotel there (1847). He also later entered the mercantile business. O.D. and his young family show up in the *1850 Federal Census* in Cass County, Georgia, where he is listed as *"merchant,"* with real estate valued at $1,000.00, which at that time was at least a modestly-respectable financial portfolio – the equivalent of slightly less than $34,000.00 in 2025 dollars.

Sometime around 1858, O.D. decided to move his family to Arkansas to follow his parents who were migrating westward. Life in the harsh realities of the west, however, apparently did not agree with O.D., though he spent nearly a year there with his family before returning to Georgia.

O.D. next appears in the *1860 Federal Census* of Adairsville, Cass County, Georgia, where he is listed as *"Postmaster."* At the time of the U.S. Civil War, O.D. – in addition to serving as postmaster – was depot agent of the newly-completed Western & Atlantic (W&A) Railroad at Adairsville.

As one might imagine, the W&A was vitally important to the war effort, and O.D.'s job shortly became a very busy post. He was refused service by the regular Confederate Army because he had a defective eye, but he did serve as a member of what was called "the Georgia State Troops," possibly a home-guard unit. It, however, was his talent in the

Oliver Davis Anderson was photographed here in 1902 at the Neel residence on South Avenue in Cartersville, GA. His skills became strategically important in the *W&A Railroad*'s use in the war effort. His family eventually refugeed southward in a railroad boxcar near the war's end.

manipulation and management of railroad rolling stock which shortly was recognized by Confederate authorities and put to use.

As the war progressed, O.D. – in addition to his other responsibilities with the W&A – was kept busy as a purchasing agent, acquiring and shipping supplies for the Confederacy via the railroad. As the battle front moved inexorably southward toward Adairsville in the war's later years, in part naturally following the route of the vital supply line

Strategic Cog – In addition to serving as the Postmaster of Adairsville, O.D. Anderson managed a portion of the *Western & Atlantic Railroad (W&A RR)*. Pictured is the locomotive *"General"* from that era on the *W&A RR*. In 1962, one hundred years after the famed "Great Locomotive Chase," the General went on tour retracing the former route of the incident from Marietta to Ringgold, Georgia. (Photo courtesy of Adairsville History Museum)

of the W&A, it soon became apparent to O.D. that his home was about to be caught within the teeth of the conflict, and he and his family would have no choice but to refugee southward down into Georgia.

Fleeing In A Boxcar

While the *Battle of Resaca* was taking place – where, incidentally, the father (***Capt. Joseph Lockhart Neel***, C.S.A.) of O.D.'s future son-in-law (***James Monroe Neel***) was involved in desperate fighting

– O.D. was preparing his family to flee southward. Due no doubt to his employment with the W&A, and the vital necessity of his professional manipulation of the rail line's Georgia rolling stock in the war effort, O.D. and his family, interestingly, were permitted to have a W&A railroad boxcar for their personal use. They loaded this unique conveyance with household goods and were soon being transported by rail southward toward Atlanta and into the lower reaches of Georgia.

Due no doubt to the severe limitations of space within the confines of the boxcar, O.D.'s young son, James, who is believed to have been approximately 13 years of age at the time, amazingly traveled *on foot* with the family's slaves through what then was the very densely-forested north Georgia countryside. Making this feat even more unbelievable for a youngster of James' age is the fact that north Georgia in the 1860s was a trackless wilderness with virtually no roads whatsoever other than occasional game trails and a few very crude wagon roads, and, of course, travel aids such as road signage – or any directional guidance of any type for a youngster or adult – were nonexistent in those dark days. It is unknown today just how James was able to navigate his way southward and ultimately reach the vicinity of Atlanta, let alone locate his family whose boxcar had been taken eastward from Atlanta to Stone Mountain, Georgia, but locate them he did.

When the Anderson family had reached Atlanta and their boxcar had been sent eastward on the Georgia Railroad – no doubt at the direction of O.D. – the railroad management responsibilities of the family patriarch had required him to chart a course separate from that of his family. While they went east, he went south.

According to family records, after reaching Stone Mountain, the Andersons spent approximately two months on a railroad siding in that small town living within the strict confines of the boxcar. It is unknown by this writer if these circumstances involved freezing winter weather within the boxcar, or the unbearable heat generated by a harsh Georgia summer. Either way, their stark existence under these circumstances is almost unthinkable – but those were

anything but "normal" times, and thousands of war-weary refugees had no roof over their heads whatsoever.

Nevertheless, the Andersons reportedly eventually tired of the harsh environment of their boxcar home, and set out northeastward on foot to Monroe, Georgia, where they somehow obtained a home in that locality – either by renting or squatting. They remained at this location until the raids by Federal troops became so frequent and deadly that they decided to move on once again – no doubt fleeing with retreating Confederate troops – into South Carolina, still amazingly traveling on foot.

After reaching South Carolina and finding the accommodations and options for survival even worse in that realm, Amelia and her children decided to return to Monroe where they remained until the end of the war. The children reportedly even went to a rustic school in Monroe and made many friends there.

Meanwhile, O.D., according to family records and lore, was in South Georgia (quite likely Barnesville), where he continued to manage what remained of the Georgia state railroad rolling stock for the Confederacy – a task at which he apparently had become quite adept – moving it continuously around the state on the rails which remained in existence, keeping as much of it as possible out of the hands of Federal troops. His work in this capacity did not cease – nor did his separation from his family – until the end of the war.

After The War

With the war concluded, both Amelia and her family in Monroe, and O.D. in south Georgia, traveled back across the war-torn, lawless, and devastated Georgia countryside to return to

Pictured is a copy of the *1860 Federal Census for Adairsville / Cass County, Georgia*, with O.D. Anderson's occupation listed as *"Post Master."* The offices and duty of the local postmaster during Civil War times often revolved around the local train depot at which much of the mail for the county/community was received. It was at the Adairsville Depot of the *Western & Atlantic Railroad* at which Anderson became adept at management of the rolling stock on that line in northwest Georgia.

their home in Adairsville to see what – if anything – remained to salvage. It is unknown today how the family members communicated with each other while separated (almost certainly not at all), or what they discovered when they arrived back at their home in Adairsville. No family lore or ancient letter has been discovered which recorded those circumstances for posterity. Suffice it to say that historic records of the war which do exist describe a totally devastated north Georgia, particularly along the route of the Western & Atlantic Railroad which would include their home in Adairsville and present-day Bartow County.

Just as did many others, the Anderson family found shelter of one sort or another, and somehow struggled along, scratching out a meager existence in what was left of a culture literally *"gone with the wind."* O.D. initially attempted to survive by farming, but when that failed, he turned back to something about which he knew a bit more – the mercantile business. Interestingly, it was the same pursuit in the same town as the father (Joseph Lockhart Neel) of his future son-in-law (James Monroe Neel).

O.D. was able to survive within that profession, no doubt due to his many and close relationships with the people of his community. At that point after the war, hard currency was nonexistent in Georgia – or anywhere in the South for that matter – so a system of "barter" took over. Those in need of items of necessity took other items of value to barter for the materials they needed. O.D. and his family survived in this same manner.

Bessie Bevins, one of O.D.'s grandchildren, described him during those days as follows: *"He had many noble characteristics. He was much more intelligent than the average man of his time, and his tiny frame bore a heart of gold. Kind and considerate of everyone, he was a very polite man and a devout Christian."*

Raised as a Presbyterian, O.D. joined the Baptist Church with his wife and was staunch in his belief. He was clerk of Oothcaloga Baptist Church outside Adairsville for many years. A friend once told him he made himself poor feeding preachers. He was a great believer in Sunday school and a faithful attendant for many years.

A description of the life these Georgians were forced to lead in these dark days during and following the war would not do justice to the struggles and horrors they faced. The marauding Union

Armies had pillaged and stolen everything in sight during the months and years of the war. Anything of value was taken – particularly foodstuffs, tools, draft animals, and any valuables which had not been hidden.

After the war, when the Union army had departed, lawlessness – which had already existed in abundance during the war years – descended upon the region with a vengeance. Law enforcement was nonexistent, and the defense of the family and its remaining pitiful possessions fell to the few male heads of household who had survived the war. This task usually fell to the younger males in the family, since most of the older men were either dead or disabled.

As such, life in north Georgia – and most of the rest of the old South – was an extremely dangerous undertaking at best. There also were very few items with which to barter for food and other necessities until gardens and livestock could be rebuilt, so hunger and lack of shelter constantly plagued the general population. For this reason, many families simply picked up what little they owned and departed for the West – usually to Texas – to begin life anew. O.D. and his family chose to remain in Georgia and struggle on.

Family Marriages

Anna Anderson, the future wife of James Monroe Neel later of Cartersville, was the third of O.D.'s six children. James Monroe Neel also grew up in Adairsville, probably in the same church as the Andersons. A daguerreotype described by the Neel sisters once showed a very pretty Anna with brown hair and eyes. She talked of wrapping bandages around the poor and desperate Confederate soldiers during the war.

Ella, O.D.'s eldest child, married *Zachariah McReynolds* in 1869, and

began the flight of some of the family to Texas with her husband – such was the desperate nature of circumstances in Georgia. Some of their descendants can still be found in that state today.

Julia Margaret Anderson who was six years younger than sister Anna, was a pretty 19-year-old at the time of Anna's marriage to James Monroe Neel. She would later marry James herself following the untimely death of her sister.

In February of 1875, sister *Laura Anderson* married a Confederate veteran and cousin, *Augustus Marcellus Foute*. They eventually moved to Cartersville, an "up and coming" town on the W&A, ultimately building a fine home there next to the home of sister Anna and her husband, James Monroe Neel, at 119 South Avenue.

Old Cass County in which Adairsville had existed prior to the war had been totally devastated, with its county seat of government – Cassville – reduced to a charred ruin, never to be rebuilt. Cartersville, also on the newly-rebuilt Western & Atlantic Railroad, was the progressive community selected as the new county seat of government, offering hope to the remaining populace of the area, including both the Anderson and Neel families.

Brother *Jimmy Anderson* who had married the previous year carried a reputation as the family mischief-maker, and was continuously keeping things lively. He lived in Kingston with his wife *Hepatia Bowden Anderson*.

O.D. Anderson shows up in the **1880** *Federal Census* of Cartersville, Bartow County, Georgia, with Julia Margaret and Frank still living at home with him and wife Amelia. O.D. is listed in this head-count as *"furniture merchant."*

Several years after the death of his wife Amelia in 1881, O.D. married her sister, **Susan Gaines**. With the struggles he had endured in Georgia since the war's end, O.D. apparently decided that he was ready to move on to a new horizon. He seemed to seek in Susan the same lust for life which he had enjoyed in Amelia, and it wasn't long before he had made the decision to uproot his family and leave Georgia himself.

One Final Adventure

No one can ever claim O.D. was not adventurous. With all of his experiences behind him to date, he chose – at almost 60 years of age – to strike out yet again in one last professional adventure. He and Susan sold their Adairsville property and purchased, of all things, an orange grove in Apopka, Florida, and moved there to raise and market oranges. Both O.D. and Susan show up in the *1885 Federal Census of Orange County, Florida* where he is identified as *"orange grower."*

No one ever accused O.D. of being lazy either, and following what must have been great labors, his orange groves flourished initially, but "Lady Luck" just did not favor the hard-working transplanted Georgian. Nothing could save him from the "great freeze of 1892." O.D. lost his entire livelihood for the second time in a little over 25 years, a situation which would have crushed and devastated a lesser man.

O.D. and Susan, however, picked up the remaining pieces of their life together and struggled onward once again. They ultimately were forced to move back to Cartersville to live with his daughter and her husband – the Foutes – next door to his daughter and son-in-law James Monroe Neel.

Those were family-centered times, when family stood strongly beside those who were struggling, and "took in" those who were homeless. Such was the case with O.D. and what remained of his family when the Foutes rescued them with domicile following their Florida losses.

After that, the seasons came and went more quickly for O.D. The year 1909 undoubtedly was yet another difficult one for the Anderson family. O.D., who had by then reached the ripe old age of 85, tragically tumbled off the high front porch of James Monroe Neel's home (which still stands on South Avenue in Cartersville as of this writing), possibly as the result of a stroke. He lingered for three days before passing.

Though the method of his death was tragic, O.D. nevertheless had enjoyed a full and rich – if oftentimes difficult – life with a large and extended family. He lived out his final years next door to the substantial Neel homestead and many nieces, nephews, and grandchildren in Bartow County.

O.D.'s lust for life had caused it to be filled with adventure – some of it good and some of it not so good – and he was remembered fondly by all who knew him. His name has been passed down more than favorably from generation to generation of family descendants. In a turn-of-the-century photograph of the extended family taken in front of the old Neel home circa 1902, O.D. Anderson is the one with the broadest smile.

(Grateful appreciation is expressed herewith for the provision of much of this material by the late Isabelle Neel Jackson and Marvin McClatchey.)

[Oliver Davis Anderson is the great-grandfather of the late Ralph Olin Jackson, Jr., formerly of Rockmart, Georgia (whose mother was O.D.'s daughter) and the great-great-grandfather of Ralph's children (Patricia, Olin, David, the late Mary and the late Guy Jackson). James Monroe Neel is the great-grandfather of these Jackson siblings.]

"They're Stealin' the Train!"

Confederate Camp McDonald and *"Great Locomotive Chase"*

Conceived as a method to sabotage the vital Western & Atlantic Railroad between Atlanta and Chattanooga to interrupt the supply of men and munitions to Confederate forces, a group of Union raiders achieved the impossible task of hijacking a Confederate locomotive parked in front of thousands of Confederate soldiers at Camp McDonald in Big Shanty, Georgia. In the end, however, the damage they inflicted was minimal to none, and many of them ended up paying with their lives.

If one visits the city streets of Kennesaw, Georgia, today, modern development and a reasonably historic town square bisected by a still-busy railroad are the basic components that will be encountered. On April 12, 1862, however, a sea of tents and other temporary structures at Confederate Camp McDonald housing thousands of troops existed on the west side of the tracks at this site, and on the opposite side, a few scant commercial buildings, a modest train depot, and the Lacy Hotel composed the hamlet of "Big Shanty" where a momentous event was about to take place.

During a twenty-minute breakfast stop at the Lacy Hotel on the morning route of the *Western & Atlantic* train out of Atlanta, a small coterie of daring Union Army spies took control of the locomotive *"General."* The chuffing behemoth already had steam in the boiler and after engaging the drive mechanism and opening up the throttle, the train began

lumbering up the track toward Chattanooga – an accomplishment made without firing a shot. A hijacking was taking place!

The parade grounds and tent city which once composed the Confederate army training site known as Camp McDonald are long gone today. Commercial buildings and the city streets of the town of Kennesaw, Georgia, have replaced the tents, pickets, horses, military equipment and temporary structures which formerly occupied this historic ground, but Camp McDonald is anything but forgotten. It is remembered as the spot where 20 Federal saboteurs stole a huge Confederate locomotive and three boxcars from right beneath the noses of thousands of bivouacked Confederate troops.

Contrary to the long-departed Camp McDonald, the line once known as the Western & Atlantic Railroad is still used today – but by modern freight instead of passenger trains. Nearby at

Questionable Judgement – In 1862 Georgia Governor Joseph E. Brown ordered that 10,000 pikes be manufactured for use in "arming" his troops when no firearms were available. His judgment in activation of this program proved to be extremely questionable (or nonexistent). He lived near Canton, Georgia, but enjoyed residing near Camp McDonald at "Big Shanty" (present-day Kennesaw, GA) to command the Georgia troops.

Kennesaw (formerly "Big Shanty"), inside a museum on the east side of the railroad tracks, the fabled *"General"* – the locomotive stolen that morning long ago – enjoys permanent display these days as the featured attraction at the site.

As for the Yankee saboteurs from that fabled day, they went down in history as *"Andrews' Raiders,"* becoming the central characters in a historically-recorded event, and even as the focus of a major Hollywood motion picture filmed in northeast Georgia in 1955 – almost 100 years after the actual event – entitled *The Great Locomotive Chase*.

Most historians today agree that the seizure of the train at Big Shanty was achieved with extraordinary daring, but

that the saboteurs actually accomplished little else in their mission. Their actions also ultimately cost many of the men their lives, so the value of the mission is – at best – questionable.

The federal agents were able to successfully achieve the locomotive hijacking in part due to the literal stupidity of the Georgia governor at that time – Joseph Emerson Brown – who "armed" the majority of the men at Camp McDonald with "pikes" – long spears with a cutting edge – instead of actual firearms which were then in short supply in the South. At the very least, the action left Camp McDonald – and the locomotive idling on the tracks beside it – in an exceedingly vulnerable defense posture.

An Absence of Logic

As the commander-in-chief of the Georgia military, Governor Brown was responsible for the local defense of Georgia. Evidence suggests that his actions and orders as commander caused Camp McDonald and the *Western & Atlantic Railroad* to be exceedingly poorly defended – despite the thousands of Confederate troops at the camp – and Federal strategists apparently had noticed.

With the war beginning to take a more serious toll upon the manpower and military munitions of the South by 1862, the Confederate War Department notified all the Confederate governors that additional numbers of troops were necessary for the war effort. Georgia was asked to supply twelve regiments which would be armed and supplied by the Confederacy, and each soldier would receive a $50 bounty for enlisting.

As a result of this action, Governor Brown ordered that Camp McDonald be re-opened in March of 1862. He had first opened the camp in June of 1861 to organize and train the 4th Brigade of Georgia Volunteers, but had closed it in July of that same year after the regiments of the brigade had been sent to the front in Virginia.[1]

As William Smedlund described in his book on Georgia's camps, there were no fortifications or walls of any kind around Camp McDonald since it was located in the "rear area" of the war effort, and was therefore considered inviolable from attack by Northern invaders. The large rolling fields made ideal camping areas and drill fields, and fresh-water springs in the vicinity provided ample water for the troops. Sentries were posted about the camp – but for guard training purposes only, since there was little to no concern about an enemy attack at this site.[2]

There is evidence that Governor Brown was more a student of the warfare of "antiquity" than that of a military strategist of the 1860s. He, in fact, is noted in history as having been the brainchild of at least one arms manufacturing enterprise which was truly bizarre.

With virtually no basis in logic whatsoever, Brown had publicly stated that any enemy upon Georgia soil must be driven away *"by the use of cold steel at close quarters."*[3] To emphasize and underline this bizarre statement – made in the day and time of gun powder arms – he introduced his dream weapon which he dubbed "the Georgia Pike." With considerable ridiculous aplomb, he assured fellow Georgians that by using this pike, any Northern invader would be driven *"from our genial territory back to his frozen home."*[4]

Instead of funding and spearheading the production of modern weapons for Georgia troops, Brown ludicrously appealed to the mechanics of Georgia to put aside all unnecessary work and

Markers of Remembrance – This present-day photo was taken looking south from the former site of *Confederate Camp McDonald* or west side of the railroad tracks at Big Shanty (present-day Kennesaw). In the foreground are three stone markers. The one on the left remembers William A. Fuller, conductor of the stolen train who gained fame for his tenacious pursuit of the raiders. The small marker in the center honors Colonel William Phillips, commander of the 4th Georgia Volunteer Brigade, who trained his men at *Camp McDonald* in June of 1861. The stone marker on the right marks the spot at which the locomotive *"General"* was seized by Federal raiders on April 12, 1862. Across the railroad tracks on the east side (in the background) is the present-day depot which did not exist in 1862. Just south of this depot, the *Lacy Hotel* (which burned in 1864) once stood. It was at the Lacy that the train crew was having breakfast when their train was stolen. (Photo by Joe Griffith)

make *"ten thousand pikes."* As an earnest advocate of the pike, he argued that *"if the defenders at Fort Donelson had been armed with pikes, the outcome of that battle would have been quite different."*

Brown backed up his claims with the assertion that *"the long-range gun might fail to fire or miss its mark, thus wasting ammunition, but the short-range pike and terrible knife. . . . wielded by a stalwart patriot's arm, never fails to fire, and never wastes a single load."*[5] He somehow blindly refused to take into consideration all those Confederate troops who were falling before the

Fateful Spot – This modern photograph looking southward, was taken from the approximate spot where James J. Andrews, leader of a band of 20 Federal raiders, climbed aboard the locomotive *"General"* and seized the train on April 12, 1862. Upon the theft of this locomotive, the fates of Andrews and his men were sealed, causing a number of them to lose their lives. A sentry at Camp McDonald, armed with a "Joe Brown Pike," stood near the locomotive at this spot. (Photo by Joe Griffith)

new rifled repeating arms of the Union Army while Southern troops were fighting with single-shot weapons – quite often little more than aged muskets – and his "Georgia Pikes." *(And still, somehow, Confederate troops amazingly won quite a few of the initial strategic battles through 1862. Even more amazing, Union armies ultimately began winning due to sheer overwhelming numbers and the starvation of the South.)*

Brown's initiative not only was amazingly naïve, it, in the truest sense, was bizarre. For each pike accepted by the Confederate Arsenal, Brown instructed the government to pay $5. For each side knife with tipped scabbard, belt, and clasp, the government paid $4.60. In all, 7,099 pikes and 4,908 side knives amazingly were actually

manufactured and received into the arsenal at Milledgeville.[6] *(In an ironic turn of circumstances, the Joe Brown Pikes today fetch breath-taking prices on the auction and collectibles market.)*

Rodney Brown, in his ***American Polearms*** reported that new recruits at camps of instruction such as Camp McDonald in Georgia were issued pikes which were used for training drills and as primary infantry weapons in sham battles. The ancient devices were also used by sentries on guard duty in rear areas, as was the case at Camp McDonald in 1862. Nevertheless, to even consider them as a training weapon was absurdly naive. Few – if any – were ever actually used. Only a fool would have so irrationally risked his life through the use of such a useless solitary weapon.

The pikes and knives were also issued to some coastal defense units as their primary weapon in lieu of a musket. On 12 February, 1862, the **Southern Banner** newspaper of Athens, Georgia, reported that *"a perfect novelty, a company of volunteers from the hills of Habersham County, Georgia, and armed with pikes, passed through town on their way to defend the coast."*[7]

According to accounts of that day, few if any soldiers were thrilled to be issued the archaic pikes. One might logically surmise that none of troops receiving the pikes preferred them – understandably – over long-guns and pistols. According to Rodney Brown, some recruits simply laughed at the idea of using a sharp pointed stick against an enemy who was armed with a large caliber "rifled" long-gun which in many cases were being updated with repeating arms. With great hilarity, the Confederate trainees who had not yet seen battle chased each other around the camp brandishing their medieval-looking weapons.

I.G. Bradwell wrote, in the **Confederate Veteran**, that when he enlisted, his regiment was promised they would be issued new Enfield rifles. However, when, instead, wagon loads of pikes arrived for issue, there was a near riot among the soldiers until the pikes were laid aside and the men were issued not the coveted Enfield rifles, but old smooth-bore muskets. In the end, the soldiers understandably treated the whole idea of using pikes in battle against an enemy with rifled and often repeating firearms as a cruel joke.[8] With logic and strategies such as this, it is amazing the South ever won any of the engagements in which it was involved.

Biographer Joseph E. Parks pointed out that Gov. Brown was particularly eager to issue his pikes and accompanying side knives to his troops because he was

Determined Leader – James J. Andrews as he appeared at the time of the daring raid at Big Shanty, Georgia. When questioned by his men as to the judgement of proceeding despite all the men at Camp McDonald, Andrews responded, *"Boys, I tried this once before and failed. Now, I will succeed or leave my bones in Dixie."* Though Andrews possibly suspected it, he undoubtedly did not know just how prophetic his words would turn out to be. He would later be hanged for his actions as a spy.

being ridiculed by members of the Georgia General Assembly for his wastefulness of scarce defense dollars on outdated and impractical weapons. As a result of this embarrassing predicament, pikes ultimately were issued only to recruits at rear area installations such as Camp McDonald, and even guard duty was performed by sentries armed with what were, by that time, being mockingly referred to as *"Joe Brown Pikes."*[9]

Camp McDonald

The troop strength at Camp McDonald, according to reports, was indeed impressive, despite the paucity of actual weapons. What was not impressive was the fact that none of these troops actually possessed legitimate arms unless they

Captain William A. Fuller, conductor of the train stolen by Andrews and his men at Big Shanty, was photographed in March of 1904, some 42 years after the raid.

had brought their own. They were bivouacked for a great distance southward along the west side of the *Western & Atlantic Railroad*. One special row of tents on the high ground to the northwest end of the camp housed the camp commander and the commander-in-chief of the Georgia Army, Governor Brown.

Brown, who lived a short distance away near Canton, Georgia, founded in the 1830s, reportedly spent a great deal of time at Camp McDonald. He thought camp life might improve his health. The dispatches he issued from there were signed *"commander-in-chief."* He, however, was not held – understandably – in great esteem by the troops inhabiting the camp with him.

Nearby were the tents of the cadets from Georgia Military Institute in Marietta. Having been professionally-trained

in the techniques of military drill on a daily basis at the Institute, they were put into service as drillmasters and instructors for the recruits.

By early April of 1862, there were at least five regiments and a separate battalion of infantry consisting of the 39th, 40th, 41st, 42nd, 43rd, and 52nd Georgia Volunteer Infantry Regiments and the 9th Battalion Georgia Volunteer Infantry undergoing training at the camp. As a result, the camp was more crowded in 1862 than when it first opened in the summer of 1861.[10]

Planning The Raid

Meanwhile, Gen. Don Carlos Buell commanded the Union Army in middle Tennessee in the spring of 1862. A spy named James J. Andrews was normally in the employ of Gen. Buell, and had traveled in disguise down into Georgia on several occasions to scout targets, as well as the potential for sabotage. Andrews had provided valuable information to the Union Army in the first year of the war, and was about to attempt an even more daring foray into Confederate Georgia.

In March of 1862, Buell had sent Andrews and a party of eight men on a secret mission to burn the bridges west of Chattanooga, but the raid had failed due to a lack of expected cooperation from local townspeople. After that defeat, Andrews had visited the Atlanta area posing as a blockade runner. He inspected all of the Confederate rail lines in that vicinity and northward to Chattanooga. He then returned to Buell with a plan for a second attempt to destroy the bridges.[11]

On the eve of his march from Shelbyville, Tennessee, to Huntsville, Alabama, Buell sent Andrews to Union Brigadier General Ormsby Mitchell who

Severing Support – This wartime illustration from *Harper's Pictorial History of the Great Rebellion,* shows Chattanooga, Tennessee from the north bank of the Tennessee River. The objective of *Andrews' Raid* was to cut off Chattanooga from support from the south.

commanded a division of Buell's troops. Andrews and Mitchell discussed the details of the proposed raid.

Mitchell ultimately approved the plan and authorized Andrews to lead a party of twenty-four men into enemy territory to capture a train, then proceed back northward on a railroad sabotage mission, burning bridges along the northern portion of the *Georgia State Railroad* and on the *East Tennessee Railroad* where it approached the Georgia border.

The destructive mission was intended to block any reinforcement from the south and thereby isolate Chattanooga. When the blocking mission was completed, Mitchell could then move into a virtually undefended Chattanooga with ease, and without further concern for a rapid enemy response by rail from Georgia. It was a bold – and perhaps foolhardy – plan.[12] And as things turned out, it not only was foolhardy, but cost Andrews his life, as well as the lives of many of his men.

For the proposed raid, 23 soldiers from three Ohio regiments were selected for their courage and combat experience. In addition to Andrews, there was one other civilian – William Campbell of Salineville, Ohio. He happened to be visiting a friend in the camp at the time Andrews was seeking men.

All of the 24 men selected were told the mission would be secret, very dangerous, and conducted behind enemy lines. According to William Pittenger, who was one of the soldiers, *"not a man chosen declined the perilous honor."* The men were also told they would not be in uniform and would wear ordinary civilian dress. In other words, they would be spies, and could be shot if captured. Each man would be provided with clothing, Confederate money, and a small caliber revolver to be carried in a holster on the rear of his belt hidden from view under his coat.

Dressed as a businessman for this trip, Andrews was adept at his disguises. He wore a top hat and frock coat, and carried saddle bags on his left arm to set him apart as a man of authority. He was

Chattanooga, Tennessee, was photographed here in 1863 during the war. Lookout Mountain is faintly visible in the distance. The objective of the raid being conducted by James J. Andrews was to cut off supply lines and the support of Chattanooga from the south. (Photo courtesy of National Archives)

tall and bearded, which added to the effectiveness of his Southern upper-crust disguise.[13]

As the men traveled southward, they passed Big Shanty – where the train was to be seized the following morning – about eight miles north of Marietta. Upon reaching Big Shanty, the men discovered to their shock and dismay that a huge sprawling Confederate camp – humming with thousands of troops – surrounded the very train they were to steal. No one had confided to them this little additional detail.

Looking out of his train window at the busy military camp, Pittenger recalled his thoughts at the time. He wrote:

"To succeed in our enterprise, it would be necessary first to capture the engine in a guarded camp with soldiers standing around as spectators, and then to run it from one to two-hundred miles through the enemy's country, and to deceive or overpower all trains that should be met – a large contract for twenty men."[14]

Pittenger also didn't mention the fact that a steam locomotive takes a certain amount of time to build up enough speed to avoid being overtaken by someone on foot. Its sluggish start would leave him and his fellow spies at the mercy of what he presumed would be the thousands of Confederate muskets opening up fire upon them as they slowly chugged away from the Lacy Hotel. Though he didn't know it at the time, he needed only to outrun the foot traffic in order to succeed in the hijacking.

By Friday night of April 11, 1862, Pittenger confirmed that Andrews and twenty-one of his raiders were staying at two different hotels in Marietta, Georgia. Most took rooms at what is known today as the Kennesaw House (which still stands as of this writing in 2025) alongside the Marietta railroad depot. The remainder took quarters at the nearby Marietta House on the town square.

The man-power of the saboteurs was unexpectedly cut from 25 to 22 (counting Andrews) – in yet another unexpected turn of events – when one man did not show up at all and two others had come under suspicion in route by Confederate officials near Chattanooga, and been forced to join the Confederate Army near Jasper, Tennessee, just as they had said they wanted to do when questioned by authorities.[15]

Determined Leader

The morning of Saturday, April 12 was cold, wet and miserable as the men were aroused shortly before daybreak at about 4:00 a.m. Always the perfectionist, Andrews left nothing to chance, going from room to room to review the details of each man's role in the raid. They spoke in whispers in order to avoid being overheard through the thin walls of the hotel rooms. According to Pittenger, Andrews quietly instructed each man thusly:

"When the train stops at Big Shanty for breakfast, keep your places till I tell you to go. Get seats near each other in the same car, and say nothing about the matter on the way up. If anything unexpected occurs, look to me for the word. You, you, and you [designating three men] will go with me on the engine; the rest of you will go on the left of the train forward of where it is uncoupled, and climb on the cars in the best places you can, when the order is given. If anybody interferes, shoot him, but don't fire until it is necessary."[16]

In his writings, Pittenger also explained that one of the men – Sergeant Major Ross – was against continuing the raid and protested that *"the circumstances have changed since we set out and . . . that many more troops were at Big Shanty than formerly; that we had noticed the crowded state of the road as we came down, and that Mitchell's movements would make it worse."* Therefore, Ross respectfully asked Andrews to either postpone or abort the raid.

Andrews, in response, quietly admitted to Ross that everything he said was true, but countered by pointing out the opportunities inherent in the situation:

"The military excitement and commotion, and the number of trains on the road will make our train the less likely to be suspected," Andrews said. *"And as to the troops at Big Shanty, if we do our work promptly, they will have no chance to interfere. Capturing the train in the camp will be easier than anywhere else, because no one would believe it possible, and there will therefore be no guard."[17]*

Pittenger reported that all did not go as planned in the attempted sabotage – in fact, very little actually went according to the method in which it had been originally conceived. Prior to boarding the train in Marietta – despite Andrews' explanation to Ross – several other raiders joined in the respectful protest against continuing with the raid. Andrews reportedly listened to their complaints and then closed the meeting by saying: *"Boys, I tried this once before and failed; Now, I will succeed or leave my bones in Dixie."* (He possibly suspected it, but did not know just how prophetic his words would turn out to be.)

At that point, according to Pittenger, Andrews grasped the hands of each of the raiders and they left the room to go next door to the depot to catch the morning train to Big Shanty as a misty rain descended upon them.[18] Their immense task yawned before them.

In order to maintain the subterfuge of their effort, the raiders had purchased tickets at the depot before 5:00 a.m., and each ticket was for a different stop farther up the line in order to avoid attracting suspicion by all going from Marietta to Big Shanty. At boarding time, two of the raiders who were staying at the Marietta House failed to appear, having overslept, thus reducing the number of raiders to 20 as the train pulled out at 5:15 a.m.

William A. Fuller was the conductor of the train on this route. Always efficient and thorough, he entered the passenger car and began collecting tickets. He was keeping an eye out for deserters because he had been warned about their possible presence on the line, but he strangely was not suspicious of the raiders even though they had all boarded the train at Marietta.[19] He did, however, recognize the "businessman" Andrews, who had previously ridden his train, but he did not know him by name, at least not yet.[20]

Sleight of Hand

The first stop after leaving Marietta was Big Shanty. After approximately a 45-minute trip at 6:00 a.m., the train approached Big Shanty and Camp McDonald. The white tents of the enemy soldiers could be seen with the sentries walking their posts. Pittenger described it thusly:

"Big Shanty had been selected for the seizure because it was a breakfast station, and because it had no telegraph office. When Andrews had been here on the previous expedition, few troops were seen, but the number was now greatly increased. It is difficult to tell just how many were actually here, for they were constantly coming and going; but there seems to have been three or four regiments, numbering not far from a thousand men each. They were encamped almost entirely on the west side of the road, but their camp guard included the railroad depot."[21]

This stop at the Lacy Hotel was a regular pause for the train crew. They made it every morning. The train had hardly rolled to a stop before the entire crew – including the engineer, fireman, and conductor, and most of the passengers – got off and went quickly into the hotel for breakfast. They all apparently relished the meal at the Lacy, and no guard was even left on the train!

Demonstrating the utmost patience in the face of mortal danger, the raiders kept their seats, awaiting a signal from Andrews. As the last passengers going to breakfast cleared the front door of the coach, Andrews and Knight fell in behind them, but instead of going off on the right side of the train, they got off on the left side next to the camp. As a result, they were hidden from the view of anyone in the hotel as they went about their espionage.

The men first had to confirm that their hijacking of the train was even possible at that point. They reportedly walked confidently forward together to see if the tracks ahead were clear. When they had confirmed that no train obstructed their departure, they walked back to the rear of the third empty boxcar where Andrews told Knight to uncouple the remaining cars and wait for him there. Then, Andrews walked back to the passenger car where the remaining raiders were waiting and, in a calm voice, said: *"Come on boys; it's time to go."*[22]

Stealth was as much a necessity as was a daring temperament. Pittenger explained that the raiders left the coach car quietly so that the remaining passengers – who had not gone up to the Lacy for breakfast – would not be alarmed. Andrews immediately went forward and Knight, seeing him coming, also hurried forward and climbed aboard the engine.

At this point, Knight cut the bell rope that was tied to the Big Shanty loading dock; put his hand on the throttle,

42

The historic locomotive *"General"* was photographed here (date unknown) with its tender still bearing the inscription *"W&A R.R."* This locomotive is permanently displayed today at the Southern Museum of *Civil War and Locomotive History* in Kennesaw, Georgia.

and stood ready, his eyes fixed on Andrews awaiting a signal to depart.[23] Andrews stood on the lower step of the engine, leaning back to see his men running forward and scrambling aboard the empty boxcars. An extra engineer and a firemen among the raiders ran forward to the engine to their posts beside Knight in the cab.[24]

Meanwhile, as Pittenger pointed out in his recounting of the incident: *"All this time a sentry was standing not a dozen feet from the engine quietly watching, as if this was the most ordinary proceeding, and a number of other soldiers were idling but a short distance away."*[25]

The late Wilbur G. Kurtz, Sr., a long-time Atlanta artist and respected historian and the son-in-law of conductor William Fuller, interviewed many of those involved in the raid. In the postscript to the MacLennan Roberts book, *The Great Locomotive Chase*, he wrote that recruits at Camp McDonald were armed with the "Joe Brown Pikes" because of a shortage of firearms. Kurtz interviewed Henry Whitley of Company

F, 56th Georgia Regiment, who was the sentry who stood and watched the raiders steal the train that day. Whitley told him that he also was armed with nothing more than a pike.[26]

Pittenger added that when everything was ready and the last raider was pulled into a boxcar, Andrews climbed aboard the engine and nodded to Knight, who opened the engine throttle. The great locomotive spun its wheels before gaining traction, then slowly began gaining momentum toward the curve in the rail line, leaving Camp McDonald in its wake and taking the 20 men to a date with destiny.

All of this happened so quickly that none of the camp's soldiers raised their useless weapons, sounded an alarm, or even showed any sign that they suspected anything was wrong as the engine – with only three boxcars attached – pulled away. The theft of a train at Camp McDonald in the midst of thousands of enemy soldiers had been done by twenty raiders *"without firing a shot or even an angry gesture."*[27]

Centennial Re-Run – In 1962, one hundred years after the famed *"Great Locomotive Chase,"* the *General* went on tour, retracing the route of the famed incident from Marietta to Ringgold, Georgia. (Photo courtesy of Adairsville History Museum)

Flight To Eternity

The remainder of this daring incident from the U.S. Civil War is a matter of history today. Though he was imminently successful in his theft of the locomotive called *General*, James J. Andrews and his men ultimately failed in their mission. After a dramatic flight northward up the railroad, the raiders eventually abandoned the train two miles north of Ringgold, Georgia, having completed only moderate damage to the railroad and failing to destroy any bridges.

The saboteurs were all eventually captured as they fled on foot into the north Georgia countryside. Several were later

The theft of a train at Camp McDonald in the midst of thousands of enemy soldiers had been done by twenty raiders "without firing a shot or even an angry gesture."

executed in Atlanta, and several amazingly even managed to successfully escape, fleeing back to the North where they later were awarded the *Medal of Honor.*

Meanwhile, back at Camp McDonald, an enraged cadre was trying to put the best face on a very embarrassing incident. The railroad raid at the camp was an extraordinary feat of daring, but as Andrews had predicted at Marietta on the morning of the event, their success in capturing the train was enabled by the lack of a local defensive preparedness by both the railroad and camp authorities. This lack of preparedness ultimately fell upon the shoulders of the lone governor of the state, Joseph Emerson Brown.

Endnotes

1/ Allen D. Candler, ed., **The Confederate Records of the State of Georgia**, 5 vols. (Atlanta, GA: Charles P. Byrd, State Printer, 1909), vol. 2, p. 187-195 (hereafter referred to as CR, 2:187-195); Joseph H. Parks, **Joseph E. Brown of Georgia** (Baton Rouge, LA: Louisiana State University Press, 1977), 182-83; William S. Smedlund, **Camp Fires of Georgia's Troops, 1861-1865** (Lithonia, GA: Kennesaw Mountain Press, 1994), 201-205; **War of the Rebellion: Official Records of the Union and Confederate Armies**, 70 vols, in 128 pts. (Washington, DC: Government Printing Office, 1880-1901), ser. 4, vol.1:902 (hereafter referred to as OR).

2/ CR, 2:89-91; Smedlund, 201-205; Sarah Blackwell Gober Temple, **The First Hundred Years: A Short History of Cobb County in Georgia** (Atlanta, GA: Walter W. Brown Publishing Company, 1935; reprint, Athens, GA: Agee Publishers, Inc., 1989), 238-241.

3/ *CR*, 2:194-198; *OR* ser. 4, vol. 1:917.

4/ Rodney Hilton Brown, **American Pole Arms** *1526-1865 (New Milford, CN: N. Letterman & Company, 1967),* 118-135; *CR* 2:199; *Parks,* 184. The "Georgia Pike" was a pole arm that had a long double-edged blade secured to its six foot wooden shaft by a ferrule made out of brass or iron and two long wrought iron side straps. The butt end usually had a cap or long cast iron shoe to prevent splintering. The Georgia pattern pikes were normally produced at the Confederate armories. The principal pike manufactured in Georgia and known as the "Joe Brown Pike" was of the "clover-leaf" design which means it had the usual ten inch double-edged blade and two additional side "bridle-cutter" blades which gave it the clover-leaf or cross appearance. The side blades were used as bridle cutters to engage cavalrymen and cut the reins of their horses, thus rendering them out of control and making the rider vulnerable to a thrust from the pike's main blade.

5/ *CR*, 2:199-200; Louise Biles Hill, **Joseph E. Brown and the Confederacy** *(Chapel Hill, NC: University of North Carolina Press, 1939),* 249.

6/ *CR* 2:349-353.

7/ "A Perfect Novelty," **Athens Southern Banner**, 12 February 1862; Rodney Brown, 134; Kenneth Coleman, **Confederate Athens** *(Athens, GA: University of Georgia Press, 1968),* 43.

8/ I.G. Bradwell, "Soldier Life in the Confederate Army," *Confederate Veteran* 24, no. 1 (1916): 21; Rodney Brown, 134.

9/ Henry H. Kurtz, Jr., "Hijack of a Locomotive: The Andrews Raid Revisited," *Atlanta History: A Journal of Georgia and the South* 34, no. 3 (1990): 2; MacClennan Roberts, **The Great Locomotive Chase** *(New York: Dell Publishing Company, 1956), postscript by Wilbur G. Kurtz, Sr.,* 155; Parks, 242.

10/ *Parks,* 151-154; *Smedlund,* 11-12.

11/ William Pittenger, "**Locomotive Chase in Georgia**," *The Century Magazine.* 36, No. 1 (1888): 141-142; Wilbur G. Kurtz, Sr., "The Andrews Raid," *Atlanta Historical Bulletin* 13, no. 4 (1968): 12.

The saboteurs were all eventually captured as they fled on foot into the north Georgia countryside.

12/ William Pittenger, **Daring and Suffering: A History of the Great Railroad Adventure Into Georgia In 1862** *(New York: The War Publishing Company, 1887),* 97; Derry, 95-96; John A Wilson, **Adventures of Alf. Wilson: A Thrilling Episode of the Dark Days of the Rebellion** *(Marietta, GA: Continental Book Company, 1972),* 17.

13/ Pittenger, **Locomotive Chase in Georgia**, *142;* Wilbur G. Kurtz, Sr., "The Andrews Railroad Raid," **Civil War Times Illustrated** 5, no. 1 (1966): 8-13; Wilson, 15-18.

14/ Pittenger, **Locomotive Chase In Georgia**, *143;* Wilson, 18-25.

15/ Pittenger, **Daring and Suffering**, *98-99;* Daniel O. Cox, Telephone interview with the author, 20 February, 2002; Wilson, 26.

16/ Pittenger, **Daring and Suffering**, *99-100;* Charles Kendell O'Neill, **Wild Train: The Story Of Andrews Raiders** *(New York: Random House, 1956),* 129.

17/ Pittenger, **Daring and Suffering**, *100-101.*

18/ *Ibid,* 101.

19/ Fuller, 10, 21; Kurtz, Sr., "The Andrews Raid," 17; O'Neill, 131-32.

20/ Pittenger, **Daring and Suffering**, *102.*

21/ Pittenger, **Daring and Suffering**, *102-103;* O'Neill, 132-133; Wilson, 28.

22/ Pittenger, **Daring and Suffering**, *102-103;* Fuller, 30; O'Neill, 135-36; Wilson, 29.

23/ Pittenger, **Daring and Suffering**, *103;* Wilson, 29.

24/ Pittenger, **Daring and Suffering**, *104-105.*

25/ *Ibid,* 105.

26/ Pittenger, **Daring and Suffering**, *105;* Lillian Henderson, ed., **The Rosters of Confederate Soldiers of Georgia**, *vol. 5 (Spartanburg, SC: The Reprint Company, 1982),* 883; Kurtz, Jr., 6; O'Neill, 137; Roberts, 155; Wilson, 28-29.

27/ Pittenger, **Daring and Suffering**, *105;* O'Neill, 137; Wilson, 29.

The Place Where Andrews' Raiders Slept

As soon as the big brick building is seen, it conjures up images of historic events in the mind of the beholder. And sure enough, if you do some checking, you'll find out that a group of espionage agents known in U.S. Civil War history as "Andrews' Raiders" once spent the night in this structure.

Joe Kirby of the **Marietta Daily Journal** once wrote, *"Few buildings anywhere in Georgia have a history as interesting as that of the Kennesaw House in Marietta. It predates the Civil War and provided accommodations for a group known as 'Andrews' Raiders' on a night in 1862 before they hijacked a Confederate train pulled by the locomotive 'General.'"* Today, this captivating structure just off the square in Marietta houses the *Marietta Historical Museum*, a non-profit endeavor offering a wide variety of historic area memorabilia for public viewing.

Beginnings and a Haunting

Prior to the war, the Kennesaw House was a summer resort for the wealthy. Many of these visitors came to partake of the waters of a unique spring in the vicinity which eventually, surprisingly, was temporarily lost to history.

Historical Museum founder Dan Cox "rediscovered" that spring in the 1980s behind present-day *Kennestone Hospital*. At the time of this discovery, he also concluded that there was a lot of interesting

history involving Marietta that was simply not well-known, and that included a "ghost" in the *Kennesaw House*.

Mr. Cox emphasized that he didn't believe in ghosts, but stated, "I think I've seen one as I've worked here." The image Cox says he 'saw' stood about 5'6" tall and wore a flat hat with a brim, a cream-colored coat that hung three-fourths of the way down the thigh, and boots that came to mid-calf. All very 19th century-ish.

Then-Cobb County Police Lieutenant Henry Higgins, a volunteer at that time at the museum, lent credence to Mr. Cox's contention. "I've seen the 'ghost' myself three times," he said. "We've attributed it to a lot of things up here - headlights reflecting on the windows, passing trains, and so forth. But just about the time you think you've got it figured out, he's gone."

Cox agreed that in the historic old Kennesaw House (Marietta Museum), imaginations tended to run wild. "Doors swing for no reason (probably actually due to the air from a heating system vent), and boards creak ominously."

> *"I've seen the 'ghost' myself three times," he said.*

Regardless of the "spirits," the developers of the museum in the historic structure seemed to be having a good time with their project and, in the process, they discovered as well as obtained a number of unique historic items which are now on display.

Early History

It is unknown for certain today whether Dix Fletcher or John Heyward Glover (Marietta's first mayor) built the old hotel in the 1850s. However, it is a matter of record that it was known as *"the Fletcher House,"* and ultimately was later renamed *"the Kennesaw House."*

As in countless towns of that era, a general hotel was almost always constructed adjacent to whatever railroad line that passed through the community, and the Kennesaw House was no different. The railroad at that time was the historic (and now long-defunct) *Western & Atlantic Railroad*. Though that rail line is now a piece of history, a modern railroad still passes on the identical railroad-bed of the old *Western & Atlantic*, right beside the hotel.

Some witnesses to the apparition in the aged structure believe it is Dr. Daniel Wilder, a Union Army physician and the nephew of Dix and Louisa Fletcher, Union sympathizers who owned the property during the U.S. Civil War. That, however, is only a matter of interest to those who actually believe in ghosts.

Dan Cox's wife, Connie, was more specific. "When Union troops looted and pillaged Marietta during General William Sherman's occupation, Wilder prevented them from absconding with the Fletcher family's belongings, including a blind horse, flour and pots," she explained. It was Connie and Henry E. Higgins who edited Mrs. Fletcher's diary for modern publication, renaming it *Journal of a Landlady*. The aged chronicle covered the years 1857 to 1883 in Marietta, and ultimately revealed a number of interesting facts about both Marietta and the Kennesaw House.

U.S. Civil War

Aside from its other early uses, the Kennesaw House also eventually was used as a Confederate hospital where wounded soldiers were fed and treated following a number of area battles – and there were a lot of them in the area, including major engagements at Allatoona Pass, Kennesaw Mountain, and all around the immediate city of Marietta.

Despite ultimately evolving into a history enthusiast, Dan Cox adamantly explained that his current fascination was a recent development. "I didn't like it until my son, Carey, had an elementary school project on researching our family history," he said. "Once I began that family project, it surprisingly generated my interest in developing the museum on the second floor of the Kennesaw House."

Cox continued by explaining that his research revealed that his ancestors could be traced back some 156 years in the Marietta area. In 1840, Dr. Carey Cox built the first hospital in the city, and specialized in homeopathic cures, particularly one using the

The railroad at that time was the historic (and now long-defunct) Western & Atlantic Railroad.

Historic Hotel – The Kennesaw House, at which James J. Andrews and his men overnighted prior to beginning their famous episode in history, still stands in downtown Marietta beside the railroad tracks. The historic *Western & Atlantic Railroad* of Civil War days is long gone, but a modern rail line still follows much of the original *W&A* road-bed today to Chattanooga.

waters from the spring Dan had recently discovered behind present-day Kennestone Hospital.

According to accounts, patients would drink the water in small quantities and many of them reportedly experienced healthful conditions thereafter. "An analysis of the water later revealed a high iron content," Cox added. "My theory is that anemic people in particular benefited from drinking the water."

Opening A Museum

Cox said that his studies of his family genealogy and other history of the Marietta area eventually bled over into the preservation of historic real estate. While driving by the Kennesaw House one day, he said his wife asked "Why doesn't the city buy that building and develop it into a museum?" Cox said he had no idea about the lack of civic interest, but it suddenly gave him an idea.

He got a city council member to set up an appointment with Joe Mack Wilson (then mayor and now deceased) in November of 1992. "I thought the process would take at least a year or two," he mused, "but three weeks later, Wilson had gotten the *Downtown Marietta Development Authority* to actually buy the building for $525,000.00 to ensure its preservation.

"And because it was my idea," Cox summed up, "I got the job of *Executive Director* of the project, but most of the work was actually done by volunteers."

The *Marietta Museum of History* opened in 1995, and was started initially with donated displays. "We were lucky in the participation of people who have been members of the community for generations," Cox smiled. "That meant a lot of donated items and volunteer help."

Civil War Railroad Legend

According to historic records, a group of Union spies – some of whom became famous for their exploits – spent the night in the corner front room of the old hotel prior to hijacking the locomotive

General from nearby Kennesaw (then called Big Shanty) the following morning and speeding northward on the *Western & Atlantic Railroad* in a failed attempt to destroy trestles and other railroad infrastructure in the now-fabled chase.

This incident was memorialized in 1956 in a major motion picture by *Walt Disney Productions* entitled *"The Great Locomotive Chase"* which was filmed in northeast Georgia's Rabun County and just across the state line in adjoining North Carolina along the recently abandoned (and now equally-historic) *Tallulah Falls Railroad.* Disney's production starred Fess Parker, Jeffrey Hunter, John Lupton, Jeff York, and Slim Pickens, and capitalized upon Parker's growing fame at the time as the star of another *Disney* production *"Davy Crockett."*

Interestingly, *The Great Locomotive Chase* cast also included a then-totally-unknown bit-part actor and recent University of Georgia graduate by the name of *John Kollock* who would go on in subsequent years to earn a measure of renown himself in the Southeast with his many artistic creations, books, and historically-accurate paintings. Despite being offered permanent employment by Disney at the conclusion of filming, Kollock nevertheless elected to remain in the hills of north Georgia.

After his arrest, Marion Ross (one of the actual spies in the historic incident) wrote Marietta's Eliza Fletcher (a dyed-in-the-wool rebel in contrast to her parents) for help. She refused him, and Ross ultimately was hanged for treason.

Information on Henry Green Cole, a Marietta businessman who married one of the Fletcher daughters, was included in what eventually was a considerable catalogue of historic items exhibited in the museum. Cole owned another hotel (burned by Confederate troops) on the south side of the Marietta town square. He was an admitted Yankee spy, but reportedly did much to help rebuild the community after the war.

Other early items obtained for display in the museum included historic memorabilia of old Marietta, period photographs, old furnishings, and, interestingly, even one of *"Sherman's hairpins"* (a twisted piece of rail from the railroad). During their scourge of the Southeast, Union Army scalawags and "bummers" had a habit of removing sections of rail from the railroads and heating them until they were red-hot, so that they could then be twisted around a tree or some other unmovable object, thereby rendering the rails useless to the Confederates.

And finally, contrary to popular folklore in the area, the Kennesaw House is one building for which there, amazingly, is no evidence that it was ever inhabited by that firebrand Gen. William T. Sherman.

> *Disney's production starred Fess Parker, Jeffrey Hunter, John Lupton, Jeff York, and Slim Pickens, and capitalized upon Parker's growing fame at the time as the star of another Disney production "Davy Crockett."*

A Southwest Georgia
Railroading Adventure

*A historic rail line, built in the 1880s during the days when Doc Holliday
and Wyatt Earp were in their prime, has been put back into use. Today,
an excursion train travels the route once again, taking sightseers to a
collection of unique destinations in the southwestern corner of the state.*

Southwest Georgia is an area rich in history and nostalgia. It is full of small towns where life moves slowly, and historic sites that have helped to shape our state's history. The *SAM Short-line* ("short" for *"Savannah, Americus and Montgomery Railroad"*) which operated daily on these same tracks in the 1880s as a passenger and freight service line, is a state-sponsored excursion train today taking advantage of the tourism opportunities offered by the three above-mentioned towns.

Referred to by some as *"Georgia's Rolling State Park,"* the *SAM Short-line* passes through two counties and a total of five towns. Its excursion passengers are able to sample some of the most beautiful scenery in southwestern Georgia.

The train ride takes passengers through fields white with cotton and orchards thick with pecan trees loaded with nuts; past aged country homes with green roofs and wrap-around porches, and across a trestle over picturesque Lake Blackshear. It has become the envy of more than one exceptional former short-line route such as the former Tallulah Falls Railroad whose tracks were abandoned and taken over piecemeal by

private landowners once that railroad fell into bankruptcy.

Just as with the *Blue Ridge Scenic Railroad* in northeast Georgia, the *Great Smoky Mountains Railroad* in North Carolina, and others, the *SAM Short-line* quickly became a popular weekend getaway opportunity. It consists of three vintage passenger cars, a commissary car which includes a gift shop and a snack bar, and the Samuel H. Hawkins dining car, which is named for the founder of the *Savannah, Americus and Montgomery Railway*.

Just a scant 40 miles or so down the road at Valdosta is the boyhood home of John Henry "Doc" Holliday, one of the participants in the Old West gunfight at O.K. Corral in 1881. There are many other historic sites and scenic attractions in the vicinity of Cordele (where the *SAM Short-line* begins) too, so any sightseer who desires to make this a week-long getaway has plenty of things to see and do.

The *SAM Short-line* is operated by the *Georgia Department of Natural Resources (DNR)* under the guidance of the *Southwest Georgia Railway Excursion Authority*. The engine which pulls the *SAM* train is owned and operated by the *Heart of Georgia Railroad Company,* which runs freight on the same lines Monday through Thursday.

The railroad's organizers have been pleased that it has brought economic development and advanced tourism to the area. Besides the regular tourists who are interested in seeing beautiful and historic southwest Georgia, the *SAM Short-line* also appeals to motor coach tours and school field trips as well. Participants can be dropped off by bus at any one of the train stops along the route and then picked up miles down the road at another stop.

On its regular excursions, *SAM* departs from Cordele and travels west with stops at the Georgia State Veteran's State Park and the towns of Leslie, Americus, Plains and Archery. Each stop offers a number of historic attractions and shopping opportunities.

Passengers may board the train at any of the aforementioned stops and return the same day. Depending upon the train's schedule, passengers may also spend the night in a town and catch the train back to their point of origin the next day.

The *SAM Railroad Company* brought growth to southwest Georgia in the 1880s, allowing local farmers an opportunity to ship their products all over the country. Many of the towns that are still along the line today originated from this burst of commerce over 100 years ago.

Another big market which this modern-day version of the railroad

expects to "farm" is the under 40ish crowd – those raised after the days when passenger trains were the main mode of transportation. For those people, the *SAM Short-line* will be a great way to enjoy the experience of a passenger train ride and the excitement it offers.

"All Aboard In Cordele"

The official starting point of the *SAM Short-line* is Cordele, Georgia, conveniently located right off of Interstate 75. Home to the Georgia State Farmers Market and billed as the *"Watermelon Capital of the World,"* Cordele has twelve hotels where out-of-towners can spend the night before catching the train. Nearby, Lake Blackshear offers fishing, boating and camping.

The first stop on the line – the *Georgia Veteran's Memorial State Park* – is barely 15 miles from the starting point in Cordele, but it could be the last stop for many passengers. Situated on Lake Blackshear, the 1,322-acre park offers an 18-hole golf course, a swimming pool and beach, nature trails, fishing, and much more.

Cottages, tents, and recreational vehicle sites are available. For those with more comfort in mind, *The Retreat at Lake Blackshear* offers 88 rooms, a restaurant, a marina, conference facilities and more, and can accommodate groups of up to 450 people.

Established first and foremost as a memorial to U.S. veterans, the *Georgia*

Just a scant 40 miles or so down the road at Valdosta is the boyhood home of John Henry "Doc" Holliday, one of the participants in the Old West gunfight at O.K. Corral in 1881.

Veteran's Memorial Park features a museum inside the welcome center which highlights America's involvement from the Revolutionary War through the Gulf War. Uniforms, guns, and other memorabilia are displayed.

An additional room celebrates the contributions of Cordele native Mac Hyman, author of the best-selling novel *No Time for Sergeants*. Based upon Hyman's own experiences in the military, *No Time for Sergeants* was turned into an award-winning Broadway play. The movie version, filmed in 1958, is considered the vehicle that launched the career of television star Andy Griffith.

Outside the museum are many other exhibits which include tanks, bombers and helicopters from World War I through the Vietnam War. A Boeing B-29 – the only one still in existence – is also located at this site.

Lovely Leslie

Leslie, a charmingly tiny community of about 455 citizens, defines small-town perfection. This little slice of Southern Americana is located half-way between Americus and Albany. "For Sale" signs on the homes in this town usually don't last very long at all. Young couples usually snap up the homes here that are close to their jobs, yet "out in the country" enough to allow a "Mayberry" sort of existence.

It might well be that any economic boom the *SAM Short-line* brings to southwest Georgia will be heard the loudest in Leslie. Many shops within walking distance of the train depot have been refurbished and opened.

Leslie is also home to the *Georgia Rural Telephone Museum*, housed in a renovated 1920s cotton warehouse. Contained in the museum is one of the largest collections of antique telephones

and telephone memorabilia in the world. Some of the pieces date back to 1876.

Admiring Americus

In Americus, the train will stop directly across from the *Habitat for Humanity's* Global Village and Discovery Center, a six-acre complex. The Global Village displays model *Habitat* homes from 40 countries and houses an international marketplace.

While Americus has always had an on-going effort to maintain the appearance and viability of its downtown area, additional revitalization has occurred as a result of the *SAM* railroad. Businesses have relocated steadily into the town as the city has restored previously-unoccupied buildings.

Downtown Americus is also within walking distance of the *Short-line's* depot, and is a shopper's dream come true. A wide variety of consumer products are available – from upscale children's clothing at the *Tot Shop* to fresh produce at the *Farmer's Market*.

Americus may be the perfect place to turn the train ride into a weekend getaway too. The *Windsor Hotel*, which opened in 1892, is the most recognizable building downtown. Right down the street from the *Windsor*, you can catch a show at the *Rylander Theater*, built in the 1920s, which offers regular tours as well as live performances and plays.

Americus is also the boyhood home of the late former *Atlanta Falcons* Head Coach Dan Reeves and former *Georgia Tech* Head Coach Chan Gailey. A number of other notables grew up in this story-book town.

A President In Plains

After visiting the town of Plains, it's easy to understand why a former *President of the United States* and his *First*

Lady would choose to live here after having lived in the *White House* in Washington, D.C. With its distinctive small-town flavor, Plains is lovely to say the least.

The *SAM Short-line* stops in Plains right across the street from *The Plains Inn and Antiques*. The inn is owned by the city and is operated under the "Better Hometown" program. It features seven suites, each decorated with items from a distinct decade from the 1920s to the 1980s, representing the decades of President Carter's life from his birth through his presidency.

The Carters were closely involved in the design of the inn. Mrs. Carter worked with a decorator designing each room in its particular furnishings – right down to the claw-foot bathtubs and the rotary dial phones.

There is also a common room where breakfast is available each morning; a television room, and the inn's most wonderful feature – a front porch on the second floor which affords a view of the entire town. The first floor of the inn is filled with antiques from over 20 dealers across the South.

School classes were still held at the Plains High School up until 1979. Today, the building houses the museum and visitor center of the *Jimmy Carter National Historical Site*. Visitors can see films and exhibits which depict the history of Plains and the town's famous son.

Other sites of interest are the *Plains Depot*, which served as the campaign headquarters for Jimmy Carter during his U.S. Presidential bid. A short distance away is the United Methodist Church where Jimmy and Rosalyn were married. Even Billy Carter's Service Station and the business district which dates back to the 1890s have been preserved.

Aiming At Archery

The final stop on the *SAM Short-line* is the first stop in the story of America's 39th President. Jimmy Carter's boyhood home in the little town of Archery is still a working farm where black-eyed peas, collards, squash and of course – peanuts – are grown each season between the house, barns, and other buildings. Carter lived on the farm until 1941 when he departed home for college.

As one walks around the farm today, he or she will hear – via recorded narratives – President Carter describe the childhood he spent there. Viewing the humble surroundings which include an outhouse and a hand-pump for water, visitors leave with the distinct impression that a good education and hard work can take anybody to the White House.

While riders are visiting the President's boyhood home, the *SAM Short-line* turns around to ready itself for the return trip back to Cordele. The train covers 69 miles of historical stops, and the entire train ride – from departure to return to Cordele – takes approximately eight hours.

Interestingly, most of the historic sites and attractions in the towns at which the train stops are free, or have only a small admission charge. The trip can be appealing to all age groups and interests. The day-long venture is also very "child friendly" with many things that reportedly will intrigue young children and teenagers.

Numerous special events are planned throughout the year in conjunction with the *SAM Short-line*, including a wine and cheese tasting event, an Easter event, special shopping excursion trips, a special Santa-train in December, and much more.

Why Early Railroads Went "Belly-Up" In Lumpkin and Dawson Counties

Following the collapse of the very substantial gold mining industries in Lumpkin and Dawson counties in the mid-1800s, area leadership sought to re-ignite commercial growth with the construction of railroads, but the idea just never seemed able to gain any traction. Though road-beds – some of which still exist today – for railroads across these two counties had been graded and partially constructed by the late 1800s, very few rails were ever laid in Lumpkin, and none in Dawson. Today, neither county has an inch of functioning railroad, a fact which continues to mystify the curious.

Even today, the absence of railroad lines across Lumpkin and Dawson counties continues to mystify newcomers and long-time residents alike. The very grand and promising commercial transportation option of the mid-1870s which had swept into most every other north Georgia county in some form or fashion, just never "took root" in these two locales, and no one seems to know exactly why.

Though a short side-track (which no longer exists) was once constructed into Lumpkin to provide access to the copper and nitrates deposits north of Dahlonega, and a temporary logging track (which also no longer exists) was constructed to the area known as "Turner's Corner" in north Lumpkin, both of these short rail lines (which were side-tracks from the former *Gainesville-Northwestern Railroad*) were in existence for only a brief period of time. Lumpkin and Dawson are two of the few counties in the state which have no railroads whatsoever today. Some people welcome the peaceful circumstances in the absence of railroads. Some businessmen, however, would no doubt like to see a change.

Since virtually none of the railroads across Georgia offer passenger transportation any longer (and haven't since the 1960s), most of today's residents consider the paucity of rail lines in Lumpkin and Dawson counties to actually be a blessing. Freight trains are noisy, often transport dangerous materials, often delay automobile traffic at crossings, and often cause property values to be depreciated, to name a few of their negative aspects.

The absence of rail transportation across these two counties – at least to a minor extent – has also helped to restrain the development and over-population of these regions (despite the growth afforded since the 1980s by modern highways such as Georgia 400), much to the additional relief of long-time residents grown cautious and fearful of the crime and congestion resulting from urban sprawl to the south.

However, to the residents of the 1870s, the railroad represented all that was good (instead of undesirable) in modern society, such as access to employment, increased access to domestic household and farming products, and dependable transportation. It offered a sense of increased civilization for what had long been a backward, semi-pioneer region.

What then happened to the construction of railroads in these two counties? Rights-of-way and rails for a major line were constructed most of the way from Gainesville to Dahlonega, and similar efforts were expended for road-beds across Dawson County, but before either of these two projects were productively operational, they strangely simply withered and died.

Were these projects an altruistic endeavor, or just another bold scheme to parlay invested stockholder monies into a fast buck? Few records exist today, and most persons involved with the projects or persons who might even remember them, have long since departed this earth.

The late Madeline Anthony, a long-time native and Lumpkin County historian, had, prior to her death, remembered what was called the *"Gainesville & Dahlonega Railroad"* (G&D RR) from old newspaper clippings she had once preserved, but was not certain of the actual circumstances surrounding the line. The late Ida Phillips – yet another long-time resident and source of Lumpkin history – had remembered excited talk during her childhood of the railroad's eminent arrival in the outskirts of Dahlonega, but little else. Yet another fount of information regarding most subjects in Lumpkin County – the late J.B. Jones – who, prior to his death,

Col. W.D. Price, a U.S. Civil War-era attorney in Dahlonega, Georgia, was a distinguished and highly-respected lawyer, businessman, investor and civic leader in the Lumpkin County area for many years. His association with the problem-plagued *Gainesville & Dahlonega Railroad* venture nevertheless did not lend it the credibility necessary to attract the additional investors necessary to give the railroad life. (Photo courtesy of the GA Dept. of Archives & History)

almost always was a well-stocked reservoir of details involving historic issues in the county, was equally at a loss when queried prior to his death.

The most notable and reliable source of such history involving Lumpkin County – the late Professor Andrew W. Cain's meticulously-documented *History Of Lumpkin County, 1832-1932* – unfortunately lists no more than a smattering of references on the subject of railroads. Cain described the initial planning and construction of the railroad to the "outskirts" of Dahlonega, but his book provides little more than brief details and the fact that financial support for the line eventually collapsed.

Prior to her death, the late Sybil McRay – long-time archivist/writer/librarian at *Chestatee Regional Library* in Gainesville – also offered information on the *Gainesville & Dahlonega Railroad*, but had no actual explanation for its demise either.

Venerable Dahlonega Lawyer – Pictured is the Price Building in which Col. W.P. Price maintained his substantial law practice on the upper level during the latter half of the 19th century. He also held a partnership in the Price & Reese Dry Goods business located on the lower level of this building which still stands on the old town square in Dahlonega, Georgia as of this writing (2025). It was from this site that Price conducted much of his business endeavors and no doubt planned and haggled with investors in the ill-fated *Gainesville & Dahlonega Railroad* project. (Photo courtesy of the Georgia Dept. of Archives & History)

"Yes, I have several references to it," she replied matter-of-factly, when, in the 1980s, she was asked about the rail line. "At one time, you could still see the pilings across the river for the railroad trestle there. It (the railroad) never made it any further to Dahlonega than that point."

Whatever the circumstances, when the first railroads were being constructed across America, it apparently was not unusual for speculation and excited enthusiasm to cloud the realities of the actual financial requirements of a venture of this nature. Such was probably the case with the Lumpkin and Dawson railroads, but didn't other counties which were successful in attracting railroads also face these same issues?

The two railroad projects, although entirely separate and distinct from each other initially, apparently became collectively associated later in their development when promoters of the lines sought to stave off financial collapse. They both originated in the late 1870s, and several newspaper accounts eventually discussed the combination of the two projects.

The railroad across Lumpkin County was initiated first in 1877-78. According to Cain's *History*, on March 7, 1879 at about 4:00 p.m. in the afternoon, a group of Dahlonega residents *"marched out"* to where the depot was to be located (never stating exactly where), to witness the completion of the *G&D Railroad*.

Cain's description of the day states: *"When the cannon had performed its part in the joyous occasion, Col. (W.P.) Price came forward with an appropriate little speech; Col. R.H. Baker set the last stake which was driven deep down into the ground by Miss Willie Lewis amid great applause. The crowd then dispersed, with plans to meet on the same spot when the first train arrived, which was apparently expected in the near future."*

Today, one can only speculate at the site of the *Gainesville & Dahlonega Railroad* depot. Accounts indicate that the railroad ended at that time somewhere in the vicinity of the western side of the Chestatee River at what was known as *"Leather's Ford"* (just east of the automobile dealership at the intersection of Georgia 400 Highway and Burnt Stand Road in Lumpkin County). Since there was no known construction beyond that point, that would have meant that the "depot" would have been quite a hike from Dahlonega.

Logic dictates that this planned depot would, almost by necessity, have been located farther north near Dahlonega since that was its original planned destination, but later news accounts of the venture indicate that contractors ultimately changed their plans, deciding instead to extend the line to Auraria south of Dahlonega. The reality of the situation meant that the rails would be graded to Auraria and then Dawson County, rather than to Dahlonega, since the most cost-effective route from the Leather's Ford termination would have followed (the already-graded) Burnt Stand Road directly to Auraria Road, which in turns leads directly to Auraria. Due to the necessity of adjoining the *Gainesville & Dahlonega* with a Dawson County line, the prospect of a depot at or even near Dahlonega apparently at some point fell out of favor and consideration.

It will likely never be known today whether it was a main line or a spur line (or no line whatsoever) that the *G&D RR*'s planners had originally planned to construct from Leather's Ford to Dahlonega. Accordingly, the actual planned site of the Dahlonega depot on the *Gainesville & Dahlonega Railroad* (if one was ever planned at all) remains shrouded in mystery.

Any further accounts of the *Gainesville & Dahlonega Railroad* are sketchy at best. According to Cain's **History**, the project suffered almost continuous financial problems and set-backs which ultimately proved insurmountable.

Dahlonega attorney Col. William P. Price was a major financial backer, promoter, underwriter and fund-raiser for the *G&D RR*. An interview with him by a reporter from the **Gainesville Eagle** newspaper in the February 21, 1879 issue (as subsequently recorded in Cain's **History**) indicates some of the uncertainty and mystery surrounding the project.

".... *You are the president of the Gainesville and Dahlonega Railroad?*"

"*Correct.*"

"*Well, ...I want some facts, and you are going around with them hid away in your bosom...*"

".... *Well,*" said the colonel, as he settled himself in a chair, "*we did not want to raise any fuss about it, or excite hopes, until we knew what we were about; but since you force me, I will give you all the facts in my knowledge.*"

"*What then are your plans?*"

"*The road can be graded by convict labor,*" Col. Price continued. "*On the first of April, there will be some changes in existing arrangements, and then I can get what convicts I want.*"

"*But you know they must be fed and clothed,*" the reporter countered.

"*The farmers of Lumpkin, Union and Dawson and other counties will advance me the provisions. One man alone said he would advance $500.00 and more if necessary in this way.*"

"*Precisely,*" said the doubting reporter, "*but they must eventually be paid.*"

"*Well, you see, with those advances, we will issue scrip, good for freight and passage. These we will make in various denominations. The consequence will be that that will be as good as money anywhere contiguous to the (rail) road, and the merchants of Gainesville and Dahlonega will take them* (the scrip) *because they will be cash to them. Why, one man – Mr. Hand, of my town* (Dahlonega), *pays $2,000 a year to get his goods here to Dahlonega.*"

"*Then you will have no stock?*" asked the reporter, as he looked ruefully at the nicket which he had saved up to invest.

"*None whatsoever,*" the victimized answered promptly. "*All we ask of the people of your city is to buy enough of the scrip, good for freight or passage, no matter into whose hands the road may fall, to give me a few thousand dollars to pay incidental expenses, guarding the convicts, etc. If they will do this, the road will be built.*"

The circumstances of the railroad as they transpired from this point are unknown today. With no stock, and the apparent lack of funds and backing, the construction of the *Gainesville & Dahlonega Railroad* no doubt continued temporarily under Col. Price's leadership, since he was widely-known and highly respected, but it was a precipitous existence at best, a reality which must eventually have assisted in its downfall.

On July 4, 1890, an advertisement describes the outright sale of the rail line venture to Col. Price. Up until this point, Price had apparently been involved in the endeavor with other individuals, but they perhaps had defaulted on their promised support.

Whatever the actual circumstances, Price reportedly purchased the railroad outright for $4,000. A newspaper account of the incident stated that he *"owned judgements and other liens on the property amounting to more than $40,000, and he was compelled to protect this large interest."*

A significant problem in the project seems to have been centered around the prospective Gainesville investors, from which a substantial portion of the railroad's funding was to have been raised. The March 4, 1879 issue of *The Eagle* (as recorded in Cain's *History*) carried a letter to the editor from W.P. Price, which, among other things, stated *"There*

A significant problem in the project seems to have been centered around the prospective Gainesville investors, from which a substantial portion of the railroad's funding was to have been raised.

is no indifference to this enterprise, except in the city of Gainesville. The people of Lumpkin and Hall counties, outside of Gainesville, so far as I could judge, are all favorable to it. A few only of the citizens of Gainesville have expressed any desire for the road. This ought not to be so, and perhaps will not be so, after they fully understand their interests in the premises."

Other references to the railroad through the remainder of the 19th Century are few and far between. The few which exist indicate that it actually provided service for the region for a short while; others suggest that it was never completed.

At some point in the construction process, a decision apparently was made to construct the railroad solely to Auraria, bypassing Dahlonega entirely, possibly in an effort to provide renewed legitimacy to the project as a connector to a similar railroad under construction through the prosperous Etowah River Valley section of Dawson County. The May 7, 1880 issue of *The Eagle* carried an article announcing the fact that *"After several experimental surveys, Col. Sage (a surveyor for the Gainesville Airline Railroad) has located the line of the Gainesville and Dahlonega Railroad to Aurora (sic)."*

On May 20, 1899, *The Eagle* carried a notice indicating that Col. Price had apparently admitted the obvious – Gainesville, for the most part, simply was not interested in investment in a railroad venture to Dahlonega. Gainesville and Hall County already had several railroads and perhaps saw little reason for investment in still more of the steel rails.

The *Eagle* article, however, provided a somewhat convoluted explanation of the lack of support: *"Application was made for charter for the Dahlonega Railroad Company* (as opposed to the 'Gainesville' and Dahlonega Railroad as it was originally billed). *It is to be 30 miles in length, and is to be built from Dahlonega to Gainesville or Lula. The capital stock of the company is to be $300,000, all of which is to be common stock. It is the intention of the company to go forward at once with the work."*

And then on June 1, 1899, *The Eagle* carried this brief notice: *"We are reliably informed that the promoters of the Dahlonega Railroad scheme have been tendered by Col. W.P. Price, free of cost, the right-of-way of the old Gainesville and Dahlonega Railroad."* Due to the use of the descriptive term "scheme" in the newspaper article, the railroad venture apparently had obtained a disreputable reputation, perhaps impacting any potential for the attraction of investors.

Regardless of the actual circumstances, the death-knell for the *Gainesville & Dahlonega Railroad* apparently had been sounded. The full financial losses of Col. Price are unknown today, but they must have been considerable.

With the advent of electricity, the age of the "electric" railway was soon ushered in. The opportunity for water power via a dam and electricity generator at Leather's Ford, coupled with the opportunity to inexpensively obtain the then defunct *"Dahlonega Railroad"* rights-of-way/etc. apparently gave rise to the creation of an electric railway system which operated for a short while on

Remnant Road – The road-bed for one of the railroads in Dawson County in the late 1800s is still faintly visible through the trees along the right side of the Etowah River in this photo. Though the route was graded, no rails were ever laid for this line. Sketchy records indicate this construction project was the work of an enterprise known as the *Gainesville, Dawsonville and Cartersville Railroad.* (Photo by R. Olin Jackson)

the existing portion of the by-then abandoned rail line.

The October 15, 1903 issue of *The Atlanta Constitution* carried an article describing that situation: *"The power now used in the city of Gainesville comes from the dam on the Chestatee River, 15 miles northwest of the city. This dam is no little one, itself. It is owned by the Gainesville and Dahlonega Electric Railway Company, and furnishes 1200 horsepower, this company being a twin companion of the North Georgia Electric Company* (which also furnished electric power for Gainesville via a dam and generator at the Chattahoochee River near present-day Riverside Military Academy), *General Warner being at the head of both.*

"The Chestatee dam is two hundred feet long, and twenty-seven feet high. The power is brought to the city on heavy copper wires strung along the right-of-way of the old Gainesville and Dahlonega Railway, an enterprise which ex-Governor Candler headed, and over which road trains at one time ran from Gainesville

In 1886, three separate railroads were planned across Dawson County. The two individuals in this photo stand at the end of one of the graded roadbeds for one of these lines. A trestle originally planned for this site would have extended this railroad across a deep ravine near the Etowah River in Dawson County. The trestle, however, was never built. Due to a lack of funding, bad economic times and other factors, no railroads were ever completed across Dawson County. (Photo by R. Olin Jackson)

to a point beyond the Chattahoochee River. The old road-bed has been reworked by the new company, and it is the intention to have cars running over this line in another year to Dahlonega. The road is graded as far toward Dahlonega as the Chestatee dam and power house, leaving only eight miles of grading necessary. The Chestatee dam cost $100,000, and was completed more than a year ago."

Interestingly judging from this news account, plans were still in the offing as late as 1903 – albeit from a different set of owners/operators – for

construction of a rail line to Dahlonega. How long and to what extent the *Gainesville & Dahlonega Electric Railway Company* operated is unknown. It apparently was not cost-effective however, because it was only operational for a few years before it too was abandoned.

Following the demise of this final reincarnation of the planned *Gainesville & Dahlonega Railroad*, the railroad rights-of-way eventually reverted back to ownership by the original titleholders of the real estate along the former route, and the rest, as they say, is history.

In Dawson County, the story was much the same, although many of the problems with this rail line seem to have centered around "too much" rather than "too little" interest in the railroad.

An article in the **Dawsonville Mountain Chronicle** of January 27, 1880, announces: *"If our people would grade a railroad and lay the ties to intersect the Gainesville and Dahlonega at Auraria, there would be no difficulty in finding capitalists who would lay the iron and put the road in operation... Owing to the natural advantages, a railroad bed can be graded from this place in Auraria at a less cost than has ever been the case with any railroad for the same distance."*

Contrary to circumstances involving the *Gainesville & Dahlonega Railroad*, investors for the Dawson County railroad were more numerous, and Dawson County apparently was a more desirable destination than Lumpkin County, because not one, but several outside railroad companies considered the extension of a rail line to it from the late 1800s up to the early 1900s.

One of the first was the *Macon and Cincinnati Air-Line Railroad*. An article in the February 24, 1880 issue of **The Mountain Chronicle** announces *"We received yesterday a letter from a gentleman* *of Brunswick reminding us of the projected Macon and Cincinnati Railroad, which will pass directly through this section. It passes Monticello, Covington, Lawrenceville, Cumming, Dawsonville or Dixon, up the Amicalola and on to Knoxville. Whilst this may not be the very best road for our people, there is more probability of it than any other now. A strong company has been organized for a long time, and have only waited for the Macon and Brunswick Railroad matter to be settled, as there was some contingency connected with that road that would affect this. But the M&B road matter has been satisfactorily settled . . . . and may now be set down as a probability."*

Another account on June 14, 1881 in **The Mountain Chronicle** proclaims: *"Less than $400,000 will grade and lay cross-ties and iron for a narrow gauge railroad from Dawsonville to Atlanta via Cumming and Alpharetta."*

In March of 1882, the **Articles of Association** for the *"Gainesville and Dalton Short-Cut Railroad Company"* were carried in **The Chronicle**. The *Gainesville and Dalton* was intended to operate in Hall, Dawson, Gilmer, Murray and Whitfield counties.

Stockholders for this venture were: Robert F. Williams (Auraria), Jacob P. Imboden (Dahlonega) and John L. Summerour (Amicalola, Dawson Co.). It (the railroad) was to connect Gainesville and Dalton, a distance of about 85 miles, and provide a shorter route between Cincinnati and Charleston.

In September of 1884, the rights-of-way for the *Gainesville, Dawsonville, and Cartersville Railroad Company* in Dawson County were also announced, and are carried in **Deed Book D** in the Dawson County Courthouse records. This railroad, based upon the land lots cited in the records, would have

followed roughly the route of present-day State Road 53, east from inside the city of Dawsonville, turning northeastward in the vicinity of the Etowah River, then following the river north into Lumpkin County. Portions of the *Gainesville, Dawsonville, and Cartersville Railroad (GD&CRR)* were graded and were still visible well into the 21st century at various sites along State Road 53, and along the northern bank of the Etowah River.

By December of 1884, the exact location of the *GD&CRR* and its depot appear to have been decided; subscriptions to the railroad had been made by some Dawson Countians, and some reservations among the subscribers had developed. The date of the completion of the line had been set as January, 1886, which, interestingly, was the same completion date as that which had been planned for the Dahlonega railroad venture.

In 1886, in fact, not one, but three separate railroads are mentioned in news accounts for construction in Dawson County:

1/ The *"Augusta and Chattanooga Railroad Company."* This project reportedly had a capital stock of $4 million, however, the board of directors, as a group, had agreed to purchase only $6,000 of the corporation's stock. It appears that the directors expected most of the money to come from "subscriptions at the county level" (which in today's language would be known as "a highly leveraged deal").

2/ A second railroad was described as *"another railroad to Cartersville, perhaps by Georgia Marble Works. . . ."* This could possibly have been in reference to the *Cartersville, Dawsonville, and Gainesville Railroad.*

3/ A third rail line was a branch railroad from Auraria to Dahlonega.

"Electric Rails" – With the advent of electricity in the late 1800s, the age of the "electric" railway was soon ushered in. The opportunity for water power via a dam and electrical power generation at Leather's Ford in Lumpkin County, coupled with the opportunity to inexpensively obtain the defunct *"Dahlonega Railroad"* rights-of-way gave rise to a new "electric" railway system which operated for a short while on the abandoned rail line. The October 15, 1903 issue of **The Atlanta Constitution** stated: *"The power now used in the city of Gainesville comes from the dam on the Chestatee River, 15 miles northwest of the city. This dam is no little one, itself. It is owned by the Gainesville and Dahlonega Electric Railway Company, and furnishes 1200 horsepower, this company being a twin companion of the North Georgia Electric Company* (which also furnished electric power for Gainesville via a dam and generator at the Chattahoochee River near present-day Riverside Military Academy)." One of the electrically-powered railway transport cars is pictured. (Photo courtesy of the GA Dept of Archives & History, Atlanta)

Judging from the amount of space dedicated to articles in the **Dawsonville Mountain Chronicle** on the possibility of railroad construction to Dawsonville, much of the talk was mere speculation and idle chatter, possibly in hopes of drumming up support for any number of several potential opportunities. Dawson County was much more accessible from several different directions than was Lumpkin, and as such, had more suitors.

The editorials, speculation, and wishful thinking may have achieved their purpose too, since by August 26, 1911, the *Etowah Valley Railway Company* had actually become a reality - at least on paper. The **Dawson County Advertiser** of August 26, 1911, carried the petition for incorporation by ten men: *G.R. Glenn, H.D. Garley* (sic) (Gurley), *John H. Moere* (sic) (Moore), *T.J. Smith, J.M. Brooksner* (sic?), *J.F.* (sic) (J.E.?) *Tate, H. Head, J.F. Sargent, W.H.* (sic?) (W.B.?) *Townsend*, and *Craig R. Arnold*. Interestingly, at least five or six of these investors were residents of Dahlonega, not Dawson County.

The corporate description reads as follows: *". . . shows that they desire for themselves their associates successors and assigns to be incorporated for the period of 101 years with the privilege of renewal as a railroad company under the name of Etowah Valley Railwsy (sic) Company, the length of said road will be about 75 miles, as nearly as can be estimated. The general direction of same will be from a point on the Louisville & Nashville R.R. at or near Ballground (sic) Cherokee County, Ga., thence along the Etowah River thru Creighton, Cherokee county, Ga. to the Northern State line of Ga. in Towns County passing thru the counties of Cherokee, Forsyth, Dawson, Lumpkin, White, Towns all in the state of Ga. Said company proposes to construct and build or purchase and acquire a railroad between the points above named along private right of way and on public roads, either or both."*

Although the *Etowah Valley Railway Company* was one of the few which were officially incorporated for business (at least on paper) in Dawson County, the actual owner of the rights-of-way and railroad line constructed in Dawson is questionable today. Some references refer to ownership as belonging to the *Etowah Valley Railway Company*, and some refer to the *Gainesville Dawsonville and Cartersville Railroad* as owner.

Although there was considerable Dawson County interest (as there had been in Dahlonega/

Lumpkin County) in bringing a railroad to Dawson, three major factors ultimately combined to deny completion into this county. These included a strong inclination for bickering and competition among the prospective builders; an inherent lack of available capital on the local level; and a fundamental lack of stable commercial industry necessary to lend legitimacy to the project and its construction. The only industry of any significance at this time in Dawson was gold mining, and it had peaked in intensity a number of years in advance of any plans for any railroads.

One of the sections graded for a railroad in Dawson ended not far from the point at which Highway 136 crosses the Etowah River today. If one stands on the bridge today during winter (when the leaves have departed the trees), this grade is clearly visible.

In the waning years of the late 19th Century, the once-explosive growth of the Lumpkin and Dawson County areas had been reduced to a fraction of that enjoyed prior to the California gold rush. The Lumpkin and Dawson County railroad ventures – however ill-conceived and mismanaged – presumably were envisioned as a means to staunch this negative growth trend, and reignite commercial development in the region. Interestingly, today, most land and home owners in the vicinity are, to say the least, probably thrilled that the aforementioned highly-anticipated railroad projects all ended in failure.

One of the sections graded for a railroad in Dawson ended not far from the point at which Highway 136 crosses the Etowah River today.

Origin Of A Town

The Railroad Comes To Blue Ridge

A number of tiny north Georgia mountain communities sprang up in the 1880s as a direct result of the railroads which passed through them. And as the years went by, if the railroad languished or died, so also did the town.

Back in the 1880s, railroads such as the line between Marietta and Mineral Bluff allowed timber to be more easily harvested in the mountains of north Georgia. Lumber and other building products were in high demand as a result of the state's burgeoning population. In those days, instead of the prefabricated building materials used today, almost everything was built of wood.

The town of Blue Ridge had its beginnings in 1887 when Colonel Mike McKinney built the first house in what then was the wilds of north Georgia. Only 50 years earlier, Cherokee Indians had still inhabited the region.

Col. McKinney's partner, C.R. Walton, a civil engineer, laid out and mapped the town. Its elevation at 1,751 feet above sea level made it the highest railroad town in the state at that time.

In 1886, steam engine Number 1, called "Little Mary," chugged into Blue Ridge.

And just as was also customary in those days, this rail line between Marietta and Tennessee was built with convict labor. The men graded the route with little more than axes, picks, shovels, wrecking bars, wheeled dumping carts, horses, mules and black powder. As a result of their harsh lifestyle, the men fought, brawled and sometimes even killed each other during the construction. It was a hard way to live, but the work of these men ushered in a new era of growth as the railroads expanded.

In 1886, steam engine Number 1, called "Little Mary," chugged into Blue Ridge. It was owned and operated by the *Marietta & North Georgia Railroad* (precursor to the *Louisville & Nashville Railroad* which would later purchase the same route) which had constructed its repair shop – the only one between Atlanta and Knoxville – in Blue Ridge.

In short order, the railroad brought about major growth in Blue Ridge, even causing the county seat to be moved there from Morganton (the oldest town and original county seat) in 1895. By the late 1890s, Blue Ridge was the bustling business center of the area.

Blue Ridge was also a resort community of sorts, and the railroad facilitated this growth as well, transporting hundreds of visitors to the site during the spring and summer months every year. Three mineral springs which had concentrated amounts of magnesium, iron and sulphur – all healthful minerals – had been discovered in the vicinity.

As word spread of the healthful waters and the attractive accommodations which were being constructed near the tracks around Blue Ridge, the railroad found itself carrying more and more visitors to the area. Interestingly, due to the concentrated minerals in the water, it smelled like swamp water, but the visitors to the spot drank copious amounts of the foul-smelling liquid, even taking jugs of it home for later consumption.

Some people took the morning train to Blue Ridge, ate lunch at the hotel, walked to the mineral springs, and then returned home via the afternoon train. It was a most unusual story, but it was one that was destined to be relatively short-lived.

As word spread of the healthful waters and the attractive accommodations which were being constructed near the tracks around Blue Ridge, the railroad found itself carrying more and more visitors to the area.

Just as the railroad brought prosperity to Blue Ridge, it also took it away. The grading of a new faster route to Tennessee, coupled with the eventual decline in rail passenger service, brought about the town's decline. In 1907, a new railroad allowed trains to travel from Marietta to Etowah, Tennessee through Cartersville, Georgia. It was a route which was on a much more level terrain, and therefore faster and safer.

As a result of this and other factors, the repair shop in Blue Ridge eventually was moved to Etowah, after that route became the more heavily-traveled rail line. The new route was a signal that the end was at hand for Blue Ridge's railroad-oriented livelihood. It would take 45 or 50 more years before the town's commerce would die out almost completely, but it was inevitable.

The once-vibrant springs deteriorated as the years went by in Blue Ridge. By the late 1930s, few individuals drank from the waters anymore. By the late 1950s, with the demise of passenger service to Blue Ridge, few travelers even went to the town anymore, and no one – save the operators of the few freight trains which still ran on the line – even traveled by rail anymore. The automobile had conquered the railroad in cost and convenience – at least for the time being.

Historic Railroad Into The Mountains

The *Blue Ridge Scenic Railway*

The old rails from the Louisville & Nashville Railroad had languished for years, and were being threatened with extinction when a group of stockholders in a small north Georgia railroad came up with a plan to revitalize the line.

The *Blue Ridge Scenic Railway (BRSR)* is a scenic passenger train service which is actually part of the *Georgia Northeastern Railroad (GNR)*. The *Georgia Northeastern* was purchased/organized in 1987 by a group of private investors who took up the task of servicing a handful of scant businesses in the timber, grain, poultry and marble products industries of northeast Georgia which still used the rail line.

The idea for the scenic passenger service was born after a substantial number of Georgia residents made known their desire for a scenic line back into the mountains. Passenger service into the little north Georgia towns was discontinued long ago, and even the railroad tracks were removed from many of the old railroads such as the famed *Tallulah Falls Railroad*.

Former passengers of some of these historic little mountain short-line railroads have mourned the loss of this romantic (and useful) form of transportation for decades, and even younger individuals have expressed an interest in rail transportation to the quaint and attractive north Georgia mountain towns from yesteryear. . . but once the railroad rails have been taken up and the railroad-bed has reverted back to private ownership, any hope of restoration of that railroad is "dust in the wind."

The old *Louisville & Nashville (L&N)* line from Marietta to McCaysville, was a lucky survivor. It, has somehow managed to weather the years and grows stronger with each passing year. The line is owned today by the Georgia Department of Transportation and is leased to the *Georgia Northeastern Railroad*.

Following a feasibility study and some cooperative efforts with the city of Blue Ridge, Georgia, the *Blue Ridge Scenic Railway* was born, and is fulfilling the dream of travelers who wish to get back to the "good old days" of rail travel. It has become a popular weekend getaway activity for Atlanta-area residents.

The train leaves the recently-restored turn-of-the-century *L&N Railroad Depot* in Blue Ridge. As it travels northward through the Fannin County countryside, passengers are treated to some of the most beautiful scenery in the state.

Train Description

The train is typically composed of a commissary car (where snacks and drinks are available) and a number of coach cars, all pulled by vintage 1960s

Holiday Celebration – Photographed on July 4, 1930, this event included a substantial barbecue, a partaking of the healing mineral waters from the Blue Ridge springs, and numerous other activities in celebration of the opening of Lake Toccoa and the completion of hydro-electric power for Blue Ridge. Many dignitaries and celebrants arrived on the *Louisville & Nashville Railroad (L&N)* (pictured), with the crowds that day exceeding well over 100 participants. The old *L&N Depot*, built in 1905, still stands as of 2025, but daily passenger service was discontinued in the 1960s. The *Scenic Blue Ridge Railroad* provides excursion services today to McCaysville, Georgia, for which tickets and other items are sold at the old Blue Ridge depot.

diesel locomotives. Each coach features traditional upholstered seats (arranged in pairs), and many of the seats face each other, a situation which facilitates and enhances conversations with other passengers.

Each coach also has a restroom, and all the cars have picture windows for unrestricted viewing of the scenic beauty one experiences along the ride. The coaches also all have air-conditioning to keep the cars cool in summer and toasty warm in the fall and winter months. And if one can get to Blue Ridge, he or she certainly has no worries about the reliability of the *Blue Ridge Scenic Railway* in inclement weather.

The coaches were all built in the 1940s and '50s, so they offer a true opportunity to savor a vintage railroad ride.

One of the coaches was built in the 1950s for the *Santa Fe Railroad* of New Mexico and Colorado fame. It was purchased from a chapter of the *National Railway Historical Society* in Greensboro, North Carolina. The commissary car was built in 1951 for the *Northern Pacific Railroad* in Washington state.

There is also one "open air" car which features padded bench seats facing to the outside and running the length of the car. This option provides an even better view of the scenery for riders who prefer the great outdoors and "open-air" transportation.

The trip is particularly popular with individuals and groups who wish to spend a day in the mountains. The scenic railway began service in June of 1998,

Ox-Power? – Photographed circa early 1900s in one of the downtown streets of Blue Ridge with an address numeral which appears to be either 1966 or 1900 or perhaps 1906, a local grocery with one of the modes of transportation of that day is pictured. Though oxen quite often were strong durable draft animals, those living in-town usually would use a horse - or perhaps even a mule - to pull a buggy of this type.

and approximately 17,000 riders made the trip during the inaugural season.

Elderly people, especially, who feared they might never have a chance to ride trains again, have expressed appreciation for the experience. "People find themselves in a gently-rocking car, with the sun shining through the windows, and the clickety-clacking sound as the train moves along the jointed track (in contrast to the continuously-welded rail used on modern lines), and it takes them back in time," one official remarked.

Scenic History

Passengers on the one-hour ride enjoy both scenery and a bit of history along the old rail line. Mile markers (which can still be viewed along the western side of the track) were installed when the *L&N Railroad* first acquired the track at the turn of the century. The markers all show the mileage from the *L&N's* corporate headquarters in Louisville, Kentucky.

Approximately three-quarters of a mile north of the historic depot in Blue Ridge, the railroad passes the site of the old engine shops which once existed in Blue Ridge. This facility was operated between 1887 and 1906, and was once a strategic service center for the locomotives on the route.

Approximately two miles north of Blue Ridge the *BRSR* passes Murphy Junction. In earlier days, the line was split at this point. A branch which continued on into North Carolina (Murphy) angled off to the right, and the main line (angling off to the left) continued (as it still does today) on to Tennessee (Copperhill).

Today, the old Murphy branch-line ends at Mineral Bluff, Georgia. The rails between Mineral Bluff and Murphy, regrettably, were taken up long ago. Had they remained in place, the Blue Ridge Scenic Railroad might have had a direct connection with the *Great Smoky Mountains Railroad* which is so popular with vacationers in North Carolina today.

Also at Murphy Junction, there is a "Y" in the tracks – or, in railroading parlance, a "wye" – which allows a train to turn around or reverse the direction in which it is heading.

On the northern side of the wye, an old family home which has long existed on the route can still be viewed today. A family by the name of Panter (pronounced "painter") built the home in the 1880s, and helped lay the track on the original rail line. Today, descendants of these railroading pioneers reportedly still live in this home.

Part of the route of the scenic line follows the beautiful Toccoa River. At one spot in the river near Curtis Switch Road, a historic landmark may be seen. Within the river, aboriginal inhabitants who resided in this area in prehistory constructed an ancient "fish-trap" with quite large rocks. This historic structure can sometimes be seen during periods of drought or low water *(requires a brief walk across private property).*

The fish trap consists of a series of rocks placed in a "V" formation on the riverbed. The aboriginal natives periodically drove fish into the large opening of the "V" and gradually forced the fish down the length of the

The *Blue Ridge Scenic Railroad* begins at Blue Ridge, Georgia in Fannin County. The historic *Blue Ridge Depot*, built in 1905, no longer dispenses tickets to customers for commercial travel destinations throughout the United States, but rather for the *Scenic Blue Ridge Railroad* excursion runs (pictured). (Photo by Martin K. O'Toole)

"V" until they were forced to pass out through the small end where they were caught in woven baskets. It was quite an ingenious design.

McCaysville Terminus

The scenic train continues northward until it reaches the Tennessee State Line (which divides McCaysville, Georgia from Copperhill, Tennessee). The train stops just a few feet short of the state line to allow passengers to disembark.

After leaving the train, all passengers have one hour to browse the many shops in McCaysville. Tourism has replaced copper as a major industry in this scenic mountain town – the county's largest – incorporated in 1902.

One unique aspect of McCaysville

Within the river, aboriginal inhabitants who resided in this area in prehistory constructed an ancient "fish-trap" with quite large rocks.

In a reflection of the increased passenger and commercial use of the *Louisville & Nashville (L&N) Railroad* through Blue Ridge, the sizeable Blue Ridge Inn was built circa 1900 near the railroad tracks in the community. It is sometimes confused with another "Blue Ridge Inn" in this vicinity.

The old Blue Ridge Hotel in downtown Blue Ridge - one of several in the town by that name over time - was photographed here circa 1930s.

has marked it as a fun spot for youngsters for a long time. Smart community promoters have painted a line across the community to mark the boundary between Georgia and Tennessee. Children just love to straddle the blue boundary, enjoying the opportunity to "stand in two states at one time." On the Georgia side, the town is called McCaysville.

On the Tennessee side, it's known as Copperhill.

The blue-painted boundary line interestingly slices through the Hometown Foods IGA in McCaysville and its adjacent parking lot, then continues diagonally across the street before scaling the yellow brick building which houses the Copper Emporium furniture store. One has to wonder how these businesses know to whom they must pay their taxes.

Folks in McCaysville like to tell the story of how the boundary line is actually not quite accurate, since the surveyors back in the 1800s reportedly spent too much time sampling from a moonshine still they had chanced upon at the time.

Whether that's the reason for the erroneously-marked boundary or not, the state of Georgia contends its border with Tennessee should actually lie farther north - at the 35th parallel, as specified in the laws of both states. *"But if*

A group of engineers with what then was known as the *Atlanta, Knoxville & Northern Railroad* (precursor to the *Louisville & Nashville RR* through Blue Ridge) posed for this photograph in Blue Ridge, Georgia, in 1897. At that time, Blue Ridge was still the center of operations for the rail line. (Photo courtesy of R. Olin Jackson Collection)

the boundary is corrected, it will shift a mile-wide strip of south Chattanooga and most of Copperhill into Georgia," said Edwin Jackson, co-author with Marion Hemperley of **Georgia's Boundaries: The Shaping Of A State**, *"and that's just not likely to happen. Even though a suit could be filed in the U.S. Supreme Court, the rulings of that court in similar situations have suggested that a boundary line which has been recognized and accepted in the past will stand, even if later found to have been drawn in error."*

Aside from the interest of the boundary line, there are numerous shopping opportunities in McCaysville. Everything from crafts, to antiques, to novelty gifts and tasty treats can be found aplenty!

It is noteworthy to point out that the former clinic of Dr. Thomas J. Hicks – who quietly operated a baby-selling practice in the 1950s and whose story

was told to a nationwide audience on programs such as *ABC Television's* **20-20** – once existed in the space occupied today by the shops in the Toccoa Center complex.

Repair Shops – This somewhat primitive photograph snapped circa 1906 shows the railroad repair shops which once existed in Blue Ridge. Known at that time as the *Marietta & North Georgia Railroad*, the line was responsible for much of the early growth of Blue Ridge.

The Railroad Comes
to Roswell – Almost

It was a landmark at the edge of the town for 40 years, and just as is
the case with most beloved short-line railroads, historic railroad enthusiasts
continue to study and enjoy the details involving this former line from yesteryear.
Interestingly, though it was officially identified as "The Roswell Railroad,"
it was never actually constructed all the way to its namesake city.

In 1863, the city of Roswell obtained a charter which provided for the organization of *"the Atlanta and Roswell Railroad Company (A&R-RR)"* which would be constructed from downtown Atlanta (actually as a branchline of the *Western & Atlantic Railroad*) to what then was the quiet country burg of Roswell. No action, however, was ever forthcoming from this charter until 1870, when the *Atlanta and Richmond Air-Line* railroad was constructing a line from Atlanta to Charlotte, North Carolina.

The original charter for the *A&R* was amended to consolidate the *Atlanta and Roswell Railroad Company* with the *Atlanta and Richmond Air-Line*, in the process providing for the creation and attachment of the Roswell rail line thereto. Despite this action, construction was still delayed, and the topic became one of frustration for the citizens of Roswell for many years, most of whom were eager to have their own railroad line for commercial and transportation needs.

A letter from the President of the Roswell Manufacturing Company dated July, 1880, stated the circumstances fairly succinctly: *"The question of securing for this Company a better connection with Commercial centres, a quicker and more economical method of transportation than by wagon, for production, supplies and merchandise, has received the serious consideration of every President who has charge of your interest at this point."* This document is the clearest indication available of the frustration felt for almost two decades by the merchants of the up-and-coming town.

Founded in 1839 by Roswell King who had moved to the area in 1836, the sleepy burg of Roswell had grown in bursts and halts since its earliest days due to its somewhat isolated location and the absence of rail or any other mode of dependable transportation. Located on one branch of the pioneer *"Alabama Roads"* at the *"Shallow Ford"* *(Readers please see "Retracing the Historic Alabama Roads" in this book)* across the Chattahoochee, Roswell enjoyed a steady supply of citizenry who nevertheless were constantly frustrated with the rough roads into and out of the town which became virtually impassable in wet weather.

Forgotten Railroad – "Old Buck" on the *Roswell Railroad* provided reliable service for many years from Atlanta to Roswell. The depot for Roswell was on the south side of the Chattahoochee River near present-day Roberts Drive. The plaque in the photo identifies "Chamblee Station" on the route.

Up to the year 1880 as stated in the Roswell Manufacturing Company President's letter: *"All freights to and from Roswell have to be transported to and from Marietta or Doraville* (Note: both of which <u>did</u> have railroads) *over common, and in winter, very rough roads by wagons, which require ten mules, five wagons, five teamsters, one smith and helper."*

A proposition eventually was made by the Roswell Manufacturing Company's president to the effect that it would pledge a payment in the amount of $10,000 to the owners of the railroad for construction of the line to Roswell, but *"only when the road is completed and in operation."* Ultimately, $7,000 of the stated amount was raised, and the president asked the company's board to authorize payment of the remaining $3,000, with the stipulation that *"not one dollar shall be paid until the road is*

finished and in operation." The emphatic nature of the statement underlines the frustration which had been endured year after year by the town fathers in obtaining the much sought-after railroad.

Following a number of legal proceedings during 1881 which included liens, foreclosures on liens, judgements, inheritances, various legal decrees, sales of interests, conveyances of properties, etc., a reorganization occurred, and the *"Roswell Railroad Company"* was formed. The new corporation renewed its relations with the *Atlanta and Richmond Air-Line* which had also been newly reorganized as the *Atlanta and Charlotte Air-Line.*

The *Atlanta and Charlotte* received 201 out of a total issue of 400 shares of capital stock of the *Roswell Railroad Company*, and thus secured control of the rail line. The road – much to

The *Roswell Railroad* was in operation for 44 years. Ike Roberts (pictured) served as engineer for all 44 years of this railway's existence. His former home still stands today on Roberts Drive, which was named in his honor.

the unbridled delight of the town's citizenry – was then finally completed as a narrow-gauge line from Chamblee to the Chattahoochee River in Roswell – at which point construction again was halted. Despite the fact that a roadbed for the railroad had been graded beyond the river almost all the way up to the Roswell Manufacturing Company in "downtown" Roswell, neither a trestle over, nor rails beyond the river were ever completed. This railroad just seemed to be constantly plagued by "obstacles," but completion of the railroad to a station just across the river at the edge of town was nevertheless a huge improvement over the sole previous option of travel over the dirt trails of the area.

Before the *Roswell Railroad* was opened for operation, the *Roswell and Doraville Railroad* had succeeded to all the rights of the *Atlanta and Charlotte Air-Line*, and had begun operation on the earlier-completed lower portion of the line. This relationship continued until 1894, when the *Southern Railway Company* succeeded to the same

relationship because of its assumption of the *Atlanta and Charlotte Air-Line*.

The *Roswell Railroad* officially began service on September 1, 1881, with Isaac "Ike" Martin Roberts at the throttle as engineer of the steam-driven locomotive pulling the train which made the twice-daily trip up and down its route. With Ike at the helm, a unique era in Roswell history began. *(Editor's Note: To add perspective to the time-period, this was approximately two months prior to the famed gunfight at the rear of O.K. Corral in Tombstone, Arizona Territory at which Wyatt Earp, his brothers, and a Georgian by the name of "Doc" Holliday, earned lasting fame.)*

Ike Roberts had been born in Gaston County, North Carolina, on February 28, 1853. He was the son of John Morgan Roberts (1827-1865) and Lucinda White Roberts (1823-1895).

When Ike was 19, he left home and walked 45 miles to Spartanburg, South Carolina, where he joined a construction gang building the *Atlanta and Charlotte Air-Line*. When the road was completed, he secured a job as "wood-passer" on one of the locomotives.

In 1874, Ike "went on the road," working as a fireman on a freight train between Atlanta and Charlotte. In the span of three short years, he rose to the post of engineer on that line.

Early on, Ike became involved with the construction work for the road-bed of the line being built to Roswell; he also worked as an agent to secure the rights-of-way for the *Atlanta and Charlotte Air-Line*. Since the headquarters of the new Roswell line was located at the railroad's junction near the south bank of the Chattahoochee River, Ike took up residence in that vicinity, living in boarding houses for a number of years.

The total right-of-way of the *Roswell*

The railroad depot in Roswell (pictured) once existed near Roberts Drive just south of the Chatta-hoochee River. For a short time, it was also a *Southern Railways* depot. Following the railroad's demise in 1921, this depot was purchased by engineer Ike Roberts and used as a hay barn for many years. Notice the heavily-forested undeveloped background scenery which today is filled with development.

Railroad was just under ten miles (9.8 miles to be specific) in length. Its former route (on what today are paved streets through Sandy Springs, Chamblee, and Dunwoody) began at the Chamblee Depot (known earlier as the "Roswell Station"). From there, the route continued to Peachtree Industrial Boulevard before angling up North Peachtree Road and passing through Dunwoody to Roberts Road, where it was graded up a long incline before ending just short of a juncture with present-day Roswell Road near the Chattahoochee.

During its days of operation, the *Roswell Railroad* passenger train would leave Roswell at 7:00 a.m., and arrive back at 10:00 a.m. Then it would leave again at 3:00 p.m. and arrive back at 5:00 p.m. The train to which most area residents fondly referred as *"The Dinkey"* (and *"Old Buck"* by others), was gratefully accepted into the community.

If "flagged," *The Dinkey* – as was the

tradition in those days – would stop at any spot along the line to pick up passengers or to let them off. Aside from these flagged stops, there were four regular stops between Roswell and Chamblee: "Powers," (near what today is the intersection of Pitts Road and Spalding Drive); "Morgan Falls Junction" (where Roberts Drive crosses Spalding Drive); "Dunwoody Station;" and "Wilson's Mill" (near Peeler Road). A branch line was also built from the Morgan Falls Junction to what today is Morgan Falls, to carry materials to construct the Georgia Power Company dam and electrical generation plant at that site.

The train had an engine with tender, a combination baggage car and coach for passengers, freight cars, and flat cars. The passenger compartment had a rest room, a heater, and a water cooler. A glass case at one end held a saw, an axe, a crow-bar, and tools for emergencies.

On the run to Chamblee, the train

Phantom Rail Line – Photographed circa 1900, the covered bridge (pictured) across the Chatta-hoochee River exists at the approximate site of the present-day Roswell Road bridge. The "shallow ford" used by Native Americans in pre-history and later by pioneers in early American history was located in this vicinity. The completed *Roswell Railroad* ended on the opposite shore of the river a short distance to the left of the covered bridge. The uncompleted road-bed for the portion of the rail-road which was to have extended across the river and up to Roswell Mill (which ironically is the only portion of the former railroad bed still in existence today) was graded in this vicinity a short distance to the left of the dirt road (present-day Roswell Road). The structures (lower left) are a portion of the Ivy Woolens Mill complex built in 1857 and operated by James R. King, son of Roswell King. The struc-ture at lower right was the Roswell Hotel. (Photo courtesy of GA Dept. of Archives & History, Atlanta, GA)

customarily pulled a number of cars – both "boxcars" and "flatcars" – load-ed with lumber, stove-wood, vegeta-bles, and fruit. On its return to Roswell, the cargo would often consist of sup-plies, manufactured goods, and fertiliz-er. Horse-drawn buggies ("taxis") would meet the train at the depot near the Chattahoochee River, and take passen-gers across the wooden covered bridge into "downtown" Roswell.

In addition to engineer Ike Roberts, the Roswell line had a crew consisting of a fireman, a conductor, a brake/bag-gage-man, and a flagman. Though these former employees enjoy a footnote in history in their association with the rail

line, it is Ike's name which inevitably is the topic of discussion when the subject of the *Roswell Railroad* is raised by the few-remaining old-timers in the area.

In 1893, Ike married Nancy Turley (1869-1924) from Roswell. In 1895, af-ter their first two children were born, they moved into their own house, newly built for them, on Roberts Road, hand-ily-located across from the train de-pot. Ike, amazingly, owned about 700 acres of land in that area which today is crowded with commercial and residen-tial development.

Ike and Nancy had five children, all girls: Lula, Laura, Edith, Sarah, and Alda. It has been said that, even though

Pioneer Roswell – Old "down-town" Roswell is pictured circa 1920s. It was the glue-like red mud and extremely poor condition of the roads - particularly during inclement weather - which "drove" area residents and businesses to clamor for a rail line. This became a particularly vocal demand as other towns nearby welcomed rail lines to their city limits.

Ike had no sons to carry on his name, he had eternal connections with many of the prominent families of Roswell through his daughters' marriages to a Foster, a Lyon, a Wing, and a Bowden.

At one time or another in Ike's lifetime, he owned two of Roswell's best-known antebellum homes – Bulloch Hall and Primrose Cottage. He also owned a lumber company, a dairy, and, in a partnership, the Civil War-era Laurel Mill complex (including the manager's office which still stands as of this writing in 2025 halfway up busy Roswell Road between the river and town.) He was also at one time chairman of the board of the Roswell Bank.

In 1905, when Ike owned Bulloch Hall, an event of unsurpassed historic significance occurred in Roswell. The president of the United States – Theodore "Teddy" Roosevelt – traveled to Roswell to pay a visit to Bulloch Hall which was originally his mother's home where she and his father had been married. Teddy, traveling to the site on *"The Dinkey"* with Ike Roberts at the helm, was visiting this historic landmark

(which also still stands as of this writing in 2025) because it was the site of birth of his mother, and had been built by his grandfather.

In 1903, in an effort to update and make the line more serviceable, heavier rails were installed on the *Roswell Railroad*, thus eliminating the original narrow-gauge tracks. This allowed the railroad access to larger rail cars and the ability to transport more gross weight.

Despite its progress and upgrades, the *Roswell Railroad* – as inevitably was the case with most short-lines – eventually literally worked itself out of a job. It helped to build highways and electrical power generation plants, and with the advent of the new-fangled automobiles siphoning off passenger service, and tractor-trailer rigs siphoning off transportation services, the *Roswell Railroad* struggled to survive. It was a problem eventually suffered by all north Georgia short-lines.

The little railroad continued to weather the years, but finally, by 1921, its usefulness had expired and the *Roswell Railroad* simply ceased operations, much to the disappointment and sadness of Roswell's citizenry. Just as had the old *Tallulah Falls Railroad* in Tallulah Falls, the *Gainesville-Midland* in Gainesville, the *Georgia-Northwestern* to Clermont and Helen, and so many other short-line railroads in other towns, the *Roswell Railroad* had become a staple of life in the community, and area residents were stunned by its loss.

Ike Roberts made a trip to Washington, D.C., and somehow came away with the deed to the Roswell Depot property, paying only $1.00 in the transaction. Thereafter, he used the historic structure as a barn. It can only be considered a shame today that this structure was not preserved for posterity as a visible reminder of the history of Roswell.

Ike continued on in the railroad business until his death. He went from *The Dinkey* to the *"Air-Line Belle,"* a line with daily runs between Atlanta and Toccoa.

When he died in 1930 at the age of 77, Ike Roberts was the oldest engineer in the Charlotte division of *Southern Railway*, both in age and in length of service. The heart attack which felled him occurred at old Terminal Station in Atlanta soon after he reported for work one morning.

Ike's obituary claimed that he was *"one of the fastest and smoothest engineers in the service of the road."* It wasn't necessarily true, but it sounded nice, and Ike was a beloved member of the community. The obit continued by explaining that even in his last years, Ike *"would set a passenger train in motion*

without a perceptible jar, and he would nurse it to a stop again with the smoothness of an automobile slowing down."

During his 58 years of service on Southern locomotives, Ike was never involved in a single major accident.

As of this writing, a number of reminders of Ike and the *Roswell Railroad* still exist. Well-known Roberts Drive on the southeast bank of the Chattahoochee River was the site of Ike's residence for many years, and bears his name. His imposing home on that road still stands, well-preserved and in continuous use since it was built.

Occasionally, during the past few decades, new home builders and/or road construction crews have unearthed a piece of track or some other artifact from the *Roswell Railroad*. And perhaps, if it was an old-timer from the area who came upon the bit of railroad memorabilia, Ike Roberts and *"The Dinkey"* were remembered in a nostalgic moment or two.

References

Fairfax Harrison, ***A History of the Legal Development of the Railroad System of Southern Railway Company***; Washington D.C.: Southern Railway Company, 1901

Elizabeth L. Davis and Ethel W. Spruill, ***The Story of Dunwoody, Its Heritages and Horizons, 1821-1975***; Atlanta: Williams Printing Co., 1975

Lois Coogle, ***Sandy Springs - Past Tense***; Atlanta: Decor Master Co., 1971

Darlene Walsh, ***Roswell: A Pictorial History*** and ***Roswell, Georgia***: Roswell Historical Society, 1985.)

(*Grateful appreciation is expressed herewith to Dr. Caroline M. Dillman who provided most of the information used in this article.*)

During his 58 years of service on Southern locomotives, Ike was never involved in a single major accident.

Early Adventures Working On *Tallulah Falls Railroad*

He was a fireman on a locomotive for many years, then an engineer on the scenic Tallulah Falls Railroad which once ran between Cornelia, Georgia, and Franklin, North Carolina. The little mountain short-line is long gone today, but Hoyt Tench remembers many adventures on the fabled line.

Railroading gets into your blood. If you don't believe it, just ask Rev. Hoyt Tench of Cornelia, Georgia, who spent thirty-eight years keeping steam engines fired and trains rolling.

Tench and his bride, Catherine Dalton, were married May 27, 1939. He admits to being only eighteen years of age at the time. "And you're not supposed to ask how old my bride was," he says, his eyes a-twinkle.

Her father, Beecher Dalton, was employed by the Stewart and Jones Company and Doubletrack, and worked in railroad construction. Mr. Dalton's work on the *Tallulah Falls (TF)* Railway made it possible for a young Hoyt Tench to be one of the first to know when an employment opening existed.

In 1942, an engineer transferred from the *Tallulah Falls Railroad* to the *Southern Railroad*. A fireman was promoted to engineer and an opening was suddenly available for a new fireman. Hoyt Tench "hired on," beginning a railroading career which lasted until 1980, a total of thirty-eight years. Of course all of those thirty-eight years weren't spent on the Tallulah Falls line, since it went out of business in 1961, but for nineteen

Railroad Reverend – Hoyt O. Tench spent 38 years as an employee on the railroads of north Georgia, a large portion of which was spent on the *Tallulah Falls Railroad*. Tench also was a Baptist minister. He is pictured with his wife, Catherine Dalton.

of those 38 railroad years, Tench said he had many adventures on the old TF.

Early Disaster

The first day on the *Tallulah Falls Railroad* almost became the last for young Tench. It began with the new fireman shoveling coal into a cart which he then rolled to the train and dumped into the engine tender (coal car). This effort was repeated four or five times until enough coal was loaded to make the

Breath-Taking – The Panther Creek Trestle on the *Tallulah Falls Railroad* was considered one of the most hair-raising crossings, but the Wiley Trestle (pictured above in 1939) with its five decks was by far the most dangerous. An area resident watches warily as the train passes one afternoon circa 1930s.

trip from Cornelia, Georgia, to Franklin, North Carolina and back.

Once the coal loading was completed, the engineer next began teaching young Tench all the things he needed to observe and do during the trip. The duties included watching the tracks ahead to make sure no obstructions were on them, as well as looking backward to insure that none of the boxcars had jumped the track or developed "hot boxes" in the wheel bearings.

Shortly thereafter on his first trip, Tench found himself making numerous interesting stops along the way at spots like Clarkesville, Demorest, Lakemont, Tiger, Clayton, Mountain City, Dillard, and on and on until they reached Franklin, North Carolina. There, the engine was turned around, the box cars were disengaged and parked for removal by another later train, and new cars were hooked to the engine for the return trip home to Cornelia.

As the train moved southward, it soon passed back through the little hamlet of Mountain City in northern Rabun County, Georgia. The train picked up speed, entered a curve, and then suddenly began to shake and rattle like an earthquake.

A backward glance by the new fireman revealed a sight which would strike terror in the hearts of even the most inveterate of railroad men. Dust was flying, cars were bouncing, and a derailment seemed imminent.

Tench immediately alerted the engineer who gradually slowed the train to a halt. Miraculously, only one boxcar had jumped the track, and it had remained hooked to the other boxcars. The task now was one of getting the heavy derailed boxcar back onto the tracks.

Crew members, accustomed to the chore, began removing huge jacks – specially designed for this purpose – from the train. It took hours of "jacking and chocking," "jacking and chocking," until the errant boxcar could again be "righted" onto the tracks, and the train allowed to proceed.

By the time the train reached Cornelia, Hoyt Tench had just about decided that railroading was a job he'd be happy to let someone else do. The work was too hard. The hours were too long. There was too much to learn, and it was just a bit too dangerous. After a good supper at home and a much-needed night of rest, however, he decided to give it another try.

The second day was much less eventful. The instructions and duties didn't seem quite so formidable this time out either. Thus began a railroad career spanning a time period from the World War II to the 1980s.

Hospitality On The Rails

Neighborliness has long been a characteristic of north Georgians. This sense of camaraderie and compassion was demonstrated many times by the people who lived along the rails, as well as by the railroad men themselves.

When a wreck or derailment occurred, citizens living nearby invariably rushed to the scene to render whatever assistance could be provided. In cases of injury, neighbors along the tracks were the first to summon help and render first aid.

Sometimes the roles were reversed too. Train workers on one occasion noted that certain families living near the tracks were clad in threadbare clothing and some children didn't have shoes, even on the coldest days of winter as they waved to the train crew.

Inquiring about the children, crew members learned that they were not in school because of inadequate clothing. The good-hearted trainmen discreetly learned the number of children, the ages, sex and approximate sizes of each, then purchased clothing and had it distributed to the parents of the children.

Though they were not present for the gifting to the children, the trainmen later learned that Santa Claus was an exciting event that year – for both parents and children at this spot.

Dealing With Danger

During the years the *Tallulah Falls Railroad* was in service, numerous frightening events occurred. Hoyt Tench, though much more fortunate than most, witnessed his share of accidents and natural disasters.

One disaster in which he thankfully was not involved,

Deadly Disaster – Accidents were an accepted potential hazard of the trade in railroading. This August 23, 1920 derailment of the *TF* south of Tiger was responsible for the death of the engineer, and the fireman was badly injured. The train was transporting children to a summer camp, and the accident was instrumental in the eventual permanent cancellation of passenger service on the *TF*. (Photo courtesy of the GA Dept. of Archives & History, Atlanta, GA)

occurred on February 7, 1927, when one of the Tallulah Falls trains was passing over the high trestle over Hazel Creek. The weakened wooden bridge over the creek, unable to support the weight of the train, collapsed, spilling the engine and its crew to the ground. Three people were killed.

The accident undoubtedly would have been even more disastrous had not a piece of timber fallen across the whistle arm, releasing steam from the engine. It otherwise, undoubtedly would have exploded, according to Tench. The engine – though severely damaged – was retrieved by a wrecker, rebuilt

The accident undoubtedly would have been even more disastrous had not a piece of timber fallen across the whistle arm, releasing steam from the engine.

A *Tallulah Falls* freight train was photographed near Demorest, Georgia in 1951. Though pulled by a more modern engine, the line nevertheless is a brief ten years from bankruptcy and cessation of business operations. (Photo courtesy of Goldman Kimbrell)

and placed back into service. Tench said he was a fireman for this rebuilt engine (#73) for a period of time.

On a return trip from Franklin on another occasion, Tench and his crew experienced a scare similar to the trestle-spill of *Engine 73*. As they approached the high trestle just north of Dillard, everything appeared to be in very good order, but in the middle of the trestle, a loud pop sounded as the train was passing over it. The engine gave a lurch, but the entire train passed over safely.

A repair crew dispatched to the trestle site discovered that a main supporting timber had indeed snapped. If the train

Miraculously, neither engineer nor fireman was injured.

had been heavily loaded as it crossed, the entire trestle would no doubt have collapsed, spilling the train and causing a loss of life as had occurred with #73.

Another experience vivid in Hoyt Tench's memory – and he had many of them – happened during a severe thunderstorm one summer afternoon. The train was returning from Franklin. Lightning flashed constantly.

Suddenly, a huge bolt of lightning struck some distance ahead of the train, then something akin to a "ball of fire" began traveling up the rails straight toward the engine. The tremendous charge reportedly passed over the driver wheels on

A *Tallulah Falls Railroad* diesel-electric mail car or "Dinky" is being loaded in downtown Cornelia in the early 1950s. (Photo courtesy of Thomas Frier)

the engine and continued along the entire train – as if it followed the rails until it reached a wheel – then flashed up, over and down the wheels, and on over the rails, continuing until it had run the entire length of the train, then continuing on beyond it farther down the rails.

Miraculously, neither engineer nor fireman was injured. At the next stop, Tench and the engineer talked to other crew members. They, too, had witnessed the phenomenon and equally amazingly were not harmed by the lightning. Amazingly, no damage was suffered by the train either.

Pranks On The Rails

"Boys will be boys," as the saying goes. Some who lived along the railroad tracks delighted in a past-time that was as dangerous and troublesome for the train crew as it was exciting and fun for the little trouble-makers who initiated it.

The deed was usually performed on a portion of the rails that were slightly inclined up a slope. Such places were easy to find along the mountainous terrain of the *Tallulah Falls Railroad*. Slight inclines were common along the route through the mountains of north Georgia and North Carolina.

Once the spot was located, the mischief-makers applied grease to the rails for a short distance. Of course, the quantity of grease necessary to achieve the wheels slippage wasn't that easy to come by from the 1930s through the 1950s, so the prank often was tell-tale for the perpetrators.

If the next train traveling the tracks was heavily loaded or proceeding slowly, the engine would immediately lose traction when the wheels hit the grease, and stall. In order to extract the train from the slick rails, the engineer had two choices. He could either reverse the engine, back it up a considerable distance on the tracks and then try to gain enough momentum to pass over the grease, or he

The dinky was photographed here in 1953 on Queen's trestle just south of Mountain City in Rabun County. (Photo by R.D. Sharpless, from the collection of Frank Ardrey, Jr.)

could stop the train so that the crewmen could wipe the grease off the rails and place dirt on them for traction.

Runaway Engine

Cold weather always presented special problems on the *Tallulah Falls Railroad*. Crew members had to check equipment to insure that it was in tip-top shape. They examined signal lights, signal flags, switch controls and the mechanism of the engines as well.

When bitter cold weather arrived, it was necessary for a crew member to remain on duty at night to keep all the engines fired so the water in them would not freeze (antifreeze being still somewhat in the future in those days) and burst sections around the boiler. One man was always assigned to watch over the engines parked in the yard at night.

On one particularly

Suddenly, Tench said he heard a strange sound and opened his door to listen.

cold night, Hoyt Tench had railroad yard-watch duty. About halfway between midnight and dawn, he returned from checking each engine and was warming himself by a coal-fired heater.

Suddenly, Tench said he heard a strange sound and opened his door to listen. All, however, seemed quiet. He closed the door and returned to his heater. Again the sound came. He opened the door again and walked a few steps into the train yard. The sound came a third time, and this time, Tench recognized it immediately. One of the engines, amazingly, was moving out of the yard!

"Somebody's trying to steal an engine," he thought, trying to decide what to do. But then, as he peered closer at the engine, he realized there was no one at the controls.

Tench then exercised the only option available to him. He made a quick dash to catch up with the locomotive, climbing into the cab as the engine gained momentum. He applied the brakes immediately, and the engine slowed to a stop.

Once it was halted, Tench released the brakes as was customary, and was amazed to see the engine lunge forward yet again, even though he had not touched the throttle. Quickly checking the device, he discovered that the throttle had been moved from the park position. He repositioned it back into park and waited. After a few moments, the engine again moved forward, and Tench realized that a valve in the throttle mechanism was leaking, thus allowing the engine to move.

As he made temporary repairs to the controls to make certain the engine was stable, he broke out into a cold sweat. He realized what havoc might have occurred had that engine moved onto the main line and met another train, or had it struck a vehicle or person at a crossing or derailed while advancing too swiftly into a curve.

Other Dangers

"Blow-up" can be a somewhat confusing railroad term. As a fireman, Tench's job was to keep the firebox hot enough to produce steam to run the train. On steep grades like those from Lakemont to Tiger, the train sometimes had to be stopped so the fireman could "double." To stop and get up double steam is known as "blowing up" (building up the steam for steep inclines).

A fireman's reputation hung on how few times he had to stop the train to blow up steam.

Photographed March 25, 1961, the final year the *Tallulah Falls Railroad* was in operation, engineer Goldman Kimbrell smiles down from the cab of one of the line's diesel-electric engines. (Photo courtesy of Goldman Kimbrell)

Fireman Tench remembers one such instance in which he almost overdid his responsibilities.

"One day, Jim Brown and I got *Engine 75* too hot," he recalled. "The engine walls never did cave in, but back in the yards at Cornelia, Noah Ward, the boiler man, had to fix all the stay bolts because they were so weak from the excessive steam (pressure) from that Tiger (Georgia) pull.

"You see, there were spaces, just like a wall (on the inside periphery of the big boiler on the engine)," he explained. "The firebox was on the inside, and there was a wall between it and the water which generated the steam when heated, and then a wall between the water and the

"One day, Jim Brown and I got Engine 75 too hot," he recalled.

Train #501 with its diesel-electric engine travels north across Tallulah Lake circa 1950s. It was at this spot that Mr. Ragsdale dumped the block of ice each day. In the foreground is the old Highway 441 bridge which still exists today in Tallulah Gorge State Park. Though the rails were removed long ago, the large concrete piers pictured on the Tallulah Lake railroad bridge also still exist today in Tallulah Lake. (Photo courtesy of Buck Snyder)

outside," he said. "Water and steam were around that stay bolt, too, that went from one sheet (of metal on the outside) to the other (on the inside of the firebox). We almost burned the stay bolts in the crown sheet, and water was leaking all in the firebox on my fire. That's when we almost blew up the engine - literally. We managed somehow to get it back into Cornelia without having an explosion."

Traveling over the many trestles between Cornelia, Georgia, and Franklin, North Carolina, was a perilous experience too. "They always said the Panther Creek trestle was the highest, but I think the Wiley trestle was the most dangerous and booger-ish-looking, because it had five decks," Tench explained.

It was on the Wiley Trestle that the cab on the TF once jumped the

Not much remains of the old TF line today.

tracks. It went on running right across the crossties according to Mr. Tench. "We just braked it light and let it come to a stop," he noted with a smile. "It never did get off the trestle.

"Mr. John Snyder was the conductor that day; Brawner Walker was the brakeman and Alec Dillard was the flagman. We used the 're-railers' to get the cab back on the tracks. As you might imagine, there was very little room to work on that trestle – it was so narrow. And one mistake could have sent men and train plummeting down into the gorge. It was scary and dangerous as all get-out."

Another danger to the railroading men, especially to the fireman, was what was known as "getting a monkey." In the peak-heat summer months, the heat in the engine and near the firebox could reach horrendous proportions, causing a condition known to-day as heat exhaustion or heat-stroke. Symptoms included delirium, hallu-cinations and other seri-ous disabilities. "But back then, we just knew it made people go crazy. That's why we called it 'getting a monkey,' I guess," Tench remembered. "You might see snakes, monkeys or all manner of other things."

Changing Times

Hoyt Tench eventu-ally worked himself up to the position of engineer. Technology was changing about that time, and steam power was giving way to diesel.

On March 25, 1961, the *Tallulah Falls Railroad* ceased operation – a vic-tim of its own good service. Highways had been built back into the mountains allowing trucking firms to move prod-ucts and merchandise more inexpensive-ly and more precisely. The timber had all been harvested and transported to mills by the TF until the supply was exhausted.

Finally, in the 1950s, passenger ser-vice was discontinued on the line, and the fabled railroad eventually was un-able to generate enough income to sup-port itself.

Hoyt Tench moved on, working as an engineer for the *Southern Railroad.* He also became an ordained minister in 1948, managing two careers until his re-tirement from the railroad.

Not much remains of the old *TF* line today. The aged depots that do still remain intact may be seen at Cornelia, Tallulah Falls, and Demorest.

Prior to the demise of the *TF*, its Demorest depot was used as a film site

Virtually any memorabilia associated with the former line is now a collectible.

for the opening scene in the major motion picture **I'd Climb the Highest Mountain**, shot in 1950 around Cleveland, Geor-gia, and starring Susan Hayward, Rory Calhoun, and William Lundigan among others. The *TF's Engine #75* was brought out of retirement so that it might provide the cor-rect period locomotive for use in this scene. In the movie's opening cred-its, *#75* is also seen steam-ing across the steel trestle over Lake Tallulah.

A former TF caboose along with other memorabilia is on display at Cor-nelia; another former caboose is on dis-play on a short piece of grade in Tallu-lah Falls. The diesel mail/express unit was purchased and placed by old US 441 north of Clayton by a local entre-preneur originally intending to open a diner.

The captivating *Tallulah Falls Rail-road* and its storybook setting provided yeoman service for many years and was sorely missed after its insolvency. Virtu-ally any memorabilia associated with the former line is now a collectible.

Sadly, so scenic was the *Tallulah Falls Railroad* that no lesser a person than showman/television and movie im-presario Walt Disney himself attempted to purchase the line after it had ceased operations. Disney reportedly had big plans to develop a rough equivalent to Orlando's **Walt Disney World** in the sce-nic north Georgia mountains, but the individuals controlling the *TF* bank-ruptcy proceedings turned down his of-fer. Just think of what might have oc-curred if that had come to pass.

Remembering Historic
Tallulah Falls Railroad

*It was one of the most scenic railroads in the entire eastern United States,
and was in operation for over half a century, but poor decisions and even
poorer funding eventually spelled doom for the fabled little short-line.*

For over half a century (54 years), an exceedingly scenic mountain short-line called the *Tallulah Falls Railroad (TF)* operated continuously through some of the most rugged and beautiful mountain vistas in the entire eastern United States, connecting Cornelia, Georgia, with Franklin, North Carolina. Though many people are not aware of it today, the north Georgia region – and indeed the entire state – lost an exceptional opportunity, as well as a unique way of life, when the final train on this little rail line whistled its way into oblivion on March 25, 1961.

Actually organized in 1881 (the same year as the Earps and Clantons shot it out at the O.K. Corral in Tombstone, Arizona), the *Tallulah Falls Railroad* was originally known as *"the Rabun Gap Route,"* indicating the original designers fully intended all along to extend the rail line at least to the Georgia state line at North Carolina.

By 1882, track had been laid from Cornelia, Georgia, to the scenic tourist town of Tallulah Falls. Since this original portion of the route was created much earlier than the ultimately-completed route between Cornelia and Franklin, North Carolina, it therefore was also obviously in business much longer (a total of approximately 80 years) than was the completed Cornelia to Franklin route.

For many years, once the train reached Tallulah Falls on the 1882-completed portion of the route, it turned around (reversed direction) on a railroad "wye" which once existed not far from the depot, and then headed back to Cornelia. During these years, the line provided passenger service for tourists and residents, as well as freight service for the timber industry and, eventually, the supplies necessary for the lake impoundments built on the Tallulah River.

Builders of the rail line advanced its construction across the Tallulah River via a wooden trestle in 1903, and the railroad arrived in Clayton in 1904. In subsequent years, track was laid to Rabun Gap and then on to Otto and Franklin, North Carolina.

Though most of this former line has disappeared completely from the landscape today, significant portions of the old rail bed can still be seen if one knows where to look. Today, some history and railroad buffs like to retrace the route of this historic line, imagining what life in northeast Georgia would be like if it was still in existence.

Many old-timers in northeastern Georgia who remember the *TF* speak

Ghost Rails – Pictured is a section of the former TF track which still stretched approximately two miles between Cornelia and Demorest when this photo was snapped in recent times. For a number of years, this track was occasionally used as a storage area for various incidentals by other railroads. Its disposition today is unknown.

almost reverently of this famed short-line whose familiar and dependable trains made daily runs through Demorest, Clarkesville, Hollywood, Turnerville, Tallulah Falls, Lakemont, Wiley, Tiger, Clayton, Passover, Mountain City, Rabun Gap, Dillard, Otto, and on to Franklin, North Carolina. Veterans of the line included individuals like Roy Shope of Rabun Gap, former trestle foreman, and Carl Rogers of Dillard, former station agent at Clayton. Just as did many others, they mourned the loss of this once dynamic railroad, and the familiar dependable service it brought to the mountain towns.

Though now completely erased from the landscape, most of the former locations of the 42 wooden trestles which once dotted the 58 miles of track

on the TF could still easily be pointed out by long-time area residents and former employees such as Shope and Rogers, but individuals such as these are fast disappearing too. Interestingly, both Shope and Rogers maintain that it was the expense of the maintenance of these trestles, coupled with other factors, which were major factors in the demise of the now-historic line.

Long stretches of the old roadbed – in various states of erosion or abandonment (or erased completely by new development) – can still be seen across three counties, clearly visible in some spots, and virtually lost in the undergrowth in others. The Tallulah Falls roadbed, sadly, was never embraced by such preservation-minded groups as the *Rails To Trails* Conservancy which has

Ghost Trestle – The only steel and concrete trestle on the *TF* stretched over Tallulah Lake, the concrete pylons of which may still be seen in the lake today. It was the constant expensive maintenance requirements of the many trestles on the *TF* line which eventually pushed it into insolvency.

preserved hundreds of other railroad beds of lesser beauty and magnificence nationwide in hiking and biking trails.

Had it been preserved, the former route of the old *TF* undoubtedly would have provided one of the most remarkably scenic *Rails To Trails* opportunities in the eastern U.S. One short portion near the rail line's namesake town of Tallulah Falls thankfully has been preserved by Georgia State Parks, but it is the lone surviving segment.

Remnants more tangible than the faded roadbeds could also be found until just recently at numerous points along the old route. Just behind the neat former *Southern Railway* station at Cornelia, Georgia, the bright red *TF Caboose #5* was lovingly maintained for many years by a railway equipment dealer with *TF* roots. Its location today is unknown.

Another portion of now-unused weed-choked *TF* track – though unprotected – still stretches (as of this writing) for about two miles out of Cornelia toward Demorest. It is unknown who owns this historic stretch today. Much of the remainder of the roadbed of the line between these two communities, however, has been buried beneath new state highways.

The old *TF* station in Demorest – one of only three still in existence – has gone through varying periods of abandonment and revitalization. It, interestingly, has been amply preserved for posterity in the film footage of the opening scene of the major motion picture ***I'd Climb the Highest Mountain***, filmed in 1950 around nearby Cleveland and Helen, Georgia, by famed Hollywood director Henry King. It starred Susan Hayward, William Lundigan, Gene Lockhart, Barbara Bates, Alexander Knox, and young rising star Rory Calhoun – now all sadly deceased.

In the opening segment of this scene at the Demorest Depot, the *Tallulah Falls Railroad* locomotive (subbing for the movie locomotive) pulls slowly into the station. As of this writing, this historic depot – its Hollywood legacy seemingly forgotten – has essentially been abandoned, but hope springs eternal.

The scenic town of Tallulah Falls, formerly one of the most splendid resorts in the eastern U.S., has another prominent depot. Today, this substantial tile-roofed former station still stands proudly at its original site alongside U.S. Highway 441 in this former resort town, and is one of the most visible – as well as best-preserved – landmarks of the railroad.

Back in its heydays, the northward-constructed *TF* tracks, clinging at one point to the very rim of the rugged Tallulah Falls Gorge – north Georgia's answer to the Grand Canyon – was an awe-inspiring ride before the train pulled into the *TF* station at Tallulah Falls. Visitors to the now historic "Scenic Overlook Loop" off Highway 441 just prior to entering Tallulah Falls can still look down in amazement at the beauty and majesty of the gorge rim section of the old railroad.

Although many of the tiles were ripped off the roof of the Tallulah Falls Depot by a disastrous tornado in March of 1994, the remainder of the sturdy structure stood firm. The current owners of the aged depot – which today is used as a unique gift shop – thankfully quickly restored it.

This former bastion on the line still boasts its station sign, and even the original chalkboard announcing the arrival and departure times of the trains. Period photographs and local paintings of the site in days gone by have captured and preserved the former activity of the locomotives which once dominated this station.

North of the Tallulah Falls Depot, the railroad at one time literally leaped over the little village via a huge wooden trestle, before crossing over Tallulah Lake on rails supported by huge concrete piers and then plunging into the woods on the opposite side. The five towering concrete piers and abutments remain today in what once represented the only steel and concrete bridge on the line – 585 feet long and 100 feet high – built when Georgia Power impounded the Tallulah River and formed Tallulah Falls Lake.

A historic marker with old photos of the *TF* has been permanently emplaced on the roadbed at the point at which the railroad once transitioned from the steel and concrete bridge back onto terra firma (at the north end of the high bridge piers across Tallulah Falls Lake). From there, the roadbed – still visible through the forest – twists around several hills as it climbs up-grade through Lakemont and Tiger on its way to Clayton.

Some years ago, the old Lakemont Depot was purchased and removed to a site on Lake Rabun where it was put

Motion Picture Moments – The Demorest, Georgia depot of the *Tallulah Falls Railroad* was - as of this writing - one of the few stations still intact from the old line. It was used as the film location for the opening scene of the major motion picture ***"I'd Climb The Highest Mountain,"*** starring Susan Hayward, Rory Calhoun, and William Lundigan, filmed in 1950. This view, looking north, clearly shows the depot agent's window, beside which the railroad passed.

to new use as a summer home. It is unfortunate that it could not have been preserved at its original location in Lakemont, just as have a number of the original Lakemont commercial buildings which have survived, and which today serve as unique shops and businesses in that quaint historic mountain fiefdom.

A similar fate befell the old Clayton, Georgia *TF* depot, which was demolished for commercial development sometime after the line ceased operations in 1961. Prior to its removal, the Clayton Depot was used as a film site for yet another major motion picture on the *TF* line – ***The Great Locomotive Chase*** (1956) – starring Fess Parker, Jeffrey Hunter, Slim Pickens and others. It was filmed in Clayton and on more northern sections of the Tallulah Falls line near Otto, North Carolina, by *Walt Disney Productions*, with the famed creator of **Disneyland** and major motion pictures himself actually visiting the site in 1956.

Disappearing Depots – Photographed in 1994, the *Tallulah Falls Depot* of the *Tallulah Falls Railroad* had recently been damaged by a tornado which had passed through the area. Notice the damaged trees to the rear and the missing tiles on the roof. Thankfully, the aged depot was undamaged beyond its missing shingles which were quickly replaced. It is one of only three former depots (counting the Cornelia station) still in existence today from the little mountain short-line.

One of the "Disney boxcars," imported for the movie and then left behind after filming was completed, could still be found south of Clayton for many years. Other remnants of the railroad can also still be seen if one knows where to look today.

Disney, who had a definite appreciation for historic and scenic rail lines, reportedly toyed with the idea of purchasing and preserving the entire scenic *Tallulah Falls Railroad* line – and he obviously had the financial backing to do it – but the plan fell through for a number of ironic reasons. Had that idea reached fruition, tranquil Rabun County might today resemble the likes of Anaheim, California, or Orlando, Florida, instead of the current sleepy confines of Clayton, Georgia. Some people

Other remnants of the railroad can also still be seen if one knows where to look today.

would have been happy with that. Others would not.

At north Clayton, the body of the gasoline-powered motor car which had performed yeoman service as the railroad's passenger train when the steam locomotives were not running, had been recycled into a unique private home for many years by one enterprising resident, but its status as of this writing is unknown.

Unbeknownst by many of the rail line's enthusiasts, a "phantom" railroad – begun in the 1850s and once planned to be routed through the outskirts of Clayton – played a vital role during the original construction of the *TF*. At this juncture, builders of the *TF* encountered – and happily made use of – a short stretch of the roadbed of the legendary, and abandoned, *Black Diamond Railroad*, also once known as the *Blue Ridge Railroad*.

The *Black Diamond/Blue Ridge* was financed by John C. Calhoun, the fiery Civil War-era senator and former vice president of the United States from South Carolina. Calhoun wanted the rail line to connect Charleston, South Carolina, with Cincinnati, Ohio, in order to redouble the commercial growth of his state. Though most of the infrastructure of the rail line was completed, bankruptcy (just as with the *TF*) and the U.S. Civil War succeeded in killing the *Black Diamond* in the tri-state area before any rails were laid.

Today, several partially-completed railway tunnels and portions of the old railroad bed can still be found near Clayton.

Though the TF itself had no tunnels, it had numerous expensive wooden trestles. Roy Shope worked

"Downtown" Lakemont – The very scenic Lakemont Depot on the *Tallulah Falls Railroad* was photographed here circa 1930s, after either a dusting of snow or sleet. Some years after the *TF* had ceased operations, this depot was relocated to Lake Rabun for use as a summer home. A few of the historic commercial buildings in Lakemont, a number of which have survived into the 21st century, are used today as popular summer shops. (Photo courtesy of the GA Dept. of Archives & History, Atlanta, GA)

for the *TF* for 21 years, much of it as the bridge foreman and as a brakeman. "We could have filled in many of those (42 trestles) for less cost than it took to maintain them," he lamented. "I don't know why the railroad never did that.

"We had seven men who worked on the trestles between Cornelia and Franklin," he continued. "Toward the end, they cut them all off (released them) before they stopped running (ceased operations), and that left only me."

Roy says he'll never forget the time several boxcars loaded with heavy pulpwood derailed atop the trestle just south of Mountain City. "Two or three cars went off, but they didn't hurt the bridge," he explained. "We didn't have a wrecker like the big railroads, so we had to use man-power and Norton jacks to raise them a few inches at a time."

At Rabun Gap, a remarkably well-preserved piece of roadbed embankment – at one time kept in topnotch condition by its owner as a memorial to the *TF* – is still clearly visible (as of this writing), marking where this section of the railroad crossed a field on its way to Mountain City.

From Mountain City to Franklin, the *TF* roadbed parallels the east side of Route 23. However, in many places, it swings far out away from the highway. At other spots, new development has shaved the roadbed down to the point that it is barely recognizable.

The Georgia Power Company played a large role in the life of the *TF*. Five separate branch lines off the *TF* were built by the big utility company to reach the new hydro-electric power plants being constructed to take advantage of the waters dammed behind several different impoundments along the course of the

Tallulah River. Georgia Power was also responsible for the construction of the railroad's only non-wood trestle spanning the Tallulah Falls Lake.

As previously mentioned, the maintenance of the many trestles along the route was a constant (and some say unnecessary) financial drain on the *TF*. On most larger railroads, trestles were laid across the low spots during the initial construction of the lines, then those spots were gradually filled in as time passed to create a permanent raised roadbed. That practice apparently was too much of a luxury for the *TF*.

The routinely-destructive mishaps and wrecks – often occurring as a result of collapsing trestles – eventually took a toll. And then there was the fact that the *TF* literally hauled in the supplies to build the new highways and hauled out the natural resources – such as timber and mining products – until they were exhausted, to eventually put itself out of business.

Passenger service (or the lack thereof) on the *TF* played a lesser role in the line's eventual bankruptcy, but had an impact nonetheless. Even though the service was important to area residents and tourists, the income generated by passengers was minimal – yet it still helped to pay the bills. In 1946, however, passenger service was abruptly discontinued forever on the line following a crossing accident with a truck that broke several coach windows, spraying the startled passengers with broken glass. For the next fifteen years, the *TF* operated without any passenger service income whatsoever.

The *TF* flirted with several brief insolvencies before it slipped permanently into its final bankruptcy in 1923 – well in advance of the *Great Depression*. It continued in financial limbo for the remainder of its life – another 38 years – until the line's credit was exhausted.

In 1961, the *TF* suffered its final indignity when a scrap dealer brought in heavy equipment to rip out the rails from the ties one by one, and then truck them out to be melted down for other products. When the rails disappeared, there was no question that the line was finished forever.

The day after the final run of the old *TF* was a sad day indeed for area residents all up and down the former route of the line. No whistle sounded any longer as no trains approached a station or road crossing. No staccato chant of the steam escaping the locomotive's jets met the ears anymore. The train which, since 1907, had daily chugged up and down the beautiful hills and around the majestic curves and precipices of the mountains of northeast Georgia from Cornelia to Franklin, North Carolina, and then back again, was no more.

Sometimes, on bitterly cold nights, the wind can be heard blowing through the Tallulah Falls Gorge. If one listens real close, interspersed with the whistling wind, the dull staccato chant of a steam locomotive can almost still be heard once again - almost.

> *The routinely-destructive mishaps and wrecks – often occurring as a result of collapsing trestles – eventually took a toll.*

The Tallulah Falls Firestorm Of 1921

To the surprise of many history buffs, in the early 1900s, Tallulah Falls in northeast Georgia rivaled such attractions as Niagara Falls in popularity. In one fell stroke on a cold winter night in 1921, however, the entire town was virtually erased and its tourism industry destroyed – quite possibly forever.

"Oh my God! How could this have happened to us?" The thought raced through Cora Ledbetter's mind as she witnessed the devastation wrought by the terrible fire that burned the mountain community of Tallulah Falls to the ground in 1921. It was a devastating blow to the acclaimed resort - one from which it has never recovered.

Cora, interviewed for this article in the early 1990s, was a student at Tallulah Falls School at the time. During the night of the fire, she was at home in Toccoa. She saw what was left of the community the next afternoon. Perhaps unaware of it at the time, she unwittingly also witnessed the end of an era for the once-mighty falls.

The Early Days

No description of the devastating fire of 1921 would be complete without an accounting of the four decades of immense development which had preceded the fire. Tallulah Falls had blossomed as a tourist mecca from 1882 - the year the *Tallulah Falls Railroad* first chugged into town - until 1921, the year of the fire. Though other factors were already negatively impacting the town's tourism

Gone With The Wind – Photographed shortly after the immense firestorm which destroyed the resort town of Tallulah Falls in 1921, the utter devastation is visible from in the ashen ruins of all the hotels, homes, and other structures and businesses which were destroyed breathtakingly quick. One or two buildings can still be seen amazingly in the background. The railroad trestle (l) which was so vital to the income and continued existence of the *Tallulah Falls Railroad* was quickly rebuilt only a couple of days after the disaster. (Photo courtesy of GA Dept. of Archives & History, Atlanta, GA)

economy by 1921 (such as the dams built on the Tallulah River by Georgia Power Company), the community of Tallulah Falls had continued to persevere due to the presence of its grand hotels which had beckoned invitingly from the mountainsides.

Out of some 17 major hotels in downtown Tallulah Falls and across the brow of the Tallulah Falls Gorge, the Cliff House was one of only a couple which miraculously survived the great blaze of 1921. Even the Cliff House itself, however, perished soon thereafter in another large fire and was never rebuilt. Today, the concrete and stone foundations of a number of the old hotels remain as remnants from this former resort town. The Cliff House was directly across the road from the *Tallulah Falls Railroad Depot* (which also survived the fire and still exists today). It was believed that sparks from the firebox of the *Tallulah Falls* train engine may have ignited the fire which destroyed the Cliff House. (Photo courtesy of GA Dept. of Archives & History, Atlanta, GA)

Tucked away in the northeast corner of the state, the popularity of Tallulah Falls had grown progressively, thanks to word-of-mouth publicity and writers such as David Hillhouse whose account of the falls was widely published in the United States. Additionally, a new trail cut through the forested mountainsides of northern Habersham County, had gradually attracted increasing numbers of visitors curious about the phenomenal stories of a huge gorge and mighty falls emptying into the precipice.

Despite the lure of the site, many travelers found they needed a guide just to help them find their way to the falls, but still they came - in droves. According to researcher and educator Dr. John Saye in his *The Life And Times Of Tallulah.... the Falls, the Gorge, the Town,* *"By 1840, visits to the falls by groups of men, women, and even children had become quite common."* By conservative estimates, nearly 2,000 visitors reportedly had journeyed to the falls in the remote corner of north Georgia by 1877.

Perhaps Tallulah Falls' resort era actually began in 1870 with the construction of the Shirley Hotel on the brow of the gorge. Just a year later, the hotel began expanding to handle the increasing numbers of visitors. With two more hotels built during the 1870s, the resort's popularity as a travel destination began in earnest.

Arrival Of The Railroad

The next decade witnessed the arrival of a convenience which brought "boom-times" to the town of Tallulah

Cliff House Proof – Engine #77 of the *Tallulah Falls Railroad* pulls into the station circa mid-1920s. This particular engine was purchased in 1923, confirming that the *Cliff House* (the corner of which is slightly visible, left) survived the firestorm of 1921. A corner of the *Tallulah Falls Depot* which still exists today and is a gift shop can be seen on the right. (Photo courtesy of the GA Dept. of Archives & History, Atlanta, GA)

Falls - the railroad. By the 1880s, travelers were no longer required to brave the trip to the falls via a treacherous unpaved mountain trail. The *Tallulah Falls Railroad* had been completed to the rim of the gorge, making the destination ever more appealing.

Travelers came by train from Atlanta and Athens to Cornelia, Georgia, where they boarded the Tallulah Falls train. An hour and fifteen minutes later, they stepped off at the breath-taking little town where they were awe-struck by the scenic vistas.

A variety of hotels offered accommodations for travelers. Author John Saye describes it this way:

"At its peak, there were seventeen hotels and boarding houses in and around town. Guests could stay in a large, grand hotel, or in a small, intimate establishment. They could stay in the heart of the bustling little town, or in the peaceful forest surrounding Tallulah Falls."

Until 1904, the railroad ended at Tallulah Falls, and the area's tourist industry had thrived. However, some seventeen years later in 1921, the lifeblood of the community literally went up in smoke virtually in the blink of an eye.

A Fire In A Windstorm

"I have never seen nor heard the wind blow so hard as it did that night," said Bertha Burrell, a Tallulah Falls resident. "That wind carried burning bark and shingles as far away as Tugaloo." Bertha had arrived home from Athens Normal School for the holidays and hadn't even unpacked.

Drucy Turpen remembered the fire all too well too. "We lived on a hill on the other side of town. I was sleeping in the front room. Granny Harvey lived just below us. She came up to the house hollering that the town was burning," Drucy said sadly, tears filling her eyes at the horrible memory. "We stood on the

Fire Source – This structure located slightly downhill from the town was the Tallulah Falls City Hall building when this photo was snapped in the 1990s. It exists upon the site where the three-story automobile service garage existed in 1921. The firestorm began mysteriously in that building. (Photo by R. Olin Jackson)

porch and watched it. It was just awful. It even burned the railroad trestle and my daddy's store."

Valiant town residents and businessmen did what they could to save their community. Some rang dinner bells to awaken the sleeping citizens. Others fired shots from rifles and pistols.

"Most everybody lost everything," recalled a still-distraught Gussie Harvey. Her father lost a store and a car in the fire. The Maplewood Inn and the Robinson Annex and some dozen other hotels went up in flames - reduced to ashes in a matter of hours.

Terrible Devastation

The actual cause of the inferno is still a matter of conjecture today. Several differing accounts exist.

One story maintains that a man whose car had become stuck in the mud had stopped at a local garage for help. The garage was on the street level of a three-story building. The owner, who lived upstairs, reportedly told the chilled stranger to come back later.

It was shortly after those remarks that the town went up in flames. Apparently angry at the lack of help, the stranger with the mired car is suspected of having torched the town.

"He broke into the garage to steal what tools he needed to repair his car," says Drucy Turpen. "Then he set fire to the garage to cover up the break-in."

Ironically, according to local sources, some years later, this same individual was himself consumed by flames when he mistakenly used gasoline instead of what he thought was kerosene to start a fire.

Regardless of the cause of the conflagration, the results were indescribable by all accounts. A barn with livestock was consumed. "I remember the screaming, mooing, and braying of those poor animals," recalled Bertha Burrell. "It was terrible." Most of the animals perished.

The J.D. Harvey Store, one of the many businesses destroyed in the firestorm once existed upon this lot. (Photo by R. Olin Jackson)

Some were more fortunate, breaking out of the barn and racing up Main Street, their hides scorched.

"There was no fire department in those days, and certainly no water mains," Bertha added. "People had spring water for their own use, but little else. There was nothing to do but watch the town burn. We saved our house by putting bags of cottonseed meal on the roof."

Gussie Harvey recalled the destruction of the railroad. "About half of the trestle was burned, stopping passenger service to Clayton, Georgia and Franklin, North Carolina," she explained, still wide-eyed at the memory. "There was a freight train that came down from Franklin, so benches were put in some of the freight cars for passengers.

"I remember," continued Gussie, "my father went to town in his bare feet. He came back the next day with badly blistered feet. To try and save the store,

Survivor – The Glenbrook Hotel was located above and behind (southwest from) the source of the terrible fire, and with the wind blowing away from it, this hotel avoided destruction by the fire even though other structures only a short distance away were totally consumed. The Glenbrook, in fact, survived right up to the 21st century before falling victim to termites, the elements, and disrepair, having been strangely abandoned for many years. It was photographed here circa 1920s.

The ornate and durable Glenbrook Hotel weathered many catastrophes over the years, including the terrible fire of 1921 and a devastating tornado, but it was ultimately unable to weather total neglect, abandonment, time, and the elements. It was photographed here in the 1990s after a destructive tornado and appears relatively intact, but since that time, has sadly disappeared from the landscape.

he had poured Coca-Cola syrup on it, but the fire was just too hot even for the syrup."

Gussie's sister remembered that the livestock ran up and down the street - many until they dropped dead from exhaustion. "Some of the animals were on fire," she said.

After The Fire

The destruction was so complete and the insurance losses so immense that little, if anything, was rebuilt after the fire. None of the hotels were ever reconstructed. The owners had no choice but to walk away and leave the town forever. Although the fire was a death blow to the town, other factors also contributed to its ultimate demise.

The extension of the railroad to Clayton and eventually to Franklin, North Carolina, inevitably lured visitors deeper into the mountains, causing

many of them to by-pass Tallulah Falls. "Many people had been coming here from South Georgia for health reasons," explains Jim Turpen, a local Methodist minister. "Once they realized they could go even further and higher into the mountains, they did."

The construction of the massive dam just above the falls and at other sites farther upriver also altered the town's character irreversibly. The once-mighty falls were virtually extinguished, eliminating much of the original attraction and beauty of the site. The focus of leisure pursuits then shifted from the falls to fishing and lifestyles around the various lakes created behind the dams. The town of Tallulah Falls was essentially abandoned as the wealthy chose instead to construct large homes around the periphery of the new lakes behind the Georgia Power water impoundments.

Cost was another reason for the

As is obvious from this aerial photograph taken circa 1950s, virtually nothing remains of the town of Tallulah Falls. The fire which struck the community began on the northwest side of this photo and swept southeastward, destroying everything in its path. To the rear of the town and Lake Tallulah, the immense wooden trestle of the Tallulah Falls Railroad is visible. This structure was destroyed by the 1921 fire, but was rebuilt in a matter of days.

town's demise. In those days, few people had insurance coverage on their homes and property, and the cost of rebuilding the hotels was prohibitive.

By the mid- to late-1930s, all of the grand hotels had completely disappeared from the brow of Tallulah Gorge. If the 1921 fire didn't get them, another fire or destructive element did.

Yet another blow came via what once had been the lifeblood of the town – the *Tallulah Falls Railroad*. By the 1950s, passenger service had been discontinued on the old *TF*, further depleting service. And in 1961, the future of the railroad was severely threatened when it went into receivership - a victim of its own success. The transportation system which had made all of the original growth at the falls possible, had literally outlived its usefulness. It had made possible the construction of the dams which choked off the beautiful falls; it

had transported the felled trees from the area until all the virgin timber had been harvested in northeast Georgia; and it had brought in the building materials necessary for the construction of U.S. Highway 441.

With the advent of the highway, trucking firms could then transport products and materials more economically and precisely than the railroad. There were no other heavy shipment needs such as the timber from the forests and the building materials necessary for the large Georgia Power Dams. Each year, the revenues from the *Tallulah Falls Railroad* became less and less, until bankruptcy was inevitable.

The Future

Today, despite its decline, Tallulah Falls still vies for a slice of the tourism pie dollars in Georgia. Travelers still want to view the beautiful gorge and the

Photographed in the early 1900s, this obviously-posed view shows the side porch and courtyard of the Cliff House which was opposite the *Tallulah Falls Railroad Depot*. The roof of the depot is faintly visible through the trees just above the top of the fence in the background. (Photo courtesy of GA Dept. of Archives & History, Atlanta, GA)

remnants of the scenic little town. It, interestingly, has now become "a historic site."

A new state park was established within Tallulah Gorge in the 1990s, to preserve as much of the gorge as possible for posterity. Area residents are hopeful the new park will continue to facilitate new growth in the little town.

The community of fewer than two hundred residents still welcomes tens of thousands of visitors who pause – if only briefly now – to admire the gorge, and perhaps reminisce a bit about the glory days of the town of yesteryear. Some of them move on farther up into the mountains; others recreate at adjoining Lakes Burton, Rabun and Seed along the Tallulah River.

The old *Tallulah Falls Railroad Depot*, which somehow survived the

firestorm of 1921, also escaped serious damage during a devastating tornado in the 1990s. It serves today as a crafts store, displaying the wares of local mountain crafts-persons.

Tallulah Falls School still attracts students from throughout Georgia and other states due to its excellent academic reputation. The area also boasts a rehabilitation center and an adult education center.

However, unless the falls are freed once again to crash and roar unrestrained into the gorge, recreating the wonderland which caused Indians to anoint the site as a sacred place and tourists to flock to the falls by the trainload in the early 1900s, it is highly unlikely that this scenic spot will ever again be the tourism destination it was prior to a terrible fire in the winter of 1921.

This Place Called "Tallulah"

By R. Olin Jackson

In forests primeval
where good and the evil
roamed earth in its
infant creation,

was a place where the Lord
waved his hand to deploy
a crashing discord
called "Tallulah"

Aboriginals awed
at the wonders they saw
in this place that they all
called "Tallulah"

So great was her might
her power and fright,
that they all feared the sight
of "Tallulah"

Loudly she roared;
from the cliffs eagles soared;
her might underscored
this "Tallulah"

Carved a realm to this day
still amazes all they
chanced to visit and play
at "Tallulah"

Though wondrous a site,
man soon scaled the height,

stole the God-given right
of "Tallulah"

Built their palaces high,
where once land, sea nor sky,
could compete nor come nigh
of "Tallulah"

Marveled though they,
their creations did flay,
all the beauty away
from "Tallulah"

All her crashing cascades
were silently stayed
in this breath-taking glade
called "Tallulah"

With her majesty gone,
man had stolen the song,
and they all ceased to throng
at "Tallulah"

With her beauty destroyed,
her realm was devoid
of the charm they so toyed
as "Tallulah"

Shackled and chained,
Soon little remained,
Of the glory once famed
as "Tallulah."

Historic Clermont, Georgia and the *Gainesville-Northwestern Railroad*

It was constructed as a transportation medium for the timber being harvested in northeast Georgia, and became a way of life for residents along the line from 1912 to 1935. When the seemingly inexhaustible timber had all been harvested by the early 1930s, the little mountain short-line was necessary no more, and ceased operation. When it departed, a way of life disappeared with it.

Just as occurred in the 1950s with a sister line – the *Tallulah Falls Railroad* – the *Gainesville-Northwestern Railroad (G&NW)* between Gainesville and Robertstown, Georgia, eventually exhausted its reason for existence as well, after the immense stands of timber had all been harvested from northeast Georgia. With the departure of the timber companies and the huge Byrd-Matthews Lumber Company which had produced and shipped the seemingly endless boards of lumber,

This photo of a new locomotive and tender is believed to have been taken shortly before delivery of the two to Gainesville. The platform on which they are positioned has a "Baldwin Locomotive Works" identification across the front.

the *Gainesville-Northwestern Railroad* found itself unable to generate enough income to survive.

By 1935, with its income severely reduced, the little mountain short-line simply went out of business. The rails were pulled up and sold for scrap iron to Japan and the property rights-of-way reverted back to ownership by the local landowners. It was a sad day for residents all up and down the picturesque little rail line into the mountains – but it had been an idyllic lifestyle while it had lasted.

In the years preceding World War I, a group of businessmen had realized the value of the immense stock of forest products available in the northeast Georgia mountains. This same timber products industry also spawned a tiny community – *Helen, Georgia* – which would later reinvent itself as a captivating Alpine village and grow into a major tourism destination which still exists today.

Beginnings

The *Gainesville-Northwestern* was incorporated on February 9, 1912, primarily to provide a viable and dependable mode of transportation for the timber products being harvested in northeast Georgia. A sizeable on-site manufacturing company – *Byrd-Matthews Lumber* – began the production of wood products from this timber, shipping its wares all across the United States via the railroad. Life was good and the income seemed endless.

The tiny short-line also provided passenger, freight, and mail service daily from Gainesville to Robertstown, passing thru numerous whistle- and flag-stops along the way. If an individual had something which needed to get to a market, or if a resident or businessman in Clermont, or Helen, or Robertstown needed to obtain a product, the *G&NW* provided the transportation.

Byrd-Matthews Lumber Company was one of the largest lumber mills east of the Mississippi in its day. It produced thousands of board feet of lumber every week which was shipped to Gainesville. After reaching that town, the lumber was transferred to other railroads and shippers for distribution throughout the nation, and to a number of foreign countries as well.

Lumber production was big business in north Georgia where virgin timber was still abundant in the early 1900s, and railroads such as the *Gainesville-Northwestern* were vital in the effort to harvest this timber. The railroad also shipped products from a limited minerals industry in the area as well.

The "passenger" aspect of the *Gainesville-Northwestern Railroad* featured what was known as "an excursion service" to and from Gainesville to and from Robertstown (above Helen), and also provided freight and postal service to all the communities in between on the line.

The run began at the old Gainesville Depot (which still stands as of this

The first post office at the community of "Dip" (present-day Clermont) was in the home of Mr. and Mrs. William Harvey Keith. This obviously-posed photo includes the Keiths seated in the chairs, and, on horseback, Mr. Josiah W. Blackwell, the first mail carrier for the area.

writing in 2025) and made stops at numerous additional depots along the way, including Bradford Street Station (removed long ago), New Holland (also gone), Clark (gone), Autry (gone), Dewberry (gone), Brookton (the ruins of which survived until just recently), Clermont (long gone), County Line (gone), Mossy Creek Campground (long gone), Meldean (gone), Cleveland (long gone), Asbestos (gone), Mt. Yonah (gone), Nacoochee (still exists as of this writing in 2025), Helen (gone), and Robertstown (also gone). Gainesville, Brookton, Clermont, Meldean, Cleveland, Nacoochee, Helen, and Robertstown were what was known as "agency stations," and the train made regular stops at them. The others were known as "flag stops," (where pauses were made only if the train was "flagged" by a customer).

Clermont had existed as a community prior to the construction of the *G&NW*, springing up in part due to the town's strategic location on an aged travel route for traditional mountain products taken to market each year in Gainesville. When the railroad was constructed through the tiny town, Clermont gained a prime supply line and became a market

This rare photograph shows *Chattahoochee High School*, an early education center in northeast Georgia, which once stood across the highway from Concord Baptist Church in Clermont. This institution was an early portion of the *Mercer University* education system, and aided in the early growth of Clermont prior to the demise of the *Georgia Northwestern Railroad.*

destination from the more heavily populated cities of Gainesville and Atlanta to the south, factors which further enhanced its growth and fostered the commerce which sprang to life in Clermont from 1912 to the mid-1930s.

Chattahoochee High School

Another growth catalyst in Clermont which preceded the railroad was *Chattahoochee High School*, established around 1890. It became a Baptist Church-supported school which belonged to the *Mercer University* system of preparatory schools in 1919. It was a four-year school, with records indicating it produced its first graduating class in 1906.

Educational institutions such as Chattahoochee High were few in number in the north Georgia mountains at

that time, and such facilities became a strong incentive for the relocation of families interested in higher education – and a presumed better life – for their children.

"My father and mother moved us to Clermont specifically so we could have the opportunity to go to a nine-month school," said the late Essie Hudgins Jordan, who was a 1919 graduate of *Chattahoochee High*. She was also a member of the faculty during the 1923-24 school year, following graduation from *Georgia Normal and Industrial College* in Milledgeville in 1923.

Miss Essie's father, James Zacheus Hudgins, had moved their family from Sugar Hill in South Hall County to Clermont in North Hall in 1912 when she was twelve years old. "Despite the fact that it meant wholly relocating a home and a profitable family business, it was important to Mother and Father that we children receive a good education," she added.

Miss Essie's beautiful old family home – built by her father in 1912 – still stands (as of this writing in 2025) on King Street in Clermont. It is one of a number of elegant turn-of-the-century homes which highlight the architectural beauty and scenic attractiveness of the town even today. While it was being constructed in 1912, the Hudgins family rented a home near Wauka Mountain.

"*Chattahoochee High School* was a boarding school at that time," Miss Essie continued. "The dormitory which housed both girls and boys was on the campus grounds. It had space for a music room and a library, as well as an apartment set aside for the school superintendent. Some of the students rented small cottages, going home on weekends and in the summer, when school was not in session."

The 1923-24 *"Annual Announcement"* booklet from *Chattahoochee High* offers a glimpse back in time at the school. It describes the institution as: *". . . located near the little town of Clermont, on the Gainesville-North Western Railroad, 16 miles from Gainesville.... This puts Chattahoochee in a few minutes of Gainesville in one direction, and a few minutes of the mountains going north. For several miles in three directions, may be seen broad fields of corn and cotton and small grain. Much of this plateau section is yet wooded....Clermont is a thriving town, built up since the school was established. The town gives many advantages: one bank, post office, hotel, drug store, furniture store, five general mercantile stores, express office, two blacksmith establishments, and a telephone exchange."*

As might be expected, social codes at the school were strict. Boys and girls

The late Essie Hudgins (Jordan), one of the first female faculty members of *Chattahoochee High School*, was photographed here in 1923, following her graduation from *Georgia Normal and Industrial College* in Milledgeville, Georgia. She also was an early graduate of *Chattahoochee*. She went on to later become a very prominent and respected teacher of chemistry and biology at *Rockmart High School* in Rockmart, Georgia, arriving in that town in 1924. She retired from teaching in 1971, and passed away in 1999, two months shy of her 99th birthday. She undoubtedly would have taught well into her 70s had she not been teaching her final 7 years while legally blind.

were expected to refrain from all communication with each other except *"that which ordinary courtesy demands."* Boys and girls were not allowed the freedom of the town, except by special permission. They were expected to remain in their rooms at night. Boys were required to *"abstain from smoking cigarettes, playing cards, profanity, intoxicating liquors and the keeping of firearms."*

An early run of the *Gainesville-Northwestern* train pulls into *Nacoochee Station* outside Helen, Georgia, circa 1930s. This depot is the only one still in existence from the little mountain short-line.

Chattahoochee High School Graduates (1906-1923)

1906 - J.T. Miller

1907 - Grover Miller

1908 - A.S. Kytle

1909 - George, Gearin, W.C. Grindle, C.W. Henderson, Fred Staton, W.L. Walker

1910 - H.W. Keith, U.A. Lawson, E.B. O'Kelley, M.K. Staton, Inez Spencer, Ruth Waters

1911 - F.L. Brown. B.J. Head, H.G. Hudgins, U.S. Lancaster, H.L. Lawson, R.H. Thomas, Minnie Head, Exer Head, Lola Staton.1912 - H.E. Buffington, A.B. Eberhart, Claude Grindle, Hubert Haynes, W.H. Lord, B.H. Robinson, Beulah Hudgins, Vivian Jarrard, Liccie Payne, Lillie Payne, Nellie Whelchel

1913 - W.T. Evans, Charles E. Hawkins, W.P. Pettyjohn, W.A. Whitmire, John Haynes, A.B. Keith, C.H. Keith, F.P.

Lockhart, Lena Hudgins, Mary Hulsey, Florence Ragan, Pink Standridge

1914 - C.J. Broom, H.T. Brookshire, O.G. Lancaster, G.F. Tyner, Salena Jarrard, Anna Belle Lockhart.

1915 - C.C. Jarrard, J.A. Meaders, M.D. Reed, Irene Bailey, Josephine Grogan, Chester Head, Iris Maddox.

1916 - Chesley Bennett, Harry Garrison, Richard Hawkins, Carl Lancaster, Elmira Grogan, Daisy Hudgins, Ethel Roark

1917 - W.E. Barnwell, R.L. Carter, Ernest Hulsey, J.L. Keith, D.T. Lawson, Y.W. Peck, H.H. Peyton, Beulah Greer, Myrtle Haynes, Ada Highsmith, Ethleen Jarrard, Florida Mauldin, Willie Staton.

1918 - Una Abercrombie, Laurie Truelove, Maude Logan, Esther Langford, Lillie Mac Culpepper, Annie Mae Haynes, Agnes Roark, Etta Chandler, Henry Reed, Clarence Puckett, Glenn

The dilapidated remains of the *Gainesville-Northwestern Railroad* depot at Brookton, Georgia, were photographed on the "wagon side" in 1972. This station, one of the last standing, has since succumbed, sadly, to the ravages of time and weathering. Out of a total of 17 stations which once existed on the *Gainesville-Northwestern* line, Brookton was one of eight "Agency Stations" which received a higher priority. The remaining nine stations were what was known as "flag stops," of lesser importance. (Photo by Grant Keene, Cleveland, GA)

Cooper, Edward Brown, Escoe Logan, Garnett Keith.

1919 - Valera Bowen, Bertie Mae Miller, Lillie Head, Sallie Hix, Hoke Grier, Homer Keith, Roy Martin, Bertha Waters, Essie Hudgins, Idell Haynes, Essie Tanner, Hester Tanner, Lucile Roark, Dewey Patten, Frank Cain, Howard Poole, Vassie Keith, Nell Whitmire.

1920 - Ernest Abercrombie, Clifton Bryson, Wallis Bennett, D.T. Buice, Nita Catlett, Callie Chandler, Adele Head, Vallie Hulsey, Floyd Hendrix, Avie Forrester, Jewell Keith, D.W. Lord, Ralph Miller, Clyde Maddox, Russell Marlow, Nellie Mae Pierce, Charlie Staton, Adelia Joe Staton, Clarence Walker, Julius Whitmire, Paul Whitmore, Edgar Hulsey.

1921 - Jarnet Carruth, Bonnie Carruth, Hugh Brice, Annie Brice, Henry Logan, Hortense Delong, Mabel Haynes, Mae Grant, Lee Grant, Herschel McGee, Seaborn Gilstrap, Y.D. Jones, Fred Moore, Ralph Thompson, J. Henry Lackey, Albert Martin, Nell Christopher, Mary Brown, Eugenia Rogers, Maudelle Pierce, Sylvia Gailey, Mary Elder, Price Bowen, Ruth Head, Michael McNeal, Texas Wallace, Herschel Davis, Laura Belle Culpepper, June Murphy, Ralph Murphy, Pearl Truelove, Pink Culpepper.

1922 - Ruth Crawford, Lee Buice, David Hudgins, Lucas Griffin, Willie Meaders, Cladith Simpson, Mozelle Marlowe, Hassie Mae Whitmire, Cordia Mullinax, Gertrude Kytle, Clarence Walker.

1923 - Cary Adams, Ernest Brown, Ralph Buffington, Lunie Mae Coker, Winnie Chandler, Kelsey Delong, Otis Dyer, Birdie Gailey, J.E. Grizzle, Clyde Hudgins, Mae Hooper, Mary Belle Jackson, Nina Keith, Vera Keith, Cora Belle

The *Gainesville-Northwestern* was built primarily to provide transportation for the wood products produced by the huge *Byrd-Matthews Lumber Mill* (later *Morse Brothers Lumber*) in Helen, Georgia, photographed here in 1912. After the immense stands of timber had all been harvested from the northeast Georgia mountains, both *Byrd-Matthews/Morse Brothers* and the *Gainesville-Northwestern* Railroad ceased business operations.

Lancaster, Myrtle Moore, Fred Orr, Turner Quillian, Emma Haynes, Marilu Hudgins, Maggie Smith, Tony Walker.

Early Clermont

In 1912, Clermont and the surrounding counties were still a very sparsely populated area, a type of pioneer country in many ways. "Father had a general store beside the railroad there in the center of town," Mrs. Jordan continued. "Clermont was a wonderful place for a child to grow up, and we had a large family – six brothers and six sisters.

"All the stories you read about pioneer life which describe the little general store where saddles, sunbonnets, barrels of apples, cheeses, dry goods, traps, and all the other staples of life in the mountains in that day and time, are very descriptive of what was sold in Father's store," she

smiled. "On cold winter days, men gathered around an old pot-bellied stove to play checkers. Father loved to play checkers," she stated in a conspiratorial whisper.

Before the railroad came through, and before *Chattahoochee High School* was constructed, Clermont's primary claim to fame had been its resort identity. The name *"Clermont"* is almost certainly a French description of "Clear Mountains." The scenic location of the town in the shadow of nearby Wauka Mountain and the beginnings of the Blue Ridge Mountains in north Georgia, led to the construction of the *Clermont Hotel* in 1911-12. This structure, now approaching 115 years in age, still stands on the old town square.

Though not luxurious by any means, the *Clermont Hotel* was elegant for its day. The *Gainesville-Northwestern*

Byrd-Matthews Lumber Mill produced a remarkable 125,000 board feet of lumber per day when operating at maximum capacity. It is not difficult to understand how convenient access to the railroad was critical in the shipment of this massive product to market.

Railroad passed right beside it and had its depot across the street. A tennis court (apparently one of the first in the north Georgia area) was available to the rear of the hotel, for guests.

Nacoochee

Up toward what then was the tiny community of Helen, Mr. T.B. Henderson owned a general merchandise store next to the *G&NW's* Nacoochee Station. Both the store building and Nacoochee Station still exist and are original to the community, being well over 100 years in age themselves. *(Henderson's former General Store is the old brick building at the intersection of Georgia Highways 75 and 17, near the Indian mound. The former Nacoochee Station building stands across Highway 75 from the old general store building.)* Mr. Henderson's daughter, Mary Lula Henderson

Davidson, provided the following descriptive details concerning early life in turn-of-the-century Nacoochee:

"The Nacoochee Post Office was located in the general store and my father was postmaster there. He also served as rail agent at the Nacoochee Station. His duties included the issuance of tickets and the posting of freight bills. Most of the merchandise in his store came in by rail from Athens or Gainesville.

"Father was one of the few persons in the area who owned an automobile. Sometimes passengers coming in on the train would need transportation to one of the 'resorts' in the area or to a friend or relative's house. After arriving at Nacoochee Station, my brother - Bon - would drive the travelers to their destinations."

Mrs. Davidson also described how she helped her father in the store, post office and at the little railroad station. She

Griffin Brothers' Cotton Warehouse on King Street was photographed here circa 1926. The *Gainesville-Northwestern Railroad* which passed through Clermont is just visible to the right rear of the warehouse. Owner John T. Griffin (far right, foreground) was remembered by one elderly resident as a stern disciplinarian and taskmaster.

Early Town Home – Essie Carroll Hudgins (Jordan) sits (far right) with two of her sisters at the home built by their father, James Zacheus Hudgins in Clermont, Hall County, Georgia, in 1913. This beautiful home - though in some disrepair at last check - still stands on King Street today in Clermont.

remembers that in the store, they sold groceries, hardware, men's, women's and children's clothing, seeds and fertilizer,

all mostly delivered by rail. She said that Mr. L.G. Hardman *(whose beautiful old home also still stands near the intersection of Georgia Highways 75 and 17, and was originally constructed by Civil War veteran Col. James Hall Nichols)* shipped butter and milk from his dairy by rail to Gainesville, and Mr. "Simp" Logan shipped asbestos from his asbestos mine by railroad.

Mr. Henry Davidson, who became the husband of Miss Mary Lula Henderson, was one of the many who helped to build the railroad from Gainesville to Robertstown. His brother, Mr. George Davidson, was an engineer on the train and Mr. Paul Westmoreland was fireman.

The railroad brought many visitors to the White County area. Major resorts included the Alley House *(still in existence as the Old Sautee Inn today)* in Nacoochee; the Henderson Hotel in

Clermont - meaning "Clear Mountains" - once thrived as a scheduled stop on the *Gainesville-North-western Railroad*. The Clermont Hotel (pictured), was built in 1912, and still stands as of this writing (2025), one of only a handful of original town buildings still in existence. The tracks of the *Gaines-ville-Northwestern* passed to the right of this structure and continued through town. (Photo by R. Olin Jackson)

Cleveland (now long disappeared); and the Mitchell Mountain Ranch (also long gone) in Helen.

Declining Years

The *Gainesville-Northwestern* continued its 37-mile run from Gainesville to Robertstown until 1930. Shortly thereafter, when the presumed-inexhaustible supply of virgin timber had nonetheless been depleted almost entirely, the railroad, with its life-blood gone, eventually became insolvent and service was discontinued. The tracks were taken up; the railroad rights-of-way reverted back to private ownership, and the *Gainesville-Northwestern Railroad* disappeared forever from the Hall and White County landscapes and faded into history.

Interestingly, businessman James Zacheus Hudgins of Clermont was noted for having provided free Christmas gifts every year at the annual Yule event at the Concord Baptist Church to poor mountain residents who, other than the celebration of the birth of our Lord, would otherwise have experienced nothing further of note on Christmas morning. Mr. Hudgins is also still remembered for his substantial benevolence regarding the many debts owed to him by residents in the community to whom he regularly extended credit and declined to seek payment – a benevolence for which he never sought, nor received, any credit during his lifetime.

Sadly, when Mr. Hudgins tragically passed away from liver cancer in 1933, his preference to show compassion to his fellow man rather than to demand payment from the many residents indebted to him for foods and other sundry

113

Old Time Religion – The original *Concord Baptist Church* sanctuary was photographed here some-time between 1882 and 1919. A brick structure replaced this building in the early 1920s. (Photo courtesy of Mr. Ralph Hampton, Gainesville)

items, unfortunately returned to haunt his family. A minor partner which Mr. Hudgins had taken in his general store business in his later years took issue with Mr. Hudgins' "negligence" in the collection of payments from those to whom he had extended credit.

This minor partner subsequently filed suit against the grieving Mrs. Hudgins for these uncollected debts, in order to gain full ownership of the family business following James' death. Mrs. Hudgins, as a result, lost not only the family business to this minor partner, but also her home and security as well, ultimately living in poverty and becoming dependent upon her children for a domicile and livelihood for the remainder of her years.

The "gentleman" who foreclosed upon Mrs. Hudgins and caused her to live in such poverty has faded into history and been properly forgotten. Mrs. Hudgins and her family, however, will long be fondly remembered for their benevolence and the kindnesses which they freely extended to others during their lifetimes.

Though forfeited long ago by Mrs. Hudgins and her family, the beautiful old family home on King Street in Clermont which Mr. Hudgins built well over 100 years ago still stands in mute testimony to his worthy Christian memory.

Last Ride of the Storied *Gainesville Midland*

For years, she worked the rails between Gainesville and Athens, hauling freight and passengers to stops along the route. Though its once-powerful locomotion has been stilled today, Engine #209 still stands near the site of the old depot in Gainesville, allowing the curious a peek at what rail travel was like in yesteryear.

She sits there in all her glory, old steam *Engine #209*, a powerful reminder of the classic days when railroads ruled the economy of America. She is, of course, retired today – a victim of progress. In tribute to her historic service as part of the long-departed *Gainesville-Midland Railroad (GMR)*, however, *Engine #209*, a mail car, and a bright red caboose have been permanently enshrined in a Gainesville city park near the old depot.

The site has become a mecca for train buffs, as well as a constant source of excitement for youngsters adventurous enough to climb to the second-story height of the old engine cab. Under the guidance of the *Georgia Mountains Museum* and the City of Gainesville, *#209* is watched over by a group of dedicated railroad hobbyists who keep the "museum" open during the year for visitors.

Not only will the volunteers enthusiastically tell you about the steam engine and the cars, but older train buffs like Forrest L. Shiver and younger ones like Jeff Puett will spin you railroad yarns just as long as you wish – if you're willing to listen. You see, railroading is more than a hobby with them – it's their life.

Engine #209 was the last "steam" locomotive to operate commercially in the state of Georgia as the diesel revolution took its toll. The old-timers from the *Gainesville-Midland*, such as Jesse Gillespie, will proudly tell you she even pulled her upstart diesel replacement into Gainesville to begin its career.

Photographed in September of 1959, *Engine #209* of the *Gainesville-Midland Railroad* pulls out on an excursion run, the last trip it ever made. The last official freight run of *#209* was made the previous June. It now gathers the years in exposition in Gainesville.

Youngsters simply can't resist climbing aboard #209 to sample the view and imagine what it was like to be an engineer on the big locomotive in days of yesteryear.

Old #209 was a working freight engine, originally built for the *Seaboard Railroad* in 1930 by the *Baldwin Locomotive Works* in Philadelphia. She was bought by the *Durham and Southern Railroad*, overhauled by the *D&S* crews, and then stored as a stand-by and never used. She later was bought by the *Gainesville-Midland*, ending up on the short run between Gainesville and Athens, Georgia.

Old #209 had some help too. Just as she was revered as a workhorse, her sister locomotive – #206 – was undoubtedly the "show-horse" of the steam locomotives operating under the *Midland* banner.

Engine #206, in fact, came into this world as royalty. She was built in 1916 for the Czar of Russia. She was a *sport* model, a Russian Decapod, and nothing defined her personality more than her sporty 10 drive-wheels which were

white-walled. She was designed to haul – at 60 miles per hour – both freight and passengers across a vast wasteland on the *Trans-Siberian Railroad*.

Interestingly, when she was finally ready for shipment to Russia, Czar Nicholas II was experiencing immense regal problems and Russia was in turmoil. In 1905, the Russians had been defeated by Japan in the Russo-Japanese War, and the czar had effectively lost control of the Pacific end of his cross-continental railroad.

Then, in 1917, the Russian Revolution was responsible for the overthrow of Nicholas, when the Bolsheviks seized power. Nicholas ultimately was executed in 1918, and the Union of Soviet Socialist Republics (U.S.S.R.) was formed in 1922.

Back in the United States, all the maneuvering in the U.S.S.R. left #206 – an engine intended for royalty – in limbo in the rail yards at the *Baldwin*

116

This early photograph of the *Gainesville-Midland* at the old *Gainesville Depot* was taken when the line still provided passenger service. Notice the crowds here waiting to board and lingering as they meet friends and family. The Gainesville town square is visible in the background.

Locomotive Works. She eventually was sold to the *Detroit, Toledo & Ironton Railroad* as *#310*. The trucks under her tender still have the *DT&I RR* visible on them.

Eventually, the *Seaboard Airline Railroad* picked up this engine, and as *#544*, she wandered over the Seaboard system until the *Gainesville-Midland* purchased her as part of their post-World War II up-grading. Today, the czar's *Engine #206* can be found in the North Carolina Transportation Museum in Spencer, North Carolina.

And the 209? In 1959, she was given to the City of Gainesville, a fitting tribute considering the fact this north Georgia city was once a busy railroad center, with a major North-South line coming directly through town, another line (the *Gainesville-Midland Railway*) connecting to Athens, and a third (the *Gainesville & Northwestern Railway*) extending through Clermont to Robertstown in nearby White County.

Today, the historic locomotive with "209" painted upon its side stands in downtown Gainesville in mute testimony to one of the great eras of north Georgia's commercial history. A group of steam engine lovers maintains her so future generations of kids – of all ages – may witness, first-hand, one of the dynamic modes of transportation of yesteryear.

Fond Memories of Old
Gainesville & Northwestern Railroad

For years, it served as a medium of transportation for the burgeoning lumber industry in northeast Georgia. And when all the timber had been harvested and the mills dismantled, the little short-line struggled on for a few more years before finally dying a slow, painful death.

Today, visitors to "Alpine Helen" in north Georgia's White County may have a difficult time picturing a huge sawmill on the east side of the Chattahoochee River in what now is "downtown" Helen. That, however, is exactly what once stood on this site. And servicing it was a now almost forgotten railroad called the *Gainesville & Northwestern (G&NW)*.

This early 1900s north Georgia rail line was completed in 1912 and began service in 1913. A typical train consisted of a steam locomotive; a coal car; a combination baggage, mail and passenger car; and another passenger car with an observation platform at the rear.

Over the years, the *G&NW* owned seven coal-burning steam "road" locomotives. *Numbers 57, 103, & 203* were "ten-wheeler" passenger locomotives built by Baldwin, while numbers *59, 60, 101* and *102* were freight engines built by Lima. *Number 101* was later renumbered *201*. The *G&NW* also owned No. *2*, a 2-truck Shay also built by Lima.

The Early Years

In its early years, the *Gainesville & Northwestern* featured excursion service from Gainesville to Escowee Falls between Helen and Robertstown, where an attractive pavilion had been built over the stream. Mossy Creek Campground was another popular excursion destination.

The *Gainesville & Northwestern* was originally built to provide transportation for the large volumes of lumber products produced by Byrd-Matthews (later Morse Brothers) Lumber Mill in Helen. In its hey-days, Byrd-Matthews produced 125,000 board feet per day when operating at maximum capacity.

The *G&NW* was also directly responsible for thriving economies in the little communities through which it passed enroute to Helen. The tracks started in downtown Gainesville where the depot and yards were shared with the *Gainesville Midland Railroad*. The *G&NW* then ran 37 miles to Robertstown (formerly called "North Helen"). This railroad was also known as *"The Nacoochee Valley Route."*

The towns of Nacoochee, Yonah, Cleveland, Clermont, Brookton and others grew significantly during the *G&NW's* glory years, and withered and shrunk just as quickly when the rail line died. A branch line extended from Clermont to the pyrites mine in Lumpkin County.

The virgin timber stands in northeast Georgia were immense, and it took a number of years to deplete them. However, the supply finally did play out in 1928, and with it, so also did the huge lumber mill, as well as the railroad in the early 1930s.

Shortly after the demise of the mill, the steam locomotive and its fine cars were sold to the highest bidders. Though the railroad essentially was "dead," the rails themselves were still usable. A temporary form of replacement transportation – which literally was a "bus on railroad wheels" – provided renewed/continued service. This "contraption" (for that's essentially what it was) was nicknamed *"The Yellow Hammer,"* and literally wobbled as it proceeded down the tracks.

Mail service (and a smattering of passenger service) was continued on *"the Hammer"* until the mid-1930s when the rails finally were removed and sold for scrap. Today, little remains of the old line except for the faintly visible outlines of the road-bed in certain locations.

To transport the harvested logs from the mountain forests, the mill owners built an extensive network of logging railroads which radiated outward from Helen in all directions. By the time logging operations ended, over 150 miles of rail lines had been built into four counties in northeast Georgia!

These logging tracks off the main *Gainesville & Northwestern Railroad* were "narrow-gauge" in size, and very temporary in nature, since their usefulness ended once the timber around them had been harvested. When the usable timber was depleted, the tracks were taken up and moved to a new location.

One unusual feature of the *Gainesville & Northwestern* was the use of three-rail (or dual gauge) track from the mill in Helen south to Asbestos Station. This track accommodated the normal 56 and one-half-inch standard-gauge trains out of Gainesville, as well as the 42-inch narrow-gauge logging trains on their way to logging sites in the mountains.

Turner's Corner & Blood Mtn.

A completely different locomotive was also used to haul the heavy log-train cars out of the mountains. These engines typically were the Shay, Climax and Heisler engines, all of which were used in the Helen operations. These locomotives had all of their wheels driven by shafts and gears, making them very slow, but extremely powerful, and capable of operation on very uneven track.

Perhaps the last area to be logged – circa 1925 to 1927 – was a tract of land northeast of Helen. Morse Brothers ran the company's railroad across the Chattahoochee River at Bell Branch, a little southeast of the Helen mill, then roughly along what today is Georgia Highway 356, then up the right fork of the Soque River, across a gap in the ridge between Habersham and Rabun Counties, along the side of the mountains west of Lake Burton, and finally up the Tallulah River to Tate City.

From this "main line," the loggers ran spur tracks up the left fork of the Soque River, Wildcat Creek and Moccasin Creek (to name a few) which are still visible today. Here, they made the last timber harvests of this era.

Despite their temporary nature, these railroad beds were of excellent quality in the days when north Georgia highways were quite primitive. Some rock retaining walls are still serviceable in the Duke's Creek Falls area. The many trestles necessary for this area were built of untreated native timbers, so most are in various states of decay today, but the rock retaining walls are quite sturdy.

After the logging rails were taken up, local residents probably carried off most of the re-usable timbers, so only the roadbeds of these interesting trails are visible today. As recently as 1987, a collapsed trestle across Goshen Creek below a beautiful waterfall still existed in Habersham County just west of what once was LaPrade's Fish Camp on Lake Burton. Back in the early 1900s, the loggers had built square log cribs on each side of the creek, then had laid huge chestnut logs on the cribs to support the tracks. This, of course, was prior to the time that the chestnut blight destroyed the chestnut trees in the Southern Appalachians.

Wildcat Creek

Another interesting area to explore is an old logging railroad in the vicinity of Wildcat Creek. The grade in this area is essentially clear of undergrowth, and is a fine "rail-trail." It follows the border of what today is a Wildlife Management Area patrolled and maintained by the Georgia Department of Natural Resources.

Little remains today of three trestles which once provided transport for the trains across the creeks, so a walk along this route today will require some climbing down to the creek beds and

then back up the other side. At one of these creeks, a side road leads up to the spring which once supplied water to LaPrade's Camp.

As you approach Wildcat Creek, the trail becomes much more overgrown, but is still quite serviceable. The grade eventually joins *Forest Service Road 26* (FS-26) which branches off *Georgia Highway 197* and runs up Wildcat Creek. This road is built on the bed of the railroad branch which once existed along Wildcat Creek.

Just downstream from where the railroad grade crosses Wildcat Creek are the ruins of the small dam and waterwheel supports for the electrical generator that once provided LaPrade's with electrical power in the days prior to rural electrification. John LaPrade's son-in-law, the late Vernon Castner, once described the building of the power plant in vivid detail.

Mr. Castner explained the plant was constructed by local craftsmen, not by the Georgia Power Company as has been rumored over the years. One tall tale maintains the plant was built by Georgia Power for Mr. LaPrade in return for his help in acquiring land for Lake Burton.

(Directions: To find the most accessible logging railroad trail, take Georgia 197 to Lake Burton. Just north of the former location of Laprade's Fish Camp, turn west on Wildcat Creek Road (Forest Service Road 26). You are now driving on the old railroad grade. After approximately one mile, look for a grassy meadow leading to a footbridge across Wildcat Creek. Park, cross the creek, and you can find the slightly overgrown railroad grade. Hike the grade south. You will encounter three old trestle locations as you hike above the LaPrade's site.)

Old West Bandit Bill Miner's Final Train Robbery

He haunted the stagecoach and train routes throughout the old West, robbing and pillaging at will, but always with a polite manner. Though captured and imprisoned numerous times, he invariably escaped to continue his high crimes... that is, until age and infirmity, and a trip to Georgia combined to bring his bandit days to a close.

George Anderson of Jackson County, Kentucky, was born in 1843. Instead of the normal law-abiding life of most citizens, George apparently decided early in life that he was best-suited to be a professional criminal. In fairness, as the son of a sometime school teacher mother and a fly-by-night father who abandoned his family before George was even ten years of age, the youngster was "running against the wind" before he ever even reached adolescence.

Without proper supervision, young George quickly earned a reputation as a dare-devil and irresponsible youth – traits by which he would live for the rest of his "devil-may-care" days. Throughout his life, in order to maintain a measure of anonymity, he used a variety of names, including George Morgan, California Billy, George Edwards, George Bud, and Louis Colquhoun, among many others, but he was known most notoriously and made famous in recent years on the silver screen as "Bill Miner."

Shortly before the U.S. Civil War, Miner (Anderson) left home for the gold

Young and Full of Vinegar - With his hat at a jaunty angle, a lit cigar, and a nice suit of clothing, a young George Anderson (alias Bill Miner) had already established himself in a life of crime when he sat (and, quite possibly actually paid) for this photo to be taken sometime earlier in his life of crime. (Photo courtesy of Robert G. McCubbin Collection)

Desperate Criminal – With a slightly more desperate look in his eye, this print of George Anderson quite likely was a prison photograph. His clothing has degenerated to the shabby level and his eyes bespeak violence and desperation.

fields of California where he landed a job as a pony express rider. He, however, either quickly tired of this job, or else it tired of him. Whatever the circumstances, he soon began robbing stagecoaches, igniting the life of crime from which he never wavered.

The nation watched in earnest as young "Billy the Kid," Jesse James, "Black Bart," Cole Younger, the Daltons, Butch Cassidy and the "Sundance Kid," and the other notorious outlaws of the old West rose to prominence and then faded into the mists of time. Miner was cut from the same mold and was considered by many to have been even more notorious than his counterparts. To be certain, he was one of the last surviving members of this fraternity, and was still robbing trains well into the 20th century.

Early on a cold February (18th) morning in 1911, Miner held up

Out of the darkness, two other men suddenly appeared, brandishing revolvers.

Southern Railway's *Train No. 36* near the White Sulphur Station north of Gainesville, Georgia. How he progressed all the way from California to Georgia in his life of crime is unknown today, but he also has a criminal record as far north as Canada where he was imprisoned (and escaped), so he was wide-ranging to say the least. He had no way of knowing it at the time, but his days of crime were fast coming to a close as this final episode of his life of thievery began unfolding in Georgia.

According to reports, at approximately 3:15 A.M. on the aforementioned morning, engineer David J. Fant of Atlanta might have cursed had he not been – aside from a railroad engineer – a Baptist evangelist minister. *Southern Railway No. 36* was already late when he took it out of Atlanta at 12:15 A.M. that morning. On this, of all mornings, Fant had H.E. Hudgens, general superintendent of the railroad on board in a private car at the rear, and now someone was flagging down the train, further delaying the train's schedule.

As Fant peered through the darkness and rain of the miserably-cold morning gloom, he saw that someone up ahead was waving a red lantern. The engineer knew he had to stop. He assumed a lineman or a farmer had discovered a broken rail and was trying to save the train from wrecking. If that was the case, the *"evangelist of the rails"* (as he was known) would issue up a prayer of thanks.

As the train coasted to a halt, Fant slid down from the engine cab and called out, inquiring if the track was being repaired. Out of the darkness, two other men suddenly appeared, brandishing revolvers. To Fant's dismay, they announced the obvious. *Southern Railway No. 36* was being robbed!

The three bandits, all wearing masks and calling each other "captain," "number four" and "number five," loudly ordered Fant's black fireman Rufus Johnson to "Disappear!" a command to which the normally affable trainman, the whites of his terrified eyes now clearly visible in the dim light, quickly complied.

While the leader of the trio with the lantern watched Fant, the other two bandits walked down to the express car with the intention of releasing the train from that point rearward, so that the robbery could be completed farther up the track, without having to contend with a lot of panicky, confused passengers.

Shortly thereafter, flagman C.H. Shirley and conductor Walter T. Mooney, both of Atlanta, began walking up to the engine to find out what was happening. Seeing the man with the lantern, Mooney called out but received no response from the suspicious-looking man. The conductor later stated *"I assumed I was dealing with a block-head."* He (Mooney) grabbed the man's arm and gave him a shove, demanding to know why the train had been stopped.

Miner immediately whirled upon Mooney and very angrily stuck a revolver in his face, formally announcing the holdup.

Thinking this was all just a bad joke, Mooney exclaimed *"Cut out this foolishness! I've got a train to look after!"* Only when the masked Miner responded with a string of obscenities and was on the verge of pistol-whipping him, did Mooney realize the full implication of

"The Grey Fox" - Just as he was described by countless lawmen and victims alike, George Anderson, alias Bill Miner, rarely appeared to be a notorious desperate outlaw, more often than not assuming the persona of a kindly elderly gentleman. He, nevertheless, robbed stagecoaches and trains from California to Georgia and was credited with more than one murder. This photo is believed to have been taken in Canada where the aging bandit was captured following one of his many robberies. He subsequently escaped from the prison there, adding further to his growing identity as *"The Grey Fox,"* and set out for the U.S. East Coast. (Photo courtesy of Heritage House Publishing Company and Art Downs)

the situation, and that he had come fearfully-near to being shot.

Mooney quickly retreated, his hands raised in submission. Once out of the bandit's view, the conductor told Shirley to try to slip past the rear of the train and go get help. The flagman did just that, running to White Sulphur Station, a small railway depot about a mile away.

Meanwhile, Walter B. Miller, in the express car, had learned of the robbery

Partners in Crime – The perpetrators of the February, 1911 robbery of Southern Railway's Train #36 were photographed during their incarceration in Georgia. George Anderson ("Miner") (center) was captured in the Nimblewill Community outside Dahlonega, Georgia several days after the robbery. His two accomplices who flank him in the photo – Charlie Hunter and James Handford – had been captured earlier. Hunter was a thirty-year-old Irishman from Michigan. Anderson (Miner) and Hunter worked for two months in a Virginia sawmill where they completed their group of partners in crime by recruiting thirty-three-year-old Handford from Nebraska.

and was desperately attempting to quickly lock all of the doors to thwart the bandits' thievery, but despite his best efforts, the men entered through a door which he had not yet latched, and demanded the keys to the two safes. Luckily, the keys were not kept on the train, so the bandits would have to use more powerful measures if they were to succeed in this theft.

Disappointed but undeterred, Miner (George Anderson) had come prepared for this possibility. He brought Fant and a shovel from the engine. With dirt from the outside, the bandits packed

dynamite under the safes, lit the fuses, and fled the car. The resulting explosion was immense. It tore holes through the roof and sides of the car, shattered the windows, and even put out the train's lights. When the smoke had cleared, however, to the bandits' immense disappointment, only the smaller of the two safes was open. The larger one yet stood firmly locked.

With time running out, "the captain" filled a bag with what little "loot" was available, and then he and his two accomplices semi-panicked, fleeing into the woods. They nevertheless made good on their escape, *"disappearing as if the earth had swallowed them up,"* according to a subsequent newspaper report.

Fant started up his damaged locomotive and since the rolling stock behind it was still operational, he engineered the train to the nearby community of Lula where he shortly telegraphed a report of the robbery. Meanwhile, ten minutes prior to Fant's report, Shirley had reached the White Sulphur Station, where he hurriedly reported the news of the robbery to local law enforcement authorities.

As could be expected under the circumstances, initial reports of the robbery became twisted and distorted as the news was passed from person to person. Two mythical additional bandits were included in early reports as having been passengers on the train. The gang's escape was described in various accounts as involving an automobile, a buggy, and even as involving a ride hitched on the underside of the very train they had robbed.

No complete account of the items/money stolen was ever made, but at the very least, approximately $800.00 in U.S. currency, $770.00 in Mexican pesos, an unknown amount in several other foreign currencies, a number of legal papers of no value to the robbers, a pair of pearl ear screws, and a watch were taken. Had the bandits known what they had left behind in the larger safe which they had failed to blow, they undoubtedly would have been truly disappointed. Still intact within the confines of that container, a total of $65,000 in gold and cash had been left untouched – an amount equivalent to approximately $1.75 million in 2025 dollars. It would have ranked among the most valuable robberies in U.S. history. Nevertheless, even the $800.00 in U.S. currency (equivalent to $21,600.00 in 2025 U.S. dollars) in Miner's loot was a nice payday for the bandits.

Miner had recruited his two accomplices for the Gainesville robbery – Charlie Hunter and James Handford – in Pennsylvania and Virginia respectively, in 1910. Hunter, a thirty-year-old Irishman from Michigan agreed, after some persuasion, to accompany the old bandit to a locale in the South, *"to try holding up a Southern train."* The pair worked for two months in a Virginia sawmill where they completed their group by recruiting thirty-three-year-old Handford from Nebraska.

The trio moved on to Georgia to prepare for what was almost unthinkable at that time – an old West-style train holdup in the East. The week before they finally struck *Southern Railway No. 36,* Hunter pawned Miner's watch in Atlanta, using the money to buy whiskey and a lantern later used in the robbery. A track wrench later found at their camp indicated that they had actually considered derailing and wrecking the train.

The first reports of the incident were met with incredulity by a disbelieving Gainesville populace. According to newspaper accounts of that day, most of

$500 Reward

The above reward will be paid for the arrest and detention of WILLIAM (Bill) MINER, alias Edwards, who escaped from the New Westminster Penitentiary, at New Westminster, British Columbia, on the 8th August, 1907, where he was serving a life sentence for train robbery.

DESCRIPTION:

Age 65 years; 138 pounds; 5 feet 8½ inches; dark complexion; brown eyes; grey hair; slight build; face spotted; tattoo base of left thumb, star and ballet girl right forearm; wrist joint-bones large; moles centre of breast, 1 under left breast, 1 on right shoulder, 1 on left shoulder-blade; discoloration left but ock; scars on left shin, right leg, inside, at knee, 2 on neck.

Communicate with

LT.-COL. A. P. SHERWOOD,
Commissioner Dominion Police,
Ottawa, Canada.

Bounty on His Head – This Canadian *"Wanted"* poster of Miner was distributed shortly after his escape from the New Westminister Penitentiary at New Westminister, British Columbia in Canada on August 8, 1907. Canadian law enforcement officials did not take lightly to his unexpected escape from their prison, and offered $500.00 for his capture. Though it may seem a somewhat paltry sum today for a reward, the $500.00 from 1907 would be the equivalent of approximately $17,000.00 in 2024 dollars, and a huge payday in 1907.

the townspeople dismissed the news of the robbery, thinking it was a joke. Most were dumbfounded when they learned the actual circumstances.

"The truth dawned at last," one newspaper intoned, *"and they were confronted with the fact that here in a free, civilized, God-fearing, and law-abiding community, a train robbery was committed that would abash the most God-forsaken Wild West country to be found. That such a daring hold-up could take place right at our doors was inconceivable."*

The Atlanta newspapers had a field

"Bill Miner Crossing" – The late Ray Shaw of Gainesville, Georgia, was an employee of the U.S. Postal Service in Hall County for many years, and was intimately familiar with the history and historic sites in the area. He was photographed above in 1987, at the spot at which *Southern Railway's Train #36* was robbed by Bill Miner and his accomplices near White Sulphur, Georgia, on a cold February morning in 1911. (Photo by R. Olin Jackson)

day with the event. The *Atlanta Journal* filled the first two pages of the February 18 issue with the news. The train crew, all of whom were Atlanta residents, were interviewed and their photographs published.

When the report of the robbery reached the Hall County Police Office in the early morning hours of February 18, Sheriff W.A. Crow was home sick with the mumps. He arose from his sick bed to organize a posse by telephone.

Assembling his deputies, Crow gave them a pep talk: "I want you to go out into the

The first reports of the incident were met with incredulity by a disbelieving Gainesville populace.

country and mountains now, and don't come back here until you bag these train robbers," he instructed. "Bring them back alive if you can. . . . But if not, just bring them along anyway."

These initial efforts in locating the bandits proved futile. Deputy Sheriff Little, with the help of county officials and railroad detectives, began a search of Gainesville, to see if the robbers might be hiding out somewhere in town.

The posse sent to the robbery site was delayed, waiting for the bloodhounds to be brought from Gwinnett

Former Depot Site – The intersection of old White Sulphur Road and what formerly was the *Southern Railway* in Hall County was photographed above in 1987. The nearby White Sulphur Springs was a resort of some note in 1911, and warranted its own train depot to service the steady stream of travelers to the site. At the time of Miner's robbery of *Southern's Train #36, White Sulphur Depot* existed at this spot, and it was to here that flagman C.H. Shirley ran to report the robbery of the train that morning. (Photo by R. Olin Jackson)

County. By the time the dogs arrived, the rain and pepper and snuff reportedly scattered by Miner and his two accomplices had effectively obscured the trail.

To Sheriff Crow's posse were added detectives from the *Pinkertons Agency*, a deputy U.S. marshal, and detectives of the *Southern Railway and Express*. All local law enforcement officials also went into the field, using the promise of a $1,500 reward (almost more than the bandits actually took) offered by the State of Georgia and *Southern Railways*, to enlist men and boys

Only a few days after the robbery, the search efforts were losing steam.

for their posse. Despite all these efforts, the ultimate capture of the train robbers was accomplished, as the editor of the 1911 *Dahlonega Nugget* explained, "*by mountaineers skilled in tracking.*"

Only a few days after the robbery, the search efforts were losing steam. Officials conducting the man-hunt were sitting around the main room of the old Dixie Hunt Hotel – their headquarters in Gainesville – so despondent, that they hardly noticed when the telephone began ringing. When one of the lawmen finally picked up the receiver,

Stocking Up On Supplies – This primitive print shows the Merritt M. London homeplace which once stood near the intersection of Long Branch Road and Highway 60 in Lumpkin County. While fleeing lawmen in February of 1911, notorious outlaw Bill Miner reportedly stopped at the country store adjacent to this home to take on provisions. Pictured in this photo are: Merritt M. London (with white beard and hat, center). His wife, Mary Neisler London stands beside the tree in the front yard. Sons Frank (in the wagon) and Bob (2nd from left) also appear. The identity of the individual in the overalls is unknown. (Photo courtesy of Annie Lou Dobbs of Toccoa, GA, daughter of Frank and Annie Kemp London)

the caller turned out to be ex-Lumpkin County Sheriff Jim Davis from Dahlonega announcing that he believed he had found the train robbers in an abandoned house nearby. How the bandits had made it through the rough north Georgia mountains toward Dahlonega in such a short time is unknown today, but they had to have been making really good travel time through some really rough country where roads were almost non-existent.

Sheriff Sergeant assembled a posse which included the aforementioned Jim Davis and Davis' two sons – Rufus and Joe.

Davis had learned of the men earlier, and both he and Lumpkin County Sheriff John Sergeant began having doubts about them. They claimed to be prospectors and had overnighted at Sergeant's Hotel in Dahlonega. However, between them, the three strangers had no prospecting tools other than one broken and split shovel.

When Lumpkin County resident Pete Carmichael reported the three men near his farm, Sergeant became even more suspicious. He set out for the Carmichael place where he picked up two sets of tracks. The bandits apparently had split up at this point, and Sergeant decided to follow the single set of tracks.

Sheriff Sergeant assembled a posse which included the aforementioned Jim Davis and Davis' two sons – Rufus and Joe. The trail at length led the group to the Elbert Kendall farm some 17 miles northwest of Dahlonega in the present-day Nimberwill community. The Kendalls reported that they did have a male boarder who was sleeping on a cot upstairs in a loft.

Davis and his sons reportedly mounted the stairs where they found a person who appeared to be asleep. As Davis pulled the blanket away, the stranger aimed the no-nonsense end of a .45-caliber revolver at him. Davis' salvation was found in his two sons who had a shotgun and a .22 rifle directed at the old man who in fact turned out to be George Anderson, alias Bill Miner.

Rufus Davis was still alive in 1987, and living in Cartersville,

Latter-day London Home – The by-then historic Merritt M. London home-place at the intersection of Long Branch Road and Highway 60, was photographed in 1993, a few years prior to its unfortunate demolition. (Photo by Anne Dismukes Amerson)

Georgia, when he was interviewed about the incident. Though in his nineties at the time, Rufus still remembered details of the exciting day. He also still possessed the actual set of handcuffs used to restrain Miner after his capture.

Jim Davis eventually collected the reward offered for the capture of the train robbers *(Miner's accomplices in the robbery had been arrested earlier in the day prior to Miner's arrest.)* Sheriff Sergeant unsuccessfully sued Davis for part of the reward, claiming the last capture was really his work.

Despite all the clamor of the event, the detectives, sheriffs, and other officials in the manhunt still had no idea who they had actually captured even after Miner was clapped in chains. The old bandit identified himself by his real name – George Anderson – and all the official Georgia police and criminal

records relating to him identified him by that name. It was probably the first time in many years that he had used his actual name for identification purposes. Interestingly, when the name by which he was commonly known – "Bill Miner" – was learned by the authorities, it was assumed that that was his actual name, and that the moniker "George Anderson" was an alias.

While waiting in the Lumpkin County jail, Anderson (alias Bill Miner) talked of the great potential of Dahlonega's inactive gold mines in such a way that the ***Dahlonega Nugget*** published his remarks as if he were a prominent geologist, stroking local civic pride. It is ironic to note that Miner began his life of crime at the site of the second great gold rush in California and ended it at the site of the first U.S. gold rush in Dahlonega, Georgia. And even as he was captured,

Manhunt For Miner – Officials managing the manhunt for the outlaw Bill Miner used the main room of the old Dixie Hunt Hotel (above, photographed circa 1900) as a headquarters. This structure, a portion of which still exists today on the square in Gainesville, was built in 1882 on the corner of Main and Spring streets. (Photo courtesy of Hall County Library)

he was preaching the merits of the gold mining industry.

After his capture in Dahlonega, Miner was transported to Gainesville for trial. His arrival in that town by automobile was greeted by crowds of hundreds of people, gathered as if to see a street parade, and caused Miner to remark *"They must think I am a bear."*

A special session of the Hall County Superior Court was held on March 3, 1911, to try the train robbers. Charlie Hunter confessed his role in the robbery, and became the state's chief witness against Miner. Hunter received a sentence of fifteen years, but escaped within a year, and surprisingly, no effort was ever made to recapture him. James Handford also pleaded guilty, received the same sentence, and was granted a parole a mere seven years later in 1918.

Miner, however, differed from his henchmen in that he demanded, for unknown reasons, a jury trial. Despite the fact that witness after witness testified against him, Miner sat impassively. Some observers believed that the old bandit believed his almost flawlessly polite manners might carry the day in the trial and somehow set him free, but it was not to be, as the Hall County jury steadfastly returned with a verdict of *"Guilty."*

Miner's only show of emotion in the verdict came when Howard Thompson, special attorney for the express company, spoke of the dynamite used in the express car potentially *"blowing into eternity sleeping women and children on the train."* A reporter witnessed Miner answer that charge *"with a most vengeful, glaring, and hateful glance."*

When Judge Sims sentenced Miner to twenty years in prison, the old gentleman bandit reportedly thanked him, stood up and turned to a group of college girls and ladies and proceeded to provide a moral for the story they had witnessed unfolding before them: *"When one breaks the law, one must expect to pay*

Early Lumpkin Jail – Photographed in front of the old Lumpkin County Jail (which still stands in Dahlonega as of this writing), are: (left to right) Sheriff James M. "Jim" Davis, Gordon Davis, Joe Davis, William S. "Bill" Davis, Charles C. Davis, and Rufus Tilman "R.T." Davis. Bill Miner was captured by Sheriff John Sergeant, Jim Davis, and Davis' two sons - Rufus and Joe. Following his capture, Miner was incarcerated in this jail. (Photo courtesy of C.C. Davis, Jr.)

the penalty. I am old, but during all my life, I have found the golden rule the best guide to man in this world," he said. He then smiled and sat down.

Though one of the most cold-blooded and notorious thugs in the colorful history of train robberies in the U.S., Miner is routinely described as *"looking less like a criminal than almost any man one might imagine."* Yet, this kindly-looking old Kentuckian reportedly methodically gunned down virtually all of a group of posse-men pursuing him from the scene of a stagecoach robbery in 1881 in California. He was also identified as associated with numerous other capital crimes throughout his life.

Books and even modern feature-length movies have been made about Bill Miner, some of them actually portraying him as somehow justified for some or all of his crimes. Though this final event in Georgia ended forever Miner's stagecoach/train robbing days, it did not bring to a close his ability to continue to cause mayhem and galvanize public attention.

Above and beyond his notoriety as a train robber, Miner was also literally a legend as an escape artist. Prior to his crimes in Georgia, he had escaped from numerous prisons in Canada and elsewhere and often boasted that no prison could hold him indefinitely. He had been so successful that he had been dubbed *"The Grey Fox"* by the news media.

Old Lumpkin Jail Today – The lock-up in which bandit Bill Miner was initially incarcerated prior to his relocation to Gainesville for trial was photographed as it appears today. (Photo by R. Olin Jackson)

William Pinkerton, head of the well-known detective agency of the same name, was a spectator at the Gainesville trial, and warned the press that he doubted that any Georgia prison could hold the old man. His comments proved prophetic. Miner escaped not once, but twice from prison in Milledgeville, Georgia, after his incarceration there. Had it not been for his aging condition and lack of resistance to exposure and the elements after his escapes, he might not have been recaptured. If anything, the man was just short of amazing.

Following the trial in Gainesville, the convicted trio were sent to Georgia's huge prison camp in Newton County. Life in the camp did not suit Miner, however. A personal appeal to Robert E. Davison, then chairman of the State Prison Board, finally earned him a transfer to the state prison farm for the infirm in Milledgeville.

While at the farm, Miner recruited the services of convicted murderers John B. Watts and Tom H. Moore for an escape. Late one night, Watts somehow managed to remove the peep-hole apparatus out of the door of his cell, and squeeze through the opening. He took the keys and a pistol from a sleeping guard, and released Miner and Moore. The trio made a clean getaway.

Following his escape, Miner was even brazen enough to mail a letter to Robert Davison, thanking him for giving him his opportunity for escape. *"My dear sir,"* he wrote, *"I want to thank you for your kindness in putting me at Milledgeville. My dear sir, don't trust a prisoner, don't matter how sick he is or makes out he is. Yours truly, B. Miner"*

The chairman's embarrassment was also the embarrassment of the state of Georgia and the newspapers and citizens as well who had urged that the *"sick*

Escape-Proof – The grave of notorious outlaw Bill Miner was photographed in the convicts burial section of Memory Hill Cemetery in Milledgeville, Georgia. It was one prison from which he finally could not escape.

old man be allowed to die in peace" at the lightly-guarded prison farm. The **Atlanta Journal** proclaimed that *"wherever Bill Miner is, he is probably grinning and the joke is on Georgia."*

It wasn't long however, before Miner was recaptured. He and Moore had headed for Augusta, Georgia. At a tiny community nearby called Keysville, a J.W. Whittle overheard a brakeman talking to two "bums" in a boxcar. When it was realized that the two matched a description of two escaped convicts, Whittle summoned help.

The boxcar was shortly thereafter surrounded by a posse, and Miner recaptured yet again. Moore, however, chose not to return – at least not alive. He reportedly fired a single shot in the vicinity of the posse, and then in turn was killed by a single shot to the face. Inside the boxcar, members of the posse found dynamite and fuses which Miner explained *"were good for catching fish."* Old Bill had been a breath away from yet another train robbery.

Returned to his prison cell in Milledgeville, Miner boasted that he would escape again at the first opportunity. His guards, understandably, took no chances against any future embarrassment. One can only imagine their total humiliation, when on the morning of June 27, 1912, they found the *Grey Fox* gone yet again, his ankle and arm bracelets locked to his bunk, the window bars sawed out, and the bedding made into a rope which he had used to climb to the ground. It was literally the stuff of legends.

Accompanied by convicts W.J. Windencamp and W.M. Wiggins, Miner was once again making good his escape. The trio took a boat into the Oconee River this time, with the plan of reaching a port where they could ship out as deck hands. However, the boat reportedly capsized, drowning Windencamp. It is not known today for certain if that was the actual circumstance.

For three days afterwards, Miner and Wiggins were lost in an almost endless boggy swamp near Oconee, Georgia, living on blackberries and unable to find safe drinking water. When they finally came out near Toombsboro, they offered no resistance to a posse which found them at a home begging for breakfast. Miner's escape this time had lasted only five days, and his age and failing constitution were fast catching up with him.

The reception the old outlaw received upon his return to Milledgeville this time even exceeded Bill's wildest imaginings. Driven in an open, heavily-guarded automobile and shackled securely, Bill was met in the downtown area by an extremely large crowd of admiring townspeople who reportedly literally applauded him and passed him money and cigars.

Always gracious, Miner stood up in the car and waved his hat to his fans. The **Union Recorder** claimed that *"for a short time, it looked like a hero had come to the city instead of a man who had wrecked and robbed trains."* This, however, was the last adventure for the grizzled old *Grey Fox* who had robbed trains from coast to coast.

Today, the exact circumstances of Miner's last days are unknown, but it is believed the hunger, exposure to the weather, and contaminated water he consumed during his escape, apparently took their toll upon him, causing him to lapse into illness.

The **Atlanta Journal**, learning that Miner was near death in September of 1913, interviewed him one last time. Before they could get the story printed, however, the *Angel of Death* had visited the cell of the *Grey Fox*, and spirited him away, granting him permanent freedom at last.

Though accounts of his actual burial site vary today, the final resting place of Bill Miner is in the old city cemetery known as *Memory Hill* in Milledgeville. Miner's grave is marked with a simple headstone, and is found on the southeast side of *Memory Hill* where the cemetery slopes toward Fishing Creek, a place where many convicts were buried when the penitentiary was located at Milledgeville. His headstone bears his pseudonym *Bill Miner*, since no one at the time was certain of his true name.

Treasure-hunters still ply the railroads and other sites suspected of holding the loot Miner supposedly left behind somewhere in Hall or Lumpkin counties in north Georgia. Interestingly, *most* of the stolen money and valuables were recovered. Miner personally provided Sheriff Crow (of Hall County) with directions to two caches of loot. Several other caches reportedly turned up later, satisfying most recovery efforts. Nevertheless, at least a portion of the cash and valuables was never recovered.

Today, the site of the famed train robbery bears mute testimony to the events of February 18, 1911. The crossing at White Sulphur is officially-known as *"Bill Miner Crossing."*

The reception the old outlaw received upon his return to Milledgeville this time even exceeded Bill's wildest imaginings.

The Day the Railroad Caused Belton to Disappear

As an early stop on the Richmond & Danville Railroad, Belton grew steadily until town leaders in nearby Lula found a way to best their up-start sister city.

Water is essential to the fabric of life for humans, animals and plants. The over-abundance of rain or snow, or a lack thereof, has sometimes changed the course of history.

Muddy battlefields or the scarcity of water for soldiers in combat can, and has, resulted in wars being won and lost.

The same analogy can be applied to civic contests. Towns can also die due to a lack of water. Belton, Georgia is a good example.

Early History

This small unassuming town once existed approximately halfway between Gainesville, Georgia, in Hall County, and Cornelia, Georgia, in adjacent Habersham County. Today, one would be hard-pressed to realize a town once existed at this site at all.

While driving through this community today, one must search closely for any road or business signage containing this town's name. As of this writing, there are approximately three: one on the "Belton" Baptist Church (churches quite often are the last structures to disappear in a dying community); another

on "Belton" Bridge; and one in the identification of "Belton" Park.

At one time, Belton and Lula were known as "twin towns." They were each located about 14 miles from Gainesville; they both faced the railroad tracks that divided Hall and Banks counties; and they were both located about three miles south of the Habersham County line.

The story of Belton and Lula is an interesting page in our state's railroading history. It is a tale which covers topics ranging from a bitter rivalry between two wealthy men, cotton production, the railroad, and most importantly - the scarcity of water in Belton.

According to *Cyclopedia Of Georgia*, published in 1906, both towns had post offices, express and telegraph offices, mercantile and shipping industries, schools and churches – all despite the fact they were separated from each other by little more than one mile. Belton was the oldest of the two. It was also the largest in the early days.

"Belton," Georgia

First named *Bellvue* or *Bellview*, the name of Lula's counterpart was later changed to *Bellton*, and then following a change in the town's charter in the early 1900s, the name was shortened to simply "Belton."

According to one account, the town was named for a John Bell who came to Georgia from South Carolina. He was one of a number of individuals who traveled to Belton as a result of early land speculation and mining activities.

The arrival of the Richmond & Danville Airline Railroad which passed through both Lula and Belton in 1873 had spurred much of the development. The railroad provided a convenient means of marketing locally-produced goods – especially cotton which was abundantly grown in the area. One old-timer, when recalling the boom-times of the town, reminisced that *"sometimes I could walk from one end of the town to the other atop bales of cotton awaiting shipment."*

Another account describes a Mr. Madison Buice who came to the area from Atlanta. He reportedly named the town after a Major Madison Bell, a former comptroller general of Georgia and a son of Major John Bell.

Buice took temporary quarters in the community while having timber sawed for his own home. According to reports, he planted vineyards and orchards and then shipped wine and fruit throughout the country.

Buice also reportedly surveyed and laid out the town, selling lots, running a steam-powered saw mill and furnishing lumber for construction. An entrepreneurial individual, he built and sold houses, promoted the community to other settlers, and indirectly influenced the construction of churches and an academy.

By 1880, the population of Belton had grown to approximately 500, and a variety of businesses were in operation. A newspaper – *The North Georgia* – was published weekly in the community, and chronicled the towns burgeoning growth.

The Northeastern Railroad

Meanwhile, things were heating up in the nearby township of Lula, where visions of greater things were on the minds of the town fathers there. It seems the railroad had expansion plans in mind in the 1870s, and both Lula and Belton were contending for a planned line (to be called the *Northeastern Railroad*) through the area which would connect Athens, Georgia with the Richmond & Danville Airline Railroad.

Joseph H. Banks and his brother, Dunstan E. Banks, sons of Dr. Richard Banks for whom Banks County was named, came from Gainesville and played a prominent role in the development of the town of Lula. In the process, they had accumulated substantial properties in the area, and it therefore became vitally important to them that the rumored new railroad line should be built through their community – and not through adjacent Belton.

As the situation evolved, both Joe Banks and Matt Buice therefore, for the same reasons, desperately wanted to attract the planned rail line, because their property values would be

According to one account, the town was named for a John Bell who came to Georgia from South Carolina.

dramatically increased (or devalued), according to the circumstances.

In a generous (but obviously personally motivated) gesture, the Banks brothers deeded a large tract of land for the railroad "provided the main and principal depot at the junction be located on land donated by [them] (the Banks brothers), and that the town of Lula will be laid out at the junction."

Prior to this inducement, Matt Buice had already provided his own gift of a depot in Belton, to attract the *Northeastern Railroad* builders. The Banks brothers, however, had offered a larger "brick" depot, winning the day for Lula.

In a twist of irony, the track was required to be forty miles in length in order to qualify for and obtain the required railroad franchise, but when surveyed to Lula, it measured only 39 miles. Rather than extend the necessary extra mile of track to Belton as well, the builders extended a branch line into an uninhabited rural area instead, and this extra portion was never used thereafter.

"Lula," Georgia

When the railroad was completed in 1876, there was an elaborate celebration which included dinner in the diner of a train which had journeyed over the line to celebrate its inaugural run. Among the young ladies in attendance that day was a Miss Lula (or Lulah) Phinizy, daughter of Ferdinand Phinizy, a wealthy Augusta, Georgia, resident and one-time owner of White Sulphur Springs,

a popular resort at that time between Gainesville and Lula. The junction and new depot were christened "Lula," in her honor.

The trains and train station were very important for the growth of Lula. It was reported that three freight train crews were stationed at Lula every night. They boarded there in a white frame hotel which was operated by Mrs. Gussie Coffee. *(Note: The hotel unfortunately, has since been demolished.)*

The town of Lula, with its big new water tank and coal chute for the steam locomotives, became an important rail junction, and quickly usurped the railroad business formerly accorded to Belton. The Richmond & Danville Airline Railroad trains had formerly stopped at the Belton Depot where the trains were laboriously refueled by water pumped from a small branch. Lula eventually attracted the lion's share of this business.

Merger By Necessity

With the demise of "King Cotton," however, both Belton and Lula suffered. Their large warehouses soon were emptied of the cash crop which had previously been such a staple commodity in the communities.

The *Great Depression* further depleted the community reserves, dealing an even worse blow to the townships. A bank in Lula, supported by Joseph Banks, was closed during the *Depression* years, and drug stores and other businesses failed as well.

With the business drought, the railroad trains had fewer and fewer

> *The Great Depression further depleted the community reserves, dealing an even worse blow to the townships.*

reasons to stop. By 1936, they stopped only in Lula.

Despite the harsh realities of life, competition between the two communities nevertheless seemed to continue. In 1911, the Belton and Lula schools were collectively consolidated. A new high school, built in 1938, was placed with one-half of the structure in the Belton city limits, and the other half in the Lula city limits.

Finally, on November 19, 1955, Lula and Belton – former bitter rivals – merged into one town. Citizens of both communities voted 150 to 3 on the consolidation. Belton, it seems, was in dire need of a number of public services, if its residents were to be able to persevere, so Lula, once again, held the upper hand.

In the process, Lula was allowed to keep its name, and Belton, in exchange for its lost identity, received the much-needed resource of Lula's water system, as well as other services. Thus, the need for water, quite literally, caused Belton to lose its name.

Today, with regular passenger service long-discontinued back in the 1960s, the only passenger-train option is Amtrak. Though Amtrak does indeed *pass through* Lula, it does not even pause, much less stop these days, as is also the case with the long freight trains which once regularly stopped in the town.

"Yesteryear" Towns

The aged old water tank from the steam locomotive days still exists up on the hill overlooking the streets and businesses of Lula – a vestigial connection to the community's historic past. Today, however, in an ironic twist of fate, all the water for Lula now comes from the Gainesville, Georgia water system.

Much of Lula's history is based understandably upon the railroad. As of this writing, the town continues to conduct a two-day observance of *"Railroad Festival Days,"* to honor the community's origin. Festivities include a parade down the town's main street, capped off by a carnival at a nearby park, but the permanency of this event is in no way guaranteed.

Years ago, a bridge was built over the railroad tracks in the middle of town, so that traffic on the street would not be interrupted nor delayed by the intermittent trains. Recently, since the train traffic has been so reduced, an effort was made to remove this bridge to better facilitate traffic flow. Interestingly, this effort was quickly squelched in typical Lula fashion.

"We saved it by proving that if there was a fire across the tracks and a train was passing through at the same time, the fire trucks would be delayed, possibly causing a calamity," explained one resident.

Today, as one of the state's early pioneer railroading communities, Belton has virtually disappeared. On the other hand, Lula continues to persevere - barely.

Years ago, a bridge was built over the railroad tracks in the middle of town, so that traffic on the street would not be interrupted nor delayed by the intermittent trains.

Historic Family Connections To Castleberry Bridge Road

As one of the first byways in Lumpkin County, Castleberry Bridge Road has witnessed the comings and goings of numerous historic figures over the years. Its builder's family is also connected to numerous historic aspects of both Lumpkin and Hall counties.

Castleberry Bridge Road which crosses the Etowah River and extends between Auraria, Georgia, and Highway 9 South in Lumpkin County, commemorates the name of one of the first settlers in the area. Elisha Castleberry and wife – Jane – undoubtedly arrived soon after gold was discovered in what then was part of the Cherokee Nation, since their daughter – Fannie – was born there in 1830.

The gold mining community which was developed at this site was without a name until the summer of 1832, when Nathaniel Nuckolls built a hotel that was soon overflowing with rooming occupants. People began calling the town "Nuckollsville" after the enterprising innkeeper until it was officially christened "Auraria" the following November. Senator (and former Vice President of the United States) John C. Calhoun, a well-known politician from South Carolina who owned gold mining property in the Auraria area had insisted upon the new name since he considered "Nuckollsville" to be too vulgar a name. Auraria is derived from Latin and means "gold" or "golden area."

Progenitor Elisha Castleberry

When the state of Georgia held a land lottery in 1832-33 to distribute the four million acres of land ultimately taken from the native Cherokees, Elisha Castleberry drew Land Lot 673 of District 12, which was located just west of Auraria. An old land lottery map shows the Etowah River running through the center of his new property. By 1850, Castleberry had acquired fifteen 40-acre gold lots in and around Auraria and many city lots as well.

Aside from being present for the north Georgia gold rush, family stories maintain that Elisha was also one of the "Forty-Niners" who traveled to California when gold was discovered there twenty years later, but he apparently didn't remain very long, since he died in Lumpkin County in April of 1850. He was buried at Antioch Baptist Church in Auraria, an appropriate final resting spot, since he had donated the land for both the church and cemetery.

In his will, Elisha left slaves, stock, blacksmith tools, furniture, and land lots to his wife Jane. When she died in 1873, she was buried beside him.

Pioneer Landmark – The original Castleberry Bridge, an aged heavy iron structure (pictured) spanning the Etowah River just west of Auraria, Georgia, disappeared years ago, and has been replaced several times, most recently by a more modern concrete version. Since the property on each side of the road at this site was originally owned by Elisha Castleberry, the original bridge (and all subsequent bridges at this site) commemorated his name and the numerous historic individuals associated with this family. (Photo courtesy of the GA Dept. of Archives & History, Atlanta)

Elisha and Jane Castleberry had five sons (Edmund, Richard J., Jackson, Samuel Guerry, and Frank) and five daughters (Phoebe, Eliza, Samantha, Fannie, and Sarah). Both Edmund and Jackson listed their occupation as *"miner"* in the *1850 Federal Census of Lumpkin County*. Edmund is buried at Antioch near his parents under a tombstone inscribed *"Rev. E.G. Castleberry."*

Eliza was never married and was still living with her mother in 1870, according to the *1870 Federal Census*.

Eliza's Famous Ears

Eliza's eyesight reportedly failed in her later years, but her hearing apparently was extremely acute. At some point in her life her neighbors realized Eliza possessed this unusual capability, and began

taking advantage of it to keep track of their cattle.

Prior to the days of the stock laws, livestock were allowed to freely roam the mountains and river valleys, except when the cows were brought home in the evening to be milked. Since their owners never knew from one moment to the next where their cattle actually were, it almost always required hours to locate the wayward beasts.

After Eliza had reached an elderly age, her neighbors in Auraria who owned the free-ranging cattle began bringing their cowbells to "Granny" Castleberry to allow her to listen to the tone of each cow's bell prior to the time it was hung around the animal's neck. When an individual's cow then needed to be located, Eliza – who by that point knew the tone of each owner's cowbell – reportedly could almost always send that owner in the correct direction of his or her cow based upon the sound (which only she could hear) of that cow's respective bell.

Years after she died, Auraria residents continued to mourn Eliza's departure – not only because she was such a likeable person, but also because of the many hours she saved them when they needed to locate their cows.

Samantha Castleberry married Thomas Christian who owned an interest in the Whim Hill Mine and other mining property in the area. Their son – Benjamin Franklin Christian – had a teaming business which hauled freight between Gainesville and Auraria by mule train. He later opened a general merchandise store and mail-order business in Auraria.

Howser Family Connection

Sarah Castleberry married Henry Howser in 1864 following the death of her first husband, L.R. Williams.

Photographed circa 1900 in Auraria, Georgia, near Castleberry Bridge Road, a black family by the name of Castleberry paused on the community's dusty main road (old "Gold Diggers' Road"). The two elderly individuals in this photo quite possibly were former slaves once owned by Elisha Castleberry. (Photo courtesy of GA Dept. of Archives & History, Atlanta)

Howser was a builder as well as a miner. He laid the foundation for the Dawson County Courthouse in 1858.

Howser also built the first schoolhouse as well as a 40-room hotel in Dawsonville. Constructed circa 1887 just south of the courthouse, the elaborate Howser Hotel unfortunately burned to the ground in 1904.

In the late 1860s, Henry Howser, his brother Thomas, and Sarah's nephew – Josephus Castleberry – built another prominent landmark in the county – Howser Mill – on Shoal Creek. At last check (2024), this historic landmark was still standing a short distance from downtown Dawsonville on Howser Mill Road.

Richard J. Castleberry, the second son of Elisha and Jane, married Martha Thompson in 1843. The ***1860 Federal Census of Lumpkin County*** shows them

living there with five children (sons Josephus, 15; Zachery Taylor, 14; Marcus, 12; Richard C., 10; and a daughter, America, nicknamed "Merrica," 6).

When Martha died in 1868 at the age of 43, she was buried at Antioch Church near the graves of her husband's parents. A year later, Richard married Cynthia Thompson, whose grandfather, Andrew Thompson, was one of the first White settlers in adjacent Hall County.

Origin of "Thompson" Bridge

Andrew Thompson built a home in Hall beside the Chattahoochee River (just across the river from Dawson County) as early as 1819 and established a trading post there for Indians and the few other White settlers in the area. His three sons – Guilford Green, Ovid, and Andrew Jackson Thompson – built and

Aged Gristmill - Historic Howser Mill on Shoal Creek in Dawson County was constructed in the late 1860s by Henry Howser, his brother Thomas, and Josephus Castleberry. The Howsers and Castleberrys were interrelated by marriage. At last check (2024), this historic landmark was still standing a short distance from downtown Dawsonville on Howser Mill Road.

operated a toll bridge across the river and established a mill nearby.

Over the years, covered wooden bridges, a pontoon bridge, an iron bridge, and a modern concrete-and-steel bridge have replaced that original toll bridge, and each one was subsequently named "Thompson Bridge."

Even though Richard Castleberry was 48 and Cynthia Thompson was only 21 at the time of their marriage, he outlived her by nine years. They did not have any children and both are buried in Alta Vista Cemetery in Gainesville, Georgia.

Richard's son by his first wife – Josephus (born in 1845) – is believed to be the J.F. Castleberry who operated two of Dahlonega's large hotels in the early 1900s. An item in the June 22, 1900, issue of

Richard J. Castleberry, the second son of Elisha and Jane, married Martha Thompson in 1843.

The Dahlonega Nugget announced that J.F. Castleberry had *"recently opened out the old Burnside House now known as the Dahlonega Hotel. Mr. Castleberry used to run the Hall House and his manner of feeding and treating people are too well-known to receive any comment from us."*

Richard's second son – Zachery Taylor Castleberry – married Nancy E. "Nannie" Palmour in Hall County. Zach undoubtedly was named for the national hero of that day who became the 12th U.S. president.

First National Bank Founder

Z.T. Castleberry was one of the founders of the First National Bank of Gainesville and served as the bank's president from 1891 to 1917. He, along with

Col. S.C. Dunlap, was also one of the organizers of the *Gainesville and Chattahoochee Power and Manufacturing Company*, a business which generated electricity for the city of Gainesville and operated an electric railroad in town.

Marcus Ferdinand Castleberry married Margaret Frances Graham in 1866. They had nine children.

Richard C. Castleberry married Mary Catherine "Kate" Prater, the daughter of Joseph and Martha Ann Hope Prater. They lived in Gainesville, where Richard C. ran a general merchandise store in a building belonging to his father-in-law.

In 1889, Richard was vying for appointment as postmaster in Gainesville. The man doling out such patronage positions was former Confederate General James Longstreet, a leading Republican who had made Gainesville his home after the U.S. Civil War.

Richard and three other individuals coveting the postmaster position were all nevertheless disappointed when Longstreet selected another individual. Richard and the other three applicants protested Longstreet's selection, but their objections were to no avail. Though there reportedly was no evidence of arson, Longstreet's expansive home in Gainesville suspiciously fell victim to a raging fire several days later.

The Texas Castleberrys

A few years later in 1894, Richard C. apparently had soured on life in north Georgia. He and wife Kate, her mother Martha Ann Hope Prater, and their first six surviving children, departed Gainesville to move by covered wagon to greener grass in Texas. Richard may have been enticed by the promise of good, cheap farmland being opened up in the state by the railroads. He farmed until his

Thomas Howser (1835-1916) - Along with his brother Henry and Josephus Castleberry, Thomas built - among many other edifices - Howser Mill in Dawson County. Notice his immense gnarled hands and fingers, signs of a person accustomed to extremely hard manual labor. The Howsers were noted as builders and entrepreneurs in both Dawson and Lumpkin counties. (Photo courtesy of GA Dept. of Archives & History, Atlanta)

retirement in 1923, and died six years later in Meadow, Texas, in 1929.

Interestingly, Richard C. Castleberry's Texas-bred grandson – Paul John – later remembered hearing stories as a child about his great-grandfather (described to him as a "mountain man" who lived near a river with a strange-sounding Indian name). He subsequently visited relatives in Georgia when he was 12 years old and was shown the home of Richard J. Castleberry whose father was the namesake of a pioneer byway in Lumpkin County whose historic roots are almost forgotten today.

Juliette's *"Whistlestop Café"* and *"Fried Green Tomatoes"*

It wasn't too long ago that tiny Juliette, Georgia, was a virtual ghost town – abandoned and forgotten in the 1950s when the grist mill closed down and the railroad ceased passenger service. However, following the release of a hugely-successful motion picture filmed at the site, the little community has sprung to life once again.

In the major motion picture **Fried Green Tomatoes**, filmed in the *Whistlestop Café* at tiny *Juliette*, Georgia, one of the lead characters comments that *"The secret's in the sauce,"* as she served a sheriff searching for the killer of a south Georgia farmer. Today, interested patrons can be served some delicious treats in the same café, and many travelers are partaking of the opportunity.

Aside from the obvious famous entrée of fried green tomatoes, patrons of the *Whistlestop* may also enjoy delicious coleslaw, gumbo, candied yams, collard greens, and cornbread. An assortment of desserts are also available, including a mouth-watering peach cobbler. The atmosphere you get for free.

The cafe uses up to 20 cases of tomatoes each week. Slices come with every order, and a five-slice side order costs $2.25.

Much of the credit for the revitalization of this once-forgotten mill-town is due to Fannie Flagg, author/producer of the movie which captured the attention of young and old alike. Miss

"The Secret's In The Sauce" – The famed *"Whistle Stop Cafe"* at Juliette, Georgia, filmsite for the major motion picture **"Fried Green Tomatoes."**

Flagg reportedly rode up and down the railroad tracks at many sites in Georgia looking for a little town to use as the setting for her fictitious community in the movie - *Whistle Stop, Alabama*. The tiny mill-town of *Juliette* finally caught her eye. It will never be the same.

In the summer of 1991, the cast and crew for the movie came to town. When the filming was completed and

A signature scene from the major motion picture *"Fried Green Tomatoes"* filmed in Juliette, Georgia, alongside the former *Southern Railways* (present-day *Norfolk-Southern Railways*) tracks.

the movie stars departed, so also did the glamour and activity with which the quiet little community had been infused.

The movie company tore down the sets used in the production. *Juliette* would have returned to its sleepy forgotten status had it not been for a few entrepreneurial spirits who realized they had a real opportunity staring them right in the face.

"The director of the movie said we ought to consider opening the place as the '*Whistle Stop Café,*'" Jerie Lynn Williams, a resident of *Juliette* explained. She and Robert Williams (no relation) quickly began thinking about opening a real restaurant in

The cafe uses up to 20 cases of tomatoes each week. Slices come with every order, and a five-slice side order costs $2.25.

the *Whistle Stop*. People thought Robert was crazy. "Who are you going to feed?" some asked.

Jerie and Robert started buying and renovating the old stores along the little main street. Jerie says she bought old fixtures at auctions that give the interior of the cafe its authentic look. She also maintains that she didn't know how to cook, but did have her grandmother's recipe for fried green tomatoes (which Jerie keeps secret, right along with her barbecue recipe...). She persuaded a cook from *Mable's Table*, the town's only restaurant (which recently had closed) to cook for her.

Living & Dying By The Railroad – *Norfolk-Southern Railroad* carried only freight on this main line in 2025, but in an earlier day and time, when it was a portion of the immense *Southern Railways* transportation system, it provided not only freight, but passenger and mail delivery services as well, which were big business on this and most other railroads in the United States until the late 1950s. Juliette received a double-blow when both passenger service on the rails and the community's gristmill ceased operations.

Jerie and Robert opened the cafe April 16, 1992, hoping immediately to ride the coattails of the movie's popularity. It, however, wasn't as smooth an entry into the hospitality industry as that for which they had hoped.

"I think I cried the first ten days," Jerie continued, remembering the early days when few if any visitors traveled to the site. Eventually, however, newspaper and magazine publicity began attracting attention, and a steady stream of customers began appearing at their doorstep.

Once inside, guests

The movie company tore down the sets used in the production.

are transported back to a bygone era. The restaurant looks much as it did in the movie, with overhead fans, clapboard walls, booths, and tables covered with green-checked oilcloths.

A small bullet hole still pierces one window, as was scripted in the movie, and movie memorabilia decorates the walls.

"When a *Southern Railways* (actually *Norfolk-Southern Railways* these days) freight train rumbles past, guests rush outside. It's amazing," Jerie laughs. "It's as if people had never seen a train before.

Early Life – The *Southern Railways Depot* at Juliette, Georgia, was photographed circa 1921 on the Depot Agent's side. The tiny town grew up on the opposite side of the river from one of the largest gristmills in the region, and thrived as long as the mill remained in operation. When gristmills became obsolete in the early 1930s, the enterprise in Juliette died a slow death with most residents eventually relocating to new jobs elsewhere. Though it is not known for certain, when one compares this photo with the previous one, it appears quite likely that the structure which was converted into the popular eatery known as the *Whistle Stop Café* was originally the *Southern Railways* depot in Juliette. (Photo courtesy of the GA Dept. of Archives & History, Atlanta)

One woman thought we had staged the whole thing!"

The first thing to do when you arrive is to put your name on the clipboard waiting list at the cafe's front door. Don't be surprised if you have a one- to two-hour wait on weekends.

To date, visitors to the site have traveled from 44 different countries - some from as far

A small bullet hole still pierces one window, as was scripted in the movie, and movie memorabilia decorates the walls.

away as Egypt and Iceland. Residents from every state in the U.S. have also visited.

As a result of the popularity of the site, *Juliette* has literally returned from the dead. At one time, it boasted the largest water-powered gristmill in the world, but by the 1950s, gristmills had become a thing of the past, bringing operations at Dr.

All-Star Cast – Some of the female cast members from **"Fried Green Tomatoes"** – Mary-Louise Parker, Kathy Bates, Jessica Tandy and Mary Stuart-Masterson – paused for a photograph.

Glover's enterprise to a close. When the mill closed, the town's residents abandoned their homes and stores in an almost wholesale flurry to find employment elsewhere.

For years, a handful of residents attempted to bring the community back to life, all to no avail. Even the construction of nearby Lake Juliette proved fruitless.

Ironically, the very quality which was working against it – its rural, scenic locale – was what ultimately appealed to the **Hollywood** movie-makers. The rest, as they say, is history.

Today, the big dam across the river in *Juliette* still offers the scenic quality that made it a highlight in a number of the movie's scenes. So also do a number of other manifestations of rural flavor which enlivened the production.

All of this, coupled

with the *Whistle Stop Cafe*, have combined to make *Juliette* a popular tourism destination. And in answer to the growing visitation to the site, other entrepreneurs have opened gift shops selling everything from antiques and crafts to collectibles and candy up and down the tiny streets of the community, so be prepared for a measure of commercialism. One shop bears the name *"The Ruth and Idgie House."*

As long as one isn't forced to endure a barrage of "less-than-intelligent **Hollywood** political claptrap," a little **Hollywood** magic will oftentimes work wonders for a town that was given up for dead in 1990.

(For more information about the Whistle Stop Cafe, contact the Monroe County Chamber of Commerce. To reach Juliette, take Exit 61 off of Interstate 75, one hour south of Atlanta.)

> *Ironically, the very quality which was working against it – its rural, scenic locale – was what ultimately appealed to the Hollywood movie-makers.*

Trails Of The Pioneers:

Retracing the Old Alabama Roads

(Part I) (Upper Route)

In prehistoric America – when the southeast was still covered by virtually impenetrable forests and undergrowth – there were no highways upon which to travel. The best opportunity existed in the game trails which had been tramped down over millennia by migrating buffalo, elk, deer, and other hooved animals who instinctively followed the routes of least resistance around hills and mountains and across bodies of water. These crude early trails inevitably were adopted by the aboriginal natives of the southeast, and later – eventually – by pioneers to our great nation traveling westward who called the byways "the Alabama Roads."

After being organized as a territory in 1817, Alabama was the first general destination west of Georgia for pioneer travelers in what came to be described as *"manifest destiny."* Many who made this trek endured the arduous trip down the eastern seaboard and then across less mountainous South Carolina to arrive at Georgia, where the Allegheny/Appalachian/Blue Ridge mountains ranges ended, allowing the pioneers to circumvent this immense obstacle. The next destination was the unsettled Alabama Territory, and the routes they used to travel across Georgia to reach the West therefore became known as *"the Alabama Roads."*

Early travelers making this trip initially referred to the destination objective as the road *"to the Alabama,"* since they were enroute to *"the Alabama Territory."* When the Alabama Territory became a state in 1819, the term was shortened to *"the road to Alabama,"* or simply *"the Alabama Road,"* a term quite often still seen today on road signs identifying many modern (albeit actually very historic) routes to the West, only by this time, these routes inevitably are now identified as the *"Old Alabama Road."*

Prior to the arrival of European settlers, the Native Americans had gradually adopted (and re-shaped) over hundreds of years the early game paths of migrating hooved animals for use as "trading paths" and "war paths" etc. In order to reach their desired destinations, the natives slightly altered the paths from time

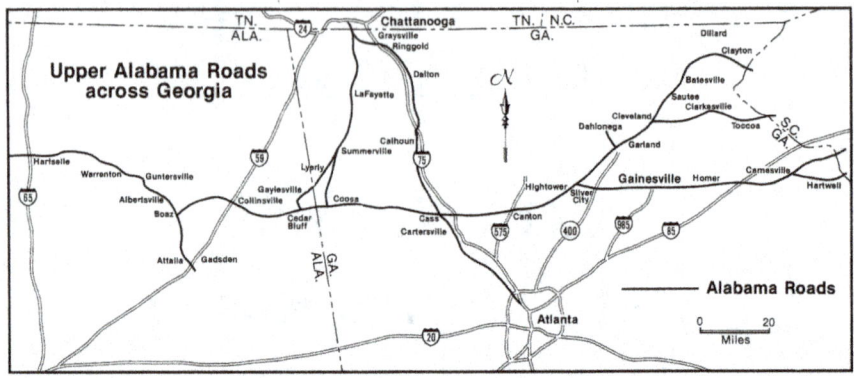

Forgotten Trails – The *Upper Alabama Road* and its "feeder roads" from Clayton, Toccoa and Hartwell are pictured, contrasted with modern highways.

to time, making use of available stream, creek and river crossings at spots such as shoals, falls, islands and shallows where fording was easier and safer, so the paths understandably were seldom the most direct routes.

With European expansion into America and the adoption of the aboriginal trails as travel routes by Whites, an innovation known as the ferryboat soon came into use for the fording of the bodies of water which were encountered westward. This innovation substantially straightened the routes when the deep sections of streams and rivers, etc., could then be easily and safely forded – as opposed to traveling "out of one's way" in order to make use of one of the aforementioned shoals, falls, or island crossing spots established by the Indians.

This straightened line of travel reduced travel time from point A to point B, but it was tempered by the fact that though the ferryboats could cross much deeper water, they also required "calm" water for safety and success. As a result of all of the above, the *"Alabama Roads"* to the west today, more often than not, are relatively straight thoroughfares which were heavily used by the pioneers.

Today, in many instances, the true original purpose of these *"Old Alabama Roads"* is completely unknown by the general public. In the stretches where these roads are still used – and oft-times even still identified as *"Old Alabama Road"* – they are nevertheless just accepted by today's travelers as yet another "modern road." The modern user is hardly aware that he or she is actually traveling upon road built upon an ancient trail from pre-history. In actuality, very few of these old routes are identified by road signage today, and historic markers have been used only sparingly to remind citizens of the once conspicuous role these routes played in the settlement of our nation.

As a result, modern-day adventurers are also oftentimes completely unaware of the sites of the former inns, former pioneer home-sites, taverns, and even the sparsely-known former sites of aboriginal Indian cabins, etc., which once existed along the route of the *Alabama Roads* in colonial Georgia. In the information which follows, a literal driving route which closely follows the former routes of these *"Alabama Roads"* will be provided for the reader, and along the

150

way, various and sundry historic sites and interesting anecdotes will be pointed out to the reader.

Interestingly, it is the exception, rather than the rule today for these early routes to coincide with our modern roads and highways – for obvious reasons. Major emphasis in this article will not be placed upon the chronological development or history of these old roads, but rather upon a re-tracing of the actual routes as they originally existed.

A particular effort has been made to name old key points along these highways, with the hope that the information may prove of value to those interested in this type of historic information, and/or who may wish to learn of the various former overnighting spots, former ferries, homes of prominent leaders, and other details which may have existed along these routes westward during the days of pioneer America. Though these routes are all collectively identified as *"the Alabama Road,"* there are also any number of various "feeder roads" to these byways of yesteryear at various points across Georgia which have been used over time, and this article will address many of these as well. These pioneer trail travel options across what today is Georgia, are collectively identified herewith as *"the Upper Alabama Road."*

The Alabama Road Via Rome and Coosa Valley

The most complicated former thoroughfares to trace westward across Georgia are the roads which utilized the natural gateway afforded by the **Coosa River Valley**. These old emigrant routes to the West are very interesting, because with the exception of stretches here and there, much of the original routes through the **Coosa River Valley** are still in use today. Significant portions of them are still known and described on road signage and mapping software as *"the Alabama Road."*

The complexities in retracing the *Alabama Roads* arise from the fact that they began at a multitude of widely dispersed origins in northeastern Georgia (and even as far back as the Carolinas), and ran westward until they merged together toward a common destination across Georgia, so there are many different variations of the "beginnings" of the avenue known as the *Alabama Road*. The initial routes included a series of cris-crossing trails – also called *Alabama Roads* – which traversed from one main pioneer thoroughfare over to another in pursuit of the most "accommodating" option for travel westward in that day and time.

The best-known of the Coosa River thoroughfares passed immediately above **Rome, Georgia**, into **Alabama** on the upper side of the Coosa River. This route had a two-pronged beginning in northeast Georgia, with the first fork – known as *"the Alabama Road"* – commencing at **Leather's Ford** on the Chestatee River in extreme south Lumpkin County. This **Leather's Ford** entry point attracted travelers via a trail from **Earl's Ford** at the mouth of Warwoman Creek on the Chattooga River in eastern **Rabun County**, Georgia. This was a natural point of convergence for the pioneers as they entered **northeast Georgia** from **South Carolina**. From there, this trail passed in the vicinity of the present-day communities of **Clayton, Batesville**, and the **Nacoochee Valley**, before moving down into **Lumpkin County** to **Leather's Ford**.

Another route used by emigrants to reach the *Coosa River Valley Alabama Road* in west Georgia ran from **Walton's Ford** east of **Toccoa** on the Chattooga River, down to **Clarkesville**.

"The Dividings" – Photographed circa 1890s, Main Street in Clayton in northeast Georgia's Rabun County, was also a feeder route for the *Upper Alabama Road*. In pioneer times, this community was known as *"The Dividings"* because it was the site at which several major Native American trails crossed or "divided." Due to this convergence - even in pioneer days - this site became an excellent site for the concentration of commerce. (Photo courtesy of the GA Dept. of Archives & History, Atlanta)

Although our description of this *Alabama Road* includes trails which began at the eastern boundary of Georgia, this *Alabama Road* option did not actually physically begin at that point. A series of introductory byways extended across the piedmont areas (down the eastern seaboard) of the Mid-Atlantic and southeastern states, all the way from **Pennsylvania**, **Maryland** and **Virginia**, to points southward. Emigrants on their way to the mid- or far-west used many of these piedmont routes which extended through what today are **Charlotte**, **Greenville** and **Spartanburg**, in order to reach the *Alabama Roads* in **Georgia**.

Interestingly, possibly the greatest users of the *Coosa River Valley Alabama Road* and its tributary connectors were not distant travelers from other states,

but rather ex-gold miners from the **Lumpkin**, **White**, and **Dawson County** areas. When these adventurous treasure-seekers decided to give up their diggings and head West during the mid to latter portion of the 19th century (and there were thousands of them leaving in particular for the **California** and **Colorado** gold fields), the *Coosa River Valley* route was the most logical path for them to take.

Because of the great importance of the many initial connectors to this *Alabama Road* option, brief descriptions of these connecting avenues are provided herewith as follows:

Connection #1

This early access route began at the *Chattooga River* in **Rabun County**, east of present-day *Clayton*, Georgia. Crossing the *Chattooga River* from *South Carolina* over *Earl's Ford* at the mouth of *Warwoman Creek*, Connection #1 paralleled and crossed *Warwoman Creek* a number of times on its way westward, continuing over *Saddle Gap* to reach *Clayton*.

Earl's Ford can easily be re-visited today in what is still a very sparsely-settled wilderness area simply by taking (from *Clayton* headed eastward) the clearly-marked routes of *Warwoman Road* to *Earl's Ford Road*. Even today, this area remains a very scenic unspoiled backwoods region for the most part, unbroken except for farmland and occasional homes.

Originally known as *"The Dividings,"* *Clayton* earned its initial moniker in the days of the pioneers due to the fact that a number of Native American hunting and trading trails crossed or "divided" there. Leaving *The Dividings, Connection #1* continued southwestward along the same general route as present-day U.S. Highway 76, passing by present-day *Fairview Church* and crossing in the vicinity of today's *Lake Burton*. In Native American days, this portion of the route was also a part of the *"Tallulah Trail,"* and was a less-desirable route to take due to the rugged country through which it passed.

Connection #1 continued on, passing the site at which famed *LaPrade's Fishing Camp* once existed (noted by the present-day *"LaPrade's Marina"*), passing into upper *Habersham County* where it followed the present-day route of *Georgia Highway 197*. Though not the most direct route in pioneer days, this route was the only practical route if one traveled through the mountainous reaches of northeast Georgia. Continuing southward past *Burton Dam*

Road, then *Batesville Junction Store* and then, at Knoll View Drive, *Providence Church*, the road left *GA-197* to turn more southwestward onto present-day *Georgia Highway 255*, and pass into present-day *White County*.

A short distance beyond "Cowart Road," *Georgia Highway 255* offers two options. One option turns left and one option continues straight ahead. In order to continue on the old route of this connection to this Alabama Road, one must use the "straight ahead" option. Continuing for a substantial but very scenic distance beyond that point, the route passed historic *Stovall Mill Covered Bridge* and the historic *Stovall House Inn* itself, *Nacoochee Presbyterian Church*, and the historic *Old Sautee Store*, where this *Old Alabama Road Connector's* former route bears to the left (not the right), remaining on *GA-255*. This portion of *GA-255* not only is the former route of the Old Alabama Road, but, interestingly, is also the former route of the very historic *Unicoi Turnpike* as well. This section continues for a substantial distance, passing *Habersham Emergency Services Station #16* (on the left), a large boat storage facility (on the left) and *Cool Spring Methodist Church* (on the right) at which point *Connection #1* of the *Old Alabama Road* reached the eastern end of the *Nacoochee Valley*, where it joined *Georgia Highway 105*, which was also the conclusion of another connector. We shall call it "Connection #2."

Connection #2

Connection #2 began at *Walton's Ford* on the Tugaloo River in eastern *Stephens County*. That location – northeast of *Toccoa* – exists today beneath the waters of *Lake Hartwell*.

Connection #2 skirted southwestward past what today is *LeTourneau*

Airport before following the route of present-day *Georgia Highway 17* in the eastern fringes of *Toccoa*. A good place to begin the adventure of retracing this route would be downtown *Toccoa* and some very interesting historic sites such as the **Currahee Military Museum** which documents the story of **Camp Toccoa**.

This World War II basic training camp for United States Army paratroopers was located five miles west of *Toccoa, Georgia*. Among the units to train at this site was the famed **506ᵗʰ Infantry Regiment**, whose Company E was portrayed in the **2001 HBO miniseries "Band of Brothers."**

From the south side of *Toccoa*, the old route of *Connection #2* to the *Old Alabama Road* continued westward on *"Locust Stake Road"* (named after a locust stake placed by an early surveyor; locust has been known to occasionally sprout and actually take root from a simple stake or pole, and the large durable locust trees made excellent boundary line markers. *Locust Stake Road* is still clearly marked by road signage just west of *Toccoa* and is easy to follow.

Continuing into **Habersham County**, *Connection #2* intersected what today is *Rock Road* before falling upon the present-day route of *U.S. Highway 123 / Georgia Highway 17* westward. Continuing for a short distance, the old route turns off at the intersection of *Glade Creek Parkway/Tommy Irvin Road* onto *GA-17 / GA-115* (the *Toccoa Highway*). Continuing westward, the old route on *GA-17* passes **Hill's Crossing Baptist Church** before continuing through *Clarkesville*, following hard on *GA-17/115* until that highway emerges on the opposite side of this town. From there, it continues out through the countryside for three or four miles before

GA-17 turns right and *GA-115* continues straight ahead. Turning right onto *GA-17* (historic pioneer *Unicoi Turnpike*), *Old Alabama Road Connector #2* continues until it shortly reaches *"Harvest"* and *"Cool Springs"* to intersect with *Connection #1* at *Sautee*.

Continuing westward past *Sautee*, *GA-17* intersects with *GA-255* (still also following not only the *Old Alabama Road Connector*, but also the *Old Unicoi Turnpike*), passing through the **Nacoochee Valley** in present-day **White County**, where the combination of *Old Alabama Road Connections #1* and *#2* turned southward on *Georgia Highway 75* to pass **Yonah** (Cherokee for "bear") **Mountain** and then pass through **Cleveland**. It was at what once was **Mountain View Church** in this area that a historic fork in the road called *"Gold Diggers Road"* once existed. *Gold Diggers Road* bore straight ahead at this point, while the combined *Connections #1* and *#2* continued hard on the route of present-day *GA-115* toward **Dahlonega**.

Gold Diggers Road is not a direct connection for the *Alabama Road*, but its route will be briefly described here since it has important historic significance. This route was – as its name suggests – a way into the gold fields of present-day **Lumpkin** and **White** counties. It continued toward **Dahlonega** from *Cleveland*, passing just north of **Dahlonega** before falling upon the present-day route of *U.S. Highway 19* just south of the simplistically-beautiful **Concord Church**. The road passed through the western fringe of **Dahlonega** and then followed the present-day route *Georgia Highway 9-E*, before finally ending at the old gold mining town of **Auraria**.

In its day, *Gold Diggers Road* was traversed by many rough-and-tumble hardy pioneers who were accustomed to an extremely harsh life, since they lived most of the time by camping out in tents and crude structures, enduring the oft-inhospitable elements of nature, vermin, and abject poverty as they staked their claims and sought their fortunes. Some located just enough gold to keep them preoccupied with seeking the precious yellow metal many years in **Lumpkin County**; some lucky few actually struck it rich and retired early, but many more endured almost endless frustration and a very inhospitable lifestyle, eventually giving up and moving westward to **California** and **Colorado**, after learning of big gold strikes there in 1849 and 1859 respectively. *Gold Diggers Road* was the route these miners took in this westward migration.

Back at the fork at **Mountain View Church** in **White County**, the collective *Connections #1* and *#2* followed the present-day route of *GA-115*, passing **Shoal Creek Church**. Just east of **Garland**, the trail turned southward, passing what today are **Hickory Grove Church** and **St. Paul Church**, both in southern **Lumpkin County**. Collective *Connections #1* and *#2* eventually crossed the *Chestatee River* at **Leather's Ford**, and then followed the route of present-day *GA 9-E*, passing into **Dawson County**.

In **Dawson**, the original route of these "connections" for the *Old Alabama Road* passed through the former pioneer crossroads of **Landrum** and **Dougherty**. It was along this stretch that the route generally ceased to be considered a "connection," and actually became commonly known as *"the Alabama Road."*

Connection #3

Connection #3 began at **Hatton's Ford** on the *Tugaloo River* northeast of **Bowersville,** and near today's **Reed**

"Mule Camp Springs" – Pictured circa 1890s is the public square at *"Mule Camp Springs,"* better known today as Gainesville, Georgia. The road passing through this site was also a feeder to the *Upper Alabama Road* on the way to "the shallow ford" across the nearby Chattahoochee River.

Creek community, all in **Hart County**. The former site of this ford is now inundated by the waters of *Lake Hartwell*.

Connection #3 continued southwestward from its river crossing, close on *Georgia Highway 51* through *Reed Creek*, where it was joined by another short connection. This latter connection ran from a crossing a short distance downstream on the Tugaloo known as **Harrison's Ferry** (later **Andersonville Ferry**), located at the site of present-day Lake Hartwell Dam. This short link ran southwestward to intersect *Connection #3* about three miles north of **Hartwell** before the combined trails continued on into that city. From there, *Connection #3* continued westward, close on present-day *Georgia Highway 77* for a short distance, before turning left onto the previously-mentioned *GA-51*.

Connection #3 continued on *GA-51* through **Flat Shoals**, **Airline**, and downtown **Bowersville**, where it dead-ends into *GA-17/51*. At that point in pioneer days, the old route continued on either what today is *Sutton Road* (which becomes *Bennett Road*) or, slightly farther down onto *Shirley Road* (which becomes *Ruckersville Road*) and proceeded across to *Georgia Highway 327* (*New Franklin Church Road*) before bearing to the right onto *Jackson Bridge Road* to *Georgia Highway 145* (*Royston Road*) into **Carnesville**. The latter portion of this stretch – from the North Ford Broad River and on into **Gainesville** – followed an old Indian trail known as *"the Toogaloo Trail"* (and sometimes *"the Pickens Trail"*). The word *"Toogaloo"* is actually a misnomer which has been perpetuated through time. The trail was so-named because it ran to the Indian town of *"Tugaloo"* (not *"Toogaloo"*) situated on the stream of the same name. This section of *Connection #3* earned the added identity of *"Pickens Trail"* from General Andrew Pickens who lived at the trail's eastern terminus in **Oconee County, South Carolina**, just across the **Georgia** state line.

Connection #3 continued on through **Carnesville**. From that point, for a short distance over to *Georgia Highway 51*, the route has been lost, but quite likely followed what today is *Georgia Highway 59* through **Ramey Farm** down to *GA-51*. From that point, the *Old Alabama Road Connector* is known to have followed closely on the route of present-day *GA-51* which, incidentally is also the former route of the historic *"Old Federal Road"* (yes the same *Old Federal Road* as that extant portion which still exists in **"Hightower"** in **Forsyth County**).

(Special Note*: The section of the Old Federal Road in Forsyth County is clearly marked with a road-sign as "Old Federal Road." It is located to the right, off Georgia Highway 369, and is exceedingly historic, being the former site of the Cherokee and pioneer community of* **Hightower**.

In this vicinity were also located **Scudder's Inn**, *as well as two stockades known as* **Fort Campbell** *constructed by the U.S. military in the 1830s.* **Fort Campbell** *was used to house native Cherokees from the area as they were collected for relocation to Arkansas and Oklahoma. Just a very short distance up the Old Federal Road, the pioneer tavern of Lewis Blackburn still stood until early in the 21st century. No remnants whatsoever exist today of* **Hightower**, **Scudder's Inn**, *Blackburn's Public House or farm, nor of* **Fort Campbell**.)

Meanwhile, back at the *Old Federal Road* section in east Georgia, the former route of the *Old Alabama Road Connection #3* continued past **Indian Creek Baptist Church** and **Plainview** before passing into **Banks County**. From there, the *GA-51* route of the *Old Alabama Road* travels a significant distance before taking a sharp left at **Redemption Church** and continuing to **Homer**, then turning left at **Mt. Carmel Baptist Church** onto *Georgia Highway 323* to **Gillsville**, thence to **Tadmore District** on *GA-323*, and thence to *Georgia Highway 11* (Athens Highway).

Due to the immense amount of construction, mining and other development just east of **Gainesville**, a short section of the *Old Alabama Road* between *GA-11* and *Georgia Highway 53* has been lost through time, but after reaching *GA-53*, the old route passed into and through **Gainesville**. The stretch west of **Gainesville** was also known as *"Shallowford Road"* (not to be confused with the *Shallowford Road* of **Atlanta**) in early days, because, just as with the *"Shallowford Road"* in **Atlanta**, the road forded (crossed) the Chattahoochee River at a "shallow ford," but this time at **Gainesville**, instead of **Roswell**. A portion of this **Gainesville** *Shallowford Road* is still marked with road signage today.

From this point, Shallowford Road in Gainesville transitions into GA-53. Some of this traffic continues straight ahead on GA-53 into Dawson County.

"Big Savannah" / Dougherty

Connection #3 continued westward from *Gainesville* to cross the Chestatee River at *Wooley Ford* (later replaced by *Bolding Bridge*), still following the route of *GA-53*, and still known as *Shallowford Road*. Passing into *Dawson County*, *Connection #3* passed across the corridor now occupied by modern *Georgia Highway 400*, and eventually intersected with present-day *GA Highway 9-E* just below *Black's Mill*, a spot which today is highly developed around the burgeoning *GA-400* corridor. The former route of this branch of the *Old Alabama Road* continued northward on *GA-53* to intersect with *Connections #1* and *#2* near historic *Dougherty*.

Some historic homes and out-buildings from pioneer days in *Landrum/ Dougherty* can still be seen in the beautiful Etowah River Valley in *Dawson County* long-known as *"Big Savannah."* Anyone who has visited this area no doubt has noticed the fine river bottomlands which stretch away from the highway up and down the Etowah River and the numerous historic homes and other structures which continue to dot this landscape.

Prior to the removal of the native Cherokee Indians from Georgia, *"Big Savannah"/ Dougherty* was the home of a number of Cherokee families, and White pioneers with whom the Cherokees had intermarried. This site is also a documented former location of a large Cherokee town in called *"Tensawattee."*

Co. Benjamin Hawkins, on his way in 1796 to take up his duties as Indian Agent, remarked that the *Big Savannah*

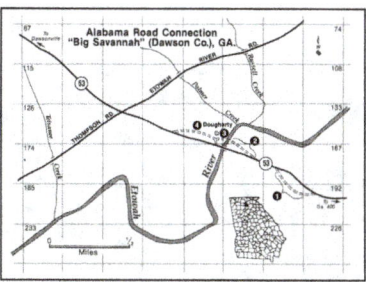

"Big Savannah" – Located in present-day Dawson County, Georgia, the community of "Big Savannah" changed its name to "Dougherty" in 1881. The numbered sections on the map identify portions of the *Alabama Road* still extant today which passed through this former township: 1/ the road over "Gober Hill." 2/ the road to the original bridge (which no longer exists) crossing the Etowah River at *Big Savannah*. 3/ the road leading from the river to the former pioneer community of *Dougherty*. 4/ the "Gober Road" portion of the *Alabama Road*. The Talley/Palmour/Gober homestead, constructed circa 1845, still exists on the road at this site. (Cartographic information courtesy of Michael Miller, Dawsonville)

area was *"a large and beautiful savannah,"* and that portions of it were *"the richest vale of land I have ever seen."* In pioneer terminology, a *"savannah"* was a moist, open, meadow-like area with very rich earth where grass or reed cane proliferated. In a heavily-forested region like early Georgia, such sites were highly prized spots for grazing stock and growing food, and were much-used for these purposes both by aboriginal natives and Whites alike.

It is interesting to note that a post office once existed at *Big Savannah* from 1869 until the community was renamed *"Dougherty"* in 1881. Records of the U.S. Postal Service indicate that the *Big Savannah Post Office* was established on August 9, 1869, with Harriet A. Barnett as the first postmistress. This

"Gober Hill" – The old *Alabama Road* over *Gober Hill* near *"Big Savannah"* plantation / *Dougherty*, Georgia, in present-day Dawson County was photographed here in 1990. Many early settlers in Georgia and travelers to states westward followed this trail to reach their ultimate destinations. Countless individuals who figured prominently in the early history of the United States traversed this byway on their way westward. In 1991, Highway 53 West was re-graded by the Georgia Department of Transportation, eliminating a substantial portion of the old *Alabama Road* in this vicinity. (Photo by Michael Miller, Dawsonville)

Palmour Gristmill – Built circa 1906, this early mill once existed beside the original bridge across the Etowah River (approximately 100 yards north of the present-day State Road 53 Bridge) at *Dougherty*, Georgia. It, quite possibly, was built on the site of an even earlier mill at this spot. Pictured in this photo are Elizabeth Hardy (l) and Dessie Black, daughter of Dick Black.

post office was discontinued on November 7, 1881, after a postal service office was established in **Dougherty** on October 19 of that year.

Robert A. Gober was the first postmaster of **Dougherty**. The historic Gober homestead still stands at **Dougherty** as of this writing in 2025. The **Dougherty Post Office** continued until January 31, 1955, at which time it was discontinued as well, and the post office was transferred to nearby **Dawsonville**.

The name *"Dougherty"* has been in use in the **Big Savannah** area since Indian days, very likely a community name held over from the days of James Dougherty, Sr., who long resided in the Cherokee nation in that section and intermarried with the Cherokees. Dougherty and his wife died there in 1837, a year prior to the Cherokee Indian removal from that area.

Old Federal Road

Meanwhile, back at *GA-53* on the west side of **Gainesville**, yet another branch of the *Old Alabama Road* diverged from the west-heading migrations on *GA-53* to instead head a short distance southeast in the opposite direction on *GA-53* until it shortly intersected with *GA-369* heading west.

Regarding the *Old Federal Road*, its former route picks up on the opposite shore of **Lake Lanier** at **Vann's Tavern Park** just south of *GA-369*. Present-day **Vann's Tavern Park** was once the site of now historic **Vann's Tavern** and **Vann's Ferry** across the Chattahoochee River prior, of course, to the construction of **Lake Lanier**. **Vann's Tavern**, interestingly, was completely disassembled

The "original" Silas B. Palmour pioneer homestead, built circa 1844 in Landrum, in the same general vicinity as Dougherty / "Big Savannah," GA, in Dawson County, was photographed in the 1980s prior to its suspected demise. It's disposition today is unknown. It was located on the old upper Alabama Road just off Highway 9-E. Silas B. Palmour was one of the early pioneers into north Georgia. He was born in 1820 and died in 1888. (Photo by R. Olin Jackson)

A later Dawson County home of Silas B. Palmour in Landrum near "Big Savannah" on the upper old Alabama Road was photographed here in the 1980s. It's disposition today is also unknown. Palmour was a substantial landowner and farmer. This home was built circa 1880 just a few years prior to his death. (Photo by R. Olin Jackson)

159

Scudder's Inn – This dwelling once stood at the present-day intersection of GA Highway 369 and the *Old Federal Road* in Forsyth County. Remnants of this structure were still visible in the undergrowth on the left side of Highway 369 at this site in recent times. Pictured in the front yard (l to r) are: Elie Sherrill (husband of Cynthia Heard Sherrill), Alice Paralee Heard (youngest child of Martha Paralee Hudlow Heard), Mattie G. Heard (with children: Pauline, Otto & Grace), George Bowman Hudlow (white-bearded family patriarch), Martha Paralee Hudlow Heard, and an unidentified young man). This structure was tragically burned circa 1941. (Photo courtesy of Don Shadburn)

at its site on the west bank of the Chattahoochee in the 1950s during the impoundment of *Lanier*. The old tavern was relocated to *New Echota State Historic Park* in *Gordon County*, Georgia where this very historic structure was reassembled and preserved.

Just a short distance beyond *Vann's Tavern*, the *Old Federal Road* continued on *GA-369* headed west, which, coincidentally was also the route of the *Upper Alabama Road*. Today, the GA-369 route (upon which both the *Alabama Road* and *Federal Road* once existed) passed over the corridor known today as *Georgia 400 Highway*, and continued to *Coal Mountain* in upper *Forsyth County* where they passed over old *U.S. Highway 19* and continued to the northwest corner of *Forsyth*.

At that point, the *Old Federal Road* which was constructed on an approximate forty-five degree angle across north Georgia, diverges to the right (away from GA-369 / *Upper Alabama Road*) to continue northwestward, crossing the *Etowah River* at the *"Frogtown Ford,"* also known as *"Blackburn's Ford."* Meanwhile, the *Old Alabama Road* continued westward on the route of *GA-369*.

The *Georgia Highway 369/Federal Road crossroads* was known in Indian times as *"Hightower,"* and exists in what today is extreme northwest *Forsyth County*. It had great significance during late Indian occupation days, because it was a focal point for the U.S. Army under General Winfield Scott while initiating the *Cherokee Removal* program.

This site was also the location of a

<u>Residents of Hightower</u> – Photographed circa 1890s at *Scudder's Inn* are (l to r): George Lumpkin, John Pinkney, Jefferson Seymour, James Linton, William Walker, Henry Arthur, and Charles Davis. A corner of the inn is visible far left. The old *Scudder Trading House/Store* at the inn is visible to the rear. It served as a headquarters of the U.S. Army in the 1830s, when troops were necessary for the relocation of resident Cherokee Indians in the area to reservations in Arkansas and Oklahoma. (Photo courtesy of Don Shadburn)

very prominent businessman of the area – Alfred Scudder. Mr. Scudder and his family had a substantial home and tavern/trading house on the left side of the Upper Alabama Road (present-day *GA-369*) at its intersection with the *Federal Road*. It was Scudder's trading house which served as a headquarters for the U.S. Army during the collection and removal of the Cherokees in that area.

Just eastward a very short distance down the *Federal Road* from **Hightower**, **Fort Gilmer** was built at the same time to house a unit of the Georgia Guard assigned by Georgia Governor Gilmer to arrest any Whites or Indians violating the laws of the state of Georgia. Since **Gilmer** was only intended as a temporary stockade, no permanent buildings were ever constructed at that site, and therefore no remnants of the fort remain today. *(Special Note: This cantonment is*

not to be confused with "Camp Gilmer," a Cherokee removal stockade built in 1838 in what today is Murray County, nor with "Fort Gilmer," a U.S. Army fortress constructed in 1814 at Standing Peachtree in what today is Atlanta. It should likewise not be confused with the stockade called "Fort Campbell" which was also constructed at Hightower and used to temporarily restrain resident Cherokees slated for removal from the area.) Though a substantial home and tavern/trading house were built by Scudder, nothing, surprisingly, remains of those structures today either. Even Alfred Scudder's once impressive tomb in which he was buried was destroyed long ago by grave-robbers.

The present-day *Old Federal Road* includes a somewhat sharp curve at the point at which **Fort Gilmer** had been constructed. Though no remnants of the fort remain, a portion of the original

Last Remnant of a Historic Landmark – Photographed at the intersection of GA-369 (originally a branch of the Upper Alabama Road) and the Old Federal Road, this site – known in pioneer days as "Hightower" – once figured prominently in the history of the area. Today, a stone pillar (visible within the undergrowth) from the old Scudder Trading House which once existed at this site, is all that remains of this landmark. Among its many historic aspects, it served as a headquarters during the removal of the Cherokee natives from Georgia in 1838. (Photo by Don L. Shadburn)

road, interestingly, does exist just to the north of the aforementioned curve. According to the late Marion Hemperley, former Deputy Survey-General for the state of Georgia, *"In this vicinity, the Federal Road ran straight and did not curve as does today's road. This straight stretch of the old road was abandoned years ago, but one can still easily see the original route as a sunken depression leading over the hill."*

Crossing the Etowah River at **Blackburn's Ford**, the old road passed through some fertile bottom-lands

before continuing up the hill on the opposite side. At the top of this hill, a very historic pioneer tavern believed to have been **Lewis Blackburn's Public House** once stood on the left. After the property was purchased by the Sherrill family circa 1960s, this historic structure was moved to the opposite side of the *Federal Road* to allow for construction of the Sherrill home upon the former tavern site. The old tavern building was used as a hay-barn and other endeavors for many years by the Sherrill family.

Though strong evidence identifies the old structure as having been **Lewis Blackburn's Public House**, it, nevertheless, was recently removed from **Hightower** and relocated to the **Forsyth County Fairgrounds** where it more recently was misidentified as **Buffington's Tavern** and the site of the 1809 murder of Cherokee Chief James Vann II. Its current disposition at the time of this writing is unknown.

It has been documented that **Buffington's Tavern** was the actual site of the murder of James Vann, and further evidence strongly supports the contention that **Buffington's** was in fact located farther up the *Federal Road* toward **Canton**, on the right side of the road, just inside the present-day **Cherokee County** line. The old tavern structure removed from the former Sherrill home was originally built on the left side of the road. Documented evidence almost certainly confirms that it could not have been the site at which James Vann II was murdered in 1809.

Through Cherokee and Bartow

Meanwhile, back at **Hightower** on *GA-369*, the *Upper Old Alabama Road* continued following that route a short distance over to *GA-20*. From the intersection of *GA-369* with *GA-20*, the

Upper Old Alabama Road is much easier to trace, simply because much of it is still in use and clearly identified along much of its route with road signage today.

Continuing westward on *GA-20*, the old road passed into **Cherokee County**, passing **Etowah School**, **Ophir**, **Orange**, and **Buffington**. The last-named community was originally *"Fort Buffington,"* another of the Cherokee Indian removal stockades of the 1830s.

The namesake of the fort is not known for certain today, but he quite likely was Joshua Buffington, a prominent mixed-blood Cherokee who lived nearby in Indian days. Interestingly, this Buffington is also of the family which owned **Buffington's Tavern** once located on the right side of the *Federal Road* just inside the present-day **Cherokee County** line as one travels to **Canton**.

The *Upper Alabama Road* continued on westward, following closely the current route of *GA-20* through **North Canton** to a crossing on the *Etowah River* known during pioneer days as **Downings Ferry**. This crossing, now beneath the waters of *Lake Allatoona*, was just downhill (in the lake-bed) from today's **Fields Church** (located on the northern side of the lake).

After passing **Fields Church**, the *Alabama Road* again followed the route of present-day *GA-20*, past the pioneer crossroads of **Laughing Gal**, and on through a rugged region which must have been a very difficult portion of the road for travelers during pioneer days. Shortly thereafter, the road crossed **Lick Creek** (now **Stamp Creek**).

The *Alabama Road* next passed above **Cartersville**, crossing *U.S. 411* at **Felton Field** to intersect *U.S. 41* at the edge of **Cass Station**. Located at that place in Indian days was *"Hawk's Store,"* where the *Alabama Road* crossed *"New Town Road."* *"Hawk's"* was a trading post which was operated by Charles Hawks, a white man who of course was residing in the *Cherokee Nation* prior to the removal of the tribe. Hawks was later appointed the first postmaster of **Cassville** when a post office was established there on July 12, 1833.

New Town Road passed by Cherokee **Sally Hughes' Ferry** on the *Etowah River* just south of **Cartersville**. From this crossing, the *Sally Hughes Road* ran on northward to the final Cherokee capital village – **New Echota**. It is for this reason that the road earned the name *"New Town Road."* This road also merits further mention because it was a crossover point from another *Alabama Road* running south of the Etowah River.

Major Ridge Home

From **Cass Station**, the *Alabama Road* (known at this point as *"the Kingston Road"* both in Indian days and today), went above Walker Mountain, but not on the course followed by *U.S. 411* today. Instead, it ran south of the modern road to a point just east of **Ransom School** near the county line, and from there into **Floyd County** and on to *"Chieftains,"* the former home of prominent

---

The Alabama Road next passed above Cartersville, crossing U.S. 411 at Felton Field to intersect U.S. 41 at the edge of Cass Station.

"Chieftains" – Major Ridge, the uncle of famed warrior Stand Watie, departed for the West in 1837. The structure in this photograph has an Indian log cabin at its core which was Ridge's home when he owned the property and resided in Indian Territory in what today is Rome, Georgia. Ridge also operated a ferry and several other business endeavors in this vicinity in the 1820s and '30s. Today, this structure is called *Chieftains Museum*, and is a National Historic Landmark dedicated to the preservation of the heritage of the Cherokees. Because of his support for the **Treaty of New Echota** which sold the Cherokee lands in the Southeast to the state of Georgia, Major Ridge was later brutally assassinated by his Cherokee brethren. (Photo by Joe Griffith)

Cherokee planter – Major Ridge – on the Oostanaula River in north **Rome**.

Ridge was intimately connected with the development of this old thoroughfare near his home, just as was James Vann II with the development of the Federal Road near his home. Ridge maintained a ferry across the Oostanaula River where the *Upper Alabama Road* crossed near his home, just as did Vann across the Chattahoochee River.

Ridge's home – **Chieftains** – is still located in the original location – today's Chatillion Road in north **Rome**. The two-story house of milled lumber built around an earlier log cabin overlooked the **Ridge Toll Ferry** across the Oostanaula.

Major Ridge, and his son – John – both were signers of the **Treaty of New Echota** in 1835, and were both assassinated for their roles in the removal of the Cherokee Nation from Georgia. Today, **Chieftains** is maintained as a very fine museum of Cherokee culture.

From Ridge's place, the original course of the *Alabama Road* is lost in a maze of modern roads and streets. It, nevertheless, continued westward, leaving the northern part of **Rome**, and, after a short distance, continued on the same route followed by *GA 20*.

Chief John Ross House

Before leaving the present city limits of **Rome** and near the intersection of *Burnett Ferry Road* and *GA-20*, the *Upper Alabama Road* was intersected by a road from the forks of the Etowah and Oostanaula Rivers. This junction, which represents the beginning of the Coosa River, is the center of present-day **Rome**, and also the former location of the Cherokee **Chief John Ross's home**.

The connecting road at this site is of significance because it was also called an *Alabama Road*, and was a link between the *Alabama Road* below the Etowah and Coosa Rivers and the upper trace under discussion. The crossing in what today is downtown **Rome** bears noting because it was also the site of the **"Widow Fool's Ferry,"** so-named for one of the two Cherokee women who operated river crossings (the other was the previously-mentioned Sally Hughes).

The Brainerd Road

The *Alabama Road* continued westward on *GA 20*, passing today's village of **Coosa**, the site during pioneer days of the **Creek Path Missionary Station**. Just beyond this point, the *Alabama Road* was joined by a prong of *"the*

Brainerd Road," another *Alabama Road* from Tennessee.

The main *Alabama Road* continued westward along the route of *GA-20* which became *AL Highway #9* when it reached that state and ran on to *Jeffersonville*, now *Cedar Bluff* in *Cherokee County, Alabama*. Just before reaching the latter city, a fork bore off to the right (approximately along the route of *AL-35*) to go to *Gaylesville* where it intersected another *Alabama Road* from *Brainerd* and *Calhoun County, Tennessee*.

The *Brainerd Road* was so named because it was one of the routes used to reach the *Brainerd Missionary Station and School*, located on *Missionary Ridge* in east *Chattanooga, TN*. That station was the headquarters of all the missionary stations in the *Cherokee Nation*. The only sign or indication today that this mission ever existed at all is a historical marker and a small cemetery at the edge of a modern shopping center.

The *Brainerd Road* (also called "*the Tennessee Road*" when followed northward from Alabama) was an *Alabama Road* and is so labeled on numerous maps – even today. It was important as a main thoroughfare for reaching *Alabama* across the northwestern tip of Georgia from Tennessee.

The *Brainerd Road* entered Georgia at two places on the Tennessee state line. One of these connections – known as "*Old Calhoun Road*" (from *Calhoun, Tennessee*) came into Georgia above *Ringgold* via present-day *GA-151* and intersected the *Cherokee Federal (Old Federal Road)* at that place. The combined roads continued a short distance before the *Alabama Road* turned southward along the route again of today's *GA-151*.

The other fork of the *Brainerd Road* entered Georgia at *Graysville, Catoosa County, Georgia*. It also intersected the *Federal Road* and ran eastward to a point just west of *Ringgold*, where the road from *Calhoun* branched off. These two trails combined to form the *Alabama Road*. The combined union ran southward into *Catoosa County*, as does *GA-151* by way of *Pleasant Grove Church*, *Wood Station*, and *Bethel*, before passing into *Walker County*. The road did not go directly through *Lafayette*, but ran just east of there through *Naomi*.

Five miles further, immediately above Cane Creek, the road forked. The left fork continued on southward into *Chattooga County*, down the east side of the Chattooga River and along the foot of Taylor's Ridge. It passed **Holland**, *Tulip*, and *Sprite*, before going into *Floyd County*, following very nearly the route of present-day *Georgia Highway 100*. It intersected the old main *Alabama Road* shortly thereafter near *Coosa* and the *Creek Missionary Station.*

The right branch of the *Alabama Road* from Tennessee bore west at Cane Creek for a short distance before turning south to strike *U.S. Highway 27* at the first fork below *Oakton*. From there, the road skirted the eastern fringe of *Trion* – not following *U.S. 27* into town – before continuing on through *Summerville*. At that city, the old road left *U.S. 27* and followed *GA-114* along the edge of *Berryton* and on through *Lyerly* and *Chattoogaville* before continuing on into *Cherokee County, Alabama* and on to *Gaylesville* via *Alabama Highway 75*.

(Grateful appreciation is sincerely expressed herewith in remembrance of the late Marion R. Hemperley for the material included in all three of the Alabama Roads articles in this series. Marion served with the Georgia State Surveyor-General Department of Georgia for 30 years, 10 years of which included service as Deputy Surveyor-General. The author rode many miles with him in yesteryear, searching out the ancient pioneer trails of Georgia to document for posterity.)

Retracing the Old Alabama Roads

(Part II) (Middle Route)

Travelers in Georgia today quite often encounter what appears to be repetitive road signage across the state's northern realm identifying roads and streets as "Old Alabama Road." This specific road identity, in fact, has very historic significance of which most travelers are completely unaware. A designation of "Alabama Road" marks the original route(s) used by both aboriginals and pioneer settlers moving across Georgia in its earliest days of settlement. The many extant individual incidences of this road clearly demonstrate that it had many different beginnings, ends, branches and connections, all of which served one purpose: they were the easiest, quickest and safest routes across the Georgia frontier to the west. Many times, these originally were ancient game trails cut by migrating wildlife which were later adopted for use by the native Indians, and then still later by white settlers. And though these roads were numerous in quantity, they all ended in "Alabama" and quite often have some interesting stories to tell.

Many people think the early pioneers and explorers just hopped into a covered wagon and headed west upon a well-established road, but it of course didn't happen that way at all. In the beginning, if they were lucky, pioneer travelers in early America were able to follow small game trails and Indian paths which gratefully traversed the contours around the hills and through the valleys, always following the routes of least resistance. If, however, these travelers were unlucky, they were forced by necessity to hack their way through intense undergrowth and thick forests and to laboriously seek out navigable spots at which to ford the countless streams, creeks, and rivers to continue their westward migration. It was an arduous task at best.

These routes westward invariably initially required these brave souls to travel down the eastern seaboard of the United States until they reached the flatlands of South Carolina and Georgia in order to circumvent the almost impenetrable barrier of the Allegheny/Appalachian/Blue Ridge Mountains range.

Some of the travelers also initially landed by ship at **Savannah, Georgia**, and then made their way northwestward across the state. As a result, there ultimately were a number of different pioneer trails across the state, all of which were called *"the Alabama Road,"* because they inevitably led to *"Alabama Territory"* – the next destination after Georgia on the road westward.

Auraria / Dahlonega

One of the first settlements in *north Georgia* was created as a result of the gold mania sweeping across the landscape following the discovery of the precious yellow metal in that locality. The community which sprang up upon a ridge between the Chestatee and Etowah rivers in northeast Georgia was called *"Nuckollsville."* Here, in 1832, William Dean built a cabin, followed by Nathaniel Nuckolls who opened a tavern and gave the community its name.

The community's main street extended along the ridge of land between the Chestatee and Etowah rivers, and everything of importance fronted on it. A stagecoach line had been established from *Athens*, Georgia, by way of *Gainesville*, for a tri-weekly run to *Leathers Ford* across the Chattahoochee River then up to *"Gold Diggers Road"* as the north-south avenue from *Nuckollsville* to *Cleveland*, Georgia, was called.

This rutted red-clay trail through *Nuckollsville* quickly became an important feeder for one of the several *"Alabama Roads"* which the pioneers used to travel westward across Georgia. During times of heat and dry weather, *Gold Diggers Road* boiled with dust, and when the rains came, it just as quickly became a gooey quagmire which made travel almost impossible.

Early Byway – This photo, snapped circa 1932, provides a view looking south down old *Gold Diggers Road* (present-day Hwy 9E) in Auraria, Georgia. This route was a direct and heavily-used feeder line for the *Lower Alabama Road*. To the right on the vacant lot once stood the Paschal Hotel. On the extreme left in this photo, the corner of a home once owned by the Brackett family during gold-rush days in Auraria is visible. Beyond it, the two-story Graham Hotel built in the 1830s is visible on the left. Fiery South Carolinian U.S. Senator and former vice president of the United States John C. Calhoun, who owned a goldmine nearby, often stayed in this hotel.

After deciding that the name *"Nuckollsville"* wasn't the most pleasant-sounding or attractive name for a community, the town fathers eventually renamed it *"Auraria,"* which, roughly translated in Latin means "gold mine."

In pioneer days, *Gold Diggers Road* was a vibrant artery of traffic moving into the bustling town, and later, of miners and travelers moving ever westward, reaching for new opportunities on the horizon. Drovers brought in hogs and turkeys to feed the growing population. The animals were herded noisily through town and then penned up on the outskirts until they could be made ready for the table.

From the earliest days, the nearby community of *Dahlonega* was the rival village of *Auraria*. When a blight was discovered upon the land lot numbering system in *Auraria*, the county seat was removed to the more stable locale

In 1990, the late renowned artist John Kollock of Clarkesville, Georgia, painted this historically correct recreation of old *"Gold Diggers Road."* This route, which passed through the former gold-rush town of Auraria, Georgia, was a portion of the *Alabama Road* westward, and can be compared with the photo of this site on the previous page. The scene depicted here is representative of the early years of the 1830s in this Lumpkin County community. The town's main street extended (and still does today) along a ridge between the Chestatee and Etowah rivers. A stagecoach line had been established from Athens, Georgia, by way of Gainesville for a tri-weekly run. On the extreme right side of the street stands the hotel operated by Agnes Paschal who is remembered for her kindness to the sick. Next door was the **Western Herald** newspaper which began publication in 1833, being edited and published by George Paschal. Steps leading into the Brackett House which stood on the extreme left in this scene are visible, and down the street from it in the distance were the post office/store and Pigeon Roost Bank. (Painting by John Kollock. All Rights Reserved)

of **Dahlonega**. When the all-important *Bank of Darien* on the Georgia coast also selected **Dahlonega** for its new inland branch, a decline in population began almost immediately in **Auraria**. Lawyers moved their practices to the new seat of government, and other businesses gradually followed.

In 1838, when the *United States Branch Mint* was built in Dahlonega, the death knell was sounded for **Auraria**. In less than ten years, the city of gold went from a rambunctious gold mining town to a quiet village, its brief moment of glory gone forever.

With this diminished community status, so too diminished the traffic on *Gold Diggers Road* through **Auraria**. In contrast however, traffic on the *Alabama Roads* across Georgia was surging by the mid-1800s, as the rush for new opportunities westward was beginning in earnest.

Warsaw

In the following article, we will focus upon the *Alabama Road* via present-day **Warsaw** and **Cave Spring**, a route also known as the "**Middle Alabama Road**." There is one additional significant "Alabama Road" across Georgia which will be covered in a later article.

Most pioneer traffic moved slowly down the eastern seaboard of colonial America, skirting as best they could the immense barrier of mountains which extends down the length of the *Coastal Atlantic States*. In so doing, most of this traffic turned west once it had reached north-central Georgia and was beyond the mountains barrier.

The *Warsaw/Cave Spring* route of the *Alabama Roads* began near the community of *Warsaw* on the west side of the Chattahoochee River in *"Old Milton County,"* (present-day *North Fulton County*). This ancient byway, by means of connections at its beginning and through tributaries which joined it along the way, received traffic from widely different areas of Georgia.

The exact date at which the *Alabama Road* via *Warsaw* came under general use by pioneer settlers is not known today. Suffice it to say, however, that this route was in use at least as early as 1825, because at about that time, one George Waters moved to the western or Cherokee side of the Chattahoochee River and began operation of a ferry at the spot.

Following his marriage to a Cherokee woman, Waters settled in the rich river-bottomlands there where he farmed and raised a family of mixed-blood children. In the *Cherokee Removal* of the 1830s when all of the Cherokee Native Americans were forced to abandon their homes and farms in what came to be known as Georgia, the Waters family was also compelled to depart.

Shortly thereafter, however, when the area on the western (present-day *Fulton County*) side of the Chattahoochee was opened for White settlement, Waters, as a White man, returned, as was his right, to settle once

again upon his former home and acreage. However, his efforts to reclaim his former home site proved to be in vain, due to the fact that by that point, it had been claimed by a new owner after Waters abandoned it.

Waters, nevertheless, was able to purchase land across the Chattahoochee River on the eastern or Gwinnett County side. He and his family lived in that area for the rest of their lives, and are buried in the cemetery of the Presbyterian Church there.

The ferry operated by Waters was first known as *"Water's Ferry,"* but in later years, it became known as *"the Warsaw Ferry,"* after the town which had blossomed in that area. This old crossing point is now spanned by *Georgia Highway 120* and *McClure Bridge*.

On the western side of the Chattahoochee, the *Alabama Road* westward came into unofficial general use just above present-day McClure Bridge over the Chattahoochee. The stretch of the former pioneer road leading away from the old ferry site does not exist today, but it once mounted the hill in front of an aged home known as *"the old Howell house"* before turning westward. The road did not pass through the tiny burg of *Warsaw*, being several hundred yards to the south of the community.

Just below the Howell house, this *Middle Alabama Road* continued westward across the state, its course virtually unaltered by modern highways except for a few stretches and minor relocations. The road is still well-known today in numerous spots across the state, including north Fulton, Cobb, Bartow, and Paulding counties where, in various sections, modern highways which still use it have retained its original *"Alabama Road"* name.

Holcomb Bridge / GA-92

Leaving **Warsaw**, the *Alabama Road* – still identified here as well with its original name today – passed *Pleasant Hill Church* and *School*, before going through the crossroads of **Newton**. One section of the road is clearly marked on mapping apps where the road begins to be identified at the intersection of *Georgia Highway 141*. At that point, it continues southwesterly briefly before branching off to the right just prior to *Concord Missionary Baptist Church* and then continuing for a considerable distance. This length of the *Old Alabama Road* then adjoins what today is known as *Georgia Highway 140* or *"Holcomb Bridge Road."* Holcomb Bridge (known as *Rockbridge Road* in pioneer days) was an out-growth of the well-known *"Hightower Indian Path"* which was the dividing line between today's Gwinnett and DeKalb Counties. This *Hightower Path* can still be seen in several areas in the

Rucker Family Home – This historic structure has stood at the intersection of Broadwell and Rucker roads in Crabapple, Georgia, for almost 200 years. Though covered with siding today, it has a two-story heart-of-pine log home at its core which was built circa 1830s when Native Americans still resided in the area. A branch of the *Alabama Road* passed very near this structure, bringing much foot and ox and cart traffic for generations. (Photo by R. Olin Jackson)

Roswell area on modern street signage as *"Hightower Road"* and *"Hightower Trail,"* etc.

Interestingly, just as with the word *"Etowah,"* the word *"Hightower"* is a pioneer-settler derivation of the indigenous aboriginal word *"Ite-wah"* which was the name the area's natives assigned to the *"Etowah"* River. All three words were/are interchangeable, whether they referred/refer to a town ("Etowah"), a river ("Ite-wah"), or a road ("Hightower").

From its juncture with *Holcomb Bridge Road*, the *Middle Alabama Road* (Holcomb Bridge Road / Georgia Highway 140) continues westward, crossing over the corridor occupied today by *Georgia Highway 400*, and passing north of old **Roswell** where, just beyond the intersection with *Georgia Highway 9 (old U.S. 19)*, Holcomb Bridge Road becomes what today is called *"Woodstock Road"* *(GA Highway 92)*. Georgia-140, on the other hand, angles off northwestward at this intersection.

Interestingly, stretches of *old Georgia Highway 19,* all the way from **Blairsville, Georgia**, in the extreme northern sector of the state down to **Atlanta**, fall upon another ancient game trail converted in prehistoric days to an aboriginal trading path. These ancient game trails/aboriginal trading paths often followed on or near the tops of adjoining ridges which made for much easier travel circumstances. Modern researchers have determined that water shed on the east side of old Highway 19 in downtown **Atlanta** drains to the Atlantic, and water shed on the west side of the road all drains into the Gulf of Mexico.

The short initial stretch of *GA-92* which begins at the intersection with *old U.S.-19*, came to be known in earlier days as *"Crossville Road,"* so-named because it runs through what once was

Photographed circa 1900, the covered bridge across the Chattahoochee River (above) exists where Roswell Road Bridge exists today. In this same general vicinity at the "Shallow Ford" across the river, a feeder of the *Lower Alabama Road* once existed. The buildings in the lower left were a portion of the Ivy/Laurel Woolens Mill complex built in 1857 by James R. King, which would soon be producing woolen uniforms for the Confederate Army. The structure right-center was the Roswell Hotel, strategically located for use by travelers immediately after fording the Chattahoochee River. (Photo courtesy of the GA Dept. of Archives & History, Atlanta)

a tiny community of that name. Little to nothing remains today of that modest burg other than the name assigned to the initial stretch of road.

Leaving Fulton County, the *Alabama Road* continued across the extreme northeast tip of Cobb County before entering Cherokee County. Continuing westward, the *Alabama Road* soon intersected with yet another ancient roadway known today as *Georgia Highway 5* just south of **Woodstock** at an intersection once known as *"Bulloch's Barn."* In prehistoric times, the route occupied today by *Georgia Highway 5* was also an ancient game – and eventually Indian – trail.

Shallowford Road

Continuing to follow present-day *GA-92*, the *Old Alabama Road* ran past **Little River Church** and what once was the tiny community of **Trickum** (located at the intersection of present-day *Trickum Road* and *GA-92).* The former route of the road next passed over the present-day *Interstate 575* and continued for another short stretch to **Carmel Church**. At that point, *Middle Old Alabama* was intersected (and also joined by some of its traffic) by its second important tributary – *Shallowford Road* – also known as *Bell's Ferry Road*. The latter name was derived from the site at which this road's travelers crossed the

Etowah River at **Bell's Ferry**, located on *Bell's Ferry Road* a few miles north of this junction with the *Alabama Road*.

The name *"Shallowford Road"* owes its origin to the *"shallow ford"* across the *Chattahoochee River* back in **Roswell**, a noted crossing point which allowed ox and mule-drawn wagons to ford the river when the water was at a normal level. The actual crossing spot was located quite near the present-day *Roswell Road Bridge* where *Georgia Highway 9* now spans the Chattahoochee just south of **Roswell**. *"Shallowford Road"* can still be found across stretches of Fulton County from points in **Atlanta** and up to the Chattahoochee River, thence all the way to *Bell's Ferry Road* in neighboring **Cherokee County**.

Beyond its intersection with *Bell's Ferry Road/Shallowford Road*, *Old Alabama* continued westward on the route of present-day *GA-92*. Just beyond *Cherokee Parkway* on the right, *Old Alabama* departed from *GA-92* by veering off to the left and heading southwestward for a very short stretch; then, just beyond *Hunt Road* (which adjoins the old road from the left), *Old Alabama* intersects (crosses over) *GA-92* and continues northwestward on the opposite side of *GA-92*.

From this point, *Old Alabama Road* again is clearly identified by the road signs, and travels for a good long stretch northwestward before intersecting with *Kellogg Creek Road*. Turning southwestward onto *Kellogg Creek*, the original route of *Old Alabama* continues for a very short distance before bearing to the right onto present-day *New Hope Road*. From there, the *Alabama Road* passed *New Hope Church* and continued until *"New Hope Church Road"* becomes *"Kings Camp Road"* before crossing *Allatoona Creek* at a spot which today has

been inundated by the backwaters of *Lake Allatoona*.

The road continued a short distance through this lake-covered stretch before picking up again on what today is *"Old Allatoona Road"* on the opposite side of the lake's backwaters where it continued its route westward. Beyond present-day *Interstate-75* and just beyond where the road passes beneath present-day *U.S. Highway 41*, the *Old Alabama Road* picks up again on the left where it again is clearly marked.

Etowah / Sally Hughes' Ferry

Traveling through present-day **Emerson**, *Old Alabama* diverged. One fork, as *"Shallowford Road"* (yes – the same road from the shallow ford on the Chattahoochee River), turned right and continued northward where it crossed the *Etowah River* at what was known in pioneer days as *"Sally Hughes' Ferry."* This *Shallowford Road* may have been renamed or perhaps it is a very minor backroad as of 2024, since its name does not seem to appear on modern mapping software (or upon any of the street signage in the **Emerson** area).

Sally Hughes was one of two noted Cherokee women who owned and operated ferries in the *Cherokee Nation*. She was living in the Indian community of **Etowah** in 1796, (as recorded in the notes of Indian Agent Col. Benjamin Hawkins when he visited that place.). The town was located in the vicinity of the present-day *Etowah Indian Mounds Historic Site* southwest of **Cartersville**.

Sally's ferry site was slightly upstream of the mounds, near the site of the present-day *Cartersville City Water Works*. Her cabin in 1832 was a short distance upstream from her ferry. According to Indian agent and valuation reports, her home was a simple log cabin on the north side of the Etowah River.

In 1832, it is interesting to note that Sally suddenly encountered competition in her ferry operation. Her competitor was a man named "Dawson." The official Georgia state valuations of properties owned by the Cherokees of that year show Sally still living at the ferry site. Just north of her cabin, *"Dawson's Ferry"* has appeared as a competitive business operation.

Sally apparently was extremely upset by this drain on her income, and forwarded a letter to the governor of Georgia in complaint. This letter is retained in the records of the Georgia Department of Archives & History in Atlanta, and it interestingly was mailed in the **Cherokee Nation** after being written by another person and then signed by Sally with an "x". Sally could not write or sign her name in English, as was the case with most Cherokees at that time. In all probability, her plea fell upon deaf ears, because it was shortly thereafter that the Cherokees were expelled from Georgia.

Continuing on northward past Sally Hughes' place, a turn-off road called *Newtown Road* closely followed the course of present-day *U.S. Highway 41* to intersect yet another *"Alabama Road"* option via **Rome**. This route, called *"the Upper Alabama Road,"* was just north of **Cass Station** and is described in detail in Alabama Roads (Part 1) in this book. Just as do old *U.S.-19* and old *Georgia Highway 5,* some of *Georgia Highway 41* also follows the former route of an ancient game, and, subsequently, aboriginal trading path.

The *Newtown Road* extended northwestward to **New Echota**, the Cherokee capital prior to 1838 near present-day **Calhoun**, Georgia. (And thus the name: *"New Town Road."*) **New**

Mystery Mission – Due west of the small community of Emerson, Georgia, the old *Alabama Road* is clearly marked, passing quite near the *Etowah Indian Mounds* in Bartow County. One of the many mysteries of the Cherokee Nation in Georgia which has long plagued historians has been the identification of the exact location of the *"Etowah Mission"* established near Etowah in the early 19th Century by Moravian missionaries. The mission is believed to have existed on the *Alabama Road* near the present-day *Etowah Indian Mounds*, but the specific site has eluded historians. Nevertheless, a very aged stone-lined well (pictured) is strongly believed to be the one which existed at the mission as identified in the valuation of the Cherokee property here by the U.S. government prior to the Cherokee Removal in 1838. This well was discovered and noted by the late Deputy Surveyor-General of Georgia Marion Hemperley. (Photo by R. Olin Jackson for Marion Hemperley)

Echota was the "new town" capitol of the Cherokees. Travelers to north Alabama or Mississippi would have logically used this connection from the *Middle Alabama Road* to the *Upper Alabama Road*, because it would have saved them distance and travel time.

Back at the other fork at **Emerson** in Bartow County, the *Middle Alabama Road* continues to be relatively easy to trace, because it is also clearly identified on road signs there today. The many persons living along that stretch will assure you that they live on *THE* Alabama Road, and few if any of these individuals know of the other *Alabama Roads* westward across Georgia via **Rome** and the **Coosa Valley**.

Etowah Mission

One of the mysteries of the former **Cherokee Nation** in Georgia has been the identification of the exact location at which the *"Etowah Mission,"* located near **Etowah** in the early nineteenth century, once existed. The mission, established by Moravian missionaries, almost certainly existed on the *Alabama Road*, directly across the Etowah River from the settlement of **Etowah** (today's Indian mounds historic site), but the actual physical site has eluded researchers.

In one of the valuations of Cherokee property by the U.S. prior to the Cherokee Removal, *Etowah Mission* is listed as *"Pumpkinvine Mission,"* so-called almost certainly for *Pumpkin Vine Creek* that empties into the *Etowah River* at this juncture (directly across from the large mounds and the former town of **Etowah** at which the mission supposedly was located). This same valuation lists a *"stone-lined well"* from which water was obtained for the mission. A very ancient well very similar to the description and which faces *Old Alabama Road* near Pumpkinvine Creek was identified by Deputy Surveyor-General

of Georgia Marion Hemperley circa 1950s. It was described by Hemperley as "almost certainly that well." It remains today in the front yard of a fine country home on the *Alabama Road* near the Mounds.

One of the out-buildings of this home is a log structure with an immense stone hearth and chimney constructed of exceptionally large field and river stones which quite likely date from Cherokee days. Although the stone fireplace and chimney are exceedingly old, the existing log building – though also appearing to be quite old – may be somewhat newer in construction, appearing to possibly have been built sometime in the late 19th or early 20th century.

Stilesboro / Taylorsville

From this point, the *Middle Alabama Road* continued westward. The road, again clearly marked with its original *"Old Alabama Road"* name, branches off from *Highway 61* just prior to the intersection of *Highways 61* and *113*. At *Richland Creek*, the road fell onto *Georgia Highway 113* for a short distance before branching off.

In December of 1796, Indian Agent Col. Benjamin Hawkins was traveling on a trail that crossed the later *Alabama Road* in the vicinity of **Stilesboro**. Hawkins' route ran directly from **Stilesboro** through the center of present-day **Taylorsville**.

Hawkins' travels bear mentioning at this point, since his notes describe a visit with a prominent Cherokee chief – *The*

In December of 1796, Indian Agent Col. Benjamin Hawkins was traveling on a trail that crossed the later Alabama Road in the vicinity of Stilesboro.

Terrapin – sometimes known as "Old Terrapin," who lived between today's **Stilesboro** and **Taylorsville**. The Indian chief's farm was on *Euharlee Creek*, which was called *Limestone Creek* in pioneer days.

Hawkins' journal entry for December 3, 1796, states that his party was *". . . continuing on 6 miles to the Old Terrapins, (we went) across a creek and passed thro' some good lands southwest by west to his house, he was from (not at) home. I visited his wife, informed her who I was, and directed her to inform her husband of it, and to deliver him a present of paint which I brought him. The old fellow lives well, the lands he cultivates are lined with small growth of saplins for some distance, his farm is fenced, his houses comfortable, he has a large stock of cattle and some hogs. He used the plow."*

Benjamin Hawkins did not get to see *Old Terrapin* that day, but the next morning, the chief caught up with the Indian agent's party and they conversed through an interpreter. It is interesting to note the thoughts of an older, and probably very wise, Cherokee during that period (the 1790s).

Hawkins records that *The Terrapin ". . . told me he was glad to see me. He knew me and rejoiced when he was informed in the talk with the President (George Washington) that I was to superintend their affairs. That their nation had been under much embarrassment from the uncertainty of their existence as a nation, as the encroachments of the whites were constantly*

growing against them, notwithstanding their treaties and the repeated promises made to them to the contrary by the agents of the government."

The Terrapin was well-informed in political matters since he had been one of the chiefs who attended the *Grand Cherokee National Council* of 1792, held in the Cherokee capitol of that day – **Ustanali (Oostanaula)**.

Meanwhile, continuing through the center of *old **Stilesboro**,* the *Old Alabama Road* angled off present-day *GA-113* at that point, continuing onto what today is *Shiloh Church Road* which, after intersecting *Covered Bridge Road*, is clearly marked as *"Old Alabama Road" (both on the actual road signage and digital mapping software)* on the opposite side of the intersection and continues for a stretch, passing just above the present-day town of **Taylorsville**.

Immediately beyond **Taylorsville**, numerous branches and brief alternative connective routes of the *"Old Alabama Road"* exist, before they collectively merge together again at the intersection with present-day *Sewell Road*.

Continuing northwestward, the *Middle Old Alabama Road* passes **Mt. Tabor Baptist Church** before reaching a four-road intersection with *Ridge Cross Road, Bailey Road,* and *Taylorsville Road*. Continuing straight ahead at this point, the present-day *Old Alabama Road* becomes *Taylorsville Road*. *Taylorsville Road* soon

Benjamin Hawkins did not get to see Old Terrapin that day, but the next morning, the chief caught up with the Indian agent's party and they conversed through an interpreter.

intersects with *Wax Road* onto which the *Old Alabama Road* route continued through what today is tiny **Wax**, *Georgia*, then the crossroads community of **Chambers** and thence to **Silver Creek**, before skirting through the lower edge of **Lindale** (known as **Courtsey** in pioneer days) before passing into **Floyd County**.

Between **Lindale** and **Cass Station** (above **Cartersville**, Bartow County), old maps show a cross-over linking the *Upper and Middle Alabama Roads*. Settlers going from **South Carolina** and northeast Georgia via **Mulecamp Springs** (**Gainesville**) and **Leathers Ford** (**Auraria/Dahlonega**, GA) on their way to **eastern Alabama**, would have found this cross-over to be a convenient alternative route.

Vann's Valley / Cave Spring

From **Lindale**, the *Alabama Road* intersected *U.S. Highway 411* just below today's **Six Mile** *(which means the old route quite probably lay on or near the vicinity of the present-day route of Booze Mountain Road)*. At this place in Indian days, there was a public stop or inn called **"Wests."** There, the *Alabama Road* was joined in early days by another *Alabama Road* coming south from the *"Widow Fool's Ferry"* (the other Cherokee Indian female, who, like the previously described *Sally Hughes*, owned and operated a ferry in Georgia) which was located at the forks of the Oostanaula and Etowah Rivers (present-day center of **Rome**).

Today, we know virtually nothing about the *Widow Fool*, other than the fact that she operated some type of boat which she used to convey passengers across the three-pronged delta formed by the junction of the Etowah and Oostanaula Rivers (which combine to form the mighty Coosa) in present-day **Rome**.

The name "Fool" was a rather common one among Cherokee men, and did not imply that the person carrying the name was in any way foolish. Instead, the name ironically was an honored war title signifying that a warrior was so brave, that he was reckless in battle.

Closely following the route of present-day *U.S. Highway 411*, the *Alabama Road* turned southwest and continued through **Vann's Valley** by **Cunningham** (also known as **Agate**) and the settlement of **Vann's Valley**, before reaching **Cave Spring**.

David Vann (1800-1863), the nephew of notorious *Cherokee Chief James Vann II* of **Spring Place**, lived at **Vann's Valley** in the vicinity of **Cave Spring** in Indian days. David was also a wealthy planter, but unlike his uncle, he was a very well-liked Cherokee. David planted 200 acres, owned 13 slaves and 17 houses on Cedar Creek in **Vann's Valley**. Local folklore in the area maintains that the stone foundation of one of his out-buildings remains today under a more modern structure there.

Just beyond **Cave Spring** and prior to passing *Rehoboth Baptist Church* (which was still active in 2024), the *Alabama Road* forked, with the left branch turning southwestward into *Polk County*, passing *Jones Church*, along the present-day route of *Jackson Chapel Road*. At *Jackson Chapel Church*, *Jackson Chapel Road* turns right and *"Old Jackson Chapel Road"* continues straight ahead. The *Alabama Road* followed the route of *"Old Jackson Chapel Road,"* turning right onto *"Lefevers Road,"* which, after a short distance, either remains as *Lefevers Road* or becomes *"Frenchman's Road."* Frenchman's / Lefevers road dead-ends into *Prior Station Road* which passes through *"Etna,"* continuing across the Georgia state line into **Alabama**.

Alabama Roads in Alabama

After passing the community of **Aetna**, this fork of the *Middle Alabama Road* turned westward to run on into **Cherokee County, Alabama**. Once in Alabama, the road becomes *"Cherokee County Road 8,"* and passed the tiny crossroads of *"Bluffton"* before falling onto another main trail just east of *"Spring Garden."* That main route was known at that time as *"the Cedartown Road,"* and extended westward from **Cedartown**, Georgia, closely following the route of today's *U.S. Highway 278* through the **Piedmont, Alabama** area.

The right fork of the *Alabama Road* (just west of **Cave Spring**) continued on the route of present-day U.S. Highway 411, entering Alabama one mile or so beyond **Rehoboth Church** and extending to **Centre** via **Forney**, **Key**, and **Bomar**, remaining on *U.S. 411* all the way. At **Bomar**, there was a left turn to old **Coloma**, a prominent community before the advent of railroads.

At **Centre**, an additional *Alabama Road* bears mentioning. It was a short, but very important link from **Rome**, Georgia. This road began at the forks of the *Oostanaula* and *Etowah Rivers* (again, today's downtown **Rome**) and ran along the south bank of the Coosa River as the "Black Bluff" or "Bluff Road." It passed **Brush Arbor Church** and ran just below **Cedar Creek Church** before crossing Big Cedar Creek at a ford located just below an old mill site known as **Foster's Mill**.

The *Black Bluff Road* continued westward by **State Line Church**, before entering into **Alabama** by an early place known as *"Blood."* From there, it ran on by **Kirks Grove**, **Alexis** and **Blaine**, before reaching **Centre**. Today, it is known as the *Rome-Centre Road*. Although this road was not included on the original Georgia and Alabama surveys, it bears the tradition of being an *Alabama Road*, and is so indicated on later maps.

From **Centre**, the old road went on to cross the Coosa River at *Hampton's Ferry*, and proceeded into present-day **Leesburg**. At this point, some travelers took the *"Old Georgia Road,"* (present-day U.S. Highway 411) to the important section which developed around **Gadsden**. Others bore right and northwestward through **Bristow** to intersect the arterial route from **Gaylesville** and **Cedar Bluff** to the **Tennessee Valley** or to **Cotton Gin Port** or **Columbus**, Mississippi. The juncture of these historic thoroughfares occurred at what is now a nondescript road fork between **Collinsville** and **Sand Rock**, the intersection of present-day *Alabama Highways 68 and 89*.

After leaving the north-central section of **Alabama**, the combined *Alabama Roads*, known from this point westward by other names, continued to other towns and areas. Westward, the old thoroughfares ran across **Mississippi** on their way to **Texas**, while those running more northwestward, led to **western Tennessee**, **Kentucky**, and the **St. Louis** region.

Today, even after the development of our modern highway systems, significant portions of the *old Alabama Roads*, much to the surprise of many individuals, remain in daily use, and even retain the original name – *"Alabama Road"* – assigned to these trails from yesteryear by the pioneers of yesteryear.

(Grateful appreciation is sincerely expressed herewith in remembrance of the late Marion R. Hemperley for much of the material included in all three of the Alabama Roads articles in this series. Marion served with the Georgia State Surveyor-General Department of Georgia for 30 years, 10 years of which included service as Deputy Surveyor-General. The author rode many miles with him in yesteryear, searching out the ancient pioneer trails of Georgia to document for posterity.)

The Route Via Villa Rica:

Retracing the
Old Alabama Roads

(Part III) (Lower Route)

*The article which follows is the third in a series of explanations of this pioneer trail –
its many different branches, connections, beginnings and ends – which collectively
came to be known as "the Old Alabama Roads." These early travel routes across
Georgia all had two things in common: the collective roads invariably began
life as ancient trails cut by migrating wildlife, which then were adopted by the
prehistoric Native Americans, and then still later came into use by white settlers.
And though there were any number of them, the roads all ended in "Alabama."
Remnants of these very historic trails can still occasionally be seen today.*

During pioneer times in our nation, the state of Georgia occupied a key geographic positon in the United States, because it was necessary for many emigrants to cross Georgia if they were to avoid extremely circuitous and often arduous travel across the towering mountain ranges which form a barrier across the eastern portion of our nation. Since the Alabama Territory – following organization in 1817 – was the first general destination west of Georgia, travelers began referring to the westward routes across Georgia as "the road to the Alabama." When the territory became a state in 1819, the term was shortened to "the road to Alabama," or simply "the Alabama Road," a moniker still often seen today on road signs identifying many

modern (yet historic) byways westward across the state of Georgia.

Since the migrating wildlife – and later the Native Americans – followed the routes of least resistance through the wilderness covering what eventually became the eastern United States, these avenues were not always the least circuitous routes. The wildlife and Native Americans also sought out the least-risky fording or crossing spots on the countless rivers and creeks across what today is Georgia. As time passed, however, and pioneers arrived who could build and operate ferries and other transportation options across deep waterways, the routes sometimes became more direct.

Today, the "old" Alabama Roads – which almost always wound around the base of mountains or followed the tops of ridges instead of proceeding up and down over each obstacle – have largely disappeared today. When they are in fact "experienced," they are largely ignored, and certainly not understood for their actual historic significance. The remnants of these routes, however, may still often be seen today if one seeks out the least resistive route in the direction of a particular destination westward. There are few historic markers to identify these old routes today, but, more often than not, the street and highway signage continues to use the identity "Old Alabama Road."

Since "Parts I" and "2" of this series on the Alabama Roads concentrated upon the "Upper" and "Middle" routes, this article will focus upon the "Lower Route," which traveled across the state toward and thru Villa Rica. Due to its location and migration patterns, it was the heaviest-used of the Alabama Roads. It was so important, in fact, that modern highways U.S. 78 and Interstate 20 both parallel – and even directly follow in some cases – portions of one of the oldest roads in the southeastern United States.

Due to its connections from the eastern area of the state, this "Lower Alabama Road" became a gateway magnet route for the small – but burgeoning – community of "Marthasville," later to evolve into Atlanta. Many of the original settlers of the piedmont section of Georgia moved on westward to locate new towns and farming opportunities by using the *Alabama Road via Villa Rica*.

In pioneer days, there were many ferries across the Chattahoochee in this vicinity, but only three were strategically important.

The *Alabama Road via Villa Rica* is sometimes also known as *"the Tallapoosa Road"* and *"the Sandtown Road,"* and was paralleled by the Coosa River route (which angled northwesterly) and *"the McIntosh"* and *"Oakfuskee"* traces which angled southwesterly. The "McIntosh" identity was the result of *"the McIntosh Trail,"* which extended from Chief William McIntosh's properties at **Indian Springs** (located near present-day **Flovilla**, halfway between **Atlanta** and **Macon**) to his **"McIntosh Reserve"** (near present-day **Carrollton**, GA) and points westward into **Alabama**. McIntosh was once an influential chief of the **Creek Nation** who was later assassinated by Creek warriors for selling away the Creek lands to the state of Georgia.

As such, the *Alabama Road via Villa Rica* had a hydra-headed beginning on the Chattahoochee River just west of **Atlanta** at various ferry crossing points ranging from **Montgomery's Ferry** (near present-day **Bolton**, GA) to as far downstream as **Campbellton Ferry** (west of present-day **Fairburn**).

In pioneer days, there were many ferries across the Chattahoochee in this vicinity, but only three were strategically important. **Turner's Ferry** crossed the Chattahoochee where the present-day bridge on *Bankhead Highway (U.S. 78)* today passes over that river. The significance of this crossing point lay in the fact that its traffic was especially enhanced by an extension from the heavily-traveled original Peachtree Road which passed by **Moore's Mill** on Peachtree Creek.

The original Peachtree Road actually began at **Fort Daniel** on Hog Mountain in present-day eastern **Gwinnett County**. It provided a route to the Indian town of **Standing Peachtree**. This virtually-forgotten historic site in **Atlanta** once existed at the site of the present-day **Atlanta** city waterworks near **Bolton**.

The original Peachtree Road was opened in 1813 as a military route from the frontier of Georgia (approximately the present-day western county lines of **Barrow** and **Jackson counties** extending northward and southward) to **Fort Gilmer** at **Standing Peachtree**. This was the more desired route by many travelers from northeastern Georgia headed to central and south **Alabama Territory**.

As its name suggests, the original Peachtree Road crossed present-day **Gwinnett County** and closely followed the present-day route of modern Peachtree Road to what today is **Atlanta's Buckhead** community. From that point, however, instead of continuing on past **Buckhead** into **Atlanta**, the original route turned westward to follow the route of present-day West Paces Ferry Road.

Many of the Peachtree Road pioneers then followed a route which branched off southward onto present-day Moore's Mill Road, continuing to an Indian town and other connections,

As its name suggests, the original Peachtree Road crossed present-day Gwinnett County and closely followed the present-day route of modern Peachtree Road to what today is Atlanta's Buckhead community.

one of which leads to the *Lower Alabama Road*.

The second ferry on the Chattahoochee was downstream from **Turner's Ferry** and just above the mouth of Utoy Creek. This was **Howell's Ferry** which later combined with **Green's** to become **Green and Howell's Ferry**, a noted crossing point just south of present-day **Charlie Brown Airport** in west **Fulton County**. The road to this ferry closely followed the route of present-day *Georgia Highway 139* (*Martin Luther King, Jr. Dr.*), and was used by travelers coming from the east via the direction of present-day **Decatur** and **Atlanta**.

Aderhold's Ferry was still farther downstream on the Chattahoochee near **Sandtown**, being located at the end of present-day Atlanta's Cascade Avenue. This was the crossing point for the noted *Sandtown Road* which had important connections from the east-central part of Georgia. It was a fork of the *Stone Mountain-Standing Peachtree Trail*, which in turn was a spur of *Hightower Trail*.

The **Stone Mountain** route continued westward, passing below Stone Mountain and through **Decatur** to a junction just east of present-day **Piedmont Park** in **Atlanta**. At that point, the *Sandtown Road* turned southward and continued through the center of downtown

McIntosh Trail – Though saplings, larger trees and undergrowth today have reclaimed the land, an abandoned and forgotten stretch of the original *McIntosh Trail* in the former *McIntosh Reserve* of present-day Carroll County, Georgia, is still reasonably identifiable through the forest. This ancient former Indian trail, discovered prior to his death by the late Marion Hemperley, former deputy surveyor-general of Georgia, is just north of and parallel to the Chattahoochee River in the *Reserve*. (Photo courtesy of Marion Hemperley)

Atlanta before again turning westward to travel over present-day Cascade Road.

Prior to being named "Cascade Road," that route was known as *"Sandtown Road,"* a name retained today in a short street just north of the site formerly occupied by what once was known as *Fort McPherson* in *west-Atlanta*.

Continuing out Cascade Road, the old trace reached *Sandtown* community on the Chattahoochee River in what today has become the *Fulton Industrial Complex. "Sandtown"* was the name of the original Indian town in that area, and was a designation retained by pioneer settlers when they moved into the locality in 1827. In earlier days (prior to 1826 when this section was ceded to Georgia), the *Sandtown* community was the stronghold of a notorious band of outlaws known as *"the Pony Boys."*

In the years when *Sandtown* was still *Indian Territory*, it was known as an extremely lawless and uncivilized region, but not necessarily because of the Indians. Prior to 1826, before the *Creek Nation* ceded this region to the United States, White authorities had no jurisdiction since the land existed within the confines of *Creek Indian Territory*. White outlaws in this vicinity therefore were beyond the reach of White authorities. *Sandtown* therefore was strategically important not only to westward travelers, but also as a profitable location for operations by outlaw groups.

Among their many crimes, *the Pony Boys* engaged in wide-ranging cattle rustling, robbery, murder and general pillaging. Westward migrating Whites weren't their only victims either. According to records, even the local Indians complained bitterly of the outlaw activities. The *Pony Boys'* outlawry was mentioned in records as late as 1836 among the Indians, but by this time, this criminal element had probably relocated their base of operations further westward into what today is *Carroll County*.

Beyond the Chattahoochee River, the roads from the three ferries (*Turner's, Howell's, and Aderhold's*) converged at a ford on Sweetwater Creek about one mile southeast of today's *Austell*. A portion of one of those original thoroughfares is still known today as *"Old Alabama Road."* The united routes continued westward over Sweetwater Creek, passing below *Austell* and following closely the present-day route of U.S. Highway 78.

The road continued on through *Lithia Springs* and *Douglasville* where it turned northwest onto today's Chicago Avenue. From this point, the *Lower Alabama Road* turned in a more westerly direction where the modern highway becomes Chicago Road before passing through the now-vanished town of *"Dark Corner."*

This former community is one of Georgia's more interesting and intriguing – yet little covered – sites. The name signifies that in pioneer days, this town was a place with a bad reputation. It is not known today just when *Dark Corner* gained its name, but the community existed prior to the

U.S. Civil War, because it appears on the maps of that day. It was physically located in Land Lot #166, District 6, *Douglas County*, at the first intersection of today's roads north of *Winston*.

On December 29, 1845, a post office – *"Dark Corner"* – was established there, with Samuel Wilson appointed as the first postmaster. The post office was discontinued in 1866, and then reestablished the following year. *Dark Corner*, however, faded into insignificance with the development of nearby *Douglasville* to the southeast and *Villa Rica* to the west. The post office was finally discontinued permanently on January 12, 1883, and thereafter, the town gradually disappeared completely. Today, little more than a couple of ancient graveyards mark the former community for posterity.

Continuing westward, the *Lower Alabama Road* followed today's *Pine Mountain Road*, passing the present-day *"Flying-S Ranch Airport"* before reaching *Old Villa Rica*, located just north of the present-day city of that name. The old town existed on both sides of today's Georgia Highway 61 just south of its junction with Pine Mountain Road. A well-beaten path was made to this locale when gold was discovered here in the 1830s, and the development of this segment of the *Lower Alabama Road* was undoubtedly enhanced by the intoxicating presence of the precious metal. The town's name, translated into English, means "Rich House" or "House of Riches."

In the 1880s, when the city of *Villa Rica* was relocated southward in order to take advantage of the commercial benefits offered by the Georgia

> *The name signifies that in pioneer days, this town was a place with a bad reputation.*

Pacific (and later the Southern) Railroad, *"old" Villa Rica* became known as *"Fullertown."* The name can still occasionally be found there today, but as *"Fullerville."*

Nearby, old *Pine Mountain Gold Mine*, an abandoned sulfur mine, and an old copper mine, all once existed. In earlier days, this mining section was a beehive of activity, particularly during *Villa Rica's* gold-rush times. It was largely for this reason that this route of the *Lower Alabama Road* came to be known as *"The Road by Villa Rica."*

Leaving old *Villa Rica*, the *Lower Alabama Road* swung northwestward for a short distance to avoid a stretch of high rugged hills which existed directly ahead. The old road passed by present-day *Willis Lake* and *Wesley Church* before turning almost directly west to pass *Fairview Church* and *Mt. Carmel School*. Passing just north of present-day *Temple*, Georgia, the *Lower Alabama Road* continued on into *Haralson County* and through *"Burnt Stand,"* one of Georgia's more enduring place-name mysteries.

"Burnt Stand. . ." What an intriguing name. What was this place? What happened to it? Why are there no signs of it today? What did its name signify?

In early pioneer terminology, a "stand" was either an inn, a saloon/

A well-beaten path was made to this locale when gold was discovered here in the 1830s, and the development of this segment of the Lower Alabama Road was undoubtedly enhanced by the intoxicating presence of the precious metal.

tavern, or a house of entertainment, and in many cases, included some of all of the above. By virtue of the clientele it attracted, a stand could be a dangerous place, particularly when it was located on the American frontier, away from civilization.

The term "burnt" obviously indicates that whatever structure(s) which once existed at the site was/were at some point in time "burnt." The designation is curious, since the name *"Burnt Stand"* is attached to any number of sites throughout Georgia. Due to the volatility of the clientele of such sites, and the fact that they were warmed by the hot hearths inside these structures, and lit by oil lamps and frequented by individuals who often smoked tobacco, there were also any number of methods that such a site could easily frequently burn to the ground.

The *Burnt Stand* in present-day *Haralson County* was located in Land Lot 62, District 7, between *Buchanan* and *Tallapoosa*. The site was in existence during the U.S. Civil War, but no record indicates that a post office was ever established there.

Just south of that area was a very interesting section that developed during the latter part of the nineteenth century. A large vineyard was planted and once flourished at this spot, providing grapes for the making of wine. Post offices named *"Nitra"* and *"Budapest"* were established for short times, and the vineyards produced large quantities of grapes for many years. On a visit to the area in 1966, one large grape vine was found to be still in existence at this site, the others having long-since completely disappeared.

Another interesting site nearby was once identified as *"Holland's Gold Mine."* A post office by that name once existed just south of **Tallapoosa** on Walker's Creek.

Continuing westward, the *Lower Alabama Road* intersected present-day Georgia Highway 120 to the southwest of **Buchanan**. This junction is in a sharp curve where Beech Creek has cut a gap through a high north-south ridge abreast of the road. In that area, *GA 120* follows, almost exactly, the original route of the old *Etowah Trail*.

Colonel Benjamin Hawkins traveled over the *Etowah Trail* in 1796 on his way to assume duties as Indian agent near present-day **Columbus**, Georgia. In his journal, Hawkins mentioned that he found the largest beech trees he had ever seen along Beech Creek. These trees were known to still be growing in this vicinity in recent times, but may now have disappeared completely.

The *Etowah Trail* used by Hawkins extended between today's **Cartersville** over a portion of the Cave Spring-Alabama Road, before turning southward to pass **Rockmart** and **Buchanan** prior to intersecting the *Lower Alabama Road*. It (the *Etowah Trail*) continued southwestward through today's **Tallapoosa** on its way to the Creek Indian town of **Arbecoochee** (sometimes spelled *"Abikudshi"*). **Arbecoochee** was situated on both sides of Tallassehatchee Creek, five miles east of the Coosa River,

just above the mouth of Wewoka Creek. The *Etowah Trail* could very well have been an *Alabama Road* itself, although no official record has been discovered naming it as such. The old trail most definitely at least was a cut-off from one *Alabama Road* to another. The *Etowah Trail* and the *Alabama Road by Villa Rica* are among the oldest roads in the Southeast.

The *Lower Alabama Road* continued on westward through **Old Tallapoosa** (located in the northern fringes of the present-day city of the same name. Leaving **Old Tallapoosa**, the *Alabama Road* was known in earlier days as *"the Jacksonville Road,"* a name still remembered by dwindling numbers of old-timers in the area today. The road received its name from pioneer White travelers who used it to reach the area in and around **Jacksonville, Alabama**.

One can thus easily see why the *Alabama Road by Villa Rica* (*Lower Alabama Road*) was so important to early travelers. The route of this thoroughfare was so logical and true that many of our modern highways make use of it today. One wonders just how many travelers today realize they are zipping along where once pioneers rode in wagons, and, before them, Indians trod quietly in leather moccasins, and, before them, hooved migrating wildlife once trod in prehistory.

(Grateful appreciation is sincerely expressed herewith in remembrance of the late Marion R. Hemperley for a portion of the material included in all three of the Alabama Roads articles in this series. Marion served with the Georgia State Surveyor-General Department of Georgia for 30 years, 10 years of which included service as Deputy Surveyor-General. The author rode many miles with him in yesteryear, searching out the ancient pioneer trails of Georgia for research purposes and documentation for posterity.)

Retracing the *Old Federal Road* Across North Georgia

It began in prehistory, first as a migratory trail for ungulates (hooved animals), evolving into a trading path for Native Americans. This simple ancient byway ultimately became a route for wheeled wagons, and witnessed historic incident after historic incident during pioneer days in America. Some of the original trail can still be seen today.

D eep in the mists of pre-history, an early migratory path was created by wandering buffalo, deer, antelope, and other hooved animals. At least as early as the late 18th Century (late 1700s), the Native Americans inhabiting the southeast region of what today is the United States began using one particular path across what today is north Georgia which later came to be known as the "Middle Cherokee Path."[1]

The path stretched from what today is Nashville, Tennessee, diagonally across Georgia down to near what today is Flowery Branch, Georgia. With additional adjoining paths, it stretched all the way down to St. Augustine, Florida.

The usefulness of this path was recognized by early American settlers who envisioned a wagon trail along the route which, following widening and improvement, would become known as *"the Federal Road."* Another branch of the road would be cleared northward to the Cherokee town of Tellico.

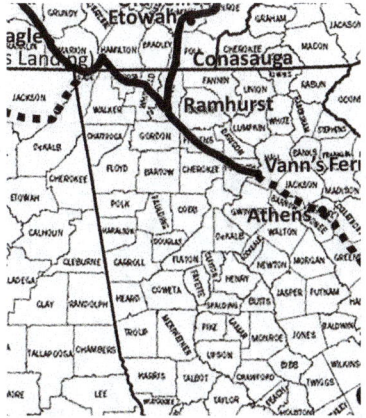

Ancient Path – The Federal Road began at a point near what today is Flowery Branch, Georgia, and extended to Nashville, Tennessee, with an additional branch extending to the Cherokee Indian town of Tellico. Its route lay on an ancient Indian trading path which was eventually enlarged into a road for carts, covered wagons and carriages.

In the early development of the United States, many settlers traveled down the eastern seaboard of the young

185

nation, following the coastal plains of Virginia, North Carolina and South Carolina to Georgia where their travel then turned westward across the Georgia flatlands. Settlers also arrived by boat to the coast of Georgia and traveled inland. The leaders of the youthful United States eventually recognized the need for legitimate travel routes across Georgia in order to populate the vast inland areas.

The inland migration of the early pioneers was continuously frustrated by the fact that at that time, much of the North American continent was covered by immensely-thick forests with even thicker undergrowth beneath them. Any travel beyond the eastern portions of the original colonies was an extremely difficult task involving the hacking and cutting of one's way through the undergrowth if no previously-developed

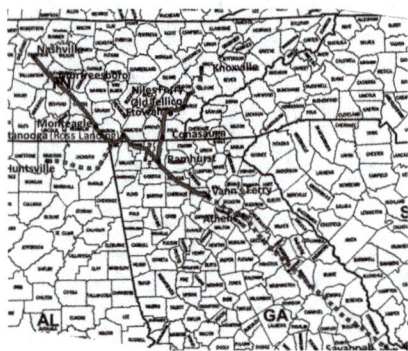

Early Route to Florida – Traveling southeastward, with associated side paths extending down the Georgia coast, the ancient trail which ultimately evolved into the *Federal Road* originated as an early trading path of prehistoric Native Americans all the way to what today is Florida. Natives traveled the byway almost to the Georgia coast, thence, by sidepaths to what today is Savannah, Georgia, and on down to Florida, or, reversing direction, northward to prehistoric Tellico or the vicinity of what today is Knoxville, Tennessee and over to Huntsville, Alabama.

Native American trading path was available for use.

With the evolution of "wheeled" transport in this inland migration, even the Native American trading paths proved to be insufficient for navigation. In order for two-wheeled and four-wheeled carts (and later covered wagons and stagecoaches) to be able to navigate the realm, it quickly became obvious to the leaders of the young American nation that any usable path first would have to be widened and cleared of trees, stumps, rocks and boulders. The 1791 *Treaty of Holston* sparked the initial planning for the road, and the nation's leaders made certain it contained the stipulation: *"citizens of the United States shall have a free and unmolested use of the road."*[2]

Road Specifications

The "Federal Road" in Georgia actually gained impetus as an official project of the federal government in 1805, following the signatory in Tennessee of the *Treaty of Tellico* between the United States and the Cherokee Nation. Interestingly, just as with the *Treaty of New Echota* which sold away the Cherokee lands in north Georgia, and the *Treaty of Indian Spring* which sold away the Creek Indian lands in south Georgia, only a fraction of the Cherokee leadership signed the *Treaty of Tellico* authorizing the Federal Road. Of the more than 100 Cherokee chiefs, only fourteen – including principal chief Black Fox – actually signed the paper document, but that was enough for the U.S. government.

Not long after the treaty for the road across north Georgia was signed, Chief Doublehead – who originally had opposed it – was murdered by his fellow Cherokees, due no doubt to the fact that he had changed his mind and become a supporter of the treaty, and thus seemed to be acting more for his personal gain than for that of the Cherokee people. Rumors of bribes and gifts to those chiefs who supported this and other similar measures were considerable.

Part of the agreement between the U.S. federal government and the Cherokee Nation included the fact that the Cherokees themselves would be tasked with expanding the *Middle Cherokee Path* to create "the Federal Road." They were required not only to make it wide enough to accommodate wheeled vehicles, but also *"those vehicles with pack animals and the wagons used by mail carriers and stagecoaches."* In return for various "incentives," the government wanted the Cherokees to be responsible for "the lion's share" of the creation of this new navigable road across Georgia. The Cherokee leadership quickly realized they would have to officially authorize this road improvement in order to obtain the necessary man-power to make it happen.

Once the Federal Road became a part of Cherokee law, the Cherokee Council detailed how the road should look: *"The road to be cut and opened twenty-four feet wide, clear of trees, and the causewaying to be covered with dirt, together with the digging of mountains and hills, to be fourteen feet wide, clear of rocks, roots, grubs, and the banks of all water courses to be put in complete order."*

As stated, the enlargement of a "path" into a "road" meant not only widening the path, but clearing the brush, obstructing stumps, fallen trees, rocks and boulders, as well as finding ways to ease the difficulties of traveling over the streams and rivers along the route. The terms also included the continued maintenance of the road, keeping it clear of new growth and/or any fallen trees or other obstacles. How the

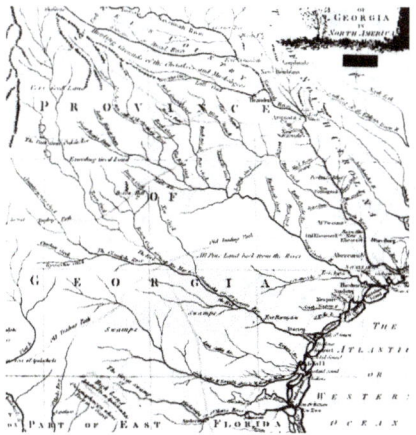

Vast Wilderness – The early maps of the state of Georgia were, as one might imagine, somewhat crude. They nevertheless do indicate that the region was composed essentially of scant pathways – mainly a few Indian trading paths. The remaining terrain was covered with thick forests and undergrowth, numerous streams and rivers.

native Cherokees were able to accomplish these tasks without road building skills or earth-moving equipment is unknown today.

As a portion of the enticement for improvement and use of this road, the U.S. federal government agreed to allow the Cherokees to operate "toll roads" on portions of the Federal Road. Rates charged by the Cherokees included: Wagon and Team: $1.00; Wagon and two horses: $.75; Wagon and one horse: $.50; Two-wheeled carriage: $.50; Man and horse: twelve and one-half cents; Loose horses: six and one-quarter cents; Hogs, sheep, goats: one cent each.[3]

Part of the problem with innovations such as the Federal Road lay in the fact that the Native Americans who actually profited from the venture tended to be the ones who were the better-educated and wealthier leaders. The average run-of-the-mill Cherokee citizen

Early Ferries – This artist's rendering shows a typical north Georgia ferryboat transporting a covered wagon and team across a river. Commercial ferryboat endeavors such as this were quite prevalent across the streams and rivers of Georgia from the late-18th century to the early 20th century, particularly along the *Federal Road* in *Cherokee Indian Territory* in the early 1800s.

gained nothing except the aggravation of overwhelming White immigrants who usurped Indian property, and, in general, made the lives of these Cherokees an unpleasant existence at best. For that and other reasons, many of the Cherokee leaders were often assassinated by their brethren.

Important Route

Over the years, the Federal Road across Georgia would eventually be used by a number of U.S. presidents traveling to various points. It also would be an important avenue in the Georgia gold rush of 1829; the removal of the Cherokee Indians on what came to be known as "the trail of tears" in 1838; the U.S. Civil War in 1864-65; and numerous other important events.

Nevertheless, prior to their removal in 1838, numerous prominent Cherokee Indians built ferries, plantations, stagecoach "stands", public houses and taverns from 1804 to 1838, a few of which can still be seen today at preserved sites. Many of these commercial endeavors eventually made the owners very wealthy men for their day and time.

Today, all along the former route of the Federal Road, highway markers identify the former byway, as well as sites of historic significance along it. Some of the former route of the road passes through what today are suburban developments, rural farmland, public parks, mountains and industrial sites. Other portions of the road still exist today on modern highways, confirming the logistical accuracy of the route.

If one drives the route across Georgia today, one should anticipate a driving tour of about three and a half hours – possibly more, dependent upon traffic and the time of day. Throughout this route, though most of them have long since disappeared from the landscape, the former sites of the early public houses, taverns, bridges, inns, historic private homes, gristmills, U.S. Army forts, missionary stations, ferries, and much more, are often indicated by historic markers along the route for travelers.

Interestingly, early U.S. government policy toward the native Indians of the Southeast was one of "encouragement" to settle upon farms, and modest commercial interests such as gristmills, inns, taverns, and ferries, moving away from the traditional "hunter-gatherer" lifestyles which had been the historic mode of existence for the Indians. It initially was believed this would aid in the assimilation of Cherokees into the White culture.[4]

Cherokee Destiny

The Cherokee Nation essentially was divided on the issue of the White incursion into the realm once completely controlled by the natives. Some – known as the *Upper Town* natives – were in favor of the creation of the Federal Road and development along the route, resigning themselves to the fact that the hoards of White settlers were endless and settlement inevitable. Others – known as the *Lower Town* natives – more generally opposed the road and any development. They were worried – justifiably so – that the Americans would not respect Cherokee sovereignty and ownership.

The leader of the *Lower Town* chiefs – Chief Doublehead – made a long statement against new roads in 1801, arguing that the Americans should not turn the existing footpaths into wagon trails, because too much violence and theft had already occurred. He would later change his tune as more incentives were directed his way.[5]

Conversely, *Upper Town* chiefs such as the prominent and wealthy James Vann, strongly supported the road because they knew that since the Americans were coming, regardless of the circumstances, the Cherokees should make the best deals possible in advance. They also saw the "civilization" of their tribesmen as necessary for assimilation into the White culture, which they felt would be the Cherokee's salvation. Amazingly, had it not been for the discovery of gold within Cherokee Indian Territory in north Georgia in 1828, this assimilatory strategy might actually have been successful.

The value of Vann's strong support of the road was not lost upon federal officials. In 1803, Indian Agent Return J. Meigs very pointedly recommended James Vann's involvement, describing him as one of numerous Cherokees certain to construct effective public houses, ferries and gristmills along the road's route. *"Vann will establish a good house of entertainment on the Chattahoochee where the road will cross that river, and*

Imposing Figure – James Clement Vann II was a very intelligent yet indomitable Cherokee leader as illustrated in this artist's rendering created shortly before his death implies. Unfortunately, he was also a legal taskmaster who brooked no violations of Cherokee laws by his people, and was quick to punish those who did. He also had the misfortune of imbibing in alcoholic beverages a bit too often, and of becoming abusive when intoxicated. He eventually met with death by an assassin's bullet, the perpetrator of which was never identified.

will keep horses always ready for the mail carriers if required," Meigs wrote.[6]

Nevertheless, well-prior to 1828, the Federal Road was built across Georgia following the route of the ancient Indian path. All along this route, commerce sprang up at every stream, river, overnighting spot, and gristmill site. In order to facilitate the cooperation of the Cherokees, enticements of many variations were offered to the more prominent leaders.

According to records, James Vann received an entire series of privileges, including exclusive ferry rights over the Chattahoochee, a contract for administration of the U.S Postal workers along the road, and also promises to provide special assistance to some of his friends in Vann's name. Rumors of bribes such as these ultimately became so widespread that the treaty was specifically written to deny such privileges, stating that the Cherokee chiefs *"were not influenced by pecuniary motives."*[7]

Located today in the northwestern corner of Forsyth County where the Old Federal Road intersects with Highway 369, the crossroads at *Hightower* (called *"Ite-wah"* by the Cherokees) was the site of *Scudder's Inn*, an early establishment on the Federal Road. Jacob Scudder was an American citizen and veteran of the War of 1812, who maintained an inn at this site from 1817 to 1831. This site was also the location for some of the early elections in 1832, following the formation of Forsyth County from a portion of Cherokee County.

Unlike many owners of "stands" and stores, Scudder was not a Cherokee, and never accepted Cherokee laws. At least once, he refused to pay a tax the Cherokees levied upon him, and they responded by fining him and seizing some of his property.

The U.S. military also established a presence at the intersection at Hightower in 1830-1831, when it constructed a small fort to protect the interests of gold miners. Named "Camp Gilmer" after then Gov. George Gilmer, this site existed – contrary to the later Indian removal forts – to protect U.S. citizens involved in conflicts with the Cherokees. One example of those conflicts was the incident in 1833, when some thirty Cherokees near Scudder's Inn adjacent to the fort fought a similar number of U.S. citizens in a serious – but ultimately not deadly

– dispute over access to nearby gold mining property.

Yet another very serious incident occurred earlier, just a few miles up the Federal Road from this site in 1809. Cherokee Chief James Vann II, as previously indicated, was one of the primary proponents of the creation of the Federal Road, and his enterprising skills at commercial endeavors continue to be reflected today in his impressive mansion which still stands in Spring Place, Georgia, near Chattsworth. He, however, fell victim to a strange murder that year.

Vann Assassination

Aside from his support for the Federal Road and the great wealth it eventually provided to Vann, he also was a strict taskmaster when it came to Cherokee law and the violation thereof. He was known to quickly administer punishments, often including very painful public whippings to those Cherokees found to be in violation of any laws. Due to this strict posture, as well as his proclivity for rash behavior when under the influence of alcoholic beverages, he was known to have made a number of enemies.

On a cold winter evening in February of 1809, Vann fell victim to an assassin's bullet at Buffington's Tavern near the present-day Forsyth/Cherokee County line in Georgia, just a couple of miles from Hightower. Though it is known – from records maintained by missionaries who lived at his home at Spring Place – that the site of this murder was "Buffington's Tavern," the physical location of Buffington's has been lost to history over the years, becoming a bone of contention among historians in recent years. The actual site of Vann's grave, strangely, has been lost to history as well.

This, and other similar incidents, are examples of the history and intrigue

Impressive Residence – As an indication of the wealth he enjoyed, James Vann contracted for the construction of this exceptional mansion at Spring Place near present-day Chatsworth, Georgia. This home and property are a Georgia historic site today, protected by the Georgia Department of Natural Resources, Historic Parks Division. (Photo courtesy of the Georgia Dept. of Natural Resources, Atlanta, GA)

which lie all along the route of the Old Federal Road in Georgia. Most all of the incidents are captivating in subject-matter, and offer an interesting glimpse into pioneer life in Georgia.

Much of the controversial issue of the location of Vann's grave stems from a tendency of the general public – and even of some respected historians – to perpetuate myths and false stories created in the absence of factual information. Vann's grave no doubt exists in the general vicinity of historic Blackburn Cemetery near a tiny crossroads community known as "Hightower" on the Federal Road. The grave site, however, has been totally confused with other graves and even possibly with the actual cemetery site.

In addition to his previously-mentioned plantations and other properties, Vann also operated a stagecoach stop ("stand"), a trading post and tavern on the Federal Road near Eton, Georgia, as well as a ferry and inn where the Federal Road crossed the Chattahoochee River in present-day Forsyth County. He also had a second plantation near that same location along the fertile river bottomlands now covered by the waters of Lake Lanier.

At the site where the Federal Road crossed the Conasauga River just west of his home at *Spring Place* Vann owned yet another ferry, as well as a mill on Vann's Mill Creek, a tributary of the Conasauga. *(Note: The Federal Road crossed the Conasauga on Lot #149, District 9, Section 3, according to the 1832 surveys of old Cherokee County by David Duke, D.S., June, 1832).*

Buffington's or Blackburn's?

Though described as having occurred at several different sites throughout most of the more than two centuries

Vann's Tavern – James Vann II was traveling to his (Vann's) public house (pictured) which once existed on the Chattahoochee River near the present-day Forsyth – Hall county line, when he was assassinated while pausing at *Buffington's Tavern* in present-day Cherokee County. Built around 1800, *Vann's Tavern* survived the ravages of time, but was about to be inundated by the rising waters of then-newly-constructed Lake Lanier in 1956 when it was rescued. It was dismantled and removed to the state historic site, *New Echota*, near Calhoun, Georgia, where it was reconstructed for permanent display. *New Echota* was the last capital of the Cherokee Nation in the southeast prior to relocation of the tribe to the West.

since it transpired, Vann's murder is believed by most researchers to have taken place at Buffington's Tavern, but beyond that point, little agreement exists regarding the actual site of this former inn. The physical remnants of Buffington's disappeared long ago, and its assumed site has become confused with Blackburn's Public House in present-day Forsyth.

Many individuals for many years identified an old log structure which once existed across the road from the old Sherrill home on the Old Federal Road in Forsyth County as the remains of Buffington's Tavern, but nothing could be further from the truth, according to the late Forsyth County Historian Don L. Shadburn who did considerable research on the topic, and who has written extensively on the Cherokees of Georgia

in his seminal *"Cherokee Planters, 1832-1838"* (1989).

"That's true," Shadburn confirmed in an interview prior to his death. "Vann was killed at Buffington's Tavern, and Buffington's Tavern was on the old Federal Road not far from the Sherrill Place, but it (Buffington's) isn't the old structure (which existed) across the road from the Sherrills. That structure is part of what used to be Lewis Blackburn's Public House built around 1820. It (Blackburn's Public House) is very historic in its own right, but it is not Buffington's Tavern."

The structure which once existed across from the old Sherrill home to which Shadburn refers was moved in recent years from that site to the Cumming, Georgia, fairgrounds where it has been put on public exposition. Some individuals have declared this structure to have been the actual site of Vann's murder. There, however, is no definitive evidence to support this contention.

Constructed of heavy log timbers 20" x 6" x 32', Blackburn's Public House is immensely sturdy, accounting for its endurance. It is awe-inspiring to stand in the doorway of this building and understand the history that has passed across its threshold over the past 200+ years.

"Part of the confusion between Buffington's Tavern and Blackburn's Public House centers around the fact that Lewis Blackburn married Tom Buffington's widow after Tom died," Shadburn added. "Lewis and the former Mrs. Buffington lived at Buffington's Tavern for a short while before moving to Blackburn's Public House when it existed at the site on which the Sherrill home later was built. (In contrast) Buffington's Tavern actually existed on up the old Federal Road from the Sherrill Place (back toward Canton), and was on the right, just across the Forsyth County line in Cherokee County."

This specification by Shadburn that Buffington's Tavern existed on the "right" side of the road is a critical detail. It is known for a fact that the public house formerly existing on the Sherrill property and later removed to the Cumming Fairgrounds was originally built on the "left" side of the road as one proceeds toward Canton, not on the right.

Ebenezer Newton's Diary

The information in *Ebenezer Newton's* (who was an eye-witness to the site in October of 1818) *Diary* provides a measure of identification of Vann's actual gravesite. In his journal describing his trip, Newton details how his travels led him to Vann's Tavern on the

Ebenezer Newton's Diary – In the early 1980s, Rev. Charles O. Walker, a noted and respected historian and illustrator recreated this historically accurate depiction of Vann's grave on the *Federal Road*, based upon a description recorded in the diary of traveler Ebenezer Newton in 1818 and other documentation. It is worth noting that the public house in this depiction is accurately placed on the "left" or "south" side of the *Federal Road* as one travels toward Canton as was noted by Newton. This location was also originally occupied by the historic pioneer public house which once existed at the old Sherrill property in Forsyth until 2004. Conversely, the site at which Vann was murdered – *"Buffington's Tavern"* – was located on the "right" or "north" side of the road, a critical detail which has left modern researchers in disagreement regarding determination of the actual murder site. (Illustration courtesy of Rev. Charles O. Walker. All rights reserved. Re-printed with permission.)

Chattahoochee River and how, the following morning, he continued on up the road toward Tennessee. *"Soon after we passed the 'High tower' by the Indians called 'It-towah'* (Etowah River), *and came to the top of the hill, we observed by the roadside on an eminence, a tomb, paled in and painted black, with an inscription at the head on a board: 'Here lies the body of James Vann who departed this life Feb. 1809, aged 43.'"* The description of this gravesite almost perfectly describes present-day Blackburn Cemetery.

The Sherrill family stated categorically that they moved the historic public house on their property, rolling it upon logs from the left side of the Old Federal Road (as one travels toward Canton) to the right, in order that they might build their home on that desirable site many years ago. The former Sherrill property public house (now on exposition in Cumming) therefore almost certainly was Lewis Blackburn's Public House, and NOT the site of Vann's murder.

Shadburn said another myth involving Vann and his death included Vann's sister – Nancy Falling/Fawling – who supposedly lived across the road from Buffington's Tavern. "That's just another case in which the facts have been embellished and twisted," he explained. "Nancy lived south of Spring Place at Vann's home (on the Federal Road) near present-day Chatsworth."

For years, local folklore has maintained that Nancy's supposed residence across the Federal Road from Buffington's Tavern in some way connected her with Vann's death. Vann was, in fact, responsible for the death of Nancy's husband – John Fawling – but no definite connection between her and Vann's death has ever been established.

Nevertheless, many historians today do agree that it quite probably was Falling's family which was in fact responsible for Vann's death, as was the Cherokee custom at that time. It was during one of his fits of anger while under the influence of liquor, that Vann reportedly was responsible for Fawling's death in a shooting incident.

It is ironic that history has chosen to characterize Vann as violent and abusive. An argument could be made for the fact that he was a victim of circumstances beyond his control in a quest to best portray his section of the Cherokee Nation as law-abiding and socially acceptable in the face of an advancing tide of White settlers who were by this time openly seeking reasons to displace the natives.

Vann Justified?

It is well documented that Vann was quick to administer punishment to criminals, a practice which no doubt enhanced his reputation as a man of cruelty. The fact that is not so well documented, is that in doing so, Vann was actually carrying out Cherokee law as decided by the entire Cherokee Nation. He also undoubtedly was helping to diminish lawlessness among his people in a desperate attempt to enhance their assimilation into the White culture.

Indeed, in the **Laws of the Cherokees**, published in the **Cherokee Advocate** at Tahlequah, Oklahoma in 1852, a glimpse into Indian life on the frontier is provided. One of the laws (in an order from the chiefs and warriors in *National Council* at *Broom's Town* on September 11, 1808, the year prior to Vann's murder) provided for the formation of *"regulating companies"* of one captain, one lieutenant and four privates each, for the purpose of arresting horse thieves and protecting property.

The penalty in the Cherokee Nation for stealing a horse was 100 lashes on the bare back of the thief, be it male or female, and fewer lashes for things of less value, and if a thief resisted the regulators with gun, axe, spear or knife, he or she could be killed on the spot. This law was signed by Black Fox, principal chief; Charles Hicks, secretary to the Council; Path Killer; and Toochalar, all of whom formed the inner circle of Cherokee leadership at the time.

Even more interesting, this same National Council barely a year and a half later on April 10, 1810 (a year after Vann's death) passed the following law: *"Be it known that this day the various clans and* tribes which compose the Cherokee Nation have agreed that should it happen that a brother, forgetting his natural affection, should use his hand in anger and kill his brother, he shall be accounted guilty of murder and suffer accordingly; and if a man has a horse stolen, and overtakes the thief, and should his anger be so great as to cause him to kill him, let his blood remain on his own conscience, but no satisfaction shall be demanded for his life from his relatives or the clan to which he may belong."

One of the more enlightened and enduring achievements of Vann was his association and support of Moravian missionaries whom he allowed to establish a mission near his home at Spring Place. Though he was not such a strong advocate or apostate of the religion they preached, Vann highly valued the educational benefits they offered to the Cherokees.

It is from the diaries kept by the Moravians that one of the most reliable accounts of Vann's murder is described. On February 21, 1809, the following entry was made:

"We received the startling news of the murder of Mr. Vann. Here and there, he and his had punished Indians for stealing. When one of them refused to surrender, Vann ordered him to be shot.

"For a few days thereafter, Vann stopped at the tavern of a half-breed, Tom Buffington, about 56 miles from here. While there, he drank heavily and became involved in altercations with some of his friends for whom he had taken a violent dislike. He feuded with them, was most abusive, and made violent threats.

"Toward midnight, Vann stepped out of the tavern and stood before the open door, when suddenly, a shot was fired from without which pierced his heart. He fell lifeless to the floor without his perpetrator being seen.

"After hearing the shot, Joseph, his son, and a Negro rapidly gathered up the belongings of father and son, including Vann's 'pocketbook' with a considerable amount of cash and bank notes. Wrapped in a blanket, Joseph with the Negro fled to his father's plantation on the Chattahoochee River, 13 miles from Buffington's Tavern.

"At the crack of dawn, Mrs. Vann and other members of the family fled to Buffington's but before they arrived, Vann's body had been buried in the woods not far from the road."

Grave Mystery

It was this and similar descriptions by the Moravians and others which have led historians and residents to believe that Vann's grave was located at the site of "Buffington's Tavern," but how can this be, if the cemetery in which he is believed to have been buried – Blackburn – exists not near Buffington's, but rather Blackburn's Public House?

"There's no doubt that Blackburn Cemetery or its general vicinity is the burial site," Shadburn added. "In Ebenezer Newton's diary of that day, he describes how he was traveling on the Federal Road from Athens, Georgia to Tennessee, and how his travels led him to Vann's Tavern on the Chattahoochee River, and the following morning to Hightower (Etowah River), where he suddenly encountered a grave on the right *'on an eminence, paled in and painted, with a headboard and inscription which read: "Here Lies The Body Of James Vann Who Departed This Life February, 1809, Aged 40.'"* Newton's description of the location of Vann's grave almost perfectly fits the description of present-day Blackburn Cemetery," Shadburn smiled.

But, the story doesn't end there. In the 1960s, when a team of what has been

Natives of Dahlonega? – This photograph, taken by A. Bogarduss of New York, was identified as having been made in "Lumpkin County, Georgia," almost certainly at some point between the 1830s and 1860. The photo was donated by *"Gaillard sisters,"* the Gaillards once being a family of note in Dahlonega. *Gaillard Hall*, a *University of North Georgia* (in Dahlonega) residence hall was endowed by the family. The first-known "photograph" in the United States was created in 1826. It is unknown whether the two pictured females were photographed prior to the Cherokee removal in 1838, or if they had later returned to Lumpkin for a visit and were photographed at that time. They, nevertheless, were almost certainly of Cherokee lineage. They may possibly have even visited from the *Qualla Indian Reservation* in North Carolina to which many Cherokees fled to freedom in 1838. The hair styles, appearance, clothing and shoes of these two females leave no doubt about their heritage. (Photo courtesy of the GA Dept. of Archives & History, Atlanta, GA)

described as "amateur archaeologists" and a descendant of Vann – Mr. J. Raymond Vann of Mt. Vernon, New York – exhumed what they and many others assumed to be the remains of James Vann, they received a surprise. According to an associated article in the *Atlanta Journal*, of August 29, 1962:

"*Dalton archaeologist Wayne Yeager has confirmed that he removed the skeleton of Chief Vann from his grave near Ball Ground, Georgia, and brought the remains to a local funeral home which he declined to name.*

"*The local archaeologist said it took seven hours to exhume the remains from the old Blackburn family cemetery on the Etowah River between Ball Ground and Cumming. Mr. Yeager said the skeleton is in good condition considering that it has been 153 years since Chief Vann's death.*

"*Mr. Yeager said he is positive that he has the right skeleton because of several factors:*

"*No. 1 is that local residents pinpointed the grave from local common knowledge, although it was not marked.*

"*No. 2, the upper right arm bone had been fractured as if by a bullet. Mr. Yeager said Chief Vann fought a political duel from horseback with his brother-in-law, John Fawling, shortly before his death, and accounts of the duel say that Fawling was killed and Chief Vann was hit in the right arm by a bullet.*

"*No. 3, Mr. Yeager has compared the shirt buttons found in the grave and the buttons of a shirt of the same era, and found them to be the same. The shirt used for comparison belonged to Tarleton Lewis, an ancestor of Mr. B.J. Bundy, (a Dalton historian).*

"***Mr. Yeager said the grave was located on property owned by Mr. and Mrs. Ernest Sherrill, and that Mr. Sherrill's 94-year-old aunt, known*** *only as 'Becky,' stated that she could re-member when the grave was marked with a wooden slab.*

"In fact, after the Georgia Historical Commission established the location of the grave, Mr. Sherrill piled brush over it and refused to tell curious historians where it was located in fear that they might dig into the grave.

"However, Mr. Sherrill did show the grave to Raymond Vann and Mr. Vann secured an order from Forsyth County Ordinary A.B. Tollison to exhume his ancestor. Mr. Tollison acted as an official witness during the excavation.

"Found in the grave were seven glass buttons, approximately 50 nails from the coffin, and a belt buckle. Mr. Yeager said the bottom of the grave was in the exact shape of the old-time wooden coffins.

"Mr. Yeager (also) said two gold rings were discovered on the hands of the skeleton, *and these rings are now being cleaned by Jack Zbar, another Dalton archaeologist and chemist. The rings appear to be inscribed, but the cleaning process has not been finished."*

On the surface, the exhumation described in the 1962 *Atlanta Journal* article sounded very conclusive, and seemed to convincingly identify Vann's grave, but was it accurate? Perhaps. Perhaps not.

In the early 1990s, Clifford Ruddell had lived in the vicinity of Blackburn Cemetery most of his life, and he well remembered the day the remains were removed from the grave site. He was one of the diggers hired to perform the labor.

"We dug for a good long while, and then all of a sudden, we were into the bones," he explained. "They told us to get out of the hole, and they jumped in with all these little tools and brushes.

"Eventually, when they had collected all they wanted from the grave; they put it in bags and then left," he

continued. "I don't remember exactly how long it was, but later on, they came back, and I think they put the bones or something back into the grave, and then they covered it all back over. That always struck me as kinda strange."

Strange indeed. For far from ending a controversy, the exhumation of this grave actually began spawning additional ones.

More Grave Mystery

In the ***Dalton Daily News*** of August 29, 1962, a bold headline proclaimed *"Vann Excavation Stirs Controversy."* The article went on to describe how state and local officials were casting considerable doubt on the findings of Yeager and Zbar as well as their credentials. The article stated:

"...Dalton amateur archaeologist Wayne Yeager has stirred a controversy among historians and archaeologists throughout the state. Doubt has been expressed on the part of at least one archaeologist, Clemens deBaillou, as to whether the remains of Chief Vann have actually been found.

"However, on the other hand, the Rev. Mr. Yeager, a Baptist minister, said today that an inscription uncovered on one of the gold rings found on the hands of the skeleton (leaves no) doubt in his mind that he found Chief Vann.

"Rev. Yeager said one of the plain, gold rings was inscribed with a 'V', and he doubts very much that anyone else buried in the Blackburn Cemetery in Forsyth County near Ball ground would have had a name starting with the letter 'V.'"

Ironically, the proclaimed discovery of the ring with the "V" inscribed in it greatly complicated (rather than simplified) the issue of identification of the remains. In the April 25, 1971 issue of

Famous Chieftain – An 1834 portrait of Major Ridge by Charles Bird King, in *History of the Indian Tribes of North America*. Ridge was a prominent leader among the Cherokees, and also made a concerted effort to assimilate into the White culture in what today is the state of Georgia. He was one of numerous Cherokees who had a substantial role in the development of the Federal Road through Cherokee Indian Territory in 1805.

the *Chattanooga News-Free Press*, Dalton Historian Mrs. B.J. Bandy said that her investigation of the census records of the early 1800s time-period indicated no one in that area had a name starting with a "V" except the Vanns. Therefore, the likelihood of anyone but James Vann being in possession of, not one, but two gold rings, particularly a ring inscribed with a "V," would have been extremely remote.

Imagine the surprise and disappointment then of all involved, when the analysis of the remains – which were supposed to have been James Vann's bones – reportedly indicated that the bones were "Negroid."

"...the man appointed by the Georgia Historical Commission had been against the whole thing from the start," Mrs. Bandy

continued. *"He was determined that it wasn't Vann. He insisted it was a slave, although I never heard of a slave with a gold ring. He turned in a documentary report against it, so there was nothing we could do.*

"I was just sick," Bandy added, *"but when you have done all you can, you can't do anything else. I took the bones back and re-buried them where we got them (in Blackburn Cemetery)."*

Where then rest the remains of Cherokee Chief James Vann? Do they lie moldering still in some unmarked grave in or around Blackburn Cemetery? Or were those actually James Vann's bones unearthed on a hot summer in August of 1962?

Could James Vann II have been part Negro, thus accounting for the bone analysis? Or could there have been a misinterpretation as Negroid instead of Mongoloid? More serious mistakes than that have certainly been previously made.

"At the very least, I'm convinced those were not the bones of Vann exhumed in 1962," explained historian Don Shadburn. "There were just too many conclusive facts to the contrary. Even the nails used in the coffin apparently were of a type not in existence in 1809. I've seen that report, (by the Georgia Historic Commission done in 1962) and their conclusions were very thorough."

Archaeologists Yeager and Zbar and Historian Bandy later returned to Forsyth County seeking another court order from County Ordinary A.B. Tollison for the exhumation of yet another grave believed to be Vann's, but by that time, Mr. Tollison had endured all he was going to allow. He denied their request.

The exact location of Vann's grave now may never be known, other than the fact that it is somewhere in or near

Blackburn Cemetery on the Old Federal Road in Forsyth County. Despite all of the above, just as some individuals have irresponsibly claimed to have "identified" a historic structure (which may actually be Blackburn's Public House) as Buffington's Tavern, these same individuals have also placed a grave-marker in Blackburn Cemetery "identifying the grave of James Vann II."

Today, the positive identification of the actual sites of Buffington's Tavern and Blackburn's Public House would, in all likelihood, be extremely difficult to ascertain. And as for the positive identification of Vann's actual remains and grave site, the only way that will occur now is if bodies are continuously exhumed in the vicinity of the supposed gravesite until remains which can be proven to be Vann's can be found, and that is highly unlikely to occur.

One important sidebar to this whole affair is that it is painfully unfortunate that a DNA comparison of Mr. Raymond Vann and his ancestor, James Clement Vann II, could not have been effected to ascertain identity at the 1962 exhumation. Under that type of examination, the entire mystery of Vann's grave might have been quickly and positively solved, but unfortunately, such an option simply did not exist at that time. Incidents such as the James Vann murder and the site of his burial lie all along the route of the old Federal Road.

"Rich Joe" Vann

James Vann II and, in turn, his son, Joseph, were easily among the wealthiest of those in the Cherokee Nation. They also rivaled a great deal of the pioneer White population of Georgia in wealth. Young Joe earned the moniker "Rich Joe" Vann by virtue of the immediate and substantial wealth he enjoyed following the elder Vann's assassination in what today is Cherokee County on the Federal Road.

The 1832 plat map for Section 3, District 9, offers a glimpse of the extent of the Vann holdings. The surveyor noted that Joseph Vann owned eight pieces of improved property, including a stand, a residence, several quarters, and land totaling about 450 acres just in this small district, all of which he had inherited upon his father's death. Joseph had also inherited from his father property along both forks of the Federal Road, as well as considerable property between the two forks.[8]

From south to north, the Federal Road passes by the Spring Place Moravian Mission, and just south of the Vann mansion. It continued to the northwest in an area where Joe Vann owned improved land both to the east and to the west. Just north of the spot that the road turns westward, he owned considerable acreage on what was identified as "the Spring Place Road."

On the northern fork of the Federal Road, Joseph owned 90 acres at a spot known as "Vann's Stand" in the vicinity of present-day Chattsworth. Numerous other Cherokees had residences and improved lots in this area as well.

In James Vann II's day, the impressive Vann House had been the site of important meetings even before the Federal Road officially existed – though it did still exist, obviously by virtue of the ancient Native American trading path.

When U.S. commissioners wished to confer with decision-making Cherokee headmen in 1802, they accidentally encountered "a number of Chiefs and head-men" at Vann's place. The commissioners, who often struggled to gain access in one location to this group of Cherokee decision-makers, seized upon

"Rich Joe" Vann – Young Joseph Vann took possession of his murdered father's estate in 1809, including the impressive mansion and holdings all along the *Federal Road*. He lived in luxury for a number of years, but by 1834, the fortunes of the Cherokee Nation as a whole in what today is Georgia were turning, and so also therefore was the wealth in property and holdings of Joe Vann. In the spring of that year, he lost possession of his gristmills and 448 acres of prime land to Georgia "legal codes." A year later, the state of Georgia totally dispossessed Joseph of his remaining property (357 acres, the ferries, the plantations, and significant additional wealth) in the Georgia state land lottery. He also suffered similar losses in his plantation and holdings in Tennessee. Joseph and his family soon were forced to flee their Georgia home and holdings forever.

the opportunity to meet with Vann *"and such other headmen, chiefs and warriors as may be present."*

Young Joe Vann's later wealth was, as described, chiefly the product of inheritance. He was a gentleman planter, slaveholder, miller, public house-keeper (public houses referring to inns and taverns of that day which he owned), a breeder of fine horses, and eventually a steamboat captain.

By 1834, as the fortunes of the Cherokee Nation as a whole in what today is Georgia were expiring, so also was the wealth in property and holdings of Joe Vann. In the spring of that year, Joseph Vann lost possession of his gristmills and 448 acres of prime land to Georgia "legal codes." A year later, he was totally dispossessed of his remaining property (357 acres), as well as the impressive brick mansion which had been constructed by his father in 1804.

The decisive blow to Joseph Vann came in May of 1834, when he filed for an injunction against nineteen White men – essentially "squatters," accused of trespassing on twenty-three lots with his buildings and other improvements. The injunction was granted and recorded in the Murray County Superior Court on June 15 by Judge John W. Hooper. This court action by a "Cherokee" plaintiff, however, was soon ruled to be a violation of Georgia law and Joseph was ordered to "cease and desist" in his legal actions.

In early 1835, with no other course of action other than violence, Joseph Vann was literally driven from his home at the hands of White Georgia Land Lottery winners. He was forced to flee with his family to another plantation on the Tennessee River in Hamilton County, approximately 40 miles distant.

Joseph Vann's story, however, was not all doom and gloom. Though his beautiful property and holdings at Spring Place, the Connestoga and Chattahoochee rivers holdings, and sites up and down the Federal Road, as well as his substantial holdings at another plantation in Tennessee were all confiscated, Joseph was nevertheless awarded substantial compensation for this property. The United States government awarded him $10,459.85

for his holdings in Tennessee, and $26,979.25 for his holdings in Georgia, for a total of $37,439.10. In 1838, that sum was the approximate equivalent of $1,235,490.00 in 2024.[10]

It is therefore somewhat difficult to mourn for Joseph Vann whose family was able to retire fairly comfortably to a new home in Cherokee Indian Territory in Oklahoma. The ones who were truly punished were the average run-of-the-mill Cherokee natives who were turned out of their homes with no place else to go, particularly those in the brutally-cold winter of 1838.

Even Joseph Vann was unable to enjoy his new-found wealth very long. In October of 1844, while racing his steamer "Lucy Walker" on the Ohio River, he over-heated the boiler, reportedly with slabs of salted pork. The steamboat subsequently exploded, killing all on board.[11]

Taloney & Sandersville

Aside from the Moravian missionaries at Spring Place, these purveyors of religion set up a number of other mission stations along the Federal Road, all of which are very historic today. One such site was in what today is Pickens County and was called the Carmel Missionary Station.

The Carmel Station site was located just north of what now is the town of Talking Rock, where the Federal Road turned west along the route of Highway 136 to Blaine. This intersection, which is marked by a highway sign for the "Old Federal Road," was the site of *"Taloney,"* where, in 1819, a Congregationalist and Presbyterian group established a missionary station. Carmel was the second missionary station to the Cherokees in Georgia, after Spring Place.

Taloney was important as a Chero-

kee Indian Territory meeting site. Cherokee and U.S. federal government officials sometimes met there on official business. The federal government placed one of the few early U.S. Post Offices in Cherokee Territory in Carmel, and another at Spring Place.[12]

In the early 1800s, the area around Talking Rock Creek was one of the more heavily settled spots along the Federal Road. Coming from the east, an establishment called *"Daniel Love's"* was located where the road crossed Love's Creek. The road passed by at least four more Cherokee homes before coming to a major intersection.[13]

The *Carmel Missionary Station* existed between the fork of the Federal Road to the west and the Ellijay Road to the north. From this point, traveling just a short ride to the west, the homes of Cherokees George and John (James) Sanders once stood, as well as one more home east of what once was called *"Sandersville."*[14]

Sanders Mill was on Mountain Creek, just northwest of the George Sanders home. George was the son of a Revolutionary War soldier and a Cherokee mother, and a tavern-keeper in Sandersville. He became one of the younger Cherokee chiefs, and ultimately was connected to several incidents of conflict. In 1807 at the Cherokee town of Hiawassee in present-day Tennessee, he, along with James Vann and Major Ridge reportedly murdered Chief Doublehead. Some quarters believe Sanders also later plotted and murdered James Vann.[15]

Since Vann and Ridge both were themselves also later assassinated (in 1809 and 1839 respectively), one cannot avoid sensing a bit of "karma" in the works. Though these men were prolific leaders in their day, pursuing a course of action which they felt was best for the

Cherokee Nation as a whole, they were also perceived by many Cherokee citizens as simply enriching themselves at the expense of the Nation.

The 1832 Land Lottery map shows that Sanders Mill was located very near the Federal Road near the homes and businesses of George and James as well as near to *Carmel Missionary Station*.[16] Cherokee "stands," stores, ferries, gristmills, and much more in fact existed along most sections of the Federal Road.

George Harlan

Just south of Chatsworth on the Federal Road, George Harlan owned a considerable amount of land, and was another of the wealthier Cherokee planters and store owners. He also joined those visionaries wise enough to realize that, if managed carefully, the coming of the Americans would be an exceptional opportunity for the advancement – not the demise – of the Cherokee Nation, and also for commercial profit, not loss for himself.[17]

During his lifetime in what today is Georgia, Harlan also owned five or six structures in the early 1830s near the site of present-day Ramhurst. Just as with the Sanders family, the James Vann family, and many others, Harlan understandably sought to take full advantage of the new commercial and personal opportunities for the Cherokee Nation.

Born circa 1781 in the Cherokee Nation (East), George Harlan was the son of Kati, the daughter of the famous Cherokee, Nan-ye-hi (Nancy Ward) and her third husband, a White man named Ellis Harlan.

George was married four times: to Nancy Sanders (c. 1801-1807); Nancy Vann (c. 1808-1813; no children); Mary Ann May (1815-?); and Eliza Riley (c. 1840; no children).

In 1817 George took a reservation on the Coosawatie River. Some 18 years later in April of 1835, having made his fortune and wise enough to know when to "cut bait," George and Mary Ann removed to Indian Territory in the West, becoming a member of the *"Old Settlers"* – those who departed on their own terms and avoided the disaster later known as *"the Trail of Tears."* George died about 1848 in the Cherokee Nation, Indian Territory, probably in the Tahlequah District of Oklahoma.

Coosawattee

At the spot where today's Highway 136 crosses Talking Rock Creek near the border of Gilmer and Murray counties, the Federal Road crossed the Coosawattee River. Present-day Carter's Dam Road passes over the dam, allowing an excellent view of the place at which all Federal Road travelers originally crossed the Coosawattee. The Cherokee town of Coosawattee was an important spot for the government in the early 1800s.[18]

Prior to the 1800s, a loose confederation of approximately 50 Cherokee towns and villages existed with little inter-community governmental activity. Coosawattee and Old Coosawattee evolved into important centers of governmental activity, serving as the site of council and judicial meetings in the 1820s.

In 1817, the Cherokees divided their nation into eight districts, including the Coosawattee District. Prior to voting upon important measures, the Cherokees conducted meetings in Coosawattee. Law-breakers charged with violations of Cherokee laws was also tried there.[19]

In and around the year 1828, gold was discovered in north Georgia. Intersecting with the Federal Road, Yellow

Vann's Station – Recreated from a historic 1832 Land Lottery plat, *Vann's Station* was once located near present-day Eton (on U.S. Highway 441 near the Georgia-Tennessee state line). According to the plat, it included an inn/tavern and at least two additional structures - possibly a cookhouse and well-house. This way-stop on the old *Federal Road* represented a portion of the financial investments and business endeavors of James Vann II, prior to his murder in 1809. (Illustration by Rev. Charles O. Walker. Reprinted with permission. All rights reserved.)

Creek Road earned its name from the gold that attracted prospectors to that area. The Federal Road was also crucial in the transport of goods to and from the mining operations in north Georgia.

Between 1829 and 1832, some 10,000 prospectors moved into Cherokee Territory in search of the precious yellow metal, many of them traveling upon the Federal Road. One of the larger and more successful of the gold mining operations near the Federal Road was the Franklin Gold Mine, located southeast of Ball Ground near the Etowah River and just southwest of the road.

Economic successes, often include tragedies. The Franklin Mine was one of the many gold mining operations which utilized slaves as primary

Prior to the 1800s, a loose confederation of approximately 50 Cherokee towns and villages existed with little inter-community governmental activity.

labor, and at least once, the timbers supporting the inside ceiling of the mine collapsed, killing a number of workers.

A new missionary station, established at Coosawattee in 1823, was led by Thomas Dawson, an Englishman. Though numerous of the Cherokees at the council at Coosawattee opposed the proposition of building still more mission schools in Cherokee Indian Territory, the Englishman found unexpected support from a wise and prosperous Cherokee Judge – John Martin. With over 60 slaves and land in excess of 300 acres, Martin was easily another of the wealthiest of the Cherokees.

The new Baptist mission under Dawson remained small until 1836, when a number of Cherokees in the area surprisingly converted to Christianity. They were baptized in Talking Rock Creek.[20]

Harnageville

Upon entering present-day Tate, Georgia, the Federal Road passes the sites of two early stands owned by James Daniel and Ambrose Harnage. These stands served as commercial stores, inns, and also as stagecoach stops for travelers, and were collectively known as *"Harnageville."*

In 1830, the governor and state legislature decreed that all Cherokee land was state-owned property. The state also began moving more forcefully to relocate all the native Cherokees to lands in the western United States.

By this point, many prominent Cherokees who had invested their lives and livelihoods into homes and businesses along the Federal Road and elsewhere in Georgia began to realize their efforts at assimilation into the White culture had been in vain. Some of them began the painful process of disposing of their Georgia properties – usually at considerably less than the actual worth – in order to migrate to the Western Cherokee reservation at Tahlequah in Oklahoma. Others continued to doggedly pursue their lives as always, hoping upon hope that an eventual forced migration would not occur.

In 1831, the state of Georgia named the entire Cherokee Indian Territory as one huge county appropriately named "Cherokee County," in preparation for further actions. Cherokee was eventually cut up into numerous smaller counties after being usurped by White owners.

In 1832, the state of Georgia divided the area that had been Cherokee Indian Territory into 160-acre lots (40-acre lots in the gold-bearing areas) and made them available to White owners in the Georgia Land Lottery. It was all very carefully orchestrated to simply take the land from the Cherokees piecemeal, particularly since gold had been discovered throughout the Cherokees' homeland in north Georgia in 1828.

Some 85,000 people submitted names in the lottery. All free White men who lived in Georgia were eligible. When the dust had cleared, 18,309 individuals had become lucky winners of the lands which had once been the sole realm of the Cherokees. Most of the land, however, was not actually made available to its new owners until 1838, when the Cherokees had been forcibly removed.[21]

Also in 1832 (February), a small number of voters from the sprawling new county gathered at *"Harnage's"* for the first elections for offices such as justice of the peace, sheriff, tax collector, and coroner. All White men.

Seeing the handwriting on the wall, Ambrose Harnage finally decided to cut his losses. He sold his business to the Tate family in the mid-1830s, and the town of Tate still bears the Tate name even today, but *"Harnageville"* has been relegated to obscurity. As in numerous other instances along the road, the historic Tate

> *In 1830, the governor and state legislature decreed that all Cherokee land was state-owned property.*

Cemetery is located along the route of the old Federal Road just to the rear of the town's tiny railroad depot.

Trippe-Simmons-Nelson Tavern

In the early 1800s, pioneer travelers on the old Federal Road in north Georgia tarried in the warm and cozy confines of a tavern of some renown in what today is Jasper, Georgia. The exact date of construction of this historic "stand" or inn/tavern is unknown today, but it almost certainly was coordinated with the Federal Road.

By 1832, General Charles Haney Nelson (1796-1848) of the Georgia Militia was occupying the tavern. He lived there with a Cherokee woman that he reportedly *"had taken up with."* This was during the period of time when the Cherokee Native Americans were being relocated to reservations in Arkansas and Oklahoma but the land was still Cherokee Indian Territory. *(In 1853 Pickens County was formed from the northern part of Cherokee and the southern part of Gilmer counties.)*

Nelson and his troops represented "law and order" in northwest Georgia, fighting running battles with greedy Whites who were attempting to illegally operate gold mines on Indian lands and to seize lands which the Indians had not yet vacated. The old tavern in Pickens existed during all this history – which was quite substantial.

Nelson's ancestors were an old-time military family. One predecessor – John Nelson – had been involved with the Revolutionary War *Battle of Kettle Creek* in Wilkes County, Georgia. Charles won his rank in the Seminole Native American wars, and later served with distinction in the war with Mexico. His family also claimed kinship to British Admiral Lord Horatio Nelson.

Historic Inn Preserved – The Cherokee Indian Territory tavern owned originally by an individual named "Nelson" is illustrated here as it appeared during pioneer days when it was located on the old Federal Road in what today is Jasper, Pickens County, Georgia. As was the case with many inns or "stands" on the Federal Road, it was designed to offer overnight accommodations, food and drink to travelers on the road. The structure pictured was later owned by the Simmons family, and still later by the Trippe family, before being abandoned and falling into disrepair. It has since been relocated to downtown Jasper where it was renovated for public exposition. It stands as of this writing near another historic structure on public exposition - the old Jasper Jail.

Charles Nelson eventually abandoned what even then was considered "an old tavern" in Cherokee Indian Territory and moved to the up-and-coming nearby town of "Calhoun." He relinquished ownership of his "Cherokee Territory" tavern to Indian trader James Simmons (1803-1894) from the nearby Cherokee community of Sandersville (aka "Sanderstown") which today is known as Talking Rock, Georgia.

Simmons expanded the durable log structure with new wings, porches, and an additional half-story which included very distinctive and attractive gables. This completed structure still exists as of 2024, but not in its original location.

Across the road from the original site of this tavern, Simmons operated a log trading post (which unfortunately

With most of its attractive gables destroyed by time and the elements and its porches sadly sagging and collapsing due to infestations of termites, virtually the only sturdy elements remaining in the historic Trippe-Simmons-Nelson House are the heavy hewn-log walls and ceiling beams so reminiscent of pioneer days construction. Though this former inn on the old Federal Road thankfully was preserved by the *Marble Valley Historic Society*, it sadly was required to be disassembled and removed from its original pioneer location on the road and relocated to a parking lot in downtown Jasper, Georgia where it was reassembled for exposition as a historic structure. (Photo by Robert S. Davis, Jr.)

disappeared from the landscape long ago). One of his store account books from the 1850s is preserved on microfilm at the *Georgia Department of Archives and History* in Atlanta. Another may be viewed at the Pickens County Public Library in Jasper.

Simmons enjoyed a long and colorful political career. During the 1850s, he headed Pickens County's local branch of the *American Know Nothing Party*, a radical third political party which attempted to unite a country which was fast coming apart at the seams over the issue of *State's*

Rights and the *Nullification Crisis* (both important aspects of Southern history).

The burgeoning local Democrat Party, led by representatives Lemuel Allred and Stephen Tate, ultimately put an end to the *Know Nothings*, but that didn't slow down Simmons one bit. He subsequently was elected to the *Georgia Secession Convention of 1860* in Milledgeville, Georgia – albeit as a "pro-Union man."

The Convention eventually voted in favor of secession, but Simmons refused to support the move, even as a sign of unity after the issue had obviously been settled. He and the other four hold-outs did however sign a document stating they would *"defend the state of Georgia against all enemies."*

Simmons apparently was good to his word too. During the U.S. Civil War, he served in the Georgia Confederate State Senate, and wrote to Georgia's Governor Brown about a critical shortage of salt in Pickens County, an item which was crucial to the preservation of meat.

Because of his political affiliations, James Simmons was appointed to the financially-lucrative position of federal postmaster. His house (the tavern on the Federal Road) served as the *Talking Rock Post Office* in Indian Territory from January 18, 1832 to July 15, 1833. It also later became known as the *Marblehead Post Office* on July 5, 1850, and was renamed the *Jasper Post Office* (for the newly-created county seat of the new county of Pickens) on June 3, 1854.

Today, the aged Dutch doors common to all old post offices of that era, are still functional in this pioneer American structure. This is just one of the many architectural elements of the old tavern which would have made it so invaluable to historians today had the structure been retained in its original location.

Among James Simmons' descendants were prominent politician Philip Rice Simmons, as well as astronaut Gordon Cooper. James is buried in the Jasper, Georgia, city cemetery.

The last family to occupy this historic old Pickens tavern on the Federal Road was the Trippe family. The current Trippe descendants, fearing further vandalism of their ancestral home donated it to the *Marble Valley Historic Society*, an organization known for the successful preservation of the 1906 Pickens County Jail. Had they also donated the small plot of land upon which it sat and retained the tavern in its original location, the gesture would have been infinitely more significant – but, alas, they did not.

Driving Tour

To take a driving tour of the Old Federal Road beginning on the eastern end:

- Beginning Point – In Hall County, take Highway 13 (the Atlanta Highway) just south of Gainesville, running just west of and parallel to Interstate 985. Just north of Flowery Branch and south of Gainesville, one will see a highway marker commemorating the Old Federal Road. Turn west briefly onto Radford Road, then south onto Highway 13-Alternate, also known as McEver Road.
- Turn west again onto Flowery Branch Road which becomes Stephens Road. Stephens winds thru rural and suburban areas for about three miles until one sees a sign for Old Federal Road.
- Turn right and continue to the intersection with "Jim Crow Road." Again, one will shortly see a sign for Old Federal Road.

- Old Cannon – Look for signage at this site which states *Federal Crossing* marked by a cannon. This designates the beginning of the Federal Road. From this point, the Old Federal Road leads to the Chattahoochee River at the *Old Federal Campground*. From this campground, one can look across the Chattahoochee where the ferryboat operated by James Vann II once took passengers across to the opposite shore.
- Vann's Tavern – One must now take a detour to arrive at the opposite shore. Return to McEver Road (Highway 13 Alternate), turning to the left (northward) and continue to the intersection with Highway 369. Turn left (west) onto 369 which is also called Brown's Bridge Road, continuing for approximately five miles before turning left at the sign announcing *Vann's Tavern Park*. Brown's Bridge offers an impressive view of the Chattahoochee as one crosses over. *Vann's Tavern Park* is the former location of James Vann's ferry landing, as well as his tavern. Following this prominent Cherokee's murder in 1809, the ferry was purchased by a new owner and renamed *Winn's Ferry*, and still later *William's Ferry*. *Vann's Tavern* which, amazingly, continued to exist at this site right up until the 1950s, was disassembled and relocated to the former Cherokee capital of *New Echota* in present-day Gordon County when the impoundment of Lake Lanier threatened to cover the historic tavern with water.
- From *Vann's Tavern Park*, return to Highway 369 (Brown's Bridge Road) and continue west. From this point to the Cherokee County line, this highway is largely faithful to the

original route of the Old Federal Road, passing through *Coal Mountain*, and then *Matt*. This stretch of Highway 369 from *Vann's Tavern Park* to the next turn-off is about 16 miles.

- Hightower – After the aforementioned 16 miles, turn right onto a portion of the old route clearly marked as Old Federal Road. This site in the northwestern corner of Forsyth County where one turns off Highway 369 onto the Old Federal Road is exceedingly historic, being the former site of the Cherokee and pioneer community of *Hightower*. In this vicinity were located *Scudder's Inn*, as well as two forts used by the U.S. military in the 1830s. *Fort Campbell* at this site was used as a stockade for native Cherokees as they were collected for the *Trail of Tears.*

- Gold Mines – Continue on the Old Federal Road at this point into Cherokee County. At *Ophir*, turn north (right) onto Yellow Creek Road. A number of the gold mines opened during the north Georgia gold rush of 1829 existed in the *Yellow Creek Road* vicinity. Continue through *Mica* and into Pickens County.

- Just inside Pickens County, the Federal Road turned westward into the mountains. Today's traveler should take a left off Yellow Creek Road onto a road called Lawson / Federal Road which winds through farmland and a nursery. *(Note: The Lawson/Federal Road does not continuously follow the route of the Federal Road.)*

- Dangerous Section – At *Four-Mile Church* and cemetery, veer left through the cemetery onto Fortner Road. *[Warning: Drivers who are uncertain about gravel roads or steep climbs may choose to skip this stretch. If so, take the right fork (instead of the left fork) at Four-Mile Church which also leads to Highway 53. Those wishing to by-pass the hilly section entirely (missing this portion of the old Federal Road) may simply continue on Yellow Creek Road to Highway 53. Be particularly aware of the fact that if one travels the incorrect direction on Fortner Road,* taking a left where one should actually go right onto Harrington Road, *the route becomes extremely hilly, dangerous, and virtually impossible for most vehicles.]* As of this writing in 2024, Fortner Road is a narrow gravel road for approximately a half mile into the mountains. After the aforementioned approximate one-half mile, drivers should veer to the left onto Pea Ridge Road, before turning right onto Harrington Road which leads northward to Highway 53. This entire section in the mountains consists of approximately six miles of somewhat slow driving.

- Travel along Highway 53 until reaching a marble factory. Go west (left) onto Highway 53, traveling up a steep hill into the town of *Tate*. *Highway 53* continues dramatically up the mountain past several attractive buildings, including a school, church, railroad depot, and other buildings into the town of *Tate*.

- Old Tate Railroad Depot – Shortly past the *Tate Depot*, turn right onto Highway 53, and continue northward for about five miles to *Jasper*, Georgia. In downtown *Jasper*, turn right onto Old Highway 5 / Main Street, passing through *old downtown Jasper* and continuing past numerous historic commercial buildings as well as a wooden bridge.

- Trippe-Simmons-Nelson Tavern – Before departing downtown Jasper, be sure to visit the old Trippe-Simmons-Nelson Tavern which once stood on the old Federal Road in town. Though relocated to a new permanent site in downtown Jasper and renovated for exposition, this historic structure nevertheless offers an able glimpse into the early pioneer life of Georgia.

- Side-Track – Just north of Jasper is a short section of road (off to the right of Highway 5) which a sign identifies as the Old Federal Road. *(This short side-track section of the road, which is approximately one-half mile in length, will be of interest only to purists who wish not to miss any sections of the Federal Road.)*

- In departing Jasper, take Highway 5 northwest to *Talking Rock. (Note: Be careful not to follow signs leading to "new" Highway 5.)*

- Taloney – Just north of Talking Rock, Highway 5 intersects with Highway 136. At this spot, the Old Federal Road turned westward along the route of Highway 136. This intersection is marked by a highway sign identifying the Old Federal Road, and was the site of *Taloney*, where the historic *Carmel Missionary Station* was established in 1819. Taloney was also important in pioneer days as a meeting site for Cherokee and U.S. federal government officials. It was here that the U.S. government installed one of the few U.S. Postal stations in Cherokee Indian Territory. Just a few miles west of this intersection (remaining on Highway 136), one of the forts used by the U.S. military (*Fort Newnan*)

to collect Cherokee citizens for transport on the *"Trail of Tears"* was located a short distance away. The fort was located on the outskirts of the town of *Blaine* off *Antioch Church Road*, south of Highway 136.

- At *Blaine*, turn north (right) onto Highway 136. Traveling from Pickens into Gilmer County, Highway 136 passes through hilly uneventful wooded terrain for a number of miles.

- Coosawattee Ford – Just before 136 intersects with Talking Rock Creek in Murray County, the road turned northward into steeper hills. In pioneer days, the Federal Road crossed the Coosawattee River prior to these hills. Today, however, the highway passes over the top of *Carter's Dam* on *Carter's Dam Road* at Carter's Lake recreational area. As one crosses on the road atop the dam, an excellent view is available of the original spot at which all **original** *Federal Road* travelers once crossed the Coosawattee.

- Fort Gilmer – To continue on the route of the road, travelers should continue westward on Highway 136 for a brief distance before turning northward on Old U.S. Highway 411 which is a very historic stretch. Approximately one mile northward in a scenic stretch of farms and woodland, a sign announcing the former site of *Fort Gilmer* will be seen. It was yet another of the sites at which the Cherokees were collected prior to embarking on the *Trail of Tears*. Continue northward until Old Highway 411 is divided into Highways 72 and 282.

- Treaty of Tellico – At this point, the Federal Road divided into two forks – one continuing northward and one heading westward. This fork occurs just south of Ramhurst. Both forks were historically important. The north fork continues to Hiwassee and Tellico in what today is Tennessee. Here, many important Cherokee political activities occurred. The *Treaty of Tellico* which authorized the *Federal Road* circa 1804 was signed by Cherokee chiefs and U.S. federal government officials at *Tellico*. The west fork is important historically regarding both Cherokee and U.S. Civil War history.

- North Fork – To take the north fork to Hiwassee and Tellico, turn right onto Highway 282 briefly, then head northward (to the left) on a road clearly marked as Old Federal Road toward the community of *Dennis*. Continue past Mountain View Church and Cemetery and then turn westward (left) onto Highway 52. Cross Holly Creek and continue into *Chatsworth*. Turn right immediately in Chatsworth onto Second Avenue.

- Chatsworth – Historic Chatsworth has two attractive options for stopping, both on the original route of the Old Federal Road. The first is a shopping and eating district and a small public park. Continuing northward, Second Avenue is re-identified as "the Old Federal Road." Continue on this road, parallel to U.S. Highway 411 just east of the town of *Eton*. Cross a small one-lane bridge. At the point that the road is situated behind *Eton Industrial Park*, the road ends at Loughridge Road. Turning left on Loughridge, the road passes through a tunnel under the railroad tracks. The traveler then will turn northward (right) onto Highway 411 into Tennessee.

- West Fork – If one instead wished to take the very historic west fork just south of Ramhurst, turn to the left onto the Smyrna-Ramhurst Road which will shortly become the Smyrna-Spring Place Road. At the signage, turn right into the small historic town of *Spring Place* on Highway 225, which, for a time, is also identified as Joseph Vann Road and Spring Place Road. Continue to the *Chief Vann House*. At this point, Spring Place Road (Highway 225) continues northward, while the Federal Road actually veered sharply westward just south of the Vann House.

- Spring Place – *Spring Place* is exceedingly historic for a number of reasons, not the least of which is the *Chief Vann House*. It was also the site of a *Moravian Christian Missionary "station."* The intersection of two important travel routes at this point, coupled with the wealth of the *Chief Vann* family and the activity of the *Moravian Mission* encouraged the U.S. federal government to place one of the first post offices in Cherokee Indian Territory at Spring Place. The U.S. federal government, coupled with the government of the state of Georgia, were not completely honest with the Cherokee Nation in such actions, since they were clearly planning for the day when the Natives could be relocated westward. Just south of the intersection of Highway 225 and the *Spring Place-Smyrna Road*, yet another U.S. military installation – *Fort Hoskins* – was constructed for use in the relocation of the Cherokees to the West in 1838.

- Free Hope Church – Turning left just south of the *Chief Vann House*, continue westward on Highway 52-Alternate. For a short distance, the former route of the Federal Road cannot be followed precisely. One can turn right (northward) onto Old Free Hope Church Road which passes through a farming and residential area, passing over Highway 76/52 and becoming Adams Road. In this approximate area, the Federal Road continued into what today is private property and crossed the Conasauga River. This section must simply be bypassed by continuing westward on either Highway 52 or 52-Alternate.

- On 76/52 or 52-Alternate, turn northward (right) onto Highway 286 toward *Dawnville*. To reach the portion of the Federal Road which picks up on the north side of the Conasauga River, head east on Mitchell Bridge Road. Mitchell Bridge will return travelers back to Highway 286 at *Dawnville*. (*Note: To skip this side trip on Mitchell Bridge, just continue on Highway 286 without turning onto Mitchell Bridge.*)

- From *Dawnville*, continue northwestward (right) on 286 briefly before turning north (left) onto the Dawnville-Beaverdale Road, then turn west (left) onto Beaverdale Road before turning abruptly back northward onto Lake Frances Road NE. Take Lake Frances to Highway 2 westward (left). The original route of the Old Federal Road shortly turns southwestward (left) for a short stretch through farming and residential areas. Highway 71 will be encountered shortly, as well as another sign identifying the Old Federal Road route. Continue briefly northward on 71 before turning left onto Highway 2 toward historic *Varnell*.

- Varnell – A number of other strategically-important historic sites will be encountered in this vicinity. In pioneer days, *Varnell* was known as *Varnell's Station,* and was important in both the *Battle of Chickamauga* in Septembr of 1863 and the *Battle of Atlanta* in May of 1864 during the *U.S. Civil War.* Between Varnell's Station and Ringgold were *Catoosa Springs*, the *Tunnel Hill Road*, the *Old Stone Church, Taylor's Station,* and *Ringgold Gap*, all of which were also strategic during the Civil War.

- Old Stone Church – Continue westward on Highway 2 to *Old Stone Church* at the intersection of Highways 2 and 41, which is a good spot for a break. Aside from the nearby Moravian missions, *Old Stone Church* was one of the first Christian churches in the area, with a congregation organized in 1837. The church was completed in 1850.

- From this point, take Highway 41 northwestward (right) most of the way to the Tennessee state line. The highway will pass through *Shookville* before reaching *Ringgold*. Travel north through *Indian Springs* and turn westward (left) onto Highway 146 (*Cloud Springs Road*). This road actually passes a bit south of the former route of the Old Federal Road, which is difficult to locate in this vicinity and impossible to travel.

- Chief John Ross House – From Cloud Springs Road, turn northwestward (right) onto Highway 27 to *Rossville* to visit the final Georgia portion of the Old Federal Road. Located here is the *Chief John Ross*

House. Ross strongly opposed the relocation of the Cherokees to the West. Just as with Chief James Vann and other prominent Cherokees, Ross's former home was once located directly on the route of the Old Federal Road in Rossville, but unfortunately has been relocated to a poorly-marked location just south of Highway 27.

- Ross's Landing – Returning to Highway 27, continue northward through the town of *Rossville* to the Tennessee border and Chattanooga. Just beyond the *Chief John Ross House* is *Ross's Landing* where he, just as Vann and others, maintained a ferryboat business for portage across the river – for a price. At this site, many of the Cherokees who ultimately were relocated to Arkansas and Oklahoma were initially grouped and organized for the long trek westward.

Endnotes

1/ Hemperley, Marion, former assistant survey-general of Georgia, *Historic Indian Trails of Georgia*, Garden Clubs of Georgia (1989), pp 22-24.

2/ *Treaty of Holston*, (1791), *American State Papers & Indian Affairs, Volume I*, p 124.

3/ Malone, Henry Thompson, *Cherokees of the Old South: A People in Transition*, University of Georgia Press (1956), pp 148-149.

4/ *Treaty of Holston*, (1791), *American State Papers & Indian Affairs, Volume I*, p 125.

5/ McLoughlin, William, *Cherokee Renascence*, p 82; McLoughlin, *Cherokees and Missionaries*, New Haven: Yale University Press, (1984), pp 72-75.

6/ Meigs, Return J., October 25, 1803 Letter, *Records of the Bureau of Indian Affairs*, U.S. Federal Government.

7/ McLoughlin, William, *Cherokee Renascence*, p 88.

8/ Duke, David, *Georgia Surveyor Field Notes, Cherokee Sections, Section 3, District 9*, Georgia

Dept. of Archives & History, Atlanta, GA, Record Group 3-3-25.

9/ Carnes, Thomas P., *Cherokee Indian Letters, Talks and Treaties, 1786-1839, Part 1*, December 22, 1802.

10/ Shadburn, Don, *Cherokee Planters in Georgia, 1832-1838*, W.H. Wolfe Associates, Roswell, GA (1990), pp 260-262.

11/ Shadburn, Don, *Cherokee Planters in Georgia, 1832-1838*, W.H. Wolfe Associates, Roswell, GA (1990), pp 262-264.

12/ *American State Papers*, Post Office Department (1827), pp 173-174.

13/ *1832 Land Lottery Maps, Cherokee County, Section 2, District 4*, Georgia Dept. of Archives & History, Atlanta, GA.

14/ McLoughlin, William, *Cherokees and Missionaries*, pp 127-128.

15/ Wilkins, Thurman, *Cherokee Tragedy: The Ridge Family and the Decimation of a People*, University of Oklahoma Press (1988), First Edition (1970).

16/ *1832 Land Lottery Maps, Cherokee County, Section 2, District 4*, Georgia Department of Archives & History, Atlanta, GA.

17/ Duncan, George M., *Surveyor's Field Notes*, Cherokee Sections, Section 3, District 8, Georgia Dept. of Archives & History, Record Group 3-3-25.

18/ McDowell, D., *Surveyor's Field Notes*, Cherokee Sections, Section 2, District 25, Georgia Dept. of Archives & History, Atlanta, Ga, Record Group 3-3-25.

19/ McLoughlin, William, *Cherokees and Missionaries*, pp 193-205, and Malone, Henry Thompson, *Cherokees of the Old South: A People in Transition*, University of Georgia Press (1956), pp 79-84.

20/ McLoughlin, William, *Cherokees and Missionaries*, pp 193-205.

21/ Perdue, Theda and Green, Michael, *The Cherokee Removal: A Brief History with Documents*, St. Martin's Press (1995); Williams, David, *The Georgia Gold Rush: Twenty-Niners, Cherokees, and Gold Fever*, University of South Carolina Press (1993), p 51; Walker, Charles O., *Cherokee Names Remain in Georgia, Volume III*, Jasper, GA, (2005), p 86; and Martin, Lloyd G., *The History of Cherokee County*, Walter Brown Company, Atlanta, (1932), p 141.

Retracing the *Unicoi Turnpike*

Ancient game trails throughout the eastern United States evolved into trade, hunting and warring routes for aboriginals from pre-history up to the early 19th century. Eventually, early American settlers also made use of these travel paths, enlarging them into wagon and stagecoach routes before they eventually fell into disuse and were forgotten. The aboriginal path which came to be known as "the Unicoi Turnpike" is one of the few which can be retraced today.

"Unicoi" is the Cherokee word for "white." Since the trail which ultimately became the *Unicoi Turnpike* reportedly has existed for well over 1,000 years, it would be safe to say that it wasn't named for the "White settlers" which began using it in the late 18th century. In all probability, the name referenced the mists and cloud-enshrouded peaks between and around which the *Turnpike* passed. The actual interpretation, however, will never be known for certain. Suffice it to say, it is an ancient trail like a number of other still identifiable ancient trails throughout what today is the state of Georgia.

Origin of the Road

Even prior to original human use by Native Americans, the travel routes which eventually came to be known as *"the Unicoi Turnpike," "the Federal Road," "the Alabama Road," "the Logan Turnpike"* and others, were initially created by large migratory hooved mammals, first including the prehistoric forerunners of horses and zebras (yes, in the United States), and later by the many elk, American bison, antelope, deer, and other hooved species which, by nature,

searched out the easiest-navigable routes around the edges of the mountains, through the mountain passes, and across the rivers and other natural water barriers in their seasonal migrations to more hospitable realms in what today is the southeastern United States.

Later, as Native Americans migrated into the area, the dense undergrowth and immense virgin stands of timber in what today is the eastern United States disallowed travel by any route other than the existing game trails which had been created hundreds – perhaps thousands – of years earlier by the aforementioned migrating wildlife. As the aboriginals populated the area, they both adopted and slightly improved upon the game trails for their own use in their hunting, trading and warfare ventures with other indigenous tribes.

The *Unicoi Turnpike* originally was approximately 150 miles (240 km) in length, and extended from southeastern Tennessee through western Carolina and diagonally across the northeastern corner of Georgia to a point slightly beyond Toccoa, where it connected with the Savannah River just below the entrance of Toccoa Creek. From this point, the river then could be navigated

The Unicoi Turnpike began life as a game trail far back in pre-history. A number of historic markers identify the ancient trail along its length.

by Native Americans and Whites alike northward and southward up and down the coast of Georgia, providing immense trading opportunities.

The specific site at which the *Unicoi Turnpike* began in Tennessee was the approximate location of the *Tellico Blockhouse* on the *Federal Road* near Nine Mile Creek in present-day Vonore. From there, the trail entered the Blue Ridge Mountains and continued to what today is Murphy, North Carolina, following the Hiwassee River toward Hayesville, before turning south to present-day Hiawassee, Georgia, where it threaded through a substantial mountain pass which came to be known as *"Unicoi Gap."* It then crossed Spoilcane Creek and the Chattahoochee

> *If one continues slowly along this route, not one, but several historic Indian mounds can actually be picked out by the discerning eye.*

River a total of eleven times, dropping approximately 800 feet on its way to the Sautee-Nacoochee Valley in northeast Georgia.

Driving the Trail

If one wishes to experience a pleasant driving tour of a portion of the former Unicoi Turnpike, a breath-taking section of the route exists in northeast Georgia in the Sautee-Nacoochee Valley. This very scenic drive offers numerous examples of early American history which have been preserved by the families which have thrived in this vicinity for generations. A number of Georgia state historical markers along the route explain portions of this pioneer history for visitors to the area.

After passing through what today is Helen, GA (following the general route of modern GA-75 southward), the *Turnpike* bore leftward near the historic Indian mound (still visible in the pasture) onto the road which today is GA-17. If one continues slowly along this route, not one, but several historic Indian mounds can actually be picked out by the discerning eye.

Continuing eastward through the scenic and pastoral Sautee-Nacoochee Valleys, the *Turnpike* route continued almost exactly upon present-day GA-17. At the intersection of GA-17 and GA-255, the trail is identified by a historic marker beside the pioneer-era *Old Sautee Store* which was constructed circa 1872, and which visitors may still visit.

Traveler's Rest near Toccoa, Georgia, gained early prominence due to its location on the Unicoi Turnpike.

Interestingly, it was in the Nacoochee Valley that the *Turnpike* connected with the ancient *Cherokee Trading Path* network, with trails which radiated to other aboriginal pre-Columbian mercantile centers in what today are Virginia, Pennsylvania and Maryland. Thankfully, much of the early history in this peaceful valley has been preserved for future generations, despite severe threats over the years from gold mining and timber harvesting interests.

From the *Old Sautee Store* the trail continued eastward on GA-17 / GA-255 for a short distance where GA-255 branches to the right and GA-17 *(the original Unicoi Turnpike route)* continues straight ahead.

GA-17 eventually joins GA-115 near Clarkesville, Georgia. A short distance beyond this junction, the old trail bore to the right in the downtown area onto what today is Washington Street.

Continuing down Washington Street, GA-17 *(and the Turnpike)* bears to the left onto East Louise Street (GA-115) which is also known as *"the Toccoa Highway"* today. After a certain distance on the *Toccoa Highway*, the exact route of this ancient byway has been lost in modern development and the passage of time, but in general, it lay in the route of present-day highways GA-17 and U.S.-123 to a point south of Toccoa.

A "Toll Road"

Permission to open the route as a "toll road" was granted by the Cherokees in 1813 to United States government representatives. Tennessee and Georgia both granted charters to the concern, and, following signatures on and execution of the *1813 Treaty*, improvement of the trace began in earnest for use by White settlers. A company led by Russell Wiley worked from 1813

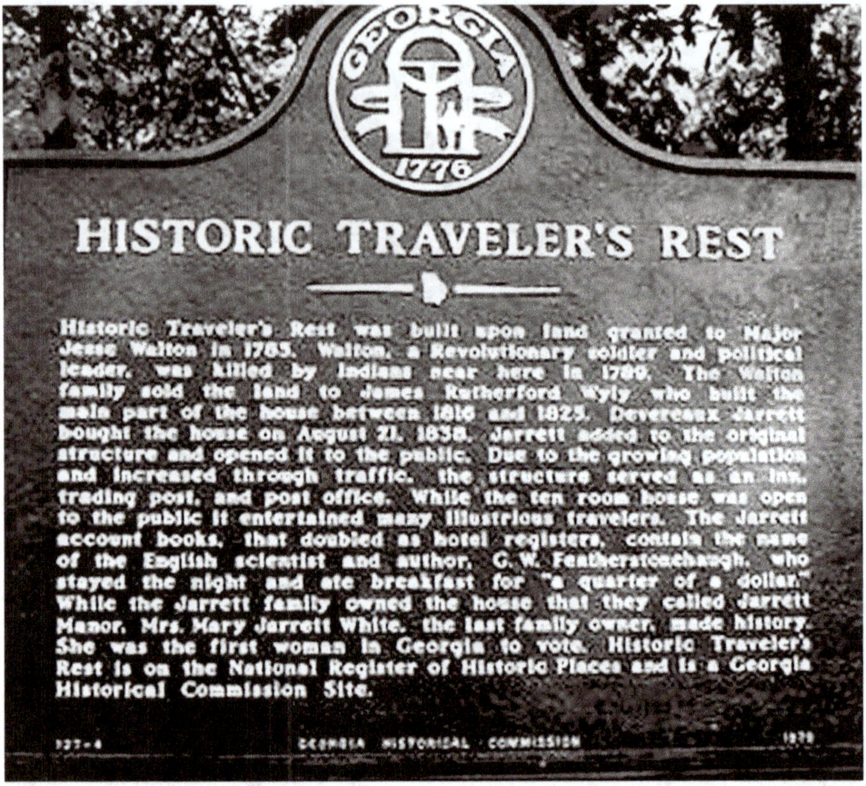
GEORGIA
1776
HISTORIC TRAVELER'S REST
Historic Traveler's Rest was built upon land granted to Major Jesse Walton in 1785. Walton, a Revolutionary soldier and political leader, was killed by Indians near here in 1789. The Walton family sold the land to James Rutherford Wyly who built the main part of the house between 1816 and 1825. Devereaux Jarrett bought the house on August 21, 1838. Jarrett added to the original structure and opened it to the public. Due to the growing population and increased through traffic, the structure served as an inn, trading post, and post office. While the ten room house was open to the public it entertained many illustrious travelers. The Jarrett account books, that doubled as hotel registers, contain the name of the English scientist and author, G. W. Featherstonehaugh, who stayed the night and ate breakfast for "a quarter of a dollar." While the Jarrett family owned the house that they called Jarrett Manor, Mrs. Mary Jarrett White, the last family owner, made history. She was the first woman in Georgia to vote. Historic Traveler's Rest is on the National Register of Historic Places and is a Georgia Historical Commission Site.
GEORGIA HISTORICAL COMMISSION

Many pioneer travelers overnighted at Travelers Rest as is explained in this historic marker at the historic inn. (Photo courtesy of the GA Dept. of Archives & History, Atlanta, GA)

GEORGIA
1776
NACOOCHEE VALLEY
VALLEY OF THE EVENING STAR
This valley has long fascinated travelers, writers and artists. It was farmed for centuries by Indians and white men alike. The valley was devastated by Spanish and American gold hunters and timbermen and has been carefully nurtured by prosperous summer residents and progressive farmers.
The valley is watered by Sautee and Duke's Creeks and the Chattahoochee River. These streams formed the rich alluvial soils, laced the soils with placer gold, and powered small industries. Longtime residents of the valley have been the Dyers, Glens, Hardmans, Lumsdens, Nichols, Richardsons and Williams.

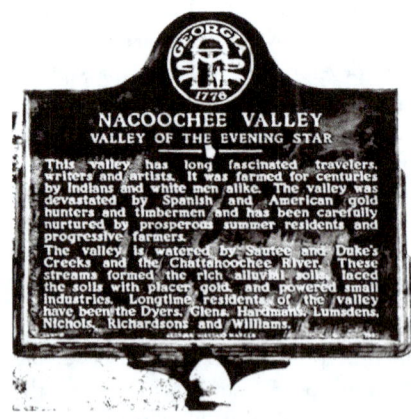

One of the most scenic stretches of the Unicoi Turnpike which can still be experienced today winds through the historic northeast Georgia realm known as the Nacoochee Valley.

to 1817 to convert the trail into a two-lane toll road for freighting wagons and other "wheeled" transport, as well as for livestock.

The route proved particularly useful to farmers raising turkeys, hogs and cattle for sale in markets both southward and northward – but mainly southward – where settlements and "civilization" were more prevalent and in need of ready amounts of food. The "toll" for travel on the road ranged from twelve and one-half cents for a man and his horse to $1.25 for a four-wheel "carriage of pleasure." Many other rates were charged for livestock and for a single horseback-mounted traveler.

Despite the income generated by the toll road, it, nevertheless was eventually beset by financial problems. In 1821, the Georgia State Legislature was forced to step in to provide support. It "loaned" the *Turnpike* Company $3,000.00 to re-stabilize the concern. Whether this $3,000.00 was ever repaid to the taxpayers of the state of Georgia is unknown today.

Allowing for inflation, the $3,000.00 loan of 1821 was the approximate equivalent of $80,000.00 in 2025 dollars, and doesn't begin to consider the raw purchasing power of that amount in 1821. The *Turnpike* therefore thrived for the bulk of the remaining 100 years it was in use before eventually being "put out to pasture" by a more modern highway system and motorized transport in the early 20th century.

Broken Promise

In return for access to and the right to improve the road, the U.S. government agreed to make annual payments in the amount of $160.00 to the native Cherokees for a period of 20 years. Following the expiration of the 20-year contractual period, the agreement was to be re-negotiated or the route would revert back to Cherokee ownership.

The annual payments reportedly were never paid by the U.S. government, but by 1833 (when the initial 20-year contractual period had expired), this payment had become a moot point anyway, since the lands of the Cherokee in Tennessee, North Carolina and Georgia were being usurped and parceled out by that point to White settlers in land lotteries and the native Cherokees were being removed to reservations out West.

By 1838, the bulk of the Cherokee Nation had been relocated from what today is the southeastern United States to

The Unicoi Turnpike was an important travel route during pioneer days in what today is the southeastern United States. (Map courtesy of Creative Commons (creativecommons.org), Mountain View, CA. Reprinted with permission. All Rights Reserved)

Arkansas and Oklahoma in what came to be known as *"The Trail of Tears."* Any thought of payments for the *Turnpike* no doubt were simply forgotten.

The contract between the United States and the Cherokees became yet another broken promise wrapped up in the unfortunate destiny of these aboriginals. Contrary to most other Native Americans, the Cherokees – particularly those of wealth – had made steadfast efforts toward assimilation into the White culture, learning English, adopting White religions, attending White schools, and, in general insinuating themselves in every possible manner into White society. It, however, was all for naught.

Early Inns

All along the length of the *Unicoi Turnpike*, small inns or "stands" which were spaced approximately 15 miles apart *(the approximate distance one could travel in one day in pioneer times)*, offered overnighting accommodations. Today, these historic "stands" *(also often called a "public house" in pioneer days)* sadly have virtually all disappeared from the landscape, victims of time, the elements, and the absence of preservation efforts. However, if one searches, occasional survivors of these early vestiges of civilization can still be found.

One example of such a surviving vestige can be seen near the Georgia state line at Toccoa. *"Traveler's Rest"* a former stagecoach "stand" and plantation, was constructed circa 1815, and is a protected state historic site today. The *Turnpike* passed beside this pioneer inn, providing it with a steady supply of customers.

Back in Habersham County just north of Clarkesville, Georgia, a stretch of the *Turnpike* has been identified by a Georgia state historic marker at the intersection of Buckhorn Road and old U.S. Highway 441 North. Numerous other visible portions of the actual *Turnpike* still exist in short spurts throughout northeast Georgia, western Carolina and southeast Tennessee.

Interestingly, aside from the handful of actual early-American "stands"/public houses which do still exist today, one will also occasionally encounter a "reminder" of the former existence of the public houses which once proliferated along the length of original pioneer travel routes such as the *Unicoi Turnpike*. These reminders exist along stretches of other historic pioneer traces across north Georgia if one knows where to look. One example is found in *"Burnt Stand Road"* in southern Lumpkin County, Georgia.

Though its history has escaped modern historians/researchers, *"Burnt 'Stand' Road"* almost certainly earned its moniker from a former inn on this pioneer route which apparently was destroyed by fire. This historic road, with a rough beginning at the pioneer ford *(Leather's Ford)* across the Chestatee River in Lumpkin County, was one of the original pioneer traces leading to

the former Georgia gold rush town of Auraria, Georgia. The actual "burned stand" which provided the identity of the road possibly existed on the west side of the Chestatee at Leathers Ford, which would have been a natural spot for gold rush miners and other early travelers to overnight prior to continuing on to Auraria the following morning.

Back on the *Unicoi Turnpike*, this travel route was used most intensely in 1828-1830s, when gold was discovered on Duke's Creek in the Sautee-Nacoochee Valley and in nearby Auraria/Dahlonega, Georgia. Prospectors, miners, land-lot and gold-lot claimants and thousands of others flocked to the region from the 1820s through the 1840s, many of them making use of the *Turnpike* in these travels.

Modern Remnants

Today, sightseers in northeast Georgia may still witness, ride and hike upon various portions of the original historic *Unicoi Turnpike* at a number of spots. Numerous state historic markers throughout this region have been placed by the *Georgia Historical Commission* for posterity. A historic marker located 0.1 of a mile north of Helen Highway in the Nacoochee Valley describes that section of the route.

As explained above, a substantial portion of the trail in fact may be experienced by automobile along the route of present-day GA 17. Original and actual dirt portions of the trail may also be experienced on foot if one wishes to venture forth on a hiking exercise. One such stretch turns off GA 17 North in Stephens County, and offers an excellent opportunity to experience what the trail might have engendered for Native and European Americans alike hundreds of years ago.

The Infamous *McIntosh Trail*

*It was an early east-west travel and trading route between "civilization"
in the east and the inhabitants of the wilderness in what was known
at that time as "the western frontier." It also led to the fateful final abode
of famed Creek Chieftain William McIntosh.*

During the pioneer days of the early 19th century, when the Cherokee, Muscogee Creek and other tribes still inhabited what today is the state of Georgia, a cross-section of much of the leadership of these Native Americans eventually came to a point of enlightenment. They finally and unequivocally grasped the fact that their homeland was being overrun by European migrants and there was absolutely nothing the native inhabitants could do to stop it. The more forward-thinking leaders such as Creek Chieftain William McIntosh therefore concluded that, rather than make war (which they could not win) against the Europeans, they should instead "assimilate" into the White culture (where possible) or simply accept the inevitable and cut their losses.

Some of the more advanced Creeks and Cherokees were successful in this enlightened endeavor initially, and proceeded with it vigorously. A few hold-over intractable leaders, however, found the "assimilation" and "capitulation" strategies completely unacceptable, and in fact believed anyone who advocated those measures were committing treasonous deeds against their people – deeds for which capital punishment should be meted out.

Today, there are still a number of examples of the advanced domestic, architectural, and landscape creations left behind by the forward-thinking leaders in their vain attempts to preserve their nation's culture and existence in the Southeast. The *McIntosh Trail* (also known as *"Oakfuskee Path"* path by the Creeks) between Indian Spring in present-day Butts County, Georgia and the McIntosh Reserve in present-day Carroll County and on into present-day Alabama, is one such remnant from those days.

William McIntosh

William McIntosh was born in 1775 in the Lower Creek Nation town of Coweta. He was the son of Capt. William H. McIntosh of Coweta *(and previously of Pine Harbor, in what today is McIntosh County, Georgia)*. Captain McIntosh originated from a prominent Savannah, Georgia family and was a Loyalist during the American Revolution.

William's mother was a full-blood Muscogee Creek named Senoia Hennenah who was a member of the Wind Clan which was prominent in the Creek Nation. Known as "Tustunnuggee Hutke," *(which reportedly translates to "White Warrior,")* young William – also a member of the Wind Clan through his mother – became a leading spokesman for the Creek Lower Towns in the early 1800s.

Trail Remnant – As of this writing in 2025, there is an area on Creek Chieftain William McIntosh's old reservation just west of the Chattahoochee River in present-day Carroll County, Georgia, where an abandoned remnant of the old original McIntosh Trail is still discernible. Turning up the hill from the river at this site, the road passes the spot at which McIntosh's home and inn once existed, and at which he was murdered.

As a result of his parentage, William was half-Creek. In their early culture, the Creeks were a matrilineal society in which the female family-heads are dominant over the household, its activities and possessions.

On the opposite side of his parentage, William was half Scottish which, interestingly, was a patrilineal society in its earlier days in which the male heads were dominant. Young William, therefore was "Patrician" on both sides of his family tree, and profited accordingly.

He rose to become one of that culture's most prominent chiefs in the early 1800s. He was also a chief of Coweta town and commander of a mounted police force.

Though the Creeks as a culture had little concept or interest in "money" or

"ownership," William very obviously was of a different mindset. His family connections allowed him to experience many of the finer aspects of the White culture and he ultimately wanted those things for himself and his wife and children. His property and possessions therefore eventually were considerable.

Some have attributed William McIntosh's business acumen to his education provided by his father in the White culture. Others have attributed it purely to his advanced intellect coupled with a very ambitious personality. Whatever the circumstances, the younger McIntosh was a very astute and successful businessman in addition to his prominence within the Creek Nation.

Aside from his standing and duties within the tribe, William eventually was also a major player in the planter elite class in Georgia, farming significant acreage through the use of slave labor. He owned and operated extensive farming endeavors on the Ocmulgee River in what today is southern Butts County, as well as three separate plantations near Carrollton and Newnan on the Chattahoochee River. Though little about it has been recorded, William almost certainly – as a result of his business ownerships and acumen – was quite wealthy for his day and time.

Aside from his plantation and farms ownership, William also built and owned a substantial and very successful inn *(often referred to as a "stand" in those days)* in Butts County at a sacred Creek Nation site which came to be known in White parlance as "Indian Spring." Travelers – both the prestigious and commoners alike – who were moving westward across Georgia often paused at Indian Spring Inn to overnight.

Young William ultimately operated an inn not only at Indian Spring in present-day Butts County, but also eventually at his home, *Lochau*, in present-day Carroll County. He also owned and operated a ferry on the Chattahoochee River near this home.

The *Lochau* inn provided accommodations for travelers using not only the McIntosh Trail, but a branch of the "Alabama Road" as well *(Readers please see "Retracing the Historic Alabama Roads" in this volume)* to travel westward. Vestiges of this historic trail near the former site of the famed chieftain's home may still be seen even today.

William's Indian Spring Inn profited from the multitudes of traffic by horseback, cart, and stagecoach since several travel and trading paths crossed at the site. A steady stream of travelers also partook of the Lochau inn as

well. And both inns profited from a new mode of travel – the stagecoach.

Stagecoaches on the Road

The route to Indian Spring and westward into present-day Alabama eventually included the travel services of stagecoaches. Interestingly, records indicate the first stagecoaches in this region were little more than "Conestoga-type" wagons that had been outfitted with crude seats for the passengers. A report of that day describes them thusly:

"These wagons had a boat-shaped body with a curved bottom which fitted them specially for mountain use, for in them, freight remained firmly in place at whatever angle the body might be (tilted). *The rear end* (tail gate) *could be lifted from the sockets; on it hung the feed trough for the horses.*

"On the side of the body was a small tool chest with a slanting lid. It held a hammer, wrench, hatchet, pincers, and other simple tools. Under the rear axletree were suspended a tar bucket and a water pail. The wheels had "steel" tires – sometimes a foot broad. The wagon bodies were arched over with six or eight bows, of which the middle ones were the lowest. These were covered with a strong pure white hempen cover, and corded down strongly at the sides and ends. Four to six tons was the usual load for such a vehicle."

In other publications of that day, the Conestoga wagon stagecoaches were described as follows:

"Long machines with seats hung on leather braces (straps), *with three seats across. These seats were of a sufficient width to accommodate three persons each, all of whom sit with their faces toward the horses. The driver sits under cover, without any division between him and the passengers, and thence there is room for*

This painting of William McIntosh was completed only a few months prior to his assassination. At the time, he, of course, had no idea that his life would be so tragically brief.

a person to sit on each side of the driver (during times of heavier occupancy)."

The later "Concord" stagecoach which is instantly recognizable as that often seen in television "Westerns," was invented and manufactured by the *Abbot-Downing Company* of Concord, Massachusetts beginning in 1827. By 1928, more than 3,000 of these vehicles had been manufactured, and they were shipped to users as far away as Europe, Australia and New Zealand. The Concord quickly became the standard stage throughout America and was soon visible throughout the growing civilization in Georgia.

Modeled after the private coaches of the aristocracy in England and France, the Concord was beautiful, durable, and featured innovation well ahead of its time. Characterized by its "bathtub shape," with ornate decorative moldings

and including custom paintings of landscapes on its exterior, the Concord often was truly a work of art as well as reliable transportation. This option eventually became a transportation method of choice for many travelers on the McIntosh Trail.

Trail Location

William McIntosh moved in high circles in both the White and Creek Indian cultures, traveling regularly between Indian Spring where his hotel existed and eastern Alabama where a concentration of the Creek Nation resided. His connections with his cousin – Georgia Governor George Troup – allowed him additional stature inconceivable to those around him.

The traffic between Indian Spring and Lochau eventually became considerable, and the route – which later came to be known as "the McIntosh Trail" – gradually was widened to a width of fifteen to twenty feet and improved to accommodate stagecoaches and other more substantial traffic.

The trail actually began at McIntosh's plantation in southern Butts County and proceeded almost due north until it joined the *Oakfuskee Path* on the southern edge of Flovilla. It then proceeded to a site just beyond the remaining *Double Cabin Inn* east of present-day Griffin where it split. One branch continued into Carroll County to McIntosh's home, Lochau, on Acorn Bluff. His total acreage in this vicinity – which was extensive – came to be known as "McIntosh Reserve."

In the early 21st century, the *McIntosh Trail Historic Preservation Society* in Georgia spearheaded an effort to have the Georgia portion of the road designated as a scenic byway by the Georgia State Department of Transportation.

From Indian Spring, the 95.5-mile-long historic road travels through Coweta, Butts, Spalding, Fayette and Carroll counties and passes through the downtowns of present-day Newnan, Sharpsburg and Senoia.

From Carroll County (and the former McIntosh Reserve), the original McIntosh Road was called *"the Georgia Road,"* since, from Alabama, it obviously led "to Georgia," just as the westward roads across Georgia in pioneer times led to Alabama and were therefore called *"the Alabama Roads."*

In order to follow the full length of "the Georgia Road" / McIntosh Trail in reverse from Alabama to Georgia, one would begin at Kymulga Ferry near Childersburg, Alabama, where the route *(portions of which are still visible today)* followed a path to Talladega, Alabama, then northeasterly along the south side of the Choccolocco Creek Valley. At that point, it crosses the ridge containing Cheaha Mountain at a pass some miles to the north. It then continued through the area known today as modern Hollis Crossroads and crossed the Tallapoosa River at Okfuskee village *(from which this historic route earned its additional identity as "the Okfuskee Road" at Indian Spring in Georgia).* From Okfuskee village, the road continued in a southeasterly direction to the Chattahoochee River near present-day Whitesburg, Georgia in Carroll County *(at which McIntosh's home, inn, ferry and the McIntosh Reserve were located).*

Treaty of Indian Spring

On February 12, 1825, McIntosh, along with a contingent of six other chiefs of the Lower Creek Nation, signed the now infamous *Treaty of Indian Spring,* so-called because the signing was conducted in McIntosh's fine home

/ inn *(which still stands as of this writing in 2025)* in Butts County, Georgia. This impressive structure, though totally unprotected in the years after McIntosh's assassination, somehow managed to survive intact into the 21st century, and is today preserved and maintained at Indian Spring by the Butts County Historic Society.

The treaty called for the Creek Nation to cede all lands east of the Chattahoochee River, including the sacred Ocmulgee site *(Ocmulgee National Monument today)* and to be relocated west of the Mississippi River to an equivalent parcel of land along the Arkansas River. In return, the U.S. Government agreed to pay the Creek Nation *(actually McIntosh)* the sum of $200,000.00, literally a fortune in that day and time, *"as soon as is practicable after ratification of this treaty."* Also in return for his cooperation in the execution of the treaty, McIntosh received other considerations as well, including his large reservation of property and another home (Lochau) on the Chattahoochee River in present-day western Georgia.

For years, a pervading myth has maintained that McIntosh was paid the $200,000.00 in person and in gold. One tale even relates how many wagons would have been necessary to transport the gold to McIntosh's Chattahoochee River plantation. No evidence, however, has ever surfaced to substantiate anything involving payments of gold, and no mention of gold was ever made in the language of the *Treaty.* Despite this fact, rumors persist to this day, and searches continue for *"McIntosh's gold"* all along the road from Indian Spring in Butts County to the site of McIntosh's Chattahoochee River home (Lochau).

The present-day fascination with the prospect of this gold is understandable.

In 1820, one Troy ounce of gold was valued at approximately $20.00, so the $200,000.00 payment would translate to approximately 10,000 ounces of gold if payment was made in that precious metal. In 2025, the value of gold is approximately $2,300.00 per ounce (and rising), so the payment to McIntosh just in the value of the gold itself, would be worth approximately $23,000,000.00 today if discovered. And if the payment to McIntosh was made in gold coinage of that day, the value would be almost incalculable. It, therefore, is small wonder that so much interest has been focused upon this presumed "treasure" over the years.

Immediately after the *Treaty* was signed, the Creek chiefs who had opposed the signing – led by the violent Upper Creek Nation Chief Menawa – met in secret at several Creek towns of east-central Alabama, where they began discussions of retaliation against those individuals who had signed away the tribal lands. It was decided that at the very least, William McIntosh would die, as would his son-in-law, Samuel Hawkins, since their actions were a capital crime under Creek law. Hawkins lived on the Tallapoosa River near the Creek towns which once existed in today's central Alabama.

Stalking McIntosh

Within the secret meetings, detailed and careful instructions were provided to a special group of the tribe's warriors on how they were to meet and advance upon McIntosh at his plantation on the

And if the payment to McIntosh was made in gold coinage of that day, the value would be almost incalculable.

Chattahoochee and how he was to be executed. The exact number of Creeks involved in this execution is unknown today; best estimates range from 170 to 400 warriors, according to several different sources through which events of that day were recorded. The mere number of warriors assigned to this task is an indication of the respect they yet held for McIntosh and his power.

The group, principally from Ocfuskee and Tookabatchie, both of which were large Creek towns in east-central Alabama, met and advanced on foot in single file toward Georgia, ironically on the McIntosh Trail / Georgia Road. They traveled so silently and efficiently that they were completely undetected on their journey, reaching the neighborhood of McIntosh's Chattahoochee plantation on the evening of the second day.

The warriors reportedly stationed themselves on both sides of an intersection about one mile northwest of McIntosh's home, and awaited the wee hours of early morning to carry out the assassination. It was at this intersection that another ironic event occurred. On the evening of the warriors' arrival and concealment in the undergrowth at this site, McIntosh and his son-in-law Samuel Hawkins – both of whom were slated for execution by their Creek brethren – met on horseback at this very spot on the McIntosh Trail. The Creek warriors were so well-concealed and noiseless and the undergrowth so dense and impenetrable on either side of the trail that McIntosh and Hawkins were completely unaware of the presence of the natives.

The two men remained upon their mounts as they conversed at length. The assassins reportedly were so near to the pair that they could almost have reached out and touched the two unsuspecting men. The warriors could easily have killed the two there on that spot had they chosen to do so, but they had been specifically instructed that for maximum effect, McIntosh was to be executed *"in his own yard, in the presence of his family, and to let his blood run upon the soil of that reservation which the Georgians had secured to him in the treaty which he had made with them."* It was vitally important to them that a message of that shocking import be made to the remainder of the tribe.

After concluding his meeting with McIntosh, Hawkins reportedly turned and started for home, with McIntosh riding a short distance beside him. Turning back toward his own home shortly thereafter, McIntosh again passed right through the hidden Indians, and again they had an opportunity to kill him on the spot, but did not.

As Hawkins continued westward on the McIntosh Trail to return to his farm on the Tallapoosa River *(near present-day Talladega, Alabama)*, a chosen few of the warriors separated from the main group and silently followed him, intent upon an equally bloody execution for him.

The Creek warrior numbers had been decimated approximately ten years earlier in 1814 by Gen. Andrew Jackson at nearby Horseshoe Bend in Alabama, where upwards of 800 of the 1,000-warrior-strong "Red-Stick" Creek Nation were destroyed. These depleted numbers no doubt lent a measure of confidence to McIntosh in his

Treaty actions. The warriors, notably, were desperate for some measure of vengeance for being so overwhelmed by the White settlers.

Assassinations

The main body of the Creek warriors reportedly remained in the woods at McIntosh's reservation until about 3:00 a.m. of the fateful morning, at which time, they gathered "fat lighter" (the highly-flammable resinous heartwood of aged pine trees) to use to ignite McIntosh's log house. They quietly surrounded the home, and at daybreak, set the structure ablaze to force the headman and his family outside.

Inside McIntosh's inn at *Lochau* on the night of the fatal attack, five persons were sleeping, including Chilly McIntosh, son of the doomed William. As he was also one of the signers of the hated *Treaty*, and undoubtedly knew his life was also in grave danger, Chilly quite likely quickly sized up the situation upon hearing the commotion outside in the yard. He no doubt decided that discretion was the better part of valor, and leapt from a rear window of the inn and then plunged into what could only have been breathtakingly-icy cold April waters in the Chattahoochee to swim to the opposite shore and safety. Better alive, cold, wet and in danger of hypothermia on the opposite shore of the Chattahoochee than temporarily warm in the inn and soon to be stone-cold dead from a savage assassination.

The Creek warriors, meanwhile, had had the presence of mind (and self-preservationist instincts) to bring a White man *(named Hudman or Hutton; records differ on the spelling of the name)* with them, in order to later certify that no harm had come to any Whites in the inn. There were Whites sleeping there,

Cheating Death – Chilly McIntosh, son of Chief William McIntosh, was sleeping in the inn at McIntosh Reserve when the Creek assassins arrived to murder his father. Chilly barely escaped meeting his own death from the same warriors by leaping from a rear window of the inn and swimming quickly across the freezing cold Chattahoochee River.

including one peddler, and accounts of this incident maintain that on the day of the furor from the assassination, the peddler *"became a most wretched man"* until Hutton assured him that no harm would come his way. The Indians, true to their word, left the peddler unharmed, but destroyed his wares nonetheless, along with everything else in sight.

Yet another of the signers of the *Treaty of Indian Spring*, a minor Creek headman named Toma Tustinugee had the misfortune to also be sleeping in the inn. The warriors, totally surprised by this additional prize, removed Toma

to the yard, where, in the light of McIntosh's burning home, they summarily executed him within McIntosh's view, firing some fifty bullets into his body. The site of his burial is unknown today.

Flames or Bullets?

McIntosh, in the meantime, was having extreme problems of his own. The flames from his home threw a bright light over the bloody proceedings in the yard below, giving his horrified family a clear view of the terrifyingly-painted warriors surrounding the house. To the warriors' credit, they allowed McIntosh's two wives and his children to remove themselves from the burning house; no harm befell them. They, however, did not allow the women or children to remove any articles with them from the burning structure. Consequently, the women were wearing only their sparse night clothing, and the children were naked in the chill early morning April air.

After the women and children were removed, McIntosh reportedly barricaded the front door and stood near it until it was forced open. He then retreated to the second floor, guns in his hands, returning the fire from the warriors. According to later reports, his attackers stood in his yard mockingly and eerily shouting *"McIntosh! We have come! We have come! We told you, if you sold the land to the Georgians, we would come!"* The Creek assassins continued to discharge their weapons into the burning house.

McIntosh's wives, meanwhile, hysterically implored the assailants to spare their husband, or at the very least to remove him from the burning house before shooting him. They screamed to the Creeks that McIntosh was an Indian like themselves, and, as a brave man, did not deserve to die a horrible death in the flames.

The burning house soon became a roaring conflagration. At this point, McIntosh knew he could either die the horrible death of being "cooked" in the blazing log house, or take his chances with the angry executioners in the yard below. Scorched and dying from the heat and flames, the Creek headman clawed his way back to the first floor where he reportedly was met by a hail of bullets. He fell to the floor severely wounded, where he was seized by the legs and dragged into the yard outside by the warriors before the flaming house could cook him any further.

While lying in the yard, and with blood coursing from numerous wounds, McIntosh reportedly raised himself on one arm and surveyed his murderers with a look of defiance. At that moment, one of the Ocfuskee assassins plunged a long knife to the hilt into McIntosh's breast. It is recorded that he took one long gasping breath before collapsing and dying.

The Indians, however, were far from finished. At that point their blood lust knew virtually no bounds. In retrospect, it is amazing that McIntosh's family survived the terrible event.

The Indians proceeded to plunder the outhouses and to kill every domesticated animal in sight. Anything they could not carry with them, they destroyed with a vengeance. Hogs were shot and left lying in the yard beside the dead men. All the peddler's goods were

Yet another of the signers of the Treaty of Indian Spring, a minor Creek headman named Toma Tustinugee had the misfortune to also be sleeping in the inn.

removed from the inn and destroyed.

One of McIntosh's wives went to the warriors and tearfully requested that they give her a white suit in which to bury her husband. This request was quickly refused. McIntosh, to the further horror of the females, was subsequently scalped and left lying in the yard where he had died. Later, after the warriors had departed, McIntosh's body was buried a short distance away, not far from where he had fallen and died.

The Aftermath

After looting and destroying the plantation, the Indians returned on the McIntosh / Ocfuskee Road to their Alabama homes, carrying McIntosh's scalp with them. It was later ceremoniously exhibited in the public square at Ocfuskee. The scalp was a further warning to others who might be tempted to take similar measures with the remaining Creek lands.

Samuel Hawkins suffered a similar fate. After following Hawkins home to Alabama, the Creek warriors assigned to him quietly surrounded his farmhouse where they remained until daybreak. Following instructions, Hawkins was not killed out-right, but was taken prisoner until the fate of McIntosh could be certified. About 3:00 p.m., after word had been received of McIntosh's death, Hawkins also was executed, being hung by the neck until dead, then scalped. The latter trophy was displayed with that of McIntosh's scalp in Ocfuskee Town.

The resulting repercussions of these killings were felt all the way to the halls of Congress. Called *"murder"* by the Whites, and *"a legal execution"* by the Indians, the incident was actually an act of desperation by a nation of people quickly being displaced from their homeland by an on-rushing tide of White settlers. It would only be a short ten years before the state and federal governments would remove the Indians completely from their remaining lands in Alabama, relocating them in an arduous journey to Oklahoma Territory.

Today, one can visit the site of the McIntosh killing in a Carroll County park located about four miles southwest of Whitesburg. With the exception of McIntosh's grave, the site holds no hint of the horrors perpetrated there in April of 1825. It is a beautiful, quiet and secluded spot overlooking the very scenic Chattahoochee River. It is small wonder that McIntosh chose this for his final home.

The remains of a later house built on or near the site of McIntosh's burned home actually stood until the late 20th century. The later structure, however, eventually was almost completely destroyed by greedy "treasure hunters" and vandals, many of whom were voraciously searching for McIntosh's mythical gold. As of this writing, a replica of McIntosh's burned home has been reconstructed yet again at the site, and is preserved there today.

If one visits the intersection of the park road with GA Highway 5 just north of the old home-place, he or she will be in the exact spot on the McIntosh Trail where McIntosh and Hawkins conversed on that fateful night so long ago.

Retracing McIntosh Trail

For those who desire to retrace the original McIntosh Road westward from Indian Spring, the following directions are provided:

Leaving Indian Spring in a south-westwardly direction, the old road passed just north of present-day Mt. Vernon Church and by Elgin and Liberty Churches, before going through an area once known as "Sandy Plains."

The road next passed through the old ghost town of Waltham, before reaching Spalding County on today's GA Highway 16. It continued by Union and Ringgold Churches to the intersection of GA Highways 16 and 156. At that crossing there was once the stagecoach stop and community of "Double Cabins" (the Militia District today retains the name: "Cabin District").

Double Cabins was due north of present-day Griffin and the McIntosh Trail in running through the former town, missed Griffin completely. Along that stretch, the old road was once known as the "Old Madison Alabama Stage Road," and also as "Upper Cabin Road."

Passing on through the upper fringes of Experiment, the McIntosh Road took the left fork at McIntosh School, before going through Rio and Vaughn and crossing the Flint River into Fayette County. It ran on westward through Brooks and Senoia, passing just north of Turin to go through Sharpsburg and Raymond, close on GA Highway 16, before reaching Newnan on McIntosh Street, a name obviously retained from the original McIntosh Road.

From Newnan, the old thoroughfare turned northwest to cross the Chattahoochee River near the mouth of Pearson's Creek. At that stream, the

McIntosh Road crossed over McIntosh's Ferry into present-day Carroll County where it reached the settlement and home of William McIntosh in McIntosh Reserve.

As of this writing, there is an area on McIntosh's old reservation just west of the Chattahoochee River where an abandoned remnant of the old original McIntosh Trail is still discernible. Turning up the hill from the river, the road passes the site at which McIntosh's home and inn once existed at the site of his murder.

Continuing northward for a short distance, the old McIntosh Trail reached an intersection just west of today's Rotherwood. This, again, is the intersection at which William McIntosh and Samuel Hawkins conversed while the silent Indians surrounding them awaited the predetermined time and place of the assassination of the two men.

From this point, the McIntosh Road turned directly westward to run on GA Highway 5 all the way into Alabama, passing through Lowell, Roopville, and Tyrus along the way. It was along the latter stretch that Sam Hawkins made the final trip to his home in Alabama before dying there at the hands of the Creek warriors.

Today, there is a great interest in the McIntosh saga. In Peachtree City, just north of the actual route of the road, there is a McIntosh Opry as well as a McIntosh High School. In fact, all along the way from Indian Spring in present-day Butts County westward, remnants of

the name are retained, and many persons living today along the original McIntosh Trail are familiar with details concerning the McIntosh legend.

Epitaph

Though he has departed this earth, and though the worldly possessions of the famous chieftain have been scattered and lost, the historic milestones of his life live on . . . as does McIntosh's legend.

Today, archived at the University of Georgia Libraries are two letters, one written by two of the three wives of McIntosh's wives, and another written by the daughter of the third wife. The letters were penned in desperation immediately following McIntosh's murder, and sent to White leaders of that day in 1825. They represented the McIntosh family's desperate pleas for help.

These sad plaintive documents vividly describe the horror and anguish suffered by Peggy and Susannah McIntosh (two of the wives), and of Jane Hawkins (a daughter of the third wife). The letters also provide a clear indication of the oftentimes harsh and unforgiving circumstances encountered by 19th century American Indian leaders (and, subsequently, their families) who dared to negotiate with and bargain away tribal lands to the U.S. government in a quest for a better life for their people.

(For more information on the life and assassination of William McIntosh, please see "Gunmen, Lawmen and Wild Men of Early Georgia" by R. Olin Jackson, available at Amazon, Ingram-Spark, Barnes & Noble, and other fine booksellers.

Continuing northward for a short distance, the old McIntosh Trail reached an intersection just west of today's Rotherwood.

The Trail-Blazer of
Peachtree Road

Prehistoric game trails which eventually were adopted by aboriginals in the region ultimately gave rise to the breath-taking metropolitan area known in the 21ˢᵗ century as the city of Atlanta.

In the midst of the creation of this book, much discussion has been made of the former wildlife and aboriginal trails from prehistory which existed (and continue to exist to some extent) in an "east-west" direction within the confines of the area known today as the state of Georgia. There were a number of prehistoric "north-south" trails as well which have evolved into the super-highways and byways used by the modern travelers of today.

Old Game Trails

More often than not – and again for the obvious reason that they originated as game trails stamped out by wildlife which instinctively followed the route(s) of least resistance in their migrations – these trails were eventually adopted by the Native Americans in pre-history, and later by European-Americans as they populated what today is the eastern United States westward.

If one examines a modern road map, one will notice several modern highways – old U.S. Highways 41, 5, 19, and 23 – which radiate in almost equi-distant bands north to south in the state. This is not happenstance. All four of the above-mentioned "modern paths" (and numerous others) follow the

approximate "prehistoric paths" which almost certainly were also created by migratory beasts – as previously stated – along the routes of least resistance around hills, through mountain passes, and across the streams, rivers and other barriers encountered along the way.

Also, as is the case with modern "old" Highways 5 and 19 in particular, these routes to a great extent simply followed the ridgetops of a long line of hills and rises as they progressed north to south. It is for this reason that the rainfall which falls on the eastern side of the pioneer community of Auraria, Georgia, in present-day Lumpkin County (through which old U.S. 19 travels) has been documented to be watershed draining to the Atlantic Ocean, and that which falls on the west side becomes a part of the watershed to the Gulf of Mexico.

The same set of circumstances exists for the "old route" of Georgia Highway 19 in downtown Atlanta. Again, the rainfall on the eastern side of this ancient route is (in general) watershed which drains to the Atlantic and that which falls on the western side is watershed draining to the Gulf of Mexico. A long ridge extends almost continuously from present-day Dahlonega, Georgia to Atlanta, and both the wildlife and Native

Pioneer Fort – This artist's rendering of "Fort Standing Peachtree" was drawn from written descriptions of this pioneer fortification. It was once located in the general vicinity of the present-day Atlanta City Waterworks near modern U.S. Highway 41 and Moore's Mill Road. (Illustration by Barbara Chastain as drawn for the Fort Peachtree Chapter of the Daughters of the American Revolution.)

Americans made use of this unique feature in their constant migrations, trading and warring activities.

An almost identical situation applies to "old" Georgia Highway 5. It was for this reason that the Louisville & Nashville (L&N) Railroad generally followed that route in its design northward to the Tennessee state line. It, quite simply, is the route of least resistance which, again, in many instances, follows a gradually rising ridgeline northward.

Old Roswell Road

Of course there are exceptions. The steep hill up which old U.S. Highway 19 travels from the Chattahoochee River to downtown "Old Roswell" being a good example. The portion of the old road from the river to the town does not follow the actual original prehistoric trail. To the contrary, when that portion of the road was "improved" by pioneer settlers populating the growing burg of Roswell, a direct route *straight up the hill* was deemed to be the most desirable route because it was the most direct and was generally manageable through the use of beasts of burden. It, therefore, became the route of general use rather than the old prehistoric route which turned right at the base of the hill and continued down the river, following the more advantageous route to the vicinity of present-day Grimes Bridge Road.

When the *Roswell Railroad* (later owned by *Southern Railways*) was being constructed from Atlanta to Roswell in the early 1860s, it followed much the same ridge from Atlanta northward until it reached the Chattahoochee River at Roswell, but it was never completed any further than that point. The reason was two-fold: the terrain across the river and up the hill into Roswell was a difficult route for railroad construction, and the U.S. Civil War ultimately interrupted any attempt to conquer these obstacles.

In 1863, the city of Roswell had obtained a charter which provided for the organization of the *"Atlanta and Roswell Railroad Company (A&R-RR)"* which would be constructed from downtown Atlanta (actually as a branch-line of the *Western & Atlantic Railroad*) into what then was a very small and quiet Roswell. No action, however, was ever forthcoming from this charter until 1870, when the *Atlanta & Richmond Air-Line (A&R)* railroad was constructing a line from Atlanta to Charlotte, North Carolina.

The original charter for the *Atlanta & Richmond* was amended to consolidate the *Atlanta & Roswell Railroad Company* within its corporate structure. This charter amendment provided for the associated creation of the Roswell rail line in conjunction with the *A&R*, thereby providing the necessary funding for the route. Despite this action, construction was still delayed, due once again to topographical and financial issues, and the topic became one of frustration for the citizens of Roswell for many years, most of whom were eager to have their own railroad line for commercial and transportation needs, not the least of which was the need to overcome the obstacle of the thick muddy intolerable quagmire up the steep hill into the town.

A letter from the President of the *Roswell Manufacturing Company* dated July, 1880, stated the circumstances fairly succinctly: *"The question of securing for this Company a better connection with Commercial centres, a quicker and more economical method of transportation than by wagon, for production, supplies and merchandise, has received the serious consideration of every President who has charge of your interest at this point."* This document is the clearest indication available of the frustration felt for almost two decades by the merchants of the up-and-coming town. It was a frustration which was not alleviated until Roswell Road "up the muddy hill" into the town was paved many years later.

The prehistoric trail down the general route of present-day old U.S. 19 was one of the more extensive of the north-south venues in the state. It provided prehistoric aboriginal inhabitants of the region not only a "warring path," but also a very important "trading path" to sites as far away as Florida.

Fort Peachtree

One portion of the present-day old U.S. 41 route included a strategically important section known to historians today as *"Standing Peachtree."* Also known as *"Fort Peachtree Park,"* this site today is a public park at the confluence of Peachtree Creek and the Chattahoochee River which places it quite near to the ridgelines carrying both the present-day old U.S. 41 and old U.S. 19 prehistoric trails.

Standing Peachtree in actuality was a Creek Indian village in prehistory and later a trading post during colonial times. The ancient Indian trail leading to this site – as previously described – existed along a prominent ridge line towards what today is downtown Atlanta. This trail later became *Peachtree Street*, named after the Indian village, not the peach trees which proliferated in the vicinity.

"Fort Peachtree," which reportedly *was* named for a large peach tree at the

site, was built in 1814, during the *War of 1812*. A reconstruction of the fort which once existed at this site was erected near the present-day Atlanta Waterworks facility, but, as of this writing, is not open to the public.

Fort Peachtree enjoys a connection to a unique figure in Georgia history. Northward, up the pioneer trail of what today is the aforementioned U.S. Highway 23 in Hall County, an individual by the name of Robert Young carved not only a home from the north Georgia wilderness, but also a significant footnote for himself in the state's history.

Young was the son of Stephen and Diana Tucker Young. He and his brother, John, came to Georgia at the time the state, through treaties, was rapidly acquiring Indian lands from the natives.

Young's Tavern

Robert Young was married in Franklin County, Georgia, to "Selah" (Celia) Strickland, daughter of Jacob and Priscilla Strickland. The young couple became the parents of thirteen children.

On his 1,600 acres of land, Robert built a large two-story log home which had twelve rooms. The chimneys, pillars, and flagstone walks were made of sandstone, cut from a quarry on the farm. The imposing structure shortly became prominently known in the region as *"Young's Tavern,"* and was frequented by guests ranging from penniless travelers to a future president of the United States.

Today, across the road from the former site of *Young's Tavern* (which has long since disappeared from the landscape), the family cemetery survives and marks the former home-site for posterity. It is located on the Atlanta Highway (Old U.S. 23) – also called, appropriately

enough, *Peachtree Road*. Robert and Selah, his mother, Diana (who died at the age of 108), and other family members are all interred in this cemetery.

For many years, the late famed Atlanta historian Franklin Garrett recorded headstones in burial plots within a 25-mile radius of Atlanta. To him, it was as much a hobby as it was an important official cataloguing of the history of the city of Atlanta.

The Young family cemetery fell outside this 25-mile radius, but for this one, Garrett made an exception in his documentation. He reportedly visited and recorded information from this cemetery on several occasions, because its inhabitants were so monumentally important to the eventual history of the city of Atlanta.

A short distance from the cemetery and *Young's Tavern*, a stockade – *Fort Daniel* – was erected in 1813 for the protection of settlers from Indian uprisings. It was located at *Hog Mountain* and was defended by troops of the 25th Regiment, Georgia Militia, along with a number of volunteer soldiers.

As a result of its accommodations and proximity to this fort, *Young's Tavern* was a place where travelers frequently paused for lodging. It also was a focal point of the area in times of unrest and war.

According to folklore, Gen. Andrew Jackson and his staff lodged at the tavern on at least two occasions – once when the famed Indian fighter's troops were marching to *Fort Early* in South Georgia on the old *Federal Road* (Readers please see *"Retracing the Old Federal Road"* in this volume) to quell an Indian uprising there.

On another occasion, Jackson was on his way to South Carolina to meet with President James Monroe to confer

Early Frontier – This illustration of Georgia during the early pioneer era shows the geographic areas which later became the states of Alabama and Georgia. At that time, the southern portion of the "western frontier" of the United States lay beyond Georgia's Ocmulgee River. The site of Milledgeville which at that time was the state capital of Georgia is pictured, as is a network of frontier outposts, including that of Fort Standing Peachtree. (Map courtesy of the Georgia Department of Archives & History, Atlanta, and Mary Frances Morrow)

with him about the **Monroe Doctrine**. While enroute to this meeting, Gen. Jackson again overnighted at *Young's Tavern*, and upon his departure the following morning – as the story goes – he paused to pay for his lodging. Robert Young reportedly declined to accept payment, and Gen. Jackson, in appreciation, presented his gracious host with a silver snuff box. The priceless keepsake reportedly has been handed down through the years, and is still in the possession of Young family members today.

Peachtree Road Origin

Young's Tavern also earned a place in the area's history for another reason. Long before there was an Atlanta, there was, as indicated above, a *Standing Peachtree* locality where *Fort Peachtree (also known as "Fort Standing Peachtree")* had been constructed for defensive purposes.

The fort occupied the crest of a commanding eminence northeast of the confluence of the Chattahoochee River and Peachtree Creek. It soon was reasoned that a road to connect this *"Fort Standing Peachtree"* with *Fort Daniel* at Hog Mountain would be very prudent for security purposes. It would reduce the rescue response time to either structure in times of emergency.

Three citizens, all of whom were stockmen familiar with the country were employed to mark out and construct the route. These three individuals were William Nesbit (associated with *Nesbit Ferry* across the Chattahoochee) and Isham Williams of Gwinnett County, and Robert Young of *Young's Tavern*.

The road builders proceeded with their task according to Franklin Garrett's now seminal volume of history entitled **Atlanta & Environs** by marking a trail from the White settlement at *Hog Mountain* to the site of what is known today as *Buckhead* in modern Atlanta. The route they carved out of the virgin forest wilderness is the highway known today as *Peachtree Road*. Since this route also follows the natural "high ground" along what today is old U.S. Highway 23, it quite probably also follows much of the route of a former game/aboriginal trail to create the easiest and most manageable route to *Standing Peachtree* (and vice versa to *Fort Daniel* at Hog Mountain).

According to accounts of this task, Augustin Young, son of Robert, and Hiram Williams, another worker, drove a cart in the project. Robert Young and Isham Williams served generally as supervisors of the project and as armed pickets, constantly monitoring the thick wilderness for any threat or danger.

According to Garrett's book, *"Robert Young was described as a character whose like is seldom seen, and whose like will seldom be seen again. . . He had no 'book knowledge' except that from the 'book of nature'. . . He was true to his word and his integrity was unquestionable. He always wore his hair – which he prized most highly and of which he was most proud – tied up in a queue."*

Young Memorials

In 1937, as a result of the historic nature of Young's life-long accomplishments, the **Georgia Historical Commission** placed a plaque at the former site of *Young's Tavern*. It reads:

"Jackson at Young's Tavern. . . Andrew Jackson, his staff and two companies of militia, spent a night on their way to the Seminole Campaign in 1818. General Jackson followed the road through Monticello and Hawkinsville, while the main body of troops went to South Georgia by way of Alabama. This was on the Federal Road, the first vehicular way in northwest Georgia, opened in 1805." (Readers please see *"Retracing the Old Federal Road"* in this volume.)

Even earlier than the above plaque, however – and unknown to many Georgians today – another more significant plaque was placed at another historic landmark. In 1935, the *Joseph Habersham Chapter* of the *Daughters of the American Revolution (D.A.R.)* of Atlanta, placed a bronze tablet upon the front of the old Sears-Roebuck building on Ponce de Leon Avenue in Atlanta. As many fans of the old minor-league **Atlanta Crackers** baseball team well remember, it was (and still is as of this writing) across

The route they carved out of the virgin forest wilderness is the highway known today as Peachtree Road.

the street from the former site of the old *Ponce de Leon Ball Park.*

(Special Note: The "Crackers" played in the Southern Association from 1901 to 1965. They famously were one of the most successful minor league teams in baseball history, winning 17 league championships, second only to the New York Yankees. Numerous later stars came up to the "majors" from their ranks.)

The plaque on the old Sears Building commemorating the accomplishments of Robert Young reads:

*This Tablet
Commemorates The Spot
Formerly Ponce de Leon Spring
Where Robert Young,
A Revolutionary Soldier
Of Cherokee, Now Hall County,
First Traded With The Creek Indians
And Built The Peachtree Trail From
Atlanta To Flowery Branch.*

Interestingly, if Robert Young could witness today the results of his early road-building and survival efforts in what now is the modern metropolitan-Atlanta area, he, no doubt, would be shocked beyond description. From his efforts – and those of his co-workers – the voluminous criss-crossing endless streets of the immense metro area and the other massive residential and commercial construction have arisen. Would he be pleased with the crime, pollution, over-population and other problems which now exist where an untamed wilderness once stood? His reaction to the circumstances of modern-day Atlanta undoubtedly would be interesting.

Early Northwest Georgia Railroad Disasters

In the early 1900s, the railroads were evolving into a huge business enterprise, much of it based upon the observance of strict time-tables as to when products and people reached a specified destination. As the speeds of the behemoths hurtling down the ribbons of rail increased to keep these arrival times, the caution of the engineers at the helm wasn't always adequate. The rail accidents in northwest Georgia which sometimes occurred as a result of this lack of caution were almost always terribly disastrous, and sometimes breathtakingly so.

"They were goin' down grade making ninety miles an hour,
When the whistle broke into a scream -
He was found in the wreck with his hand on the throttle,
Scalded to death by the steam."
- From "The Wreck of Old 97"

On the crisp autumn morning of October 23rd, 1903, there was no hint of the unfolding disaster waiting ahead. All witnesses to that terrible event have now passed on into eternity, but the written records of the incident describe a calmness which belied the onrushing horror. *"Train Number 81, southbound on the Southern Railway, had a few minutes to get in the clear at Dallas for Number 18 northbound vestibule Sunday morning,"* according to a news report in a 1903 issue of the **Dallas New Era**. The men on board did not know it at the time, but a sizeable disaster was only a few moments away. . .

The article continued by explaining *"Engineer Jim Nichols opened the throttle of his monster engine on the summit one mile south of McPherson. Engine 345 never acted better. The big machine moved forward at a terrific rate with twenty-five cars behind. The engineer looked at his watch and knew that time was precious."*

Pumpkinvine Creek Trestle

The disaster which broke the stillness that quiet Sunday morning occurred approximately one mile north of the tiny community of Dallas in northwest Georgia. It was the type of accident that, unfortunately, was not unusual on

Trestle Disaster – For reasons still unknown today, the Pumpkinvine Creek Trestle collapsed beneath the weight of Train #81 of *Southern Railways* on October 23, 1903, killing the fireman of the train. The engineer miraculously guided *Engine #81* safely to the opposite side as the trestle and numerous freight cars collapsed behind it. (Photo courtesy of Duane Mintz & Jack Howel)

lonely mountain trestles in the early days of railroading. It was also the type of accident which immortalized the trainmen who traveled these dangerous routes – often at excessive speeds – day after day until fate finally overtook them.

Train Number 81 was a very heavy locomotive. It included some twenty-five cars, and was hurtling down the track at approximately 60 miles an hour when the monstrous engine rolled onto the high steel bridge over Pumpkinvine Creek. The engineer later said he felt the trestle lurch from the weight, and he quickly throttled back, but it was too late. Behind him, six spans of heavy steel trestlework began collapsing with a thunderous roar into the creek-bed seventy-seven feet below, taking thirteen freight cars, the engine tender and the fireman with it into eternity.

Then, just as suddenly as the horrifying accident had begun, it ended, bringing a deathly silence to the spot. As he brought his locomotive to a screeching stop, Nichols reportedly turned and looked desperately for his faithful fireman, John Fagala (also reported as *"J.M. Flagler"* in the news article), who had been standing on the tender when the collapse began. After a quick but futile search around the tight confines of the locomotive, Nichols next went back to the edge of the broken trestle high above the flowing creek below, where his eyes landed upon the sight he feared he would find in the ravine below.

The tender had been ripped from the engine coupling as the track collapsed beneath it. It was lying far below in a tangle of trestle steel and freight cars. John Fagala (Flagler?) undoubtedly

Disaster Trestle Today – The trestle over Pumpkinvine Creek at the site of the 1903 disaster was photographed in 1997. Many trainmen remain uneasy about traversing it even today. (Photo by Gordon Sargent)

never felt the impact when he struck the bottom of the chasm. He may have jumped free of the tender, hoping for the best, or maybe he had simply been tossed off the precipice as the tender was snatched from the engine. Whatever the circumstances, his body was found in the wreckage, his neck and leg broken. He had been killed instantly.

Miraculously, the last cars of the train had somehow remained intact upon the track on the opposite side of the chasm. Consequently, the conductor and flagman in the caboose survived the devastation without a scratch. The reason for the salvation of this portion of the train is unknown today.

The 360-foot bridge across Pumpkinvine Creek was one of the longest and highest in northwest Georgia. It had safely carried hundreds of fast trains in the late 1800s. Today, no one knows what caused the bridge to suddenly collapse, but many individuals knowledgeable of rail accidents have speculated on the cause. One report indicated the large locomotive had simply been traveling too fast and had jumped the rails on the curved trestle, leading the cars behind it to devastation.

"The first time I heard of the Pumpkinvine trestle collapsing was from Mr. Paul McDonald, Southern Railway's third trick operator at Rockmart," explained the late Duane "Cowboy" Mintz, a former conductor on Southern Railways, who said he passed back and forth across the Pumpkinvine Creek trestle continuously himself during his career.

"Later, after I went to work for Southern, I mentioned the incident while dead-heading to Chattanooga on (Train) Number 32, Rockmart's four o'clock train in the afternoon. I was rebuffed by some of the veteran railroaders who seemed to be irritated at me for passing on tales of which they had never heard. The old head conductor, Mr. E.E. (Emmett) Whittle, however, came to my rescue. 'The boy's right,' he told them. 'It happened not long after I went to work (for Southern). I almost quit the railroad on account of that accident.'"

The Pumpkinvine Creek trestle is located on the rail line between Atlanta, Georgia and Chattanooga, Tennessee on the route once known as the "Georgia Division" of Southern Railways. Even today, trains still pass over a steel trestle (one of the longest and highest on the division) at this same site above the creek many times a day. "I, as well as a lot of

The old *Southern Railways* depot in Rockmart, Georgia, a short distance from the Pumpkinvine Creek trestle was photographed circa 1905. *Train #81* stopped regularly at this station.

others, never did like crossing it," Mintz added. "I personally don't like any trestle that is built as part of a curve, especially like that one is."

Braswell Mountains Culprit

The Dallas to Rockmart portion of the Georgia Division has long been a dangerous one. As a part of the Atlanta to Chattanooga line in Southern Railways' network it was completed on July 1, 1882. There have been at least four major disasters on the Dallas to Rockmart segment alone in the past 90 years, and possibly numerous others.

Break-neck speed and a tight railroad time-table undoubtedly were major factors in several of the incidents. In 1902, Southern Railways obtained a contract to haul the mail between Washington, D.C. and Atlanta, Georgia, on the New York to New Orleans line. The U.S. government wanted the best means possible for quick transport

of the mails, and fast locomotives were the answer. In return, Southern Railways earned $140,000 a year for this service. In those days, that was big money – the rough equivalent of $4,483,000.00 in 2025 dollars.

But it was a double-edged sword. If Southern couldn't keep up with the schedule, it was penalized $100.00 for every thirty minutes the mail was late at every destination. That was more than enough incentive for rail management to impose heavy, heavy pressure on trainmen to maintain schedules. This almost always meant exceeding the speed limit by many miles an hour more than the speed at which a stretch of rails and their supporting components such as trestles were designed to be used. And the fact that some trains were traveling on dangerous stretches of track to begin with, only added to the propensity for disaster.

One such example is the stretch of tracks between Dallas, Georgia and

Rockmart. On the evening of December 23, 1926, on the outskirts of Rockmart, the Ponce de Leon passenger train, traveling in excess of 50 miles per hour, collided head-on with the Royal Palm passenger train because of confusion exacerbated by excessive speed.

This disaster resulted in at least 19 – and possibly 20 or more – fatalities (the exact number is unknown today), and at least 113 passengers, 4 Southern Railways employees and 6 Pullman employees were seriously injured. This wreck remains as one of the worst disasters in the history of the railroad in the United States.

At least part of the reason for these accidents outside Rockmart stemmed from the fact that trains have long been able to build up considerable speed coming down out of the Braswell Mountains outside Rockmart, and engineers were loathe to cut this speed once having built it up along this stretch. It has happened time and time again, and even today, the big freight trains hurtling toward Chattanooga often pass through Rockmart at far higher rates of speed than necessary and safe.

Big Raccoon Creek Trestle

Another accident (on that same dangerous stretch between Dallas and Rockmart) which caused the death of several individuals occurred nearby at Big Raccoon Creek trestle in February of 1883. The bridgework at this site was practically new at that time, and railroad historians have long pondered the reason for its collapse. "It's just another of the many puzzling events in the annals of railroading in the early days," Mintz continued matter-of-factly.

The 44-year veteran of the rails served on the Georgia Division Safety Committee of Southern for ten years. "I wrote, printed and distributed a safety newsletter, and one of the articles I carried in the newsletter was a description of the Big Raccoon Creek accident," he smiled.

The trestle at Big Raccoon Creek is seven miles north of Dallas. The creek itself is just a small stream, but the heavily eroded creek-bed is significantly deep with high bluffs on either side. At the time of the accident, the trestle at this site was a three-deck trestle, spanning 1,480 feet from bluff to bluff and rising 94 feet from the creek-bed.

Mr. Mintz's newsletter article of this disaster, reprinted from a news report in the February 22, 1883 issue of the **Dallas New Era** newspaper, described the accident as follows: *"Last Saturday morning, about 10:30 a.m., as Train Number 59, a through-freight of the E.T.V. & G. R.R.* (East Tennessee, Virginia & Georgia Railroad) *was leaving the switch at the tunnel, south-bound. Conductor Bob Shoemaker boarded the engine, as it was convenient for him at the time, and (he) remarked to his engineer that he would ride with him down to Dallas rather than drop back to his caboose.*

"All went well until the train, running at the rate of 7 or 8 miles an hour, ran upon Big Raccoon Trestle. . . Having passed across to within a few yards of the south side with his engine, Mr.

This wreck remains as one of the worst disasters in the history of the railroad in the United States.

Neeley gave her a little more steam in order to pull over the grade in front. Almost immediately, a severe shock being felt, Mr. Shoemaker, (comprehending) the cause and looking back, shouted, 'Pull her open! Pull her open! The bridge is going!' . . . The terrible crash that followed left them standing upon the very brink of a yawning abyss - the bottom of which was covered with ruins, all within a moment of time.

　　"*The (collapsed) section consisted of ten or eleven cars laden with merchandise, and the caboose. There were three men in the caboose and a Negro brakeman about midway of the train. . . The unfortunate brakeman was killed outright. Mr. R.P. Kidwell . . . was on board, enroute to Atlanta to visit his family. He too was so fatally injured that death came as a relief to his sufferings very soon after being removed from the debris to the car in waiting. Mr. John Cox . . . also in the caboose, sustained injuries that proved fatal to him as well, living until Saturday night totally unconscious all the while. Mr. Charles Camp, flagman . . . remained unconscious for several hours, then awoke to the realization of his remarkable escape . . . (He had) a scalp wound, a crushed ankle, and a dislocated elbow, (but he was alive!).*"

　　The heavy train had passed across the trestle until the caboose was immediately over the creek. At that point, according to the news account printed in the *New Era*, section after section of the trestle began giving way somewhere near the center of the train. The general collapse of the trestle was very similar to

On December 23, 1926, a devastating collision between the *Ponce de Leon* and the *Royal Palm* passenger trains resulted in one of the worst rail disasters in U.S. history. This accident in Rockmart, Georgia, occurred only a short distance from the Pumpkinvine Creek trestle disaster site. (Photo courtesy of the GA Dept. of Archives & History, Atlanta, GA)

the collapse of the trestle just six or seven miles away at Pumpkinvine Creek in 1903.

Common Cause For The Disasters?

　　The 360-foot trestle across Pumpkinvine had safely carried hundreds of fast trains over the years. The cause of its collapse is still unknown also, but the news account in the 1903 *New Era* speculates upon the possibilities. "*Some think train wreckers had removed a rail causing the wreck, while others believe that the high rate of speed caused the terrible disaster,*" the newspaper intoned.

　　Duane Mintz said he didn't think a missing

The general collapse of the trestle was very similar to the collapse of the trestle just six or seven miles away at Pumpkinvine Creek in 1903.

rail had caused the accident at all. "If a rail had been missing, the whole engine would have gone over the side of the trestle, and it wouldn't have caused much trestle damage either," the trainman explained. "I think simple structural weakness caused both the Raccoon Creek and Pumpkinvine Creek disasters."

A very similar accident, which was highly publicized across the United States, had occurred on a Southern Railways line just three weeks earlier. The wreck of the "Old 97" which occurred in Danville, Virginia, became the subject for a popular ballad which is still remembered by many railroad enthusiasts today:

Steve Broady, the engineer of the Old 97, was pushing the mail train faster and faster to make up lost time. Witnesses claim the train reached ninety miles an hour as the 80-ton behemoth swept down a grade and struck the "curved" timber trestle. A flange on one of the wheels reportedly broke off, and the engine with its cars plunged seventy-five feet into the creek below.

Twelve of the nineteen individuals on board Old 97 were killed. The engineer and fireman were found with the skin flayed from their bodies by the super-heated steam from the crushed boiler. It was a fate from which the engineer at Pumpkinvine Creek had mercifully been spared, but there's no arguing that the Danville, Virginia and Pumpkinvine Creek, Georgia disasters were eerily similar in nature.

Whatever the cause of the wreck at Pumpkinvine, rail officials were determined not to allow the accident to keep the line out of service any longer than absolutely necessary. Service between Chattanooga and Atlanta was

temporarily rerouted through Rome, while a huge work crew labored feverishly to repair the damage. Every hour the line remained out of service represented a great financial loss for Southern.

"Two wrecking crews reached the scene about 12:00 p.m., six hours after the occurrence, and more than two hundred men were clearing away the debris," the **Dallas New Era** explained.

Even this amount of man-power, however, apparently was not enough, and still more men were dispatched to the site to help. Working around the clock, the men had the track and trestle repaired three days after the disaster. By Wednesday morning, the first train steamed safely over the repaired bridge, heading north to Chattanooga.

Once the wreckage had been cleared away and the repairs had been made, the scene at Pumpkinvine Creek quickly returned to normal too. Earlier on that fateful Sunday, sightseers had streamed out of Dallas to view the site of the disaster. And with the crowds came scavengers who dug through the wreckage in search of booty.

The atmosphere, no doubt, was somewhat like a country carnival. The crushed freight cars had spilled their cargoes of corn, oats, cotton, and apples, and according to one wag, a load of *Bull Durham* tobacco. It was reported with some mirth, that virtually every boy in Paulding County learned to smoke as a result of this wreck.

Meanwhile, in sleepy Varnell, Georgia, near the Tennessee state line, the festivities were not quite so lively. . . A railroader – the poor fireman at the Pumpkinvine Creek Trestle accident – had been killed. The grieving wife – with her two small children – received their loved one home from the railroad for the last time.

The *Silver Comet* Rail Trail

The old Seaboard Railroad – a victim of time, progress, and business mergers - ceased operations in Polk County, Georgia, in 1971. As such, the tracks of Seaboard in most of Polk were taken up and sold for scrap. However, a growing phenomenon in the great outdoors has breathed new life into the former road-bed of the old rail line, preserving it for future generations.

Outside of a once-thriving stone products industry, a championship high school football team or two over the years, a terrible train wreck in 1926, and a sensational murder or two, there haven't been many things to focus regional attention (and certainly not national attention) upon the small mill-town of Rockmart, Georgia. That, interestingly, may be changing, however, with the advent of a substantial new hiking and biking trail through the county on an abandoned rail line.

Called the *"Silver Comet Trail,"* this twelve-foot-wide multi-use byway is built on the former road-bed of the old *Seaboard Airline Railroad*. The trail has proven to be a big hit among exercise and outdoor enthusiasts – particularly those of the bicycle-riding class.

This new addition to the *Rails-Trails* phenomenon has rescued the memory of the rail line and its historic former passenger service on the famed *"Silver Comet."* The *Silver Comet Trail* (obviously named in the train's honor) will ultimately adjoin several other similar "rails to trails" projects to stretch a total of approximately 100 miles as a scenic byway for the enjoyment of walkers, bicycle riders, horseback riders and skaters from throughout the state.

On almost any given weekend (and often on weekdays as well), trail users may be seen enjoying this scenic avenue. The trail has not only attracted hikers and bikers, but nature and history enthusiasts as well, since the old *Seaboard Railroad* bed snakes through some very scenic and historic terrain in Cobb, Paulding and Polk counties. It also hasn't done any harm to the commercial life of the sleepy towns on the route either.

The Silver Comet

In 1904, construction of the Seaboard subsidiary Atlanta and Birmingham Air Line Railway was completed, extending the Atlanta route to Birmingham, Alabama, the largest center of iron and steel production in the South at that time, and a valuable endpoint for the Seaboard. With that new rail line, the sky seemed the limit for Seaboard.

In 1947, the famous *Silver Comet Train* – one of the finest forms of

Oft-Mistaken Identity – The Pumpkinvine Creek trestle (pictured) of the old *Seaboard Airline Railroad* (and *Silver Comet Trail*) is often confused with a similar trestle a short distance away on the *Southern Railways* line. Both trestles bridge Pumpkinvine Creek, but are separate and distinct. On October 23, 1903, the trestle on the *Southern Railways* line collapsed beneath the weight of a heavy southbound *Southern* freight train, plunging the fireman of the locomotive to his death and destroying a number of the freight cars, but miraculously sparing the locomotive which somehow made it safely to the opposite side of the overpass. (Photo by Gordon Sargent)

transportation in the southeastern United States at that time – made its maiden journey. Traveling through such major cities as Birmingham, Atlanta, Washington D.C., and Philadelphia, this luxury passenger train was considered an elegant and speedy mode of transportation for travelers between the above metropolitan cities. Along the way, the passengers were treated to many scenic rural areas such as that offered by Polk County.

The *Silver Comet* consisted of three day-coaches, a dining car, a tavern car, and several sleeping cars. Each of the sleeping cars was named after towns along the *Comet's* route, such as *"the Atlantan,"* or *"the Cedartown,"* and the train flourished for a decade or more before passenger rail travel fell out of vogue.

With the advent of dependable interstate highways, better and more comfortable automobiles, and more affordable air travel in the 1960s, rail transportation suddenly became passe' and patronage of the once-elegant passenger trains swiftly declined.

Sadly, the once majestic rail transportation options such as the *Silver Comet* eventually were unable to generate the revenues necessary to warrant continued existence. The *Comet* made its final run in 1969, and passenger service was discontinued entirely in 1971 when Seaboard turned all of its passenger business over to AMTRAK. As a result of the loss of these revenues, even the rail lines such as the once high-traffic route between Smyrna and

Rockmart eventually found themselves being abandoned.

Luckily for the communities along the old Smyrna-Rockmart route, a movement called *"Rails-To-Trails"* became interested in the *Comet's* former road-bed. In 1989, the Georgia Department of Transportation purchased the rights-of-way of the former Seaboard route to Rockmart. Approximately ten years later in 1998, an organization by the name of *"PATH"* agreed to oversee the construction and completion of what was being called the *"Silver Comet Trail"* from Smyrna to Cedartown, and the stage was set for a whole new life for the revered old Seaboard Airline Railroad bed.

The *PATH* foundation is a nonprofit organization dedicated to the conversion of old railways to metro-wide trail systems. In the process, the foundation seeks to enhance community spirit and bring neighborhoods together. The *Silver Comet* is just one of a number of successful similar projects undertaken by *PATH* in the foundation's endless pursuit of *"Rails-To-Trails"* opportunities.

A short distance beyond Cedartown, the trail will continue across the state line into Alabama. At this point, the *Silver Comet Trail* will connect with the *Chief Ladiga Trail* in Alabama for a combined total of approximately 100 miles of hiking and biking enjoyment.

Points Along The Trail

From the Rambo access point in Dallas, Georgia, the first scenic stop on the trail is the Pumpkinvine Creek Trestle at mile marker 23.02. Here, the traveler passes over a 750-foot-long, 126-foot-high historic trestle. In its final years of use by the railroad, this viaduct was rebuilt with reinforced concrete and heavy steel, and, just as did railroad passengers

Sneaky Snakes – One of the "denizens of the deep" along the *Silver Comet Trail*, Mr. Copperhead is almost perfectly camouflaged as he slithers into the undergrowth to the side of the trail. One must always be on the alert as snakes – including this poisonous specimen – will frequently pass over the trail in the heat of the summer.

in the late 19th and early 20th centuries, patrons on this route can again admire quite a view from this spot.

This trestle site on the old *Seaboard* line is often confused with a nearby trestle on the *Southern Railways* line which, on October 23, 1903, was the scene of a major railroad disaster. On that fateful day, *Southern's* trestle – also over Pumpkinvine – collapsed beneath the weight of its Train #81, a heavy early steam freight train. Many of the trailing rail cars in this disaster plunged to the bottom of the gorge.

The fireman on #81, John Fagala (identified as "Flagler" in some reports) accompanied these freight-cars into the depths, losing his life in the massive pile-up. Miraculously, the engine of #81 continued right on across the gorge just ahead of the collapsing trestle, and made it safely to the opposite side.

As stated above, the trestle on the old *Seaboard* line is entirely separate and distinct from that of the trouble-prone

Brushy Mountain Tunnel once reverberated with the sounds of huge locomotives thundering through its length as the *Silver Comet* passenger train sped across the Georgia countryside enroute to Atlanta, Philadelphia, Washington, D.C. and points in between. Today, the lighted passageway is quiet as patrons of the *Silver Comet Rail Trail* stroll and ride bicycles casually through its cool confines.

Southern Railways trestle. The two are approximately two miles apart on Pumpkinvine Creek, with the *Silver Comet* trestle located further south near GA Route 278.

The next scenic locale on the *Silver Comet Trail* is *Brushy Mountain Tunnel*. Here, visitors are treated to an 800-foot-long lighted tunnel nestled beneath the beautiful hardwoods and lush waterfalls of Brushy Mountain. Trail hikers sometimes pause here to explore the adjacent natural environment.

During the *Atlanta Campaign* in the U.S. Civil War, the *Battle of Brushy Mountain* occurred very near to this vicinity. General James McPherson's Union troops, fresh from their ransacking of nearby Van Wert and Cedartown, were moving in conjunction with General William T. Sherman's overall army

bearing down on Marietta and Atlanta. Sherman had maneuvered General Joseph Johnston's Confederate Army out of several defensive positions in this area by performing successive flanking movements. The Confederates had dug in all the way from Brushy Mountain to Lost Mountain, but it was to no avail as Sherman ultimately moved inexorably toward Atlanta.

As a portion of the Silver Comet Trail development, a man-made pond with goldfish has been creatively constructed near the entrance to Brushy Mountain Tunnel. Frogs and turtles doze fitfully along the pond's perimeter, enjoying the sunlight until being interrupted by human traffic.

Leaving the coolness of the deep forest at Brushy Mountain, it is approximately three miles to the next stopping

Refreshing Dip? – Coot's Lake, skirted by the *Silver Comet Trail*, has been a gathering spot for Rockmart area residents for generations. Patrons of the trail can cool off in the waters at the Coot's Lake Beach in the summertime if they so desire.

point. Along the way, it is not uncommon to encounter abundant wildlife, including deer, turkeys, snakes, armadillos, foxes, and other denizens of the forest.

In short order, the traveler will reach the *Coot's Lake Rest Stop*. This local attraction in Polk County includes a lake for swimming and relaxation, a nice beach area, and a snack shop for treats. A modest fee is charged for admission to the lake and beach during the summer months, and any *Silver Comet Trail* patrons are always welcome to pause (for the cost of admission) to cool off in the lake if they so desire.

There is also ample parking at this stop *(which is the trailhead just prior to the main Van Wert Trailhead a short distance away)*, and if the snack shop at Coot's Lake is closed, a convenience store at the *Van Wert Trail Head* offers an additional opportunity for food, refreshments and supplies.

Historic Van Wert

From Coot's Lake, the trail winds down to the historic community of Van Wert. Some bikers may wish to take a side trip at this point to visit this tiny town. *(Then again, they may not, since there is not a great deal to do or see here except possibly visit a fragment of history.)*

In the near vicinity of Van Wert, a Cherokee Indian village once existed. Numerous Indian artifacts ranging from pottery fragments to arrow and spear points, and even atlatls and war axes have been discovered here by area residents over the years. A collection of such items discovered at this site by the author in his youth bears mute testimony to this fact.

In pioneer days, Van Wert – which was in existence well before the U.S. Civil War – was known derisively as *"Clean Town."* According to folklore, the *Clean Town* moniker was used by both the resident Cherokees and pioneer settlers due to the decidedly filthy nature of the

Pioneer Burg – The tiny town of Van Wert originated from an Indian village. In its earliest days, the pioneer community was so filthy that the natives and settlers referred to it derisively as *"Clean Town."* By the time it was burned by Union army troops during the U.S. Civil War, Van Wert included a courthouse and jail, four saloons, two drug stores, a Masonic Hall, a blacksmith shop, at least one hotel, a school (Williams Academy), and a number of lovely homes. Today, aside from a small portion of the old jail, the forlorn historic structure built as the Methodist Church (foreground) in 1846 is the only remaining original public building in the town. Numerous pioneers lie buried in the graveyard at this site. (Photo by R. Olin Jackson)

initial trading post and its rowdy (and often-criminal) early inhabitants.

As the young state of Georgia was being settled, Van Wert existed within the confines of what then was Paulding County (prior to the creation of Polk County), and as a result, the small but growing town of Van Wert was named as the county seat of Paulding.

According to records, in its early days, this tiny community boasted a county courthouse (through which Union troops fired their weapons piercing holes in the walls in 1864), four or five general stores, four barrooms/taverns, at least one hotel, an education institution (*Williams Academy*), two churches, a Masonic Hall, a blacksmith shop, a jail, and many surprisingly nice homes. A few of these homes, the Methodist Church, and a remnant of the old jail are virtually all that remain there today, historically-speaking.

Much of the town reportedly was burned by the aforementioned Gen. James McPherson and his Union troops (which comprised the right flank of Gen. William T. Sherman's Union Army during his 1864 military invasion of Georgia). McPherson's army, which numbered approximately 35,000 troops, camped around the periphery of the town for several days, laying general waste to the area. A bayonet, lost by one of these troops, was discovered years later by the great-uncle of the author. Numerous Civil War relics, in fact, have been discovered over the years by individuals with metal detectors exploring this area adjacent to the *Silver Comet Trail* in Van Wert.

The aged remaining church in Van Wert – once the town's Methodist facility – includes a very historic adjacent cemetery with headstones which date back to the early 1800s. Many of the headstones are from Welch miners who emigrated to Van Wert to be employed in the nearby slate mines. The historic church at this site also enjoys the distinction of having been the sanctuary at which famed (and nationally-renowned) evangelist Sam Jones began his ministry in the late 1800s.

Van Wert remained the county seat of government for many years until the creation of Polk County in 1851, and the subsequent naming of Cedartown as the seat of that new county. When it lost its status as the county seat of government, Van Wert withered and died.

There are a number of historic homes remaining today in the little

Famed Pulpit – The membership of historic Van Wert Methodist Church was photographed circa 1923. This interesting structure was the first church of renowned evangelist Samuel Jones (1847-1906) who went on to nationwide fame, and is just a short walk from the *Silver Comet Trail*. (Photo from R. Olin Jackson files)

town, but the old Methodist church and the jail remnant are the most historic *public* structures still in existence as of 2024.

Other Historic Sites

Approximately one-half mile from the *Van Wert Trailhead, Silver Comet Trail* patrons will pass a site to which many long-time Rockmart locals still refer as *"Ma White's Bottomlands,"* (and to which some over the years have referred amusingly as *"Ma White's Bottoms"*). Here, visitors will see the fertile alluvial creek soils which were tilled by the owners of a Civil War-era plantation which once existed on this site in the 19th century.

As stated above, numerous Indian artifacts have been discovered in this vicinity over the years by area residents, and an Indian village has been documented by professional researchers as having existed nearby.

The plantation home at this site was originally owned (and built) by Judge Wiley Crawford Barber. Though its original owner is known, the exact date of construction of the rather substantial structure which once existed at this site is not. Conflicting records indicate it was built sometime between 1848 and 1863.

It was the Barber family which endured the several days of torture meted out by Gen. James McPherson's abusive troops in 1864 who had burned Cedartown several days previous. Upon discovery of the Barber estate, a group of McPherson's men crossed the creek separating the town from the plantation and took up quarters across the road in front of the Barber house (which still stood until 1985 when it tragically was consumed by fire).

When the troops made their intentions of terrorizing Barber and his family known, the judge moved feather beds

Former Indian Village – Inhabited by Native Americans in pre-history and later cultivated as a plantation for many years by White settlers, the rich creek bottom lands once owned by the White family offer additional scenic beauty to one stretch of historic Silver Comet rail-trail. Known down through the 20th century as "the old N.A. White home," this structure was first owned (and built) by Judge Wiley Crawford Barber. Conflicting information places the construction date of this landmark between 1848 and 1863. Various members of the White family were photographed here circa 1921. Pictured (L-R) are: Thelma White Randall, Newton Alexander (N.A.) White, Fannie Talitha Cline White ("Ma White"), Lena "Grace" White Kirk, "Ethel" Leona White Jones and her two girls. In front of her are: Frances "Fern" Jones Langston, Mary Hoyle Jones, and grandchildren (left down the row): Parks Henry Durham, husband of "Ella" Martha Matilda White Durham, their two children, Wylie Newton Durham, and Ruth Durham Groves, Frances Pearl White Paris, Roscoe Newton "Bill" White, Mary Lou White Mintz and Levi Johnson "Buck" White. Pictured in the distance to the rear of the circa-1930s vehicle are the extensive plantation bottomlands which produced the abundant corn, cotton, syrup cane, and other products once grown on this plantation. Voluminous Native American arrow tips, spear tips, tomahawks, cooking implements and other relics discovered in this vicinity by the author confirm the former existence of aboriginals at this site in prehistory.

down into the immense cellar of the large house then huddled there in the darkness with his family to endure whatever abuses the troops intended to mete out. Fortunately, McPherson's troops made an exception with this home, and chose not to set it ablaze, a circumstance which was rare for Gen. Sherman's army of thieves and firebrands.

On day two of the troops' encampment, after everything of value on the Barber property had been stolen or destroyed, the troops aimed an artillery piece at the home and set off a charge. The ensuing cannon round passed through the front door and exited near the rear door. Amazingly, no one was injured, but the missile left a hole in the outside rear wall large enough to easily accommodate a man crawling through it. Today, as a result of the disastrous fire of 1985, no sign of the immense farmhouse remains at the site. The only remnants of the old plantation are a couple of outbuildings and the crumbling foundations of an ancient gristmill.

A short distance from this spot, travelers on the *Silver Comet* will pass the historic *Rockmart Slate Quarry* at mile marker 36.8. Here, at the junction of Thompson and Euharlee creeks, park benches offer a cool, quiet place to pause for a moment. It was to this site that the Welch miners traveled to be employed in the slate mines prior to the 1860s.

A historic marker at this spot explains the history of the pre-Civil War slate industry which once existed here. This vicinity became world-renowned for its bricks, slate and limestone products in the 20th century. The roofs of numerous homes in Polk County and elsewhere in the state still contain the original slate shingles from this quarry which were installed more than 120 years ago, and the Rockmart bricks (with the imprinted Rockmart logo) have been found over the years at sites as far away as St. Augustine, Florida. *(Just imagine a roof which could survive high winds, hail, and much of what Nature could hurl at it, and still survive intact for several hundred years.)*

Also near this spot, the historic *Rockmart Seaboard Depot* still stood into the 21st century beside the railroad, but unfortunately was, for unknown reasons demolished shortly thereafter. From this point to the nearby city of Cedartown, an active *CSX Railroad* still exists (as of 2025). For that reason, the *Silver Comet Trail* skirts and exists adjacent to the railroad on a short stretch before turning to the right to proceed beneath a small railroad trestle and continue on to the shady confines of downtown historic Rockmart.

The Riverwalk

Advancing into old downtown Rockmart, the *Silver Comet Trail* takes the traveler to many of the historic buildings *(yes, with the historic slate shingles)* of the town. At this point, one is on the leg of the trail known as *"Riverwalk Trailhead."*

Rockmart Seaboard Depot – Photographed circa 1926, a locomotive idles beside the *Seaboard Airline Railroad Station* (left center) at South Marble Street in Rockmart. This historic *Seaboard* depot still existed into the 21st Century, but – unfortunately for the civic value of the town – was demolished shortly thereafter due to abandonment and dilapidation. Today, the rails passing beside this former depot site have not been removed because the tracks from this point westward, owned by *CSX Railroad*, are still in use. On the opposite side of this depot and paralleling the present-day *CSX* tracks, the *Silver Comet Trail* is routed for a brief distance before turning to the right to pass beneath a short *CSX* trestle (visible far right, center) over Euharlee Creek. After passing through the edge of old downtown Rockmart, the *Silver Comet Trail* today roughly parallels the *CSX* track between Rockmart and Cedartown. This short-line (known as CSX's "Cartersville Subdivision" today) extends between Cartersville and Cedartown, with Stilesboro, Taylorsville, Aragon, Rockmart and Fish Creek along the route which ends at Mile Post SG632.3 in Cedartown. Originally organized as the "East and West Railroad" circa 1900, it is one of several railroads that were constructed to Polk County in the late nineteenth and early twentieth centuries. It passed through downtown Rockmart, with a small depot which once existed where the old original Rockmart City Hall building exists today. During passenger service days (circa 1900-1950s), "flag-stops" existed at Stilesboro, Taylorsville and Aragon. (Photo from R. Olin Jackson files)

Old Cattle Barn – *Wayside-Seaborn Jones Park* is visible (far-left) along the *Riverwalk* portion of the *Silver Comet Trail* in downtown Rockmart. Jones donated the land for the park, the town square, and the first railroad depot, and as such, was responsible for much of the early growth of Rockmart. A holding barn at which cattle were temporarily housed – presumably prior to being loaded into cattle-cars on the nearby railroad – once stood in the background (right-rear) at this site. A portion of this same barn was later used as the "pool-house" for the Rockmart swimming pool which was built at this site circa 1950s and razed circa 1980s.

This scenic vicinity is also used in Rockmart's annual *Homespun Festival* activities. *Riverwalk* ends at *Wayside-Seaborn Jones Memorial Park* in the center of old downtown Rockmart, and has been a popular site for picnics and festivities for well over 100 years.

Many *Silver Comet Trail* travelers also pause at this point to visit the small town's unique museum just a few yards away in the center of town (in the old original city hall building). It was at this as well as numerous other sites

This is the old historic "downtown" portion of Rockmart, so a number of the buildings in this vicinity are well over 100 years in age.

in the historic downtown area in 2020, that comedian *Jon Stewart* brought a production company to film the major motion picture **Irresistible**, starring *Steve Carell* and *Chris Cooper*. Many of the scenes with Carell and Cooper were filmed inside this structure.

On either side of the old City Hall site and up and down the Main Street *(Marble Street)*, there are numerous sites at which one may take refreshment in restaurants, shops, bakeries, and other eateries.

This is the old historic "downtown" portion of Rockmart, so a number of the buildings in this vicinity are well over 100 years in age.

Back down on the Riverwalk, some trail patrons enjoy hopping into the scenic shallow areas of the adjacent *Euharlee Creek* just a few yards from the trail near the bridge for cool refreshment. Others enjoy relaxation in the shady confines of the adjacent park.

If not for pioneer Seaborn Jones, the *Silver Comet Trail* quite likely would never have come into existence. Mr. Jones, who had reportedly become wealthy from mining gold in the area, donated land for many important sites in Rockmart, including that of the original railroad depot, an event which precipitated the ultimate development of a town beyond Van Wert, and which also subsequently attracted the rail line upon which much of the *Silver Comet Trail* exists today.

Sometimes described as a "town father," Jones provided land not only for the first railroad depot *(which, incidentally, existed where the aforementioned former City Hall now stands)*, but also for several churches, the town square, the city park, and *Rose Hill Cemetery*. Today, his monumental gravestone is still the most prominent in this cemetery beside which the trail passes.

Also at the *Riverwalk Trailhead* in downtown Rockmart, many other opportunities for a leisurely pause are available for trail patrons, including picnic tables, and commercial items of all make and description at local businesses. As of this writing, the *Silver Comet Depot* shop offers bike rentals, ice cream, *Silver Comet* souvenirs and more.

Group activities are often on-going in the park at *Riverwalk*, and professional photographers are sometimes

Town Father – Seaborn Jones, early Rockmart, Georgia resident and businessman, donated land for many civic needs in the town, including that on which the train depot in the community was built. (Photo from R. Olin Jackson files)

available here since this trailhead is one of the most beautiful and delightful to visit.

Rockmart Entertainment

The slow-paced confines of old downtown Rockmart offer a safe, wholesome area to pass time prior to departing the trail and heading homeward. The *Impala Grill*, a 1950s-style diner complete with nostalgic decorations of hotrods and muscle cars from yesteryear is located within easy pedaling distance (a couple of city blocks) of Riverwalk on North Marble Street. For classic automobile enthusiasts, a *Hot Rod Cruiser Show* is periodically held in front of the *Impala*. (*Elvis has even been known to return from the dead and make an appearance here on occasion!*)

Other restaurants within bicy-

Old "East & West Railroad" – The present-day *CSX* tracks between Rockmart and Cedartown (known today as *CSX's "Cartersville Subdivision"*) were originally laid circa 1900, having been officially organized as the *"East & West Railroad."* Though the old depots on the *E&WRR* gradually disappeared over the years after passenger service was discontinued on the line in the late 1950s, scheduled stops once were made at Stilesboro, Taylorsville, Aragon, Rockmart and Fish Creek, with the route ending at Mile Post SG632.3 in Cedartown. The *E&WRR* is one of several railroads that were constructed to Polk County in the late nineteenth and early twentieth centuries as commerce ramped up in Georgia. This early railroad passed through downtown Rockmart where its original depot once existed on the spot at which the old original Rockmart City Hall building exists today. Pictured are laborers constructing the *E&WRR* circa 1900. (Photo from R. Olin Jackson files)

cle-riding distance as of this writing include *Hometown Pizza, Bar-L Barbecue, Chocolate Café, T's Seafood, Pizza Depot, Sidekicks, House of China* and others.

Rockmart is also home to several local festivals, so those who might enjoy attendance of events such as this should plan their trip accordingly. The annual *Homespun Festival* hosted by the local Rockmart Chamber of Commerce occurs the second week in July each year. Located at *Riverwalk* and *Seaborn Jones Memorial Park*, visitors to this event can enjoy a morning parade, a 5-K footrace and other festival activities right on the trail.

Also scheduled is a complete lineup of entertainment from morning to night at the gazebo, arts and crafts items for sale, barbecue plates, games and rides for the children and much more. The grand finale is a late evening fireworks celebration which can be seen for miles around.

A growing event a short distance off the trail after the *Coot's Lake* trailhead is *"The Rock."* This gathering is held the first weekend in October each year, and, in years past, has been the site of a popular arts and crafts festival as well as substantial musical entertainment.

Departing Rockmart

Departing the downtown Rockmart district and heading west, trail patrons encounter an attractive iron bridge with the *Silver Comet Trail* logo over Euharlee Creek. The view from this bridge back toward Riverwalk offers the opportunity for scenic photos of Euharlee Creek, the bridge and Riverwalk itself.

This short leg of the trail skirts the edge of the aforementioned *Rose Hill Cemetery*, the final resting place of a number of Rockmart's most prominent citizens from years past. At this vicinity, the trail also intertwines around one of the still active railroads on which freight trains pass daily through Rockmart.

Patrons on the trail next encounter *Nathan Dean Sports Complex*. Here, many athletic activities take place on well-manicured and maintained baseball and softball fields. From this point, the trail continues much of the distance to Cedartown, and the *Chief Ladiga Trail* in Alabama.

Take advantage of the *Silver Comet Trail*. You'll be glad you did.

(For more information on the above events and the Silver Comet Trail in Polk County, contact the Polk County Chamber of Commerce at (770) 684-8774.)

The Horrible 1926 Rockmart Wreck

Exactly two days before Christmas of 1926, a lot of the passengers upon the northbound Ponce de Leon passenger train in northwest Georgia had happy plans for the upcoming holiday season. Little did they know, they not only would never enjoy those plans, they would never see Christmas on this earth again.

"I heard the shrill whistle and saw the headlights ahead, but the northbound was not slowing. . . . When I saw the collision was certain, I slammed on my brakes and called to my fireman to jump."
-Arthur M. Corrie
Engineer of the Royal Palm

The tiny township of Rockmart, Georgia, in the northwest quadrant of the state was very sparsely-settled in 1926. It was a very uneventful place where a major disaster had simply never occurred. That changed on December 23rd of that year as two immense passenger trains crashed head-on in one of the worst disasters in U.S. railroad history.

Interestingly, though it was a tiny town, Rockmart had enjoyed passenger rail service since the 1870s, when philanthropist Seaborn Jones, according to tradition, donated land to Southern Railway for a rail line right-of-way through the county at no cost – with the stipulation that Southern would guarantee passenger service to Rockmart as long as the company existed. It was the strict timetable required for this passenger service which quite possibly became the catalyst for disaster in 1926.

That December evening was a dark and rainy night in the foothills of north Georgia, as are many days in the autumn and early winter months of that region. Despite the miserable weather and gloom outside, the Pullman coaches in the Ponce de Leon were nevertheless filled with warm diners and, no doubt, lively Christmas cheer.

Both the Royal Palm and the Ponce de Leon were crack passenger trains of Southern Railway, and were regularly patronized by many travelers, since the 1920s was a time when the rapidly-growing network of railroads in our nation dominated the travel industry. Both trains were renowned for their

False Promise – According to tradition, early resident Seaborn Jones provided land for the rights-of-way for the railroad with a stipulation that passenger service always be available in the small Polk County community. Despite the stipulation, passenger service was discontinued at all towns along the route in the 1960s, but freight trains still rumble down the same track where the 1926 disaster occurred. (Photo by R. Olin Jackson)

good food, accommodations, and timely schedules. December 23rd was no exception, as both trains hustled to remain on schedule.

It was at a long side-track at Rockmart that the Royal Palm and the Ponce de Leon regularly passed each other on this route, so it was a common occurrence. The Southern railroad through Rockmart was not double-tracked, so the side-track a short distance from the Rockmart depot made it possible for these two luxury trains to pass each other and then continue on to their destinations in opposite directions.

In order to prepare for this maneuver, Engineer Arthur M. Corrie on the Royal Palm had throttled back to slow his big locomotive down to approximately 4 miles per hour to give the Ponce

de Leon ample time to take the siding. All seemed normal until Corrie realized to his shock that the on-coming train was not slowing at all; nor did it seem that engineer Robert M. Pierce of the Ponce even intended to take the siding at all. To the contrary, a horrified Corrie realized that the Ponce was bearing down directly toward the Royal Palm at an incredible rate of speed.

For many years, engineers negotiating the Braswell Mountains just prior to Rockmart had become accustomed to increasing speed down the leeward side into the little town. This was particularly true – and to a greater degree – when there was no oncoming train requiring a pause on a side-track. All the engineers were constantly working to stay on schedule, because a timely delivery of passengers and postal materials meant "money."

As could best be determined in the after-accident report, the engineer of the Ponce apparently was simply unaware of the need to take the siding at Rockmart, and was taking advantage of the acceleration opportunity down from the Braswell Mountains in order to make up for some lost time on his schedule. That misunderstanding, coupled with the poor visibility caused by the drizzling rain and fog, led to a disaster of immense proportions.

The late Leonora (Mrs. Robert Henry) Mintz was seventeen years of age on the day of the accident. Prior to her death, she lived not thirty feet from the tracks of the Norfolk-Southern Railroad (formerly Southern Railways) in Rockmart for many years, and approximately one mile from the scene of the terrible 1926 disaster. When interviewed in the early 1990s, she stated that she could still clearly remember that fateful Christmas.

"At that time, we lived on our family farm (near the site of present-day East Side Elementary School) in Rockmart," Mrs. Mintz explained. "We heard the crash all the way from there. It was so loud, we thought it was thunder."

As an experienced trainman, Corrie knew that he had just enough time to yell a warning to his fireman, pull on the whistle-cord as another warning to his passengers, and then to leap from the train to attempt to save himself. After he had jumped, the next thing Corrie heard was the horrendous blast from the collision, the grinding

Early Landmarks – Downtown Rockmart was photographed here in the early 1900s. A trestle for *Southern Railways* is visible in the distance. The large building visible below the trestle is the old *Commercial Hotel*, and the building in front of it is the original Rockmart Depot of the East & West Railroad (E&WRR) from Cartersville in the middle of downtown Rockmart. The former *Rockmart City Hall* building exists on this depot site today.

of metal, and the horrible screeching of the train trucks on the twisting, ripping rails.

According to reports, Corrie later told Interstate Commerce Commission (ICC) investigators that he turned and watched as the Ponce de Leon, traveling at approximately fifty miles an hour or better, crashed head-long into his beloved Royal Palm.

"I will never forget it," Corrie later stated. "It sounded like the heavens had split open. I don't want to ever hear anything like that ever again."

Despite the enveloping darkness and miserable cold rain on the fateful evening, the noise of the crash immediately brought local residents running to the crash site. The provision of help to the injured and dying proved

"We heard the crash all the way from there. It was so loud, we thought it was thunder."

Repetitive Accidents – The site at which the *Ponce de Leon* and the *Royal Palm* passenger trains collided in 1926 was photographed here in 1994. At least one other major train derailment – which fortunately was a freight train – occurred in this exact same location in 1961, scattering freight cars haphazardly for almost half a mile. Some railroad professionals have speculated that at least part of the problem included trains which were hurtling down from the Braswell / Brushy Mountains into Rockmart at an excessive rate of speed. (Photo by R. Olin Jackson)

a challenge for the citizens of the tiny, poorly-equipped community, for the carnage at the wreck site was absolutely overwhelming.

"When the Royal Palm and the Ponce de Leon collided, we weren't allowed to go up there to see it, because it was just too horrible," Mrs. Mintz explained emphatically, still shaken by the tragedy. "A friend of mine told me she and some other friends went to the wreck, and she said they saw the best-looking gentleman in a car. All of a sudden, it seemed like his head just rolled off his shoulders. He had been decapitated.

"Rockmart was a very rural area back then," Mrs. Mintz continued. "People were begging for help. We had no ambulances here at that time. Some people were carried in private automobiles

A side-track, photographed here in 1994, still exists in almost the exact same spot as the fateful siding involved in the 1926 disaster. (Photo by R. Olin Jackson)

The *Southern Railways Depot* in Rockmart was photographed circa 1920s. A locomotive, very similar in class to that of the *Royal Palm* or *Ponce de Leon*, idles at the station. Notice the old well (left foreground). (Photo courtesy of Polk County Historic Society)

to Rome (Georgia); others were carried as far away as Atlanta. It was just chaos."

One can only imagine today the misery and pain endured by the injured as they were carried out of the wrecked train cars and laid upon the ground in the rain until they could be huddled into automobiles for what then was a long, bumpy ride on dirt roads to a hospital many miles away. It is not known today how many victims died of their injuries "enroute" to hospitals and doctors, but there no doubt were many.

Mr. Hal Clements, a retired educator and a native of Rockmart said he was a lad of 11 at the time of the disaster. He and his family resided on Bluff Street in Rockmart. He remembered traveling

Depot Departure – With the cessation of passenger service in the 1960s, the old *Southern Railways Depot* building became obsolete and therefore was demolished. A replacement structure for the monitoring of freight trains was built quite near the same site and photographed here in 1994. (Photo by R. Olin Jackson)

Eyewitness Account – Arthur M. Corrie was the engineer of the *Royal Palm* on the night of the accident. His counterpart on the *Ponce de Leon*, Robert M. Pierce, was killed in the wreck. As he saw the crash unfolding, Corrie leapt from the engine cab at the last possible moment, and watched in horror as the two monstrous locomotives collided with what he later described as a deafening crash. He provided much of the eye-witness testimony on the disaster.

with his father to the wreck shortly after it occurred.

"It happened just east of (what today is the former) Goodyear Mill complex in an area we used to call 'Barber's Woods,'" Clements explained. "I was only eleven years old, so I don't remember a lot. One of the things I do vividly recall, however, is the steam that was still rising from the locomotives. And I remember later that they brought a lot of boxes down to Cochran's Funeral Home.

"My father drove immediately to the accident, because he wanted to help in any way he could," Clements continued. "As I remember, I held onto my

father's hand the whole time. I knew instinctively that there were a lot of bodies in those crushed cars."

Much of the horror of the disaster was caused by the Pullman cars of the Ponce de Leon which had "telescoped" into each other when they met the immovable force of the huge locomotive which suddenly had come to a halt. The impact was horrendous – a crushing and mutilation of passengers – as the heavy cars smashed one into the other and then were each crushed as the heavy wooden housings collapsed, piling up against the locomotive.

After the shock of the initial crash had passed, the screams and moans of the dying and injured passengers – many of whom were trapped beneath the huge weight of the wreckage – horribly filled the night. The **Associated Press** reported *"The screams of women pinned beneath the wreckage were mingled with the hoarse shouts of men and the prayers of a Negro waiter when he was released, uninjured, from a hole in the side of the dining car."*

According to the **Rome** (Georgia) **News-Tribune**, *"The scene. . . . tested the strength of strong men. Bodies of victims crushed and mangled beyond description were . . . unreachable because of tons of weight upon them. The roof of the diner was rolled up like paper. The body of one man was hanging from a window, his legs pinned beneath the heavy weight."*

Most of the residents of Rockmart were unprepared for the trauma involved in a disaster of the magnitude of the 1926 wreck. Some rescuers went about their work numbly; others found themselves simply unable to continue as the shock set in.

Most sources today agree there were approximately 20 fatalities as a result of the collision. The official Interstate Commerce Commission report,

Devastating Damage – Photographed shortly after the December 23, 1926 wreck, the heavy damage inflicted upon the *Ponce de Leon* (r) is visible in this photo. The *Royal Palm*, however, due to its slow rate of speed, suffered far less damage. (Photo courtesy of Atlanta Historic Society)

filed January 11, 1927, reported that 11 passengers, 7 Southern Railways employees, and 1 news agent were killed (a total of 19 deaths as of that date; others may have died at a later date as a result of their injuries.). The report went on to explain that 113 passengers, 4 Southern Railways employees and 6 Pullman employees were injured in the wreck. It was miraculous that the death toll was not higher.

On December 24, the front page of the

An arm and a leg were amputated from Pierce in a futile effort to save his life, but he succumbed shortly thereafter.

Atlanta Georgian trumpeted *"18 Dead In Wreck."* Due to the confusion which reigned at the scene of the accident and the inaccuracies in news reports of that day, several variations of the death count were published.

The dead in the Ponce de Leon included Road Foreman of Engines, Robert M. Pierce, who had assumed the engineer's duties from the regular engineer shortly before the crash. An arm and a leg were amputated

Curious bystanders watch as a crane works at the front end of the *Ponce de Leon*. The day-coach pictured here telescoped into the dining car, and was the scene of many mutilated bodies. (Photo courtesy of the Atlanta History Center)

from Pierce in a futile effort to save his life, but he succumbed shortly thereafter. Also dead was the fireman in the engine with him – H. R. Moss – who was killed instantly. W.H. Brewer, the baggage-master, died a few hours later.

Others listed as dead in the December 24, 1926 issue of the ***Atlanta Georgian*** were:

- Dr. P.T. Hale, 69, a professor of evangelism at Southern Baptist Seminary in Louisville, KY.
- W.L. Dynes, 56, an Atlanta real estate developer who lived at 951 Courtney Dr.
- J.E. Frost of 509 Foster St., Chattanooga, TN.
- L.B. Evans of Lebanon, KY, Kansas City and Jacksonville, FL addresses.
- Mrs. J.W. Whitaker of Chattanooga, TN.

- Goldie Williams, the infant daughter of Mrs. Alice Williams of Detroit, MI.
- J.W. Whisenhunt of Aragon, GA.
- W.I. Dowie, Jr. of Jacksonville, FL.
- A young boy, age approximately 8 years, believed to have been the son of Mrs. George Hardy of Toronto.
- A young girl, age approximately 10 years, with the initials H.M.H. on a bracelet, believed to have been the daughter of Mrs. Hardy.
- Six other individuals were unidentified: two white and four Negro.

Those listed as injured in the same article were:
- Mrs. George Hardy of Toronto.
- J.W. Dosser of Chattanooga, TN.
- F.W. Swann of Bolton, GA.
- Will Kuhn of St. Louis, MO.

Residents from miles away traveled to Rockmart to view the disaster for several days. (Photo courtesy of the Atlanta History Center)

- L.I. Seibert of Chattanooga, TN.
- Corporal Gus Rusts of Ft. Oglethorpe, GA.
- Dan Lobrugh of Cincinnati, OH.
- Robert Hilty of Lansing, MI.
- Edward Wiseman of Louisville, KY.
- H.E. Bullis of Lexington, KY.
- R.L. Bateman of Macon, GA.
- Mrs. J.J. Finlay of Chattanooga, TN.

As for the Royal Palm, the injuries were much less severe, and there were no fatalities. Much of this was due undoubtedly to the slow speed of the Royal Palm as its heavy engine impacted the Ponce de Leon.

"The hand of providence guided the destiny of the Royal Palm last night," Corrie told a reporter at his home Friday morning following the accident. *"I was barely moving, pulling my engine along about 4 miles per hour as I neared the switch at the siding.*

"I was obeying orders to await the Ponce de Leon which was to pull up and go into the siding so I could pass. When I saw the collision was certain, I slammed on my brakes and called to my fireman to jump.

"I jumped to the ground and rolled down a steep embankment. I don't suppose I was 30 feet away when the two engines met. . . . I fully expected the engine and cars to topple over and roll down upon me, but they didn't."

The Royal Palm consisted of one club car, five regular Pullman sleeping cars, one dining car and two Pullman sleeping cars of all-steel construction. They were pulled by Engine #1456.

The Ponce de Leon consisted of one combination car (half baggage & half coach), one coach, one dining car, and seven Pullman sleeping cars, all of steel construction, pulled by Engine #1219.

Following the impact, both engines were derailed, but somehow remained upright. Engine #1219 (Ponce de Leon) was badly damaged and its tender was torn from its frame and thrown down the embankment on the inside

Death Cab – Some onlookers posed for photographs in front of the battered *Ponce de Leon* at the fateful site. It is easy to see how the impact from the wreck severely mangled the bodies of both Engineer Robert M. Pierce and Fireman H.R. Moss, both of whom were inside this locomotive at impact. Pierce lived for a few hours following the wreck, but Moss was killed instantly. (Photo courtesy of the Atlanta History Center)

Rapid Repair – *Southern Railways*, in a perpetual race with time, began clearing and repairing the rail line into Rockmart almost immediately to allow for the continuation of traffic. Amazingly, both locomotives from the Rockmart collision were ultimately repaired and put back into service – even the severely-battered *Ponce de Leon* (pictured), as badly damaged as it was. (Photo courtesy of the Atlanta History Center)

of the curve. The combination car was telescoped at its forward end nearly the length of the baggage compartment. The coach immediately following it telescoped into the dining car.

Though there has been much speculation, the positive cause of the accident is still not known to this day – or if it is, it has not been reported – and many questions linger:

What about the switch controlling the entrance to the siding? Much speculation has centered around this device. It is not known today if it (the switch) was even open to admit the Ponce de Leon to the siding, but even if it had been open, the Ponce de Leon was moving at an incredible rate of speed far in excess of that which would have allowed it to negotiate the arc of the turn leading into the switch.

Another view of the wreck was photographed across a cotton field from the approximate site at which a Goodyear Mills complex was later constructed. (Photo courtesy of Rockmart Library)

Another question centers around the speed of the Ponce de Leon. The descent down from the Braswell Mountains into Rockmart can be a perilous route. As recently as 1961, another train – this time a freight – was derailed in almost the identical spot as the 1926 disaster, causing an immense catastrophe in its own right. Speed and a lack of familiarity with the incline from the Braswell Mountains into Rockmart quite possibly played a role in that accident, and are suspected as prime catalysts in the 1926 disaster as well.

Just a few moments prior to the 1926 accident, S.J. Keith, the regular engineer, was directed by Pierce to *"go back into the train."* According to Keith's later statement, Pierce was running behind time, and therefore

Another question centers around the speed of the Ponce de Leon.

had advanced the speed of the Ponce de Leon to an excessive rate, *"dropping down off the mountain below Rockmart."*

According to the 1927 Interstate Commerce Commission report on the accident, *"When it (the Ponce de Leon) stopped at McPherson, 11.4 miles south of Rockmart, for the purpose of meeting an opposing train, Road Foreman of Engines Pearce, who had been riding in the combination car, boarded the engine and took charge of it, Engineman Keith going back to ride in the combination car.*

"Train first No. 2 (the Ponce de Leon) departed from McPherson at 6:23 p.m., 15 minutes late, passed Braswell, 6.4 miles from McPherson, at 6:35 p.m., 16 minutes late, passed the south passing track switch at Rockmart and collided

265

Heavy-duty railroad cranes labor to re-rail the battered *Ponce de Leon* locomotive. (Photo courtesy of the Rockmart Library)

with train #101 while traveling at a speed believed to have been approximately 50 miles per hour."

Some individuals have speculated that the blinding rain, coupled with Pierce's unfamiliarity with a newly-installed switch-head, were responsible for the tragedy. Others have maintained that in the driving rain, Pierce mistook a freight engineer's signal from a siding

Terrible Suffering – Not only was the wreck horrendous and the wrecked cars exceptionally difficult to search, the bitter December weather took a turn for worse as well, adding further gloom to rescue efforts. By the time survivors had endured the biting cold drizzling rain as they were extricated and transported from the wreck, they were then required to suffer through transport across rough dirt roads in mostly-unheated automobiles to available hospitals.

further up the line as the Royal Palm's signal that all was clear. This, at the very least, might provide a measure of explanation for Pierce's obvious decision to continue on at top speed without instead taking the side track.

The Interstate Commerce Commission report, however, concluded that the wreck occurred because Road Foreman of Engines Pierce, who had relieved Engineman Keith, either failed to have a thorough understanding with the engineman as to the contents of Train Order #92 (requiring him to take the siding), or else simply forgot it.

The true reason for the tragedy may never be known, since this information departed with Robert M. Pierce when he succumbed to his injuries shortly after the wreck. However, over the ensuing years of time, there have been some long-time former employees who have developed interesting opinions and theories concerning the accident.

Mr. H.D. "Cowboy" Mintz, a retired Southern Railways senior conductor and the son of Mrs. R.H. Mintz of Rockmart, says passenger train crews always consisted of the oldest men on the seniority list. Therefore, most of the Southern Railways employees from the Ponce de Leon and the Royal Palm who were involved in the accident were either deceased or retired by the time he was employed by Southern in the mid-1940s. However, "a few were still around," he said, and they – from time to time – shared their thoughts with him.

"I worked with Nath Turner, an engineer on the Royal Palm; Henry Sorrells, the conductor; and Harry Smith, the flagman," Mintz related. "Harry told me he and Henry were up in the cupola on the caboose on the rear of the Royal Palm, and they could hear the Ponce de Leon 'still working steam' as it was approaching. The whole train should have been coasting down the grade by that point. He always thought Bob Pierce was attempting to make up the lost time the train was suffering from."

But Mr. Mintz also says there have been rumors over the years of a personal vendetta between Keith and Pierce, and speculation regarding the possibility that this may have played a role in the disaster.

When Keith was relieved of control of the engine by Pierce at McPherson, could he (Keith) possibly have intentionally neglected to inform Pierce that the Ponce de Leon was to take the siding in Rockmart? Surely Keith would have known that failure to communicate these instructions to Pierce would have meant almost certain death or injury to himself.

The Interstate Commerce Commission report however, states unequivocally, that *"After the accident, Mr. Copeland assisted in removing Road Foreman of Engines Pearce from his engine and he said the road foreman asked him how the accident had occurred. When told that he had failed to take the siding for train #101 (the Royal Palm), he replied that Engineman Keith, Fireman Moss and everyone concerned had told him that he was to hold the main track."*

"Harry Smith's personal observation, Engineer Keith's statement that he explained the conditions of the orders to Pierce, and the theory of a personal vendetta between Keith and Pierce will always add to the mystery of the Rockmart wreck," Mr. Mintz added. "We'll never know the answer for certain."

Today (as of this writing), trains – albeit freight trains – still pass swiftly down this same single-tracked railroad from the Braswell Mountains into Rockmart. They often are moving at what almost anyone would deem to be an excessive rate of speed, causing automobile drivers at the Rockmart track intersections to cautiously stop far in advance of the crossings.

And to the rear of the former Goodyear Rubber Company building in Rockmart, a lone siding still exists today in virtually the identical location as the 1926 siding, almost as a harbinger of the terrible 1926 disaster, and reminding the trainmen to "slow down."

> *Today (as of this writing), trains – albeit freight trains – still pass swiftly down this same single-tracked railroad from the Braswell Mountains into Rockmart.*

Recollections of An RPO Clerk On the Old Tallulah Falls Railroad

*A Railway Mail Service worker gained the opportunity
of a lifetime when he was granted a temporary job working
on the historic Tallulah Falls Railroad in the 1950s.*

For many years, first as the *North-eastern Railroad* chartered in 1856, later as the *Blue Ridge and Atlantic Railroad* in 1887, and finally as the *Tallulah Falls Railway (TF)* beginning in 1897, a very scenic and historic railroad ran through several extreme northeastern Georgia counties. Sadly, the fabled *Tallulah Falls* line went into receivership in 1923, but managed to last another 38 years before finally whistling its last run in 1961. Prior to that time, however, a number of individuals experienced many adventures on this colorful railroad.

A *Tallulah Falls Railroad* diesel-electric mail-car or "Dinky" is being loaded in downtown Cornelia in the early 1950s. It was this conveyance in which Mr. Ragsdale traveled and worked in 1951. (Photo courtesy of Thomas Frier)

On Sunday morning, May 27, 1951, Harold Bell, the regular mail clerk on the *Tallulah Falls Railroad* woke up and reached under the bed for his trousers. He forgot that the last thing he had done before dropping off to sleep was to place his revolver under the bed – on top of his trousers. As he picked up his pants, the gun tumbled to the floor, discharged, and the bullet shattered the shocked trainman's shin bone, crippling him.

Bell was able to get medical attention, and no doubt was greatly relieved once the pain had subsided. He, however, would be unable to continue his duties on the *Tallulah Falls Railway* until his leg healed, and that assuredly troubled him considerably.

The district office of the *TF* immediately began assigning substitute clerks to fill Bell's vacancy, but the substitutes all requested to be relieved after two weeks, because that was the limit of time that they could draw subsistence pay for having to spend the night away from their normal jobs in the Atlanta headquarters, and money was money – especially in those days.

Train #501 with its diesel-electric engine travels north across Tallulah Lake circa 1950s. It was at this spot that Mr. Ragsdale dumped the block of ice each day. In the right foreground is the old Highway 441 bridge which still exists today in Tallulah Gorge State Park. Though the rails were removed long ago, the large concrete piers (pictured) which once bore the weight of the *Tallulah Lake Railroad Bridge* still exist today in Tallulah Lake. (Photo courtesy of Buck Snyder)

As a result of this unstable situation, the office approached mail employee Theron Ragsdale about moving back to Banks County where he had been born. They wanted him to make Cornelia his headquarters so that no subsistence pay would be necessary.

So it was, that Mr. Ragsdale, only a substitute clerk with less than three years' seniority, became the Railway Post Office (RPO) clerk on the Franklin and Cornelia run until Harold Bell's one year of disability leave was up. Some of his experiences and remembrances from this period in his life are as follows:

Learning The Job

"The work was drastically more complicated than what I had been doing in the Railway Mail Service stationary unit in Atlanta," Ragsdale explained in an interview, "so I wisely requested that I be allowed to ride without pay and assist the current substitute – a Mr. Sarrett – for two days before tackling the job solo. Sarrett was a good instructor, and because of the tips he gave me, I felt much more confident when I had the job to myself on Monday morning, July 30.

"There was, however, one problem about which Sarrett never warned me. The "Dinky," a diesel-powered, single-unit car, the middle portion of which served as my railway post office, was to remain in Cornelia for repairs that first day. I would have to perform all distribution of mails in the unit before leaving Cornelia, and then the railroad had arranged for a local trucker to carry me and the mail to Franklin and back on the highway.

"Now in those days, railroad regulations forbade the railroad repairmen from beginning work until I had left the car. Those workmen all were well aware of this requirement too, and, as a result, they obviously had decided to have a little fun with me. As I labored to sort and organize the mail, they stood around – looking as idle as possible – every time Bob Addington, the president of the railroad, came by.

"As I worked frantically at my job, I heard Mr. Addington yelling at the men, but they simply responded with, 'We can't jack the car up, because the mail clerk hasn't finished working his mail.' Needless to say, when I finally got all the

Strange Depot – The distinctive *Tallulah Falls Depot* was photographed in this peaceful setting circa 1950s. The dinky on which Mr. Ragsdale worked stopped here daily. This photo will appear strange to many today, because modern U.S. Highway 441 today passes beside the depot on the approximate same route on which the railroad tracks exist in this photo. This depot, the most ornate of all the *Tallulah Falls Railroad* structures, was expected to provide service for a substantial portion of the mail and passenger service on the line, but after the tragic fire in the town of Tallulah Falls in 1921, and the resulting disappearance of the summer crowds which had flocked to the once-numerous hotels along the brim of the gorge, this depot unfortunately was little-used thereafter. (Photo courtesy of Bob Whittaker)

mail 'worked' and loaded on the truck, I was a nervous wreck and exhausted to boot.

"I think it was Thursday of that first week before the dinky was fixed and on the road again. When we arrived in Cornelia at 5:20 pm and I off-loaded all mails for transfer to Charlotte & Atlanta Train #39, a man in a brown suit came into the mail compartment and started looking in a first aid box on the wall. He was acting like he didn't notice me, but I thought I ought to at least make him identify himself, so I asked him, 'Do you work for the railroad?'

"I was mildly confused when this fellow touched the tip of his finger to his hat, and said something that sounded like 'See?' The next morning I mentioned this incident to Mr. Snyder, the conductor of the dinky, and he explained that the railroad was in receivership, and that the man in the brown suit was Henry Brewer, the person appointed by *Southern Railways* as the Receiver of the *Tallulah Falls Railroad*. When

I misunderstood him to say 'See,' I guess what he really said was 'Receiver.' Maybe there was an emblem on his hat that indicated his position. I still don't know. The *TF* was plagued by financial problems for much of its existence.

"I believe it was on the morning of that first day of riding the Dinky solo that we were passing through a woodsy area somewhere above Clarkesville, when suddenly I heard two shotgun blasts in rapid succession just outside the mail car door.

"In a flash, I thought about the one time I had ridden the *Tallulah Falls* train in 1941 to visit relatives near Turnerville. While crossing a trestle, I had looked out the window and seen a man in wading boots, lying on the ground beside a stream, with one of his boots actually in the stream. He evidently was drunk – or at least I hoped that was all that was wrong with him. He might also have been shot for all I knew.

"In that same flash, I also thought briefly about Jesse James and his feud with the railroads. I dropped on the floor in case the shotgun outside contained another shell. The Dinky slowed, but didn't come to a stop, and a few minutes later, Mr. Snyder appeared in the doorway, smiling, and explained that the track maintenance workers had put down a couple of torpedoes (audible alert devices) to warn us that they were working on the track up ahead. The track was clear, but they hadn't had time to go back and retrieve the torpedoes.

John B. Snyder

"As I got to know Mr. Snyder, I realized he was the same conductor who had taken my ticket on that trip I had made in 1941. He wore overalls and a felt hat as conductor on the Dinky, but as conductor on the passenger train in 1941, he had worn an immaculate navy blue conductor's uniform and the official conductor's billed hat. His career as a conductor included some of the years when Tallulah Falls was a popular tourist attraction, and on Sundays, excursion trains to 'the falls' departed from both Atlanta and Athens. Entire cars would arrive at Cornelia – loaded with tourists – to be hooked onto the TF engine. Thus, Mr. Snyder had become an experienced tour guide as well as conductor.

"He had grown up near Sylva, North Carolina, and had started working for the TF as a young man, I suppose about 1913, at which time he was 21 years old. He worked his way up to conductor as a freight train crewman. He said that at first, he was frightened by the prospect of being conductor on a passenger train, but it was a promotion, so he tackled it. He told me that once he got into the swing of it, he had rather enjoyed conducting the excursion trains.

"Mr. Snyder always had a ready smile, and was friendly, so I thought it

Photographed March 25, 1961, the final year the *Tallulah Falls Railroad* was in operation, engineer Goldman Kimbrell smiles forlornly down from the cab of one of the line's diesel-electric engines. As the clock was winding down for the existence of the old *TF*, there were a lot of sad faces all up and down the line of the historic mountain railroad. (Photo courtesy of Goldman Kimbrell)

was a shame the railroad no longer had an opening for his services as a passenger train conductor. As it was, since the Dinky did actually offer minor passenger service (passengers occasionally rode in the forward compartment with the engineer and conductor), he drew more salary than Brawner Walker, the freight train conductor.

"I don't know how much money Mr. Snyder actually made, but it's a fact that he never owned an automobile. Maybe traveling 114 miles a day six days a week left him feeling that he didn't need any additional transportation.

"Mr. Snyder would frequently inquire of people at Otto, Prentiss, and Franklin (North Carolina) if they had

The Dinky was photographed in 1953 on *Queen's Trestle* just south of Mountain City in Rabun County. The breath-taking scenery all up and down the old TF was awe-inspiring, and the motivation for its use as background scenery in a number of major motion pictures which have been filmed in the area over the years. (Photo by R.D. Sharpless, from the collection of Frank Ardrey, Jr.)

any eggs or other produce to sell. I suspect that, being from North Carolina and remembering the days when the area was hungry for trade and contact with the outside world, he wanted to grab every chance available to throw some trade to his fellow North Carolinians.

Honest Working Folks

"I presume that the salaries of the railroad employees were set by railroad regulations, even though the railroad was in 'Receivership,' but one morning when I had been on the line about three weeks, I got to wondering. Shortly after I had climbed into the mail compartment and started preparing for the day's work, Earl Ward, one of the yard crew, called to me. 'Hey, mail boy! Come out here!'

"Now I didn't know what he wanted so I came to the door. There, I saw that the entire yard crew – about ten men including Mr. Snyder and Goldman Kimbrell, the engineer – were standing in a small semicircle, looking up intently at me. 'Mail boy' Earl repeated. 'Have you lost anything?'

"I examined the eyes in the semicircle, and it looked to me like they were expecting a confrontation, maybe a fight. I couldn't think of anything I might have lost, and I didn't want to admit that I was so careless that I didn't know whether I had actually lost anything or not, so I tried to sound confident when I replied with a somber 'No.'

"Earl then related to me how he had found a ten-dollar bill on the floor of the mail compartment the previous evening when he was sweeping it out. He said he just wanted to be sure it wasn't mine before claiming it for himself. I nervously repeated my denial that the money was mine, and as Mr. Snyder walked away, he said, 'Well, it couldn't be mine, because I don't have that much.'

"The next morning I was to discover just how honest and good these folks could actually be. Earl came walking up to me that day and said he just didn't feel right about keeping the ten, and I admitted, 'Well, I did a little figuring, and I believe I am about ten dollars short.' He handed me the ten and that was that.

Postal Regulations

"Another time, the Dinky broke down near Franklin, (NC) and we had to wait for the freight train to come along so it could pull us back to Cornelia. As we headed back, some of the stops we made were mail stops, and some were freight stops, involving the shuttling to and fro of cars onto sidings. This made the freight train even slower than it normally would have been.

"By the time we got to Clarkesville, it was pitch dark, and a hard rain had set in. Broughton Ward, who usually worked with the yard crew in Cornelia, was in the passenger compartment with two other yard crewmen.

"I don't know why they were on the train, but they must have been on duty, because as soon as the train came to a stop, they ran out into that pouring rain to get the mail from the Clarkesville Post Office. The mail messenger who normally passed the mail to me at the mail car door had left it with the station agent, who in turn had locked it up with a railroad lock before going home for the evening. I guess the agreement between the Post Office Department and the railroad required that the railroad guarantee that the mail would be brought to the mail car door. Apparently Mr. Ward and the crewmen knew about the mail requirement. They had allowed me to stay warm and dry while they got soaked to the bone carrying the mail to the Dinky.

"Many of the rules which governed the RPO clerk's interactions with the railroad had been drawn up many years earlier. I'm sure that Mr. Brewer's inspection of my first-aid kit was a standard operating procedure to make certain the kits were in compliance with the rules.

"Another of these rules was surely a carryover from the days before

This somewhat dramatic photograph shows a Tallulah Falls train at Wiley Junction in 1939. Today, this immense trestle – just as almost all of the rest of the old *Tallulah Falls Railroad* – has disappeared from the landscape forever.

refrigerators were invented: Every morning the yard crew placed a five-pound block of ice in my lavatory so that I could have the luxury of a cold drink at lunch time every day. I wish I had told them not to bother, because it actually was a nuisance to me. The drip from the ice itself went down the lavatory drain, to be sure, but the condensation that formed on the outside of the lavatory dripped on the floor, and I had to carefully avoid storing any mail in that area, or it would get wet. Those railroaders however, didn't ask me what I wanted. They just blindly fulfilled the requirements of the postal contract.

"At the stationary unit in Atlanta, I had carried a thermos of coffee in my lunch-box every day, but I found where I could get a pint of buttermilk in Cornelia every day, and the ice in the lavatory kept it good and cold. I usually finished my buttermilk about the time the train was crossing the high concrete-pillared trestle across Tallulah Lake, and to stop the incessant drip from the ice, I would throw the remainder of the block out the door and watch it splash into the lake waters far below.

A Tallulah Falls freight train was photographed near Demorest, Georgia in 1951. It was on this train that Mr. John B. Snyder and many other friends of Mr. Ragsdale worked. (Photo courtesy of Goldman Kimbrell)

Mail Call

"Improperly addressed mail was a problem on the *TF*, just as it was throughout the Post Office Department (the nomenclature 'U.S. Postal Service' didn't come into use until 1972). Some guy named Pasquale in Hollywood, California, was always getting mail in a blurred type that made it difficult to determine whether the state was CA or GA. Harry Dover, a WW I veteran Hollywood Postmaster would simply dispatch these letters to me without making any notation. It was up to me to surmise that there was no Mr. Pasquale in Hollywood, GA, and that I needed to write 'Calif' under the address and then place this mail in the slot for "Western States."

"Outside my mail car door was the notation '*United States Railway Post Office*,' and underneath was a slot for receiving letters to be mailed. One day, just before the Dinky started moving out of Mountain City, headed north, Mr. Snyder happened to notice a fat boy starting to insert a letter in the drop slot, and he stopped him, saying, 'Let's give it to the mail clerk.'

"I came to the door, and took the boy's letter. It was for his girlfriend in Rabun Gap, just three miles up the road. If he had put it in the slot, it would have silently landed on the floor under my work table, and I probably wouldn't have noticed it until the next morning – on my work table – where Earl Ward would have placed it when he was sweeping up. The drop slot on the RPO car was grossly unworkable.

"One of the entrepreneurial opportunities which opened up with the construction of the railroad was the illegal removal and sale of shrubbery from the nearby National Forest lands. Someone would occasionally have fairly large shipments of laurel, rhododendron and other shrubs from the post office at Tallulah Falls. The shrubs were tagged with the return address of 'Nature's Greenhouse.' I was told that state inspectors would occasionally come to inspect this business at Nature's Greenhouse, but this individual apparently always either bluffed or bought his way out of the situation.

"A sawmill run by Ritter Lumber Company in downtown Mountain City had about done all the logging that was practical in the area by 1951, but at that time, it was still in operation. The home office of the company was in Cincinnati, and the mill would send reports in a cardboard cylinder about once a month. Earl Dotson, postmaster, would hand me these cardboard cylinders outside the pouch. I thought he did this because they wouldn't fit inside, but after letting one or two of them get by me, I realized they were registered mail, and required my signature as well as the recording of their dispatch.

"The mail messenger at Franklin was John Pennington. He used a ton-and-a-half truck to carry mails between the train and the Franklin Post Office. He was always in a hurry to get to the post office with his mail. Maybe his girl-friend was timing him. . . I never knew.

"One day when Mr. Pennington backed his truck up to the mail-car door, I had a crate of baby chicks, and I wanted to give them to him first thing, to be sure I didn't forget them. John said, 'Save those dern chicks for the last; otherwise, I'll be having to work around them.' As I started handing him the other stuff, I said, 'Well, help me remember them.'

"We spent about ten minutes loading his truck with outside parcels, parcel post sacks, newspapers, pouches, rose bushes, tail pipes and whatever, then he said hurriedly, 'Is that all?'

"As was my habit, I quickly replied, 'Yes,' and he was off like a bullet. I had already passed Prentiss – the first post office south of Franklin – when I heard the first 'peep peep' coming out of the crate with the baby chicks. They had been making a continuous racket prior to the time I set them out of the way for John, but had become silent thereafter – until I had left the station. I was just angry enough with John for not taking the chicks when I first handed them to him that I put them off at Otto, North Carolina, and told the mail messenger to call John Pennington in Franklin and tell him to come get them.

Tornado Tales

"On February 29, 1952, a tornado hit the Banks County house where I was living with my parents, and in order to have some protection from falling timbers in case the house collapsed, I had crawled under an oak table. As I sat there, I could feel the floor shaking as the wind whistled and growled outside. For weeks afterward, whenever the Dinky would go down a grade, the vibrating floor of the mail-car frightened me so that I became nauseated.

"Compounding my problems with this phobia, was the fact that at this same time the Dinky actually did jump the track on one of those dangerous grades. Luckily, the rear truck twisted, straddling the rails, so that two wheels were on the right and two wheels on the left of each rail. This kept the dinky from leaving the roadbed and turning over, but it really was a bumpy ride on the cross-ties till we came to a stop.

"We soon discovered the cause for the wreck. A rail that wasn't sufficiently spiked down had leaned to the outside and caused the truck to twist. I thought we would have to wait for a railroad crane to come and set us back on the track, but as it turned out, Mr. Snyder had what was known as a 'derail' in his compartment up front. This was a piece of metal that fitted onto the rail. It had a groove that would catch the flange of a railroad wheel and force it off the rail as the train passed over it. They simply turned this derail around backwards so that it became a 're-rail,' forcing the wheel back onto the rail. We were on the go again in about thirty minutes, but what a scare for a guy who had recently been in a tornado.

"One day, there was a thick large brown envelope on which I just happened to notice the return address. It read 'Lillian Smith, Old Screamer Mountain, Clayton, GA.' I was struck by the name of the sender. I knew she was the well-known author of a popular novel at that time, *Strange Fruit*. This package was evidently another manuscript on its way to a publisher, and I felt honored at being in the position of providing her with a service.

"Also at this time there were lots of airmail letters to and from Oregon and Washington State. Harold Bell explained to me that the local boys had

Though virtually all the rails from the Tallulah Falls Railroad were removed and sold for scrap almost half a century ago, one or two short stretches still existed in recent years. This photograph of a partial remnant of the track being used as siding for the temporary storage of rolling stock was taken outside Cornelia in the mid-1990s.

been sent out there by the Civilian Conservation Corps, and they had married females from that area and had remained there, but were keeping in touch with their northeast Georgia relatives. The longer I worked the TF line, the more attached I became to the local people of the area.

Tango Uniform (Time Up)

"It surprised me how fast time passed. One day I noticed that Harold Bell's registry book was still in the drawer of the letter table. His last entry bore the date 'May 26, 1951.' I knew that as that date approached in 1952, I would have to be reassigned back to the Atlanta, Georgia Terminal RPO, and I wasn't looking forward to that.

"Today, as I record these memories, I am surprised to discover that all my recollections from my days on the old *TF* are of bad things that happened to me.

But in retrospect, a part of me actually died the day I had to leave the old Dinky for the last time.

"After I went back to Atlanta, my old-timer co-workers in the Terminal related to me how, when the RPO was discontinued on the *Toccoa & Elberton Line*, the mail clerk there had committed suicide to keep from having to return to the Terminal. I knew the feeling. Being the sole representative of the Post Office Department on a one-man run gave a man an independence and prestige that was not to be had in a larger facility.

"For example, on one of the days back on the Tallulah Falls run I was carrying the mail in the truck. There was an auto accident on the highway between Habersham Mills and Clarkesville. Gawkers had lined the shoulders of the road with their parked vehicles, and then had filled both lanes of the highway itself, just so they could get out and take a close look at the poor unfortunate souls in the wrecked vehicles.

"I was already behind on my schedule, and it looked like the accident was going to cause a long delay. I swung down from the cab of the truck and started walking toward the wreck, thinking I would ask the sheriff or patrolman – whoever was in charge – for some help getting through.

"As soon as I got six feet in front of the truck, the teenager who was driving the truck gunned the motor loud enough to get the attention of the entire crowd. I suddenly saw people pointing at me and murmuring to each other.

"In order to appear non-confrontational, I looked down at the ground as I walked. When I looked back up, I saw the highway was almost completely clear. Those gawkers who had parked in the middle of the road had seen my shiny RMS badge and the RMS revolver on my belt, and they immediately had assumed I was in charge. They had gotten into their cars and moved on. I felt like Gary Cooper in *High Noon*.

"A large part of my love for the *TF Line* was from childhood conditioning. From my earliest recollections, watching the trains cross the Hazel Creek trestle was a highlight of every visit to my grandparents' house in Demorest. I followed the smoke coming up through the trees before and after the crossing, and the loud Huff! Huff! Huff! which told me the train was moving again after stopping at the depot.

"My mother told me the train went to Franklin, North Carolina, and to me, that sounded like some wonderful enchanted land, where I probably would never have the good fortune to visit. So, getting the RPO clerk's job was virtually the realization of a life-long dream.

Bell/Snyder Last Days

"The last time I saw Harold Bell, he was still using crutches to get around. I feel sure he was still using them when he reported to work on Monday morning after I had put in my last day on the route on Saturday. Despite the crutches, Harold loved the route too, and I'm sure he didn't want to retire, so he gave it a good try.

"Harold's regular clerk's schedule called for three weeks on and one week off. The off-week would be filled by a substitute clerk. When Harold's three weeks were up, I was asked if I would like to go back to the Franklin and Cornelia route (called the Frank & Corn in RMS parlance) on the old *TF* and do Harold's off-week. It was a temptation, but at that time, Ethel and I had been married just one week, and I would have been ashamed to leave her for a week as a newlywed.

"I later had second thoughts about the offer, however, and the next time I thought Harold Bell was due for a week's layoff, I inquired about the substitute's job. To my disappointment, I learned that Harold had been granted another one-year disability leave, and John Carroll, the substitute who had taken the first layoff fill-in, was now assigned to '*Frank & Corn*' for the one-year period.

"Much to his despair, I'm sure, Harold Bell ultimately was forced to retire. I don't know if he ever even reported for work again. Interestingly, shortly after Harold retired, the Dinky was discontinued forever. Harold was a good friend of the district supervisor, Mr. Stevens, and I suspect he had been using his influence to keep the *Frank & Corn RPO* going just to accommodate his old friend.

"With his seniority, Mr. Snyder obtained a freight conductor's job. This was shortly before *Walt Disney Studios* began filming **The Great Locomotive Chase** on the Tallulah Falls route. Walt Disney promoters had learned of the scenic railroad and had gone to a great deal of trouble to ship in a vintage locomotive and build sets to use to film the movie on the TF line.

"With filming in progress, the freight train had more than normal difficulty moving along the tracks. Mr. Snyder was exposed to the rain and cold more often than normal. Tragically, he caught pneumonia and died. I don't remember what year it was, but if it was 1956, he would have been only 64 years old. His last thoughts probably involved the railroad which he loved dearly.

"As long as I live, I'll never forget my days on the *Frank & Corn RPO* job, nor the colorful *Tallulah Falls Railroad* either." – Theron Ragsdale

Retracing the Former Route
of the Old *Blue Ridge Railroad*

*Planned as direct competition for the Central Railroad between Macon
and Savannah, the Blue Ridge Railroad from Charleston was "side-tracked"
by the U.S. Civil War and never re-started. Though it never reached fruition,
the engineering marvel which was surveyed and partially-built through Rabun
County, Georgia, utilized almost indestructible granite in its construction which
undoubtedly would still be in use today, had the line ever been completed.*

A portion of an abandoned pre-Civil War-era railroad – much to the surprise of many today – still exists in northeast Georgia's Rabun County. Called the Blue Ridge Railroad (BRR), it was designed to extend from Charleston, South Carolina to Knoxville, Tennessee to enhance the commerce of the Charleston seaport in competition with the Savannah seaport in Georgia. But, just as occurred with many plans made prior to 1860, the BRR died aborning with the advent of the U.S. Civil War.

The Blue Ridge Railroad was originally conceived by fiery U.S. Senator and former vice president of the United States John C. Calhoun of South Carolina. He and the line's financiers promoted it tirelessly, but following Calhoun's death in 1850, a huge and important "political" element of the line entered the grave with him.

Calhoun had watched in frustration as development of the neighboring port of Savannah, Georgia, had threatened to siphon off the cotton product and prestige from the port of Charleston. The South Carolina Railroad connecting Hamburg, South Carolina to Charleston had been built in 1830 in a futile attempt to counter that competition, serving for a short while as a viable alternative for the massive shipments of Southern cotton which had begun flowing to the seaport of Savannah.

To counter the South Carolina Railroad, a group of Savannah officials obtained a state charter, and, by 1843, had constructed the Central Railroad 190 miles to Macon with a connection there to the Western & Atlantic Railroad (W&A) for transport of cotton and other products all the way from Chattanooga, Tennessee, with stops all along the route to Atlanta and Macon to Savannah gathering, among other things, the cotton "cash crop." This new railroad took on rapid growth, as did the Savannah rail yards and associated industry.

It is not difficult to imagine the competitive wrath this new railroad undoubtedly reignited in Senator Calhoun. This new competitive advantage in Georgia could not be allowed to continue. His counter-stroke had been the Blue Ridge Railroad.

Researcher Ruddy Ellis pauses at *"Observation Point"* in Rabun County. *Dick's Creek Falls* are visible (right foreground), and the Chattooga River in the background. The *Blue Ridge Railroad* bridge across the Chattooga River would have been just downstream from this site, and would have been an amazing 450 feet long and 100 feet high had it been completed.

Suffice it to say, that in the 1850s, residents of Georgia's Rabun County – through which the BRR had been surveyed and designed to pass – such as "Colonel" Henry T. Mozeley and James Bleckley were thrilled and captivated with the idea of this railroad and all it represented for the advancement of their mountain county. Mozeley was one of the incorporators in the Georgia Charter of 1838, while Bleckley was a director.

These same two gentlemen also obtained a charter for the Georgia Northeastern Railroad from Athens *"so as to strike the Blue Ridge Railroad at or near the town of Clayton,"* but that venture obviously never came to fruition either. However, interestingly enough, the portion of this railroad from "Rabun Gap Junction" (present-day Cornelia,

Georgia) on into Rabun County later of course did become the fabled Tallulah Falls (TF) Railroad. The historic TF, however, was still a number of years into the future at that time.

Though advanced in years, Calhoun over in South Carolina maintained a steady determination to orient the route of the new Blue Ridge Railroad through Georgia's Rabun Gap and then down the Tennessee River, instead of acquiescing to the wishes of fellow South Carolina statesman Robert Y. Hayne, whose vision involved taking the line through the mountains near Asheville and down the French Broad River. Calhoun, of course, ultimately gained the upper hand in that contest, but his death in 1850 coupled with the war in 1860, ended any hope whatsoever for completion of the BRR

The graded road-bed of the *Blue Ridge Railroad* alongside *Warwoman Creek* in Rabun County is still clearly visible through the forest. Despite the immense investment made in infrastructure, no rails were ever laid for the line. (Photo by Ruddy Ellis)

which was abandoned and forgotten in the dark days of the 1870s in Georgia.

Hiking the old BRR

Today, the now-aged tunnel at Stumphouse Mountain in South Carolina, and the amazingly massive stone masonry works (which the Blue Ridge Railroad used instead of trestles) are some of the more visible reminders of this surprising relic from yesteryear. The builders of this line obviously intended for it to handle a significant amount of freight, and they were building it to last indefinitely.

In retrospect, it is almost shameful that the builders of the later Tallulah Falls Railroad – a tremendously-scenic route passing through Norman Rockwell-quality mountain towns – were not equally dedicated to such construction quality. The TF might still be in operation today as a wonderful scenic tourist train had that been the case.

Despite the huge investment of time and money, the efforts of the BRR's builders toward this project ultimately were all for naught. Though records

indicate it was 80% completed by 1859, the outbreak of the U.S. Civil War interrupted funding and the devastation and poverty of the South were so impactful that construction on the line was never recommenced.

One massive tunnel (through Stumphouse Mountain) had been a particularly difficult obstacle. By the time other developers (after the war) got around to reconsidering renewed construction on the line, its usefulness had been eclipsed by other railroads and its day had passed.

Remnants of the Line

The unfinished portion of the BRR begins in Walhalla, South Carolina. In the little community of West Union (a suburb of Walhalla), an old siding for the BRR leads, as of this writing (2025), to the former site of a saw-mill. This short stretch of rails had been the starting point for the aforementioned unfinished portion of the Blue Ridge line planned across northwestern South Carolina, northeast Georgia, western North Carolina, and on up to Knoxville.

At the time of its last inspection, this section of siding did not appear to have been used in quite a long while, as the rails were heavily coated with rust and debris, and the sawmill was closed. However, the rails in the first part of the siding were fairly heavy and there was evidence that this was originally one leg of a "wye" (a triangular arrangement of rails which once allowed the heavy steam locomotives to reverse direction in earlier days).

The first 300 feet of the siding at this site appear to have been laid on the original main line grade towards the mountains. There is evidence still of this grade across the road from the saw-mill and on through a residential area. The former grade of the old BRR beyond

Though "soil-slides" from above the tunnel opening have almost obscured the west portal of *"Middle Tunnel"* through a ridge near Stumphouse Mountain, spelunkers keep the opening just large enough for explorers to continue slipping inside. The Stumphouse Mountain tunnel of the *Blue Ridge Railroad* (also known as the *"Black Diamond Railroad"*) ultimately proved to be too long and laborious to complete, and with the on-set of the U.S. Civil War, work on the line was discontinued, dooming it to abandonment.

this point has largely been erased by new construction.

Yet another section of the old grade which once existed down from the mountains and around a horseshoe curve is still partially visible. A substantially-long driveway leading to a home at this site exists almost exactly upon the original route of the old grade today.

If one searches a little further, he or she will also find a "cut" (a portion of the line where the original railroad bed required excavation through high ground) to the north of this aforementioned home, as well as a "fill" (a portion of the railroad bed where low ground or a ford across a ditch or chasm must be "filled in") leading to a culvert site to the south.

When one returns to the paved road in this vicinity, he or she will discover a deep, apparently unfinished cut which stops at the driveway of the aforementioned home just before the paved road. Next to this cut are little signs marking the grade as an official Boy Scout hiking trail. It follows the old line all the way down from what today is known as Stumphouse Tunnel Park. Little evidence of the line south of that point exists today due to modern development in the area.

Stumphouse Mountain

Explorers of the old BRR often wish to visit the site of Stumphouse Mountain Tunnel. At the time of its attempted

Located on *Warwoman Creek* near Houck Road, the old mill pictured here was built by Samuel Beck, a captain in the Confederate Army during the U.S. Civil War. It is located in the general vicinity of the east bridge abutment of the *Blue Ridge Railroad* in Rabun County.

construction (in the 1850s) – if it had been completed – it would have been (at 5,863 feet) one of the longest railroad tunnels in the world (over one mile in length).

There are two shorter tunnels through smaller mountains leading up to Stumphouse Tunnel: "Saddle Tunnel," which is 616 feet long, and "Middle Tunnel," which is 385 feet long. The approaches to these tunnels have collapsed into the mouths of the tunnels, rendering them almost unrecognizable today.

Visitors to Stumphouse – who enter at their own risk – should wear rain gear and water-tight boots, and should also obviously carry flashlights. (The Walhalla Light and Electric Company has for some reason not gotten around to stringing exterior illumination into this tunnel.)

The completed portion of Stumphouse Mountain Tunnel measures some 1,600 feet. The interior dimensions of the tunnel are 16 feet wide and approximately 20 feet high.

Another characteristic of Stumphouse Mountain Tunnel (and the reason for the rain gear) is the continuous misting rainfall within its confines, which is a phenomenon in itself. Heavy moist air sinking down vertical airshafts bored from the top of the mountain, cools below the dew-point as it sinks, creating a steady rain inside the tunnel.

Even more interesting, the original tunnel drilling crews dug a total of four of these vertical air shafts from the top of the mountain down to the interior of the tunnel. The shafts ranged from 161 to 228 feet deep, and enabled the work crews to dramatically increase their work

A *Blue Ridge Railroad* culvert over a small stream alongside Sandy Ford Road just east of the second ford across *Dick's Creek* is pictured. Notice the immensely-fortified nature of this construction accomplished with native stone.

pace. The shafts also provided vents for the wood-burning locomotives' smoke to be vented.

These "exhaust and breathing holes" were not completed without a heavy price. Several workers, according to reports, were killed in accidents. Some either fell into the shafts, plummeting the several hundred feet where they were dashed into the tunnel floor, or else died after being struck by objects falling through the shafts. One individual was scalded by steam from one of the engines used to hoist the buckets of "spoil" from the tunnel which was lifted through the exhaust holes to be discarded outside.

Visitors to this tunnel may also be interested in hiking the short distance over to beautiful Isaqueena Falls, where the ruins of the old Walhalla Water Works dam may be seen.

Middle Tunnel

Energetic hikers can next advance down the Blue Ridge grade to what was known as "Middle Tunnel," a shorter tunnel southeast of Stumphouse Mountain. Middle Tunnel is included in the aforementioned Boy Scout Trail which passes through breath-taking cuts and fills of the old line.

If one visits in spring, wildflowers are in abundance along the trail, including many beautiful "Jack-In-The-Pulpit" flowers. There, however, is also a lot of poison ivy in this vicinity, so hikers beware!

Additional exploration opportunities in this vicinity require a drive around to a spot near the northwest end of Stumphouse Mountain Tunnel and its long approach cut. This site today is flooded by Crystal Lake. The portal of the tunnel

The immense east bridge abutment of the Blue Ridge would have been a portion of the span across *Warwoman Creek* in Rabun County. This abutment was completed circa 1859, just prior to the outbreak of the U.S. Civil War which halted construction.

is completely full of water, mud and debris, so that only the rock face above the portal is visible.

If one walks southeast from this portal along a dirt road which appears to run almost exactly above the tunnel, he or she will encounter a crater in the ground which is probably the remains of shaft #4. Approximately 1,200 feet from the portal the hiker will encounter several small piles of rock here and there in the woods, but no real evidence that a lot of digging once took place at this site.

Blue Ridge RR In Rabun

At Stekoa Creek north of Clayton, Georgia, both the "plan" for the Blue Ridge Railroad and, ultimately, the actual route of the historic Tallulah Falls Railroad (TF) passed over this stream. One can only consider it ironic today that the TF – completed in 1907 from Cornelia, Georgia, to Franklin, North Carolina

– succeeded in reaching Rabun County and the Blue Ridge Railroad did not.

The irony of the situation stems from the fact that the 58 miles of the TF included some 42 "wooden" trestles – all of which constantly required maintenance and repair, and constantly engendered danger for the trains and occupants. The trestles were a tremendously expensive proposition which ultimately aided in the demise of the little mountain short-line.

The Blue Ridge Railroad by comparison, whose failure was caused by the advent of the U.S. Civil War, was being built with solid stone culverts and earthen fills across chasms and streams, and was designed to have no wooden trestles whatsoever. Had it been completed, it might very easily still be operational today.

In crossing Stekoa Creek in the 1890s, the TF built a trestle some 30 feet high. A good 50 years earlier, the

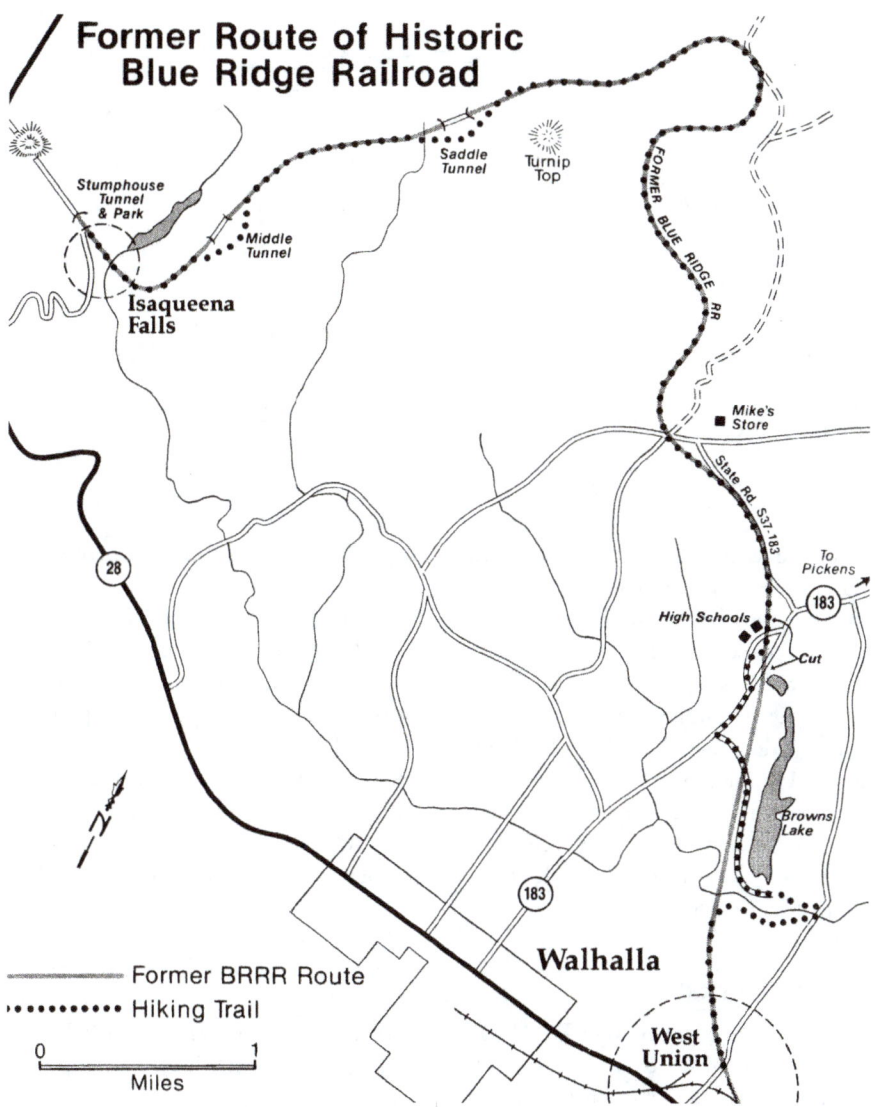

Former Route of Historic Blue Ridge Railroad

Stumphouse
Tunnel
& Park

Middle
Tunnel

Isaqueena
Falls

Saddle
Tunnel

Turnip
Top

FORMER BLUE RIDGE RR

Mike's
Store

State Rd S37-183

28

To
Pickens

High Schools

183

Cut

Browns
Lake

183

Walhalla

━━━━━ Former BRRR Route
•••••••• Hiking Trail

0 ━━━━━ 1
Miles

West
Union

Blue Ridge had built stone walls on both sides of the creek about 100 feet long. The Blue Ridge Railroad only planned to build bridges over the largest of the creeks such as Stekoa – a circumstance which therefore required the stone walls on either side of the creek.

For any smaller streams, the BRR planned to construct stone culverts covered by massive earthen fills. Amazingly,

all of the stone culverts had to be built by hand using only animal-drawn carts! A number of these completed culverts may still be seen today, all built of large rectangular stone blocks set without any mortar. This type of fine craftsmanship was standard procedure in the first-class engineering involved in the construction of the Blue Ridge line – sadly, all wasted.

Up at Warwoman Road at Saddle

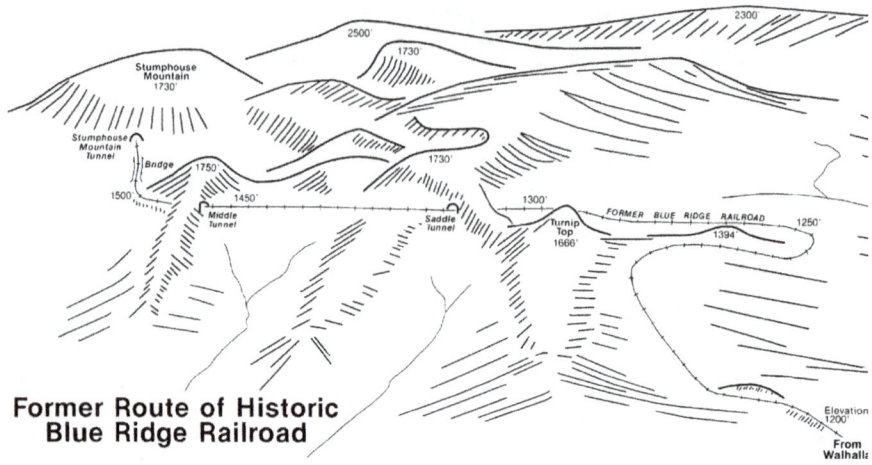

Former Route of Historic Blue Ridge Railroad

Gap, rail enthusiasts may look down upon the eastern approach cut to Warwoman Tunnel on the BRR. Grades and culverts constructed for the line extend almost as far as the Chattooga River.

A long-standing legend in this vicinity maintains that in the late 1850s, some 41 immigrant Italian laborers were buried in a cave-in inside Warwoman Tunnel. According to the legend, the bodies were left there since work on the project had ceased at about that same time.

More BRR In Rabun

If one drives down Sandy Ford Road (off Warwoman Road), the massive 94-foot long stone culvert of the Blue Ridge represents the last known remnant of the line in Rabun County.

If one is searching for the spot where the Blue Ridge Railroad had been designed to span the very substantial Chattooga River gorge, he or she must drive to and park at the spot where Bartram Nature Trail intersects with the road. From that point, one needs to hike down to Dick's Creek, then follow the stream to where it flows down Dick's Creek falls

into the Chattooga. It was at this spot that a BRR bridge would have crossed the wild and scenic Chattooga.

Construction of the BRR route never reached this point, but a bridge across the Chattooga at this juncture would have been a massive undertaking, particularly for 1850s contractors. Just judging from the topographic maps of this site, the landscape would require a bridge in the neighborhood of 450 feet in length built 100 feet above the river!

Judging from the remoteness this site must have enjoyed in the 1850s, particularly since there were few if any roads – or even pig-trails – in Rabun at this time, the BRR builders quite likely became bogged down in the tunnel at Stumphouse Mountain, and, as such, could not get heavy equipment or building materials around to the Chattooga River gorge, and therefore, no remnants of the line exist at that site today. The most likely bridge site exists between present-day Earl's Ford and Sandy Ford, but there is no indication that any construction whatsoever was attempted in this vicinity.

It seems almost unbelievable today

to understand that the charter for the Georgia portion of the Blue Ridge Railroad was granted in 1838, the same year the Cherokee Indians were herded out of Georgia on the shameful "Trail of Tears."

It also seems almost tragic that the Blue Ridge line was never completed, particularly since virtually all of the culverts – constructed of huge indestructible granite stone blocks – are virtually all still serviceable today, an engineering marvel.

Directions:

To reach Stumphouse Tunnel Park, take Interstate 85 north into South Carolina. Take SC 11 to Walhalla, then SC 28 to the park. The entrance to the park will be on the right prior to reaching the Stumphouse Ranger Station.

To reach the Blue Ridge Railroad remnants in Rabun County, take U.S. 23/441 to Clayton. Turn east onto Rickman Road, which joins Warwoman Road. Just beyond the Stockton House Restaurant (a good spot for lunch, incidentally) a side road runs north along Norton Creek. There are stone culvert walls (from the railroad) in the creek and the end of a high fill on the other side of the road.

Continue eastward on Warwoman Road, turning right into the park and drive to the end of the park. Walk up the steps to the railroad grade and read the information signage there. A nature trail leads to the rock face which would have been the east portal of the 1,700-foot long Warwoman (Stekoa) Tunnel.

Continue eastward on Warwoman Road (about six miles from Clayton) and turn right onto Sandy Ford Road. At the point where Sandy Ford Road take a hard left across Warwoman Creek, continue straight on John Houk Road until you reach the old mill. You will be able to see the old railroad bridge abutment there.

Double back to Sandy Ford Road and continue east. A few miles further, you will be driving upon the old railroad grade. Shortly after that, the grade swings off to the north and to the uncompleted 2,300-foot Wall Mountain (Dick's Creek) Tunnel.

A bit further on, the grade crosses the road and the adjacent creek over another stone culvert.

After fording two creeks, you will see the last stonework at about 9.8 miles from Clayton. Beyond this point is Dick's Creek Falls into the Chattooga River. Good luck!

A long-standing legend in this vicinity maintains that in the late 1850s, some 41 immigrant Italian laborers were buried in a cave-in inside Warwoman Tunnel.

(Grateful appreciation is expressed herewith in remembrance of the late Rutherford L. "Ruddy" Ellis, Jr., a former electrical engineer who was active in the Atlanta Chapter of the National Railway Historical Society for many years. Ruddy learned to love and treasure the north Georgia mountains as a child while visiting his grandmother's cottage on Lake Rabun and attending what once was known as "Camp Dixie" at Wiley. His great-grandmother, Mary Ann Lipscomb, owned a summer home in Tallulah Falls and was a founder of Tallulah Falls School. Ruddy provided most of the information used in this article.)

The Historic *Macon &*
Western Railroad

It arose in the earliest days of railroads construction in pioneer Georgia, so its history
is noteworthy, and its patrons have included the noteworthy as well.

One of the lesser-known and yet important short-lines in Georgia history was the *Macon & Western Railroad* between Macon and Atlanta. Founded in December of 1832, it provided an important connection to the still-more important *Western & Atlantic Railroad (W&A)* between Atlanta and Chattanooga, and was therefore a vital link between two of the most significant and historic cities in Georgia.

Origin of the Railroad

Originally chartered as the *"Monroe Railroad and Banking Company"* in December of 1833, it was not until 1838 that the first rails were actually laid. In due time, the line – with a 5-foot gauge rail – was completed from Macon northwest to Forsyth, Georgia.

On November 22 of 1838, the railroad received its first piece of rolling stock, and its engine was christened *"Ocmulgee."* The heavy locomotive was transported from the Georgia coast at Darien, up the river which gave it its name, where it amazingly was pulled up the riverbank onto track by teams of oxen. As track was laid before it, the engine was laboriously towed forward, the used track from its rear being taken up and relocated back to the front of the behemoth continuously until it had reached a specially-constructed side-track adjoining the main line approximately one mile from the river.

The first coach on the new Macon line arrived December 3, 1838, and on December 10, one day after the track had been completed to Forsyth, the first train steamed up these rails with an enthusiastic delegation of Maconites, and the fledgling enterprise was declared open for business.

The Macon line was extended to Griffin in 1842, but, much to the dismay of its ownership, fell into bankruptcy shortly thereafter. Purchased in foreclosure, the transportation venture's name was changed to the *"Macon & Western Railroad"* in 1845.

In 1846, the new *Macon & Western Railroad (M&WRR)* was extended from

> *On November 22 of 1838, the railroad received its first piece of rolling stock, and its engine was christened "Ocmulgee."*

The abandoned rails of a side-track near the terminus of the *Macon & Western Railroad* were photographed (date unknown) at "Railroad Gulch" in Atlanta, in front of the first Union Depot. Also pictured are buildings on the north side of Alabama Street near the intersection of Pryor Street (right) which had been rebuilt after the U.S. Civil War upon old foundations, including that of the former *Atlanta Intelligencer* newspaper. (Photo courtesy of GA Dept. of Archives & History, Atlanta)

Griffin into Atlanta after 21 more miles (34 km) of rails had been laid. That gave the railroad a grand total of 102 miles of rails.

In 1872, though it retained the *Macon & Western* moniker, it was purchased by the much larger *Central Railroad & Banking Company of Georgia* following recovery from the devastation of the U.S. Civil War. The *"R. R. Cuyler"* and the *"Emerson Foote"* were two of their more well-known dependable engines which were put to use on the *M&WRR*.

The consolidation of the *Macon & Western Railroad Company* with the *Central Railroad and Banking Company* was officially approved by the Georgia General Assembly Aug. 24, 1872. At this point, the *Central of Georgia* – after securing entrance over the river into Macon – boasted a continuous line all the way from Savannah to Atlanta.

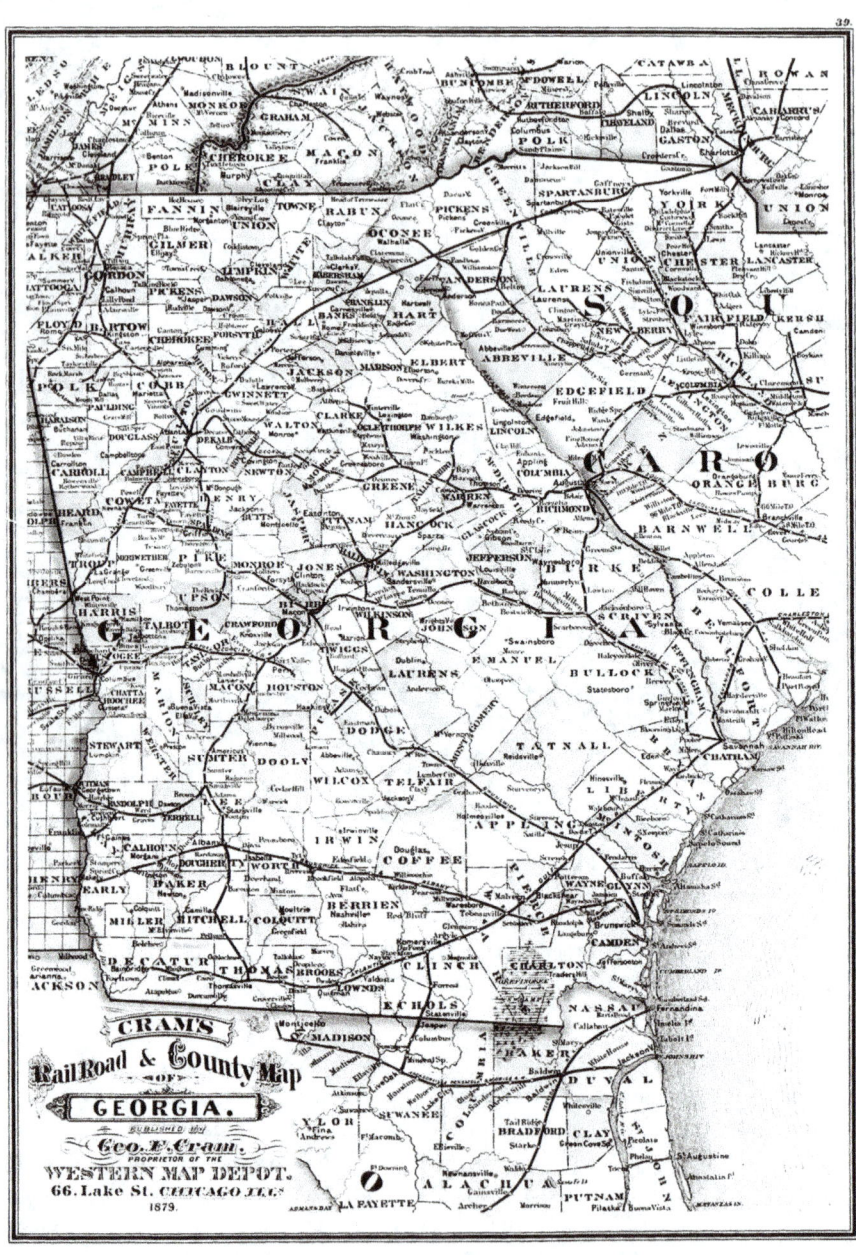

An 1879 map of the railroads in Georgia, showing the *Macon & Western Railroad.*

A Feat of Design

At that time, the Savannah to Atlanta route was considered to be something just short of an engineering marvel. The grades are exceptionally smooth and transitional, and the curves, where necessary, were broad, allowing for safe and trouble-free transportation. The most remarkable aspect of this route, however, is that in laying out the line, *"the engineer dragged his chain along the dividing ridge which forms the watershed between the Gulf of Mexico and the Atlantic Ocean, allowing the rail line to reach its terminal without crossing a single stream of water, and thus did not require the construction of a single bridge or trestle."*

As a result, throughout its history, this rail route has recorded exceptionally-few serious accidents and delays. Speeds of almost a hundred miles per hour have also been recorded on the line, and it has never suffered a single washout of any of its rails in even the most inclement of weather. In 1889, when Georgia was hit by record-breaking floods, there were many days when there was only one train arriving in the City of Atlanta – the *Macon & Western* train from the south.

Though few individuals pause to consider it today, rail transportation was extremely vital to the development of the fledgling United States in the early portion of the 19th century. Prior to that point, the only feasible means of transportation over great distances was either on horseback or by stagecoach. Both methods were rough and extremely uncomfortable over great distances. Further, the stagecoach routes in pioneer days were very limited regarding long-distance travel.

Long-Distance Travel

One also often does not consider the "logistics" of long-distance travel on horseback in the 18th and 19th centuries. If one was traveling an exceptional distance, it not only was an uncomfortable affair physically, it was also extremely arduous and dangerous. One was "open to the weather," as well as to Indian attacks, wild beasts, tainted water, and constant and endless other challenges, requiring relentless alertness.

One also had to consider the human biological "necessities" of long-distance travel by horseback. There were no comfortable rest stops or options for restrooms when "nature called," nor readily-available food or purified water. One simply paused wherever necessary to move one's bowels or empty one's bladder and took one's chances with whatever wild game one might be able to procure to eat and whatever chancy water from every questionable stream one "might" encounter.

If one was traveling by stagecoach, the circumstances were no better. They, in fact, were even more uncomfortable and dire. Stagecoaches had "schedules" to keep, rarely making "toilet stops"

Speeds of almost a hundred miles per hour have also been recorded on the line, and it has never suffered a single washout of any of its rails in even the most inclement of weather.

for anyone – particularly male passengers. If nature called during this form of transportation, one usually had no choice but to suffer in silence – many times for long hours at a time – before a stage stopped to change horses, or to pause overnight at a stage "stand."

As a result, anytime one could travel by rail, it was a much more highly preferable mode of travel – at least when considering speed and safety. The problem of toilet facilities, however still persisted. And just as with the stagecoaches, commercial rail travel functioned on a time-table with rigid schedules, so there very obviously was no such thing as a pause for a toilet stop with this mode of travel either. Again, one simply suffered in silence.

This lack of amenities was a common feature of early train travel, and passengers simply were required to plan accordingly (and be prepared to suffer if nature called), particularly during long-distance travel. *Occasionally,* if one was fortunate during these early days of rail transportation, a train might be equipped with a device providing little more than "a privy-hole through the floor" for emergencies. But that was rare.

It was only later in the development of rail travel, beginning roughly in the early 20th century that trains began to be equipped with restroom facilities for passenger convenience. Even those "toilets," however, were anything but "commodious" or comfortable. Nevertheless,

Did any famous individuals ever patronize the Macon & Western Railroad? The answer to that question is a resounding "almost certainly."

the addition of any type of facilities for relief of this nature on trains made long journeys immensely more comfortable, convenient and dignified for the rail-traveling public.

But then there was the matter of the "cost" of rail transportation. Long-distance rail trips were anything but inexpensive in the 19th century. A ticket between *most* destinations in that day and time could be purchased for approximately two and one-half cents per mile. That may seem amazingly inexpensive to today's traveling public, but in 1850, two and one-half cents was the equivalent of approximately one dollar in 2025, so a ticket in 1850 between even Macon and Atlanta would cost the equivalent of approximately $102.00 in 2025 dollars, and that was a considerable amount of money in those days. One therefore had to be reasonably wealthy to afford "long-distance transportation" on a railroad in the 1800s, and passengers on such a lengthy route were understandably few in number.

Famous Patrons

Did any famous individuals ever patronize the *Macon & Western Railroad*? The answer to that question is a resounding "almost certainly." So who might those individuals have been?

Well, though it is possible that he traveled by stagecoach – as he was regularly want to do in his later years – Georgia native John Henry "Doc" Holliday (who would soon earn Western fame as a noted gunman) was required to travel between Philadelphia (where he attended the *Pennsylvania College of Dental Surgery*) and Valdosta, Georgia (to which his family had fled in 1864 to escape the onslaught of General Sherman's invasion of Georgia during the U.S. Civil War) by some mode of travel, and it quite possibly was occasionally by rail.

In 1872 (when Holliday was graduated from college), his family obviously was financially able to send their son to an institute of higher learning which was a rare occurrence at that time. It therefore is possible that he also was possessed of the funds to travel – at least occasionally – back and forth between Valdosta and Philadelphia by rail. If so, the only feasible route northward (and southward back to his home) was via the *Western & Atlantic Railroad* (between Chattanooga and Atlanta) and then the *Macon & Western Railroad* (from Atlanta to Macon, at which point he would have changed trains to travel to Valdosta).

Indeed, Holliday had spent the first twelve years of his life on his father's farm in Griffin which was bordered by the *Macon & Western*. A few years prior to his death in 2020, Doc Holliday historian and chronicler Bill Dunn had rediscovered the original rusted and forgotten ancient rails of the *Macon & Western* hidden beneath the thick forested undergrowth on the periphery of the former 147-acre Holliday property north of Griffin. Nearby, following extensive research, he and an assistant also documented the discovery of the foundation stones of the old Holliday farmhouse at which a young Doc Holliday had lived and watched countless daily trips of the *M&WRR* in the late 1850s and early 1860s.

Still later, after John Henry had benefitted from a substantial inheritance via the sale of a multi-storied commercial office building in downtown Griffin, Georgia (from which he is also believed to have practiced dentistry a short time), he most certainly was possessed of the funds to enable him to travel back and forth by rail between Griffin and Atlanta (where he was employed as a dentist). The only possible railroad which might have provided this service was the *Macon & Western*.

Did Holliday in fact actually make use of that railroad for these purposes? Well. . . . He had the funds. He had the need. And he was accustomed to the finer aspects of life, so it's a safe bet that it quite possibly was the *Macon & Western* which provided him with at least some of this transportation, but actual proof of those circumstances is yet to be obtained.

There were also many other famous travelers on this line at one time or another. The 32nd President of the United States – Franklin Delano Roosevelt – made use of at least a portion of the route with his Presidential Train each time he traveled to his *"Little White House"* at Warm Springs, Georgia and other sites around the state.

Indeed, Holliday had spent the first twelve years of his life on his father's farm in Griffin which was bordered by the Macon & Western.

Engineer David J. Fant and the *"Valley of Death"*

Famed railroad man David J. Fant was known as "the evangelist of the rails" during his lifetime, because he was a Baptist minister in addition to his railroading duties. On a cool spring morning in 1910, his faith undoubtedly earned him deliverance from disaster.

David J. Fant – "the evangelist of the rails" – knew he had a serious problem when old No. 37 began to shake and vibrate terrifically as the huge train he was controlling approached Toccoa Falls in northeast Georgia. The car immediately behind the great engine and tender bobbled and bounced as it left the tracks and began dragging the train down a steep embankment.

Fant had been on the rails long enough to have witnessed his share of the end results of disasters such as this. He had only a moment to utter a quick prayer before yelling for his fireman to jump. Time was obviously of the essence, as they say, and it was quickly expiring for these two men.

Fant was well aware that the huge steam locomotive was about to roll over. It was simply the nature of the beast. When these mechanical giants leave the rails, they rarely remain upright, and when they roll over and hit the ground, the boiling water tanks filled with super-heated steam are always ruptured, and anyone within 50 to 100 feet invariably is delivered to the hereafter, the skin from their bodies instantly boiled and flaying off.

In his desperation in the moment, Fant cried out to the Lord, threw on the emergency brake then closed his eyes and awaited the inevitable. . . .

Dangerous Rails

Seven years earlier in 1903 and almost at this same spot near Toccoa, Georgia, Fant had watched in helpless horror as his dear friend and fellow engineer Ed Miller had died tragically in a similar derailment. Then, only one year later in 1904 – again near this exact same spot – Fant himself miraculously had escaped injury in a similar derailment. Did fate hold a winning hand against him now in 1910?

Fant's exciting adventures upon the endless ribbons of rail and his compassion for his fellow man ultimately earned him a spot in the annals of railroading folklore for all time. And today, as his immense engine leaned to the right side, he was about to add to that legend. . .

There was a pall hanging over the scenic Blue Ridge Mountains as the railroad rose up from the lowlands and forested terrain along the North Broad River south of Toccoa. It was almost like a funeral dirge marching the railroaders to a final destiny.

In today's modern world, rail accidents, comparatively-speaking, are rare. For that reason, when an accident does occur, it's usually a big one, becoming statewide, if not national, news.

Back in Fant's day in the early 1900s – prior to the age of the automobile and practical air travel – the railroads were the only quick means of long distance transportation. And since the science of safe rail travel had not yet been perfected, railroad mishaps were much more common – yet they were still big news when they occurred, since they were just as devastating as modern accidents.

In the early 1900s, passenger rail cars were all constructed of wood, not metal. Consequently, when a rail disaster occurred and the momentum of the train was suddenly halted, these wooden cars filled with flesh and bone human passengers would "telescope" or collapse into each other as they collided, crushing each car in succession and mangling the unfortunate passengers inside.

As if that was not bad enough, a wrecked steam locomotive meant a horrible death for many a brave engineer, his fireman, and anyone else within 50 to 100 feet of the steam escaping from the locomotive's ruptured water tanks. If they were not crushed and killed immediately, the steam would horribly scald them to death. It was a death, the thought of which, caused even tough and hardened trainmen to shudder in fear.

Atlanta-Charlotte Route

The real culprit in these disasters in the early 1900s was the routes traveled by the trains and often the speed at which the trains were required to travel. The railroad construction contractors invariably were forced to wind the route of their rail lines around mountains and

Engineer David J. Fant

across deep chasms, often using construction technology and materials which were destined for eventual certain failure and catastrophic accidents.

In 1856, a company was formed to build a railroad through the Toccoa (Stephens County) area to connect Atlanta and Charlotte, North Carolina with steam locomotive rail transportation. However, according to historian Kathryn Curtis Trogden, a national depression and the Civil War held up this project until sometime around 1873-74.

This Atlanta to Charlotte route was and still is a heavily traveled line even today (2025), since it is the shortest route by rail from the Deep South to the North. It became so popular in the late 19th century that the iron rails were replaced with steel from 1878 to 1887, and the line was double-tracked in 1917.

The "Air-Line," as this railroad was known, skirted the edge of the mountains, a dangerous route in the days

A *Southern Railways* passenger train steams down Currahee Mountain (background) in Stephens County, circa 1911. (Photo courtesy of GA Dept. of Archives & History, Atlanta, GA)

prior to the safety measures taken by today's rail transportation companies. In the Toccoa area, the railroad had sharp curves, high wooden trestles, steep banks and other characteristics which made it a perilous trip, especially during heavy rains which caused landslides and destabilized trestles.

Famous Fant

David Jones Fant, an engineer from Atlanta, had earned a place in the folklore of railroading because, aside from his employment as an engineer, he was also a Baptist minister, preaching wherever his time and schedule would allow him. While many of the railroad employees in the early 1900s were a rough, tough, profane lot, with a "live for today" attitude, Fant was a family man, close to both his family and his ministry.

Fant had even met his future wife on the railroad while on a short run on the Atlanta to Toccoa route. He also often ministered to the students at Toccoa Falls Bible College, and would blow his engine's whistle each time he passed by the school, as a call to prayer for his friends there.

As a result of his many and varied railroading experiences, Fant – as much as anyone – was well aware of the

dangers of steaming up the Toccoa run. His knowledge of the danger this route represented constantly plagued him, and he also knew that he could be the inadvertent cause of the death or injury to others because of this peril.

In addition to the normal dangers of this route, Fant also had to be on the lookout for other steam locomotives on the tracks, as well as the people and livestock which often strayed accidentally onto the rails. Livestock were big enough to actually derail a train themselves, although it was considered good luck (and good eating) for the engineer to catch poultry in the grill of his engine.

Fant had witnessed the devastating derailment involving engineer Ed Miller, a friend of his, who – only one day previous (through Fant's persuasion) – had attended railroad church for the first and only time in his life. Fant was running a fast freight and had sidetracked at Toccoa to allow the northbound No.36 passenger train under Miller to pass.

His fellow engineer, however, never arrived. At Ayersville, six miles up the mountainside from Toccoa, a landslide had caught and derailed the locomotive of the No. 36 at Currahee Crossing.

Wreck of No. 36

Upon learning of Miller's fate, Fant waited only long enough to take on local doctors and nurses, before going to his friend's rescue. As suspected, the wreck was a terrible one.

The huge locomotive with its white-hot steam-filled tanks had been turned over by the force of the landslide, trapping Miller and his fireman beneath it. Unfortunately for them, they were not killed by the impact, but were slowly dying from a complete scalding they had received from the ruptured tanks of

Photographed circa 1940s, this *Southern Railways* passenger train makes its way through Stephens County, Georgia.

boiling water in their engine. The skin, reportedly, was sliding off their bodies, and the colors of their eyes had faded by the time Fant reached them.

The dying Miller, in horrible agony, feverishly beseeched Fant to pray for him. The evangelist engineer pulled out his worn, grease-stained Bible which he always carried with him, and began to read:

"Yea though I walk through the valley of the shadow of death, I will fear no evil, for thou art with me..." Fant read steadily, as Miller's life slowly ebbed away.

On April 28, 1910, near the anniversary of Miller's death at the site, Fant passed through that same "valley of death" once again on a run to Atlanta. He was at the controls of No. 37, heading for Atlanta with his friend and black fireman - Rufus Johnson.

Deliverance

After passing through Toccoa, Fant pushed the old engine up to its cruising speed of 50 miles an hour, in order to accelerate for the climb through the edge of the mountains. Toccoa Falls Bible College rushed by, and it was shortly thereafter, that Fant's world turned topsy-turvy.

Since he was going south on a banked curve at such a high rate of speed, the engine of No. 37 *should* have turned over on the outside of the curve, derailing and trapping Fant beneath his engine. Miraculously, however, the engine fell instead over in the opposite direction, and when it finally came to rest seventy feet below, the evangelist of the rails amazingly emerged from the tangled wreck above the wheels uninjured. Was it a miracle? You be the judge.

Fant immediately began a feverish search for his devoted fireman, Rufus Johnson. He finally found him a short distance away. He, just as amazingly, was also unharmed, but in a state of shock.

The conductor and flagman arrived soon afterwards, and not finding Fant and Johnson, assumed they had met their fate trapped beneath the huge engine. Somehow, this false assumption was reported down the line. The wreck drew headlines in the ***Atlanta Journal*** where Fant's assumed death was unfortunately reported therein, a mistake which was not corrected before Fant's young son had read it in the newspaper.

Fant's wife, however, had been spared much of the shock. She and their three-year-old daughter, Mary, were on a passenger train that ironically was following Fant's No.37. Not only did they get to see that he was alright, but were given a tour of the wrecked engine and cars.

The derailment had been a terrible wreck, but, amazingly, no one was killed. Little Mary wasn't even shocked or impressed, remarking simply: "Daddy turned his engine over."

Arriving safely in Atlanta with his family, Fant stopped at the terminus long enough to send a telegram to his friend Rev. R.V. Miller in Hendersonville, North Carolina. It read *"Saved from a serious wreck. Psalms 91:9-12. Continue to pray."*

Miller's reply was: *"Have just learned of your deliverance. Psalms 91:9-12. God answers prayer."*

The passage cited by both these God-fearing men reads as follows:

"Because thou hast made the Lord which is my refuge, even the most High thy habitation; there shall be no evil befall thee, neither shall any plague come nigh thy dwelling. For he shall give his angels charge over thee, to keep thee in all thy ways. And they shall bear thee up in their hands, lest thou dash thy foot against a stone."

A Legend Retires

The late Atlanta historian Franklin Garrett once wrote that the stretch of Southern Railway between Charlotte and Atlanta has never been quite the same since David J. Fant made his last run on September 22, 1939, retiring at the age of 71, after 47 years of service. His narrow escape from the wreck of the *Southern Crescent* in 1910 made him a legend, familiar to evangelists and trainmen alike throughout the United States.

Interestingly, news media coverage of Fant's miraculous survival of that train wreck was dwarfed the following year by the media circus surrounding the fabled engineer as he had the dubious honor of watching his train being robbed at gun-point near Gainesville, Georgia, by one of the last remaining notorious bandits from the old West – Bill Miner. The *"Gentleman Bandit,"* as Miner was dubbed in newspaper coverage, had migrated to the eastern United States after numerous robberies and murder in the western United States and Canada had made him a *"Wanted"* man in those areas.

David J. Fant died in 1965 at the ripe old age of 97. The rails through Toccoa today are not the same in many ways as they were in Fant's day. Modern safety measures and advanced engineering of the routes have virtually eliminated most of the danger, but old-timers still close their eyes when they hear a train approaching, imagining that it is a steam locomotive from yesteryear about to pass through the "Valley of Death." They silently pray that the next sound they hear is not a crash. . . .

Former Stagecoach Route Through the Mountains

It began as a pathway in pre-history, traversed periodically and seasonally by migrating wildlife. In pioneer days, early travelers and, later, stagecoaches, often converted these routes to their use.

It takes a keen eye today, and a reasonably good knowledge of the pioneer history of our state, to find traces of the early toll-roads, but if one knows where to look, they can still be seen in the backwoods. The *Logan Turnpike* (known originally as *"Union Turnpike"*) was once a well-traveled wagon road over Tesnatee Gap, providing a lifeline for commerce and transportation between Blairsville (in Union County) and Gainesville (in Hall County).

To pay for its construction and maintenance, the *Logan* had both a toll-gate and a gate-keeper who collected a fee from everyone who used the road. Modern highways built across the north Georgia mountains in the 1930s ultimately eliminated the need for most of the old toll-roads, and it wasn't long before routes like Logan fell into disuse and abandonment, but they once were vital travel venues.

Today, very few north Georgians are even aware the old toll-roads ever existed at all, and fewer still can claim to have traveled over one of these old routes prior to the time that our modern highways usurped the usefulness of these early thoroughfares. One individual who could however, was Charles Roscoe Collins of Choestoe.

Known to family and friends as "Ros," Mr. Collins was appointed official historian of Union County by Georgia Governor Zell Miller during his term in office. Interviewed for this article prior to his death, Ros's memories provided a colorful roadmap for a time in our state's history which has long departed.

"I went over the *Union Turnpike* many times with my father, James J. Collins, in our two-horse wagon," recalled Collins. "My job was to 'brake' the wagon. I'd cut some blocks of wood to use in scotching the wheels down the steep grades. In the wintertime, I had to go ahead and break up the ice on streams so the horses could get across. These were hard jobs for a slip of a boy."

Once, before the turnpike closed (circa 1925 when U.S. Highway 129 was being opened across Neel Gap in north Georgia), Ros Collins made a wagon trip on the old trail by himself. He was about seventeen years of age at the time.

Though remnants of the old pioneer-era *Logan Turnpike* are still visible in the mountains of Union County, much of the route has been obscured by logging roads and access trails. One distinct characteristic of the turnpike, however, is the many boulders lining the route which were regularly removed to the sides of the road each year as cattle, horse, and wagon traffic wore down the trail to reveal them.

"The experience was a sign of 'having arrived,' of being grown up and responsible enough to manage the team and wagon alone, sell the farm produce at the market in Gainesville, and purchase 'store-bought' supplies at wholesale houses for re-sale in father's country store at Choestoe," he smiled in remembrance. "The round trip took five days."

Origin of the Routes

The *Union Turnpike* over Tesnatee Gap is one of the earliest official travel routes ever cleared in the state. In the ***Digest of Laws of the State of Georgia for 1821***, the following notation may be found: *"John Lyon, Joel Dickerson and Company shall hereafter be a body corporate by the name and style of the Union Turnpike Company, for the purpose of constructing a turnpike road from Loudsville in Habersham County, through the Tesnatee Gap in the Blue Ridge Mountains, by way of Blairsville to some eligible point on the northern boundary of this state in a direction toward the Tellico Plains in the state of Tennessee."*

Specifications for the turnpike were for a width of twenty feet with twelve feet of causeway. The owners/contractors of the route forbade any canal, railroad or other road being constructed within ten miles laterally of the turnpike for a period of fifteen years. This no doubt was done to discourage competition against this toll-road, at least until its owners could make back their investment in this public conveyance.

Construction of *Union Turnpike* apparently began immediately. Indians were still in the mountain areas in 1821, and, as often occurred in road-building projects of that day and time, the course of the *Union Turnpike* followed an Indian trail.

The early footpaths of the Native Americans were routinely adopted from trails through the mountain passes which had been originally trampled down by animals – usually buffalo, elk, or some other hooved animal – in their seasonal migrations. These animals instinctively knew the easiest and safest routes across the mountains, and their trails subsequently were naturally adopted by the Native Americans for their trading and warring purposes.

Union Turnpike was completed the same year it was chartered. Despite its early construction, it was paralleled across another ridge by an even older road, chartered in 1813, known as the *"Unicoi Turnpike."* The course of this early mountain road extended from Tennessee down across Unicoi Gap, through Nacoochee Valley (in present-day White County, GA) and on into present-day Clarkesville in Habersham County and Toccoa in Stephens County.

Remnants of the Unicoi Turnpike may still be viewed today in the Sautee-Nacoochee Valley. Though chartered in 1813, the route was actually cleared in 1812 by a group of coastal merchants seeking an inland trade route into the area.

The early mountain turnpikes usually acquired their names from a prominent mountain gap through which they passed, from a nearby landmark – or from a prominent landowner.

Logan Turnpike

Frances Logan was born July 18, 1802. He was the son of James and Nancy Edgerton Logan. He had migrated

Photographed here circa 1920, are Homer Nix and a "Miss Satterfield." They stand in front of the old Logan home near the toll-gate of the *Logan Turnpike*. Travelers - both coming and going - were required to pause at this spot to pay fees, and any avoidance was a crime. The ten-room log lodge at this site known appropriately as *"Logan's Lodge"* reportedly was a favorite of South Carolina Senator and former U.S. Vice-President John C. Calhoun who often traversed the turnpike in traveling to the Calhoun Gold Mine in Dahlonega.

from Rutherford County, North Carolina, leaving March 1, 1822, and arriving on March 10 at Nacoochee Valley in north Georgia's present-day White County.

Logan had made the trip to Georgia via the *Unicoi Turnpike*, and was one of a number of pioneer settlers who had chosen to leave North Carolina for the valleys along the Chattahoochee River in Habersham County (in a section later renamed White County).

Frances Logan's land was physically located north of Cleveland in the Loudsville community. According to records,

A pioneer view of the Gainesville, Georgia town square at which much of the products produced in Tennessee and extreme north Georgia were sold. Gainesville was the southern terminus of the *Logan/Union Turnpike.*

he married Hulda Powell on August 12, 1825.

Three years later in 1828, an event on the Logan farm set off a chain reaction which was unprecedented in the area. One of Frances Logan's slaves discovered a gold nugget in nearby Duke's Creek. The precious lump weighed some three ounces, and ignited a gold rush of amazing proportions at the same time as a similar strike and rush were occurring just a bit southward in what came to be known as Dahlonega, Georgia.

Other discoveries were soon made along the Chattahoochee River, Bean Creek, Black Branch, Hamby's Ford, Town Creek and adjacent locations in White. Within a short period of time, the "North Georgia Gold Rush" was in full swing, and thousands of gold-hungry prospectors and businessmen were setting up operations from all directions to seek a share of the riches.

Gold played an important role in the development of both the Union and Unicoi Turnpikes. Gold ore obtained in the early days of mining in the area was hauled over both routes to Bechtler's Mint in Rutherford County, North Carolina, where it was processed. The valuable cargo was guarded with great caution along the trip. This arduous trek later became unnecessary with the construction of the U.S. Branch Mint in nearby Dahlonega, Georgia.

When Major Willis Logan, a son of Frances Logan, purchased extensive lands on the south slope of the Blue Ridge Mountains in western White County, the name of the *Union Turnpike* over Tesnatee Gap was changed to *"Logan Turnpike."* Records show that Major Logan paid $3,000 for the rights to the road. He then owned a charter to its operation for some thirty years. Members of his family continued to operate it right up to the days when U.S. Highway 129 was opened across Neel Gap in 1925.

After Major Logan's ownership was established, the route of *Logan Turnpike* extended from Loudsville in White County northward over Tesnatee Gap, by Ponder Post Office, on into Choestoe, where it connected with the old *Union Turnpike* – a length of seven and one-half miles.

A stagecoach line eventually provided transportation from Augusta, Georgia, to Athens, Tennessee, on this turnpike. Major Logan had a stagecoach stop or "stand" (as it was called in pioneer days) on the route, and frequently accommodated overnight boarders.

Tolls for the road were collected at Major Logan's stop. The charges varied according to the type vehicle, the purpose of the travel, and the number of livestock used to pull the vehicle:

Wagons with four wheels and drawn by four or more horses or oxen were charged two cents per mile.

Four-wheel carriages termed "pleasure vehicles" paid three cents per mile.

Jensey wagons (those drawn by only two horses or mules) and pleasure carriages with only two wheels (buggies) were clocked for one and one-half cents per mile.

Ox-drawn carts were one-half cent per mile.

Cattle driven over the turnpike had additional special rates.

Jack Shuler and his family lived at the foot of Tesnatee Gap on the Logan Turnpike. They operated the Ponder Post Office and a store, and farmed the nearby bottomlands.

Shuler was employed by Willis Logan to maintain the turnpike. He worked for seventy-five cents per day. When his sons worked, they received ten cents per day for their labor, even when they were grown to manhood and could pile rocks and move brush with the best of workers.

Edward Shuler, a son of Jack, remembered working on the turnpike. "While our bottomlands were drying out before another plowing, we boys put in time with Father, working on the *Logan Turnpike* from its foot to its top at Tesnatee Gap.

"We took up large rocks from the road which had sharp points poking out of the ground and piled them or threw them over the banks down the mountainside. We opened ditches that had become clogged with rocks and sticks and leaves. We filled up low places that had been washed out by rains or hollowed out by wagon wheels, and smoothed them out."

Legends on the Turnpike

A favorite story of both Ros Collins and Edward Shuler about *Logan Turnpike* happened at the point called Big or Spiva Bend. A man named Newt Spiva was a deserter during the U.S. Civil War.

He had been hiding out in the mountains. The "Home Guard," (a group of men loosely organized on the pretense of protection for the homes and property of those who had volunteered for service in the Confederate forces), surprised Spiva as he sat on a big rock outcropping. They ordered him to raise his hands and surrender, but he refused to be taken captive, preferring instead to die at that spot, and they accommodated him.

Spiva Bend on the *Logan* had the most hazardous curve to negotiate – particularly if one was transporting a large load. Ros Collins tells of a huge steam boiler constructed at the gold mines in Coosa District of Union County west of Blairsville. Tom Collins (Ros' older brother) and two others, Perry Hood and Tom Calloway, had been hired by a Mr. Jarrard to transport the bulky contraption across Tesnatee Gap to his place on Town Creek near Collins Mountain in White County.

A special wheeled vehicle had been made to bear the boiler. Three yokes of oxen (large steers) pulled the unwieldy rig onto which the boiler was strapped.

When the men arrived at Spiva Bend, it appeared that they would have to dismantle the boiler to get it around the gigantic rock alongside the narrow road. With true mountain ingenuity however, the men used a series of winches in strategic locations to move the boiler past Spiva Bend. The effort required so much time and energy that the men camped at the Bend that night, and proceeded on across Logan Turnpike to the Jarrard place in White County the next day. The precious cargo arrived safely and in one piece.

Tesnatee Gap rises 3,138 feet, the highest point on the toll-road. The famed Appalachian Trail now crosses near this spot. Ros Collins identified another milepost near here.

"The Runyon boys were hanged from a chestnut tree here," he explained, matter-of-factly. According to folklore, the Runyons were also hiding out in the mountains for a transgression, and apparently were also captured by the Home Guard. They were hanged as an example from the branches of the giant chestnut.

"As a lad, every time Dad and I came along this place, I had a horror of seeing the Runyon boys' ghosts seeking revenge," he said.

(Editor's Note: It seems proper to point out here that in many instances, the "Home Guards" of Civil War days were often only a self-appointed group of opportunists supposedly serving duty by defending the home front. In reality, they many times represented little more than an assemblage of vigilantes and outlaws, taking the law into their own hands and taking advantage of unprotected property, guarded in most instances by little more than women and children.)

As might be expected, the few old-timers who still remember Logan Turnpike have colorful stories to tell of the early days along the historic route. Characteristically, a number of the common stereotypes of wagon-train travel also hold true for the trail.

Life on the Turnpikes

Travel along the turnpike usually followed a pattern. Wagons banded together and journeyed as a group from Choestoe to Gainesville, according to Mr. Collins. The largest group usually consisted of approximately thirty wagons (which would have been quite a procession).

The first day's travel took the wagon train to Mile Branch north of Cleveland, where the group camped for the night.

The next day got them to Gainesville where they stayed overnight at either Bell's or Simon's Wagon Yards. There, they sold chestnuts, animal skins, farm produce, and sorghum syrup. They traded as much as possible for merchandise to stock the country stores.

The return trip also took two days. The entire episode was usually planned to extend from Tuesday through Saturday. Mondays were used to load the wagons for the outgoing trip, because the mountaineers were strongly opposed to working on Sunday, considering it the Lord's day, Collins noted.

Jud Duckworth once made his living as a wagon driver on the turnpike. Employed by merchant Virge Waldroup, Duckworth made weekly trips across Tesnatee to Gainesville. His large covered wagon, drawn by four iron-gray mules, regularly transported heavy loads.

On the way south, Jud said he carried live chickens, eggs, and various produce from mountain farms received "in trade" at Waldroup's General Merchandise. On the return trip, the wagon was loaded with hardware, dry goods, and staples such as coffee, sugar, and rice. The driver also became the source of news from "down south," so he had to have a good memory.

Ros Collins and others in Blairsville today remember the first automobile driven over *Logan Turnpike*. The year was 1917, and the car was an Overland Country Club Roadster owned by Mrs. Roxane Durfee of Atlanta.

When Mrs. Durfee – an obvious adventuress – came to the toll gate at Loudsville, the gatekeeper reportedly was perplexed, because no fee had ever been established for motorized vehicles. After much argument, an agreement was struck for a fee of fifty cents – a cost

Early ATV – The ever-adventurous Roxane E. Durfee drove her *Overland Roadster* - an early version of "off-road vehicle" - over Tesnatee Gap on the *Logan Turnpike* in 1917. It was the first time an automobile had ever even attempted, let alone navigated, rough terrain of that magnitude. After successfully completing her trek, she parked the vehicle (pictured) on the town square of Blairsville, Georgia.

which remained in use for the remainder of the life of the old turnpike.

Following a great deal of trouble with overheated brakes, dangerous potholes, hazardous curves and frequent stops, Mrs. Durfee finally appeared at the Christopher Hotel in Blairsville – nerves somewhat frayed and frazzled. Her snappy gray roadster, however, with its red wire wheels and white convertible top, seemed none the worse for wear. Mrs. Durfee probably didn't know it at the time, but her trip undoubtedly signaled the beginning of the end for the turnpike, since the age of motorized transportation inevitably required a more accessible route.

To reach the site where the old *Logan Turnpike Toll Gate* and the stagecoach stop once stood, travel northwest from Cleveland, Georgia, on U.S. Highway 129 for approximately eight miles.

Turn right onto Kellum Valley Road and proceed northeastward for approximately two miles. On the right, a sign with the words "Toll Gate" marks the historic spot.

The two-story Logan home-place which served as a hotel, stagecoach stop and toll-gate, is long gone today. On its former site, a newer home erected at a much later date and the adjoining toll-gate site were purchased in 1947 by Mary Mathis of Americus, Georgia, and Washington, D.C., as a future retirement residence. Four Mathis sisters – Mary, Rebecca Kimmel, Sarah Ethier, and Lynn McKay – spent May through October there annually until all of the sisters had passed away with the exception of Sarah. Sarah continued to live – well into her 90s – at the old Toll-Gate site in a modernized home with her daughter, Marion Crawford.

The *Logan Turnpike* was officially closed on Independence Day, 1925, but until the U.S. Forest Service barricaded the road in 1981, four-wheel-drive vehicles still traveled the 7.5 miles of the route regularly.

Today, a hike up the old road is still a challenge, but well-worth the trip, offering numerous scenic vistas of small waterfalls and the flora and fauna of the Blue Ridge Mountains along Town Creek. All along the old turnpike, piles of rocks and boulders serve as silent reminders of the days long ago when Jack Shuler and his predecessors kept the old *Logan Turnpike* passable by piling the obstructing stones to the sides of the road. Today, the old route has receded into the mists of time.

The Pigeon Mountain Railroads

It may be something short of a world record that has stood unrecorded and unchallenged for over 80 years. Northwest Georgia's Pigeon Mountain may contain the most railroad tunnels of any such summit in the world.

No less than eight railroad tunnels pierce various ridges and spines of the rugged defile that extends southward from Lookout Mountain across the northwest corner of Georgia. Two railroads in this vicinity owed their existence to an early 20th century iron industry which once flourished in this locale.

This railroad network and the iron mines that gave them life are located about eight miles west of LaFayette in northwest Georgia's Walker County. Pigeon Mountain was once a bustling beehive of iron ore mining and narrow

Last Remnant - The only tunnel on the *Tennessee, Alabama & Georgia (TAG) Railway* is still visible today through the undergrowth on Pigeon Mountain. It can be reached by hiking from Georgia Highway 193. The rails on this line, however, were taken up long ago.

gauge steam railroading activity. All of it was built using little more than black powder, mules, carts, hand tools and back-breaking labor. Insects, snakes and other unhappy disturbed wild creatures no doubt contributed to the miseries of those laboring at this site.

Today, a portion of this mining area – the old Estelle Railroad – is an excellent "Rails-To-Trails" hiking venue. GA Highway 193 twists its way through Dug Gap to reach the Cloudland Canyon area. Unknown to many travelers in this region today, this road passes over the top of an abandoned railroad tunnel once used by the standard gauge Tennessee, Alabama & Georgia Railway – known simply as the TAG line. The north portal of this tunnel is just off the north side of the highway.

Not far from the south side of the highway through Dug Gap is the site of two former ore loading tipples at Estelle, once a company town of the Chattanooga Iron & Coal Corporation (which preferred to be called "The Corporation" in the 1920s). Diminutive steam locomotives and trains of the Estelle Railway ran over small three-foot gauge track, extending six miles south on the west flank of Pigeon Mountain, to trundle iron ore to these tipples and crushers. The

Ghost Road – Much of the former route of the *Estelle Railway* is used as a biking trail as of this writing, and is known as *Estelle Mine Trail*.

crushed ore was then loaded into cars on the TAG line.

TAG Railway

Although one would be hard-pressed to find it on most maps today, there are two railroad stations just over one mile apart on this line. One is called Kensington and the other is called Hedges which is located near Davis Crossroads. Today, Hedges is the end of the line on a 23-mile branch line of the Chattooga & Chickamauga Railway (C&C), headquartered in LaFayette.

The C&C took over operation of both the old Central of Georgia main line

For nearly 70 years, heavy trains thundered over the TAG line connecting Chattanooga and Gadsden.

from Chattanooga to Lyerly, Georgia, and the remaining stub of the TAG line from Chattanooga to Kensington and Hedges in 1989.

Until about 1980, the TAG line rails continued unbroken for 92 miles, starting at Chattanooga and continuing through High Point and Kensington to eventually reach Gadsden, Alabama. The first through-train ran on the Chattanooga Southern Railway on June 25, 1891. This railroad was reorganized in 1911 as the Tennessee, Alabama and Georgia.

For nearly 70 years, heavy trains thundered over the TAG line connecting Chattanooga and

Old mine shafts opened in the 1920s still dot the mountainsides in the vicinity of Pigeon Mountain. Most of the mining activity in this area ceased in the 1930s.

Gadsden. From the start, the steel mills at Gadsden were the reason for the road's existence.

Interestingly, there was also passenger travel on this railroad too, but it was accomplished in small gasoline-powered motor cars which were referred to derisively as "doodlebugs." It must have been quite a thrill in the 1920s to ride in one of the diminutive gasoline cars as it hurtled through the damp pitch black darkness of the 1,648-foot-long Pigeon Mountain Tunnel.

Several long side-tracks extended off the TAG line near Kensington and Hedges to reach Estelle. From these side-tracks, the Estelle Railway dumped the crushed ore into cars on the TAG line which then took the ore to the steel mills.

Southern Railways purchased the TAG line on January 1, 1971. By then, the iron ore business on Pigeon Mountain had been no more than a memory for nearly four decades.

Changing patterns of railroad activity ultimately doomed much of the TAG line beginning about 1980. Southern Railways had

a parallel line to Gadsden via Fort Payne, Alabama. As a result, the track south of Hedges was gradually abandoned in stages. Today, the rails have been removed and a silent road-bed yawns into the distance from Hedges to Gadsden.

TAG Tunnel

The only tunnel on the TAG line is located about two miles south of the current end of the track at Hedges. It is one of the more tangible remnants of this now forgotten railroad. The long curved shaft into Pigeon Mountain is partly filled with water and debris today.

The north portal of the tunnel can be reached by hiking in from Route 193. However, hikers are discouraged from entering this tunnel, particularly in warm weather, when snakes and other wild animals may inhabit its dark and musty recesses.

At one time, the north portal was once the site of a small servicing facility. A water tank quenched the thirst of steam locomotives laboring to the entrance. Some old footings from a former building at this site can still be seen in the tall grass.

Estelle Railway

The little burg of Estelle was located immediately southwest of Kensington, and gave its name to the three-foot gauge railway which extended six miles back along Pigeon Mountain. Estelle was dominated by a large ore crusher and tipple which loaded the iron ore from the ten-ton cars of the Estelle Railway into the cars on the TAG line.

Little remains to mark Estelle today. A few concrete footings from the twin crushers can be found in the undergrowth, and several

Little remains to mark Estelle today.

The tiny town of Estelle was once located immediately southwest of Kensington, Georgia. It gave its name to the three-foot-gauge railway (photographed here circa 1924) which ran into Pigeon Mountain.

nearby small hills are really mine tailings. The village was dismantled and virtually erased from the face of the earth when the ore mining ceased.

Iron mining began on Pigeon Mountain as early as 1884, but the Estelle Railway was not built by The Corporation until after 1910. Much of the mining and railway activity appears to have ended sometime around the Great Depression of the 1930s.

The Corporation reportedly went bankrupt about 1927. The scrap drives of World War II, stripping the mountain of all the steel rails and other equipment, kept things going for awhile, but it didn't take long to remove the usable and recyclable raw materials.

Numerous clefts in the mountainside are left from former mining activities.

Starting at Estelle, the six-mile Estelle Railway extended along the west face of Pigeon Mountain. According to a guidesheet prepared by the Georgia Department of Natural Resources which manages the Crockford-Pigeon Mountain Wildlife Management Area, the railroad followed the mountainside.

Hiking In

On a recent autumn hike along this route, two railroaders experienced with this area – Harold Holiman, general manager, and Randall Magnusson, superintendent of the Chattooga & Chickamauga Railway - revisited the area. These two knowledgeable veterans of the rails pointed out the remains of numerous remnants of this aged line. Today, these sites would be discernible only to experienced eyes.

Much of this roadbed is now known as the Estelle Mine Trail, marked by orange paint splotches on the trees along the route. The trail is passable by hikers, horseback riders and mountain bike riders - but not by motor bikes or motorized vehicles of any type.

Numerous clefts in the mountainside are left from former mining activities. Mining was done both by boring shafts (which have collapsed into the mountainsides as time passed), and by stripping exposed iron ore from the surface.

The Estelle Railway was a private, non-common carrier operation. As a result, it was not required to file reports of its development and/or its activities, so little information exists on it today.

One level area along the steep mountainside between two of the tunnels appears to have at one time been the site of small rail yard, probably about three or four tracks wide. Here, the tiny dinkey steam locomotives of the Estelle Railway marshaled the 10-ton cars of ore into trains to take them to the crusher.

Estelle Railway Tunnels

Then, there are the tunnels. When they encountered an obstructing ridge on the mountainside during construction of the rail line, the road crews simply dug and blasted a short tunnel through it, rather than divert the tracks around it. This practice was repeated seven times as the railway was extended southward from Estelle, and was the reason for the

Since their abandonment during the Depression, many have been reclaimed by nature.

many tunnels in Pigeon Mountain.

Most all of the tunnels are approximately 500 to 1,000 feet in length. Since their abandonment during the Depression, many have been reclaimed by nature. Some have collapsed along much of their length.

The tunnels were often bored through well-fractured shale rock. Since abandonment, this rock has continued to erode from the walls and ceilings of the tunnels, often nearly completely filling them. Any wood shoring used for support inside the tunnels rotted away years ago.

As a result of the extreme danger of these tunnels, the Georgia Department of Natural Resources strongly discourages exploration inside them. At the site of each tunnel, the orange Estelle Mine Trail markers are diverted around the tunnels by a steep curving trail which climbs and twists over each ridge.

DNR management officials claim that a few of the narrow gauge cars which were used to haul the iron ore from the mines to Estelle Railway are still located inside one partly-collapsed mine at the far end of the Estelle Mine Trail. Due to the thick undergrowth and remote location, this mine is almost impossible to locate today, and even if located, would be extremely dangerous to enter.

Today, eight tunnels and miles of vacant roadbed aside, little remains to indicate that this once was a bustling industrial area. Mother Nature has reclaimed her own on Pigeon Mountain, but a good hiking opportunity awaits those who wish to venture onto the Estelle Mine Trail.

Early Life in Historic Helen and the *Gainesville & Northwestern Railroad*

Built in the early 1900s, this mountain short-line railroad was a mainstay for mountain communities between Gainesville and Robertstown for some 37 years. In the early 1930s, with its lifeblood gone and suffering from the effects of the Great Depression, the line went out of business and slipped into history.

Byrd-Matthews Lumber Co., one of the largest lumber mills east of the Mississippi in its day, opened in Helen, Georgia, White County, in 1912. It was the same year the hydroelectric dams were built on the Tallulah River to silence the great falls there. These were very "industrial days" in the once-quiet and sleepy confines of northeast Georgia. Along with the harvesting of the huge stands of virgin timber in White County, came a "first" for the county – the railroad.

In order to get the huge harvested trees down to the mill, and then to get the lumber products to market after they had been milled, Byrd-Matthews Lumber had to have a reliable method of heavy transportation. A new railroad – the *Gainesville & Northwestern* – fulfilled this need.

Lumber production was big business in north Georgia when virgin timber was still abundant in the early 1900s.

The advent of this railroad was a momentous occasion, because it brought with it the capacity not only for hauling heavy loads of lumber, but also for the provision of passenger train service as well. Suddenly, area residents all up and down the line could obtain products which had previously been completely unavailable to them, and they also were able to send their own products to new markets back down the line. And they could even travel back and forth to these markets themselves now.

After reaching Gainesville, Georgia, the thousands of board feet of lumber from Byrd-Matthews were then transferred to other railroads for distribution throughout the United States as well as to foreign markets. Lumber production was big business in north Georgia

Engine #203 of the *Gainesville-Northwestern Railroad* pulls into Nacoochee Station in the early 1900s. The depot pictured here still stands as of this writing.

when virgin timber was still abundant in the early 1900s.

The "passenger" aspect of the *Gainesville & Northwestern Railroad* (called G&NW) featured what was known as "an excursion service" to and from Gainesville from and to Robertstown and all points inbetween, and also provided freight and postal service to these areas as well. The run began at the old Gainesville Depot (which still stands as of this writing in 2025) and made stops at Bradford Street Station (removed long ago), New Holland (also gone),

"Back in the day," Mr. T.B. Henderson owned a general merchandise store next to the Nacoochee Station. This building still stands today (as of this writing).

Clark (gone), Autry (gone), Dewberry (gone), Brookton (remnants still survived until just recently), Clermont (long gone), County Line (gone), Mossy Creek Campground (long gone), Meldean (gone), Cleveland (long gone), Asbestos (gone), Mt. Yonah (gone), Nacoochee (still exists as of this writing in 2025), Helen (gone), and Robertstown (also gone). Gainesville, Brookton, Clermont, Meldean, Cleveland, Nacoochee, Helen, and Robertstown were agency stations, and the train made regular stops at them. The others were known as "flag stops," (where stops, interestingly, were made if the train was "flagged").

"Back in the day," Mr. T.B. Henderson owned a general merchandise store next to the Nacoochee Station. This building still stands today (as of this writing). It is the old brick building near the intersection of Highways 75 and 17, near the Nacoochee Indian mound. Mr. Henderson's daughter (a Mrs. Davidson) provided the following information:

"The Nacoochee Post Office was located in the general store and my father (Mr. Henderson) *was postmaster there. He also served as rail agent at the Nacoochee Station. His duties included the issuance of tickets and the posting of freight bills. Most of the merchandise in my father's store came in by rail from Athens or Gainesville.*

"Father was one of the few persons in the area who owned an automobile. Sometimes passengers coming in on the train would need transportation to one of the 'resorts' in the area or to a friend or relative's house. After arriving at Nacoochee Station (which also still stands across Hwy 75 from the old general merchandise store), *my brother – Bon – would drive the travelers to their destination."*

Mrs. Davidson explained how she helped her father in the store, post office and at the little railroad station. She remembers that in the store, they sold groceries, hardware, men's, women's and children's clothing, seeds and fertilizer, all mostly delivered by rail. She said that Mr. L.G. Hardman (whose beautiful historic home – once known as *"West End"* – also still stands

near the intersection of Hwy. 75 and 17) shipped butter and milk from his dairy by rail to Gainesville, and Mr. "Simp" Logan shipped asbestos from his asbestos mine by railroad. This, of course, was long before science had revealed the destructive aspect of asbestos to human lungs.

Mr. Henry Davidson, who became the husband of Miss Mary Lula Henderson, was one of the many who helped to build the railroad from Gainesville to Robertstown. His brother, Mr. George Davidson, was engineer on the train and Mr. Paul Westmoreland was the fireman.

The railroad brought many visitors to the White County area. Major resorts included the *Alley House* (present-day *Old Sautee Inn*); Nacoochee; the *Henderson Hotel* in Cleveland; and the *Mitchell Mountain Ranch* in Helen. Most of these historic structures – save the *Old Sautee Inn*, the historic *Hardman House* and its out-buildings, the old depot building, and a few others – are now sadly long gone.

The *Gainesville & Northwestern Railroad* continued its 37-mile run from Gainesville to Robertstown until 1930. Shortly thereafter, when the seeming inexhaustible supply of virgin timber had in fact been depleted almost entirely, the railroad, with its life-blood gone, was discontinued. The tracks were taken up; the railroad rights-of-way reverted back to private ownership, and the *Gainesville & Northwestern Railroad* disappeared from White County and receded into history.

> *The Gainesville & Northwestern Railroad continued its 37-mile run from Gainesville to Robertstown until 1930.*

Remembering Old Dalton Depot

For almost 180 years (as of this writing in 2025), the historic structure alongside the railroad tracks in Dalton has withstood the ravages of time and war. Railroad buffs can enjoy not only the railroading history, but of Civil War soldiers as well who once trod that site.

When Mark Thornton sold a plot of land in Whitfield County to the state of Georgia in 1846 for $100, he clearly stipulated the property could only be used for one purpose: to build a railroad station which would provide rail transportation to other sections of the state. Eight years earlier, Georgia's *Western & Atlantic (W&A) Railroad* had been established to connect the Chattahoochee and Tennessee Rivers in a trade route between the Atlantic Coast and the West, and Thornton wanted to establish the Dalton area as an important stop along the way. It wasn't long before his dream became a reality.

Prior to construction of the Dalton Depot, trains had been rumbling into the area for seven years. When the tracks from Dalton to Atlanta were completed in 1847, the town as yet, had no depot.

The first train from Atlanta arrived in Dalton on July 22, 1847, paving the way for the arrival of many more locomotives in future years. And though they did not know it at the time, the *Western & Atlantic Railroad* would generate a variety of emotions ranging from joy and excitement to tears and fears in the Dalton community in the years ahead.

Following the erection of the Dalton depot in 1852, the station quickly became the focal point of life in Dalton. Soon after the depot's completion, the population of the town soared from 300 to 1,500.

Today, travelers are attracted even more to the site since it is one of only two surviving original *W&A* passenger depots in the state. An extensive $1 million renovation in 1990 by two Rome, Georgia, developers – Walter Hackett, Jr. and Mike Wrobel – transformed the 10,550-square-foot building into *The Dalton Depot Restaurant and Trackside Cafe*. Town fathers had hoped this hospitality development would enhance the stability of the site.

In order to maintain the unique dining experience of the site, very little was changed architecturally. The one-story brick structure with its shallow-hipped roof, overhanging eaves and arched loading doors, remains typical of a nineteenth century train depot. The restaurant/cafe' concept, however, as of this writing, was short-lived, since it eventually ceased operations. As of this writing, the subsequent use of this historic structure is unknown.

Despite its spotty commercial use, this building houses some of the area's most significant history. Edward White, an entrepreneur from Massachusetts who named the town after his mother's family, hammered a circle of nails into the depot to mark the center of the town in 1852. Measuring from the nails in a one-mile radius, White established the first city limits from Dalton in a circular fashion.

Although records do not reveal the name of the depot's architect, many believe Eugene LeHardy, a *W&A* civil engineer and designer of the old Chattanooga depot erected in 1859, served as the designer of the Dalton station.

During the U.S. Civil War, soldiers frequently boarded trains at the Dalton Depot. On June 10, 1861, Private Eli S. Stanford boarded a train there with his company, headed for Big Shanty in present-day Cobb County's Kennesaw. During the march into Dalton, however, Stanford reported in his diary that his comrades *"stopped and took some refreshments about two miles from town. After we got to Dalton, the boys increased refreshment and kept up quite a ruckus all night. At 4:00 a.m., boarded train at Dalton for Big Shanty, arriving 2:00 p.m. It was obvious some of the boys had too much of the old Billy Patterson (a local moonshine) in them."*

The Dalton Depot played a role in the now-famous wild ride of the *"General,"* the *W&A* locomotive which was stolen by the Yankee saboteurs known today in historic lore as "Andrew's Raiders." Here at the Dalton Depot, a 17-year-old telegraph operator was dropped off from the pursuing engine, *"Texas,"* to send a message to Confederate forces in Chattanooga to warn of the *General's* approach.

In later Civil War action, railroad officials suspect the depot may have received some damage when Union troops entered Dalton in 1864 and set fire to several buildings. Although the brick exterior remained virtually unharmed, ornamental brackets beneath the overhanging eaves were added during later repairs to the roof, representing stylistic features normally in vogue after the construction of the original building.

Today, trains still rumble down the tracks beside the old depot which is owned by the City of Dalton and leased to private business owners. At last check, the structure still retained the station's original freight scales and other railroad memorabilia, and visitors could also watch trains zooming by the window.

Surprisingly, the activity on the tracks outside the depot usually does not disturb visitors to the facility. The 1852 builders of the depot specially designed the structure to isolate it from ground vibrations.

Placed on the ***National Register of Historic Places*** in 1978, the antebellum Dalton Depot still maintains an important role in the heart of the city's downtown district. It is located at the east end of King Street, and by the time you read this, it may once again be opened for use as a restaurant or other attraction. Stay tuned.

Despite its spotty commercial use, this building houses some of the area's most significant history.

The Wreck of the *W&A*
At Willowdale

A group of picnickers from Calhoun, Georgia, set out on a special excursion train for an afternoon of adventure, bound for Chattanooga, Tennessee. They never made it. On a section of the track near Willowdale, fate dealt them a hand which turned a happy afternoon into a frightening trip into destiny.

"Onward thundered 179,
With hundreds of souls on behind.
Faster and faster it sped the rail,
'Til it reached a place called Willowdale."
(From "The Wreck Of The Willowdale" by T.B. Kendrick)

On the morning of June 12, 1912, a beautiful summer day dawned for a group of some 400 residents from Calhoun, Georgia, who were heading for the *Western & Atlantic Railroad's (W&A RR)* Train Number 179. The occasion was a picnic for members of the Knights of Phythias Lodge with their friends and families. For one of this group and two of the trainmen, it would be their last day on this earth. They just didn't know it yet.

Travel by train in the 19th and early 20th centuries was the rough equivalent of air travel of today. And when disaster struck a train, it was just as compelling as are the air-travel tragedies of today.

When the excursion was planned, a special passenger train had been hired for the day. The group planned to visit the Civil War battlefields in Chattanooga. At that point, the war had ended only a mere 47 years earlier, and there were still many relics left on the huge battlefield – free for the taking. Unfortunately, the only memories this group would retain of this day would be of suffering and death.

A cross-section of Gordon County was represented that morning as the train departed the Calhoun station amid much jubilation. Spirits were high. All indications pointed to a very memorable day. As things turned out, it was indeed memorable – just not the type memories one wishes to have.

The group departed Calhoun early, and by 8:00 a.m. were on the siding in Dalton some 20 miles north in Whitfield County. A southbound train was

Engine #179 of the *Western & Atlantic Railroad* was photographed here on June 12, 1912. It was the passenger cars pulled by this engine that derailed tragically near Willowdale in Whitfield County.

due through Dalton at 8:08, and once it had passed, the Chattanooga delegation continued their journey.

Approximately two miles north of Dalton, in an area known locally as Willowdale, a work crew was performing routine maintenance on the tracks. At the sound of the approaching northbound passenger train, the three men – Arthur Pilcher, Bill Richards, and John Shuman – quickly ceased working and moved with their tools to an area they presumed would be safe, waiting for the train to pass.

As the train neared the workers, the locomotive suddenly erupted from the tracks without warning. The cars which followed gyrated into tangled masses of splintering wood and buckling steel, their crumpled remains scattered about the hillside on either side of the tracks.

As the train neared the workers, the locomotive suddenly erupted from the tracks without warning.

The horrified three unsuspecting maintenance workers were immediately engulfed in the avalanche of wood, iron, and spewing debris. Richards and Shuman, amazingly, were not seriously injured by the wreckage. Section hand Pilcher, however, was killed, a victim of traumatic injuries from which he could not recover.

The fireman of the ill-fated #179 – Claud Holcomb of Resaca – was horrifyingly completely buried beneath the engine of the train. He reportedly died instantly of massive injuries.

Though there was understandably an intensive investigation into the cause of the tragedy, the explanation was met with doubt and even outrage from some. The investigators had suggested the cause of the accident was *"a spreading of the rails at the point of derailment."* It was speculated that

317

Photographed June 12, 1912, is a view of the tragic accident at Willowdale. Many passengers who were injured were enroute to a picnic in Calhoun. A section hand (Arthur Pilcher) working on the rail line at the time of the accident perished, as did the train's fireman, Claud Holcomb, and a passenger, Mrs. John A. Ray. (Photo courtesy of GA Dept. of Archives & History)

the high temperatures of the week previous could have been the culprit.

Skeptics, however, were quick to point out that the Willowdale curve had in fact been the scene of many serious wrecks in the past. Though none of the previous wrecks had equaled the magnitude of this disaster, it was reasoned that all the mishaps could not have been the result of "spreading rails," and many of the trains sped down that section of track much too swiftly.

Other doubters noted that the engine pulling No. 179 had earlier been in a serious accident south of Dalton. Could there have been a problem with it which caused it to initiate the accident by jumping the rails?

Eyewitness accounts of the wreck stated that immediately following the crash, the passengers showed great calmness and presence of mind. Within

This was back in the day when in times of emergency, everyone volunteered to help.

minutes, a make-shift emergency ward was assembled on the hillsides adjacent to the disaster site.

Within an hour, as soon as word had reached Dalton, all available physicians were rushed by special train to the Willowdale area. Much of the credit for this quick response was given to the local telephone exchange which voluntarily took the responsibility of locating the doctors and advising them of the needs involved.

Those victims most seriously injured were returned to Dalton on the train which had carried the physicians to the wreck site. Many victims interviewed in later days emphasized that it was the sight of so many injured bodies being loaded onto the train that brought the scope and magnitude of the catastrophe home to them.

In Dalton, all available hotel rooms were quickly occupied. There were in fact so many serious injuries that the local First Baptist Church was pressed into service as a hospital, as was the city park downtown, where rows of cots and litters revealed an all too graphic scene of injury and despair.

Scores of Dalton females volunteered their services as nurses for the injured, and as babysitters for the children – both injured and unscathed – who had been on board, since many of the parents of those children were hospitalized.

This was back in the day when in times of emergency, everyone volunteered to help. No one just stood around watching. One such lady, a Mrs. Statem whose home was in the vicinity of the derailment, donated her entire

Another view of the still smoldering ruins of the *W&A Railroad* wreck near Willowdale. (Photo courtesy of GA Dept. of Archives & History)

supply of linen for bedding and bandages. The ***North Georgia Citizen***, Dalton's weekly newspaper, reported that *"Mrs. Statem busied herself, despite the fact that she was in a 'delicate condition' (emphasis added), in assisting in caring for the injured, her work and generosity showing the noble woman she is."*

In all, four cars jumped the tracks that fateful day. The baggage car followed the engine down the eastern slope of the steep embankment, while the other cars fell to the right.

Engineer Charlie Kitchens was at the throttle and stayed his post, escaping with only a badly bruised and lacerated head and a broken arm. The conductor, A.W. Hill, escaped uninjured.

Those most seriously injured were evacuated to Dalton first, with a second run following shortly thereafter.

Meanwhile, back in Calhoun, word was filtering back via a special long distance telephone line established by the Dalton Telephone Company. This courtesy was extended to the victims without charge, and allowed the two cities to remain in uninterrupted communication.

In Calhoun, rumors were as rampant as fact, and a sense of shock pervaded the town. According to accounts in the next day's ***Calhoun Times***, townspeople were *"completely stunned by the news."* Later dispatches during the ensuing days detailed how the town seemed unable to come out of the stupor thrown over it by the serious injury to so many of its distinguished citizens.

In the aftermath of the disaster, the presence of "ambulance chasers" and other profiteers – those who attempt to turn another's tragedy into their personal gain – abounded.

> *In Calhoun, rumors were as rampant as fact, and a sense of shock pervaded the town.*

Photographed in 1990, the site at which the W&A Railroad train wrecked at Willowdale is pictured. Willowdale is just north (2 miles) of Dalton.

One enterprising photographer filmed stereopticon views of the horror only a few hours after it happened. Calhoun people reportedly turned out in record numbers to see the show, just to see how close they themselves had come to serious injury, even death.

Another scavenger, who, incidentally was never identified, went about the wreck site collecting edible food items from the many picnic baskets and undamaged items of passengers' personal property. He later was seen hawking his bounty around the wreck site and about Dalton during the days which followed.

"Enterprising" individuals unfortunately seemed to abound at the wreck site. One small girl, amazingly judged to be only about ten years of age, reportedly busied herself helping those critically injured, and then helping herself to their jewelry at the same time!

Two young boys who had escaped unscathed, evidently were determined not to miss the picnic they had been promised. Reports indicate that they collected a picnic basket and a blanket and spread their repast on the hillside amidst the pallets of the suffering.

Thankfully, more numerous than those who sought to profit from the wreck were those who gave unselfishly in this time of need. Many deeds of heroism were recorded, and physicians who were first on the scene credited many of the passengers with saving the lives of many who might otherwise have perished.

In all, eight individuals out of a passenger manifest of some 400 people were considered seriously injured. Of those, Mrs. John A. Ray, who sustained a serious back injury, was the only passenger who died. Others considered seriously injured were Dr. G.A. Anderson, a representative to the state legislature from Gordon County, and prominent Calhoun matron Mrs. Kate Littlefield. It was judged amazing that more passengers were not seriously injured or killed, such was the extent of the destruction.

First-hand reports from those who experienced the horror tended to be the most reliable. One account was rendered by Captain A.H. Hill, surprisingly a Civil War (Confederate) veteran: "I was at Gettysburg, but believe me, it was nothing like this. I'd rather go through another such battle as that one than to be in another accident like this."

It was judged amazing that more passengers were not seriously injured or killed, such was the extent of the destruction.

Miss Tilla Rooker, who with her brother Bart and sisters Ola Belle and Maude operated Calhoun's famous Rooker Hotel, was a passenger on the train. Accompanying her for the day's outing was her brother and Joshua Hamilton, Mr. Rooker's Negro man-servant. "It (the train) was just going too fast around a curve near Willowdale. . . and went off the rails," she explained some 77 years later. "Joshua in the baggage car was killed (and) my brother was injured. I was not injured, just scared half to death." That day, she would later testify, was her "most exciting event."

Once the initial shock of the tragedy had subsided, Calhoun residents began efforts to repay those Whitfield Countians who had so generously given of their time and resources. A purse containing nearly $100.00 was collected in Calhoun for Mrs. Statem who had donated all her linens. Though that seems like a paltry sum today, in 1912 it was a significant amount of money, the equivalent of approximately $2,700.00 in 2025.

The city of Calhoun, led by Mayor J.F. Allison and the aldermen; Col. J.G.B. Erwin, superintendent of the M.E. Sunday School; H.J. Roff, chancellor-commander of the Calhoun Lodge No. 264, Knights of Pythias; W.L. Hines, superintendent of the Baptist Sunday School; and Mrs. C.C. Harlan, president of the Calhoun Woman's Club, presented the city of Dalton with a formal resolution which concluded that the heroic, benevolent actions of many in Dalton had demonstrated *"for us and yourselves, woman in her*

> *Today, most prognosticators would surmise that simple excessive speed was the actual cause.*

gentlest and truest and man in his noblest aspects."

Regarding the officially-stated cause of the accident, follow-up investigations were conducted – such as could be done – but no definite cause other than "the spreading rails" was ever declared the culprit in the accident. Today, most prognosticators would surmise that simple excessive speed was the actual cause.

The tracks northward to Chattanooga remarkably were cleared and repaired that same day, and by nightfall, it was "business as usual" for the W & A.

On Friday following the wreck, the locomotive was raised from the ravine where it lay, and by noon, it was at rest on a side track, awaiting shipment to the factory where it would be rebuilt for further service in the W&A network.

That same Friday afternoon, the body of fireman Holcomb, having been prepared for burial, was shipped south to his home in Resaca where funeral services were held shortly thereafter. Mrs. Ray, the only fatality among the passengers, died several days later and was buried in a family cemetery in Gordon County. No report exists on where section hand Pilcher lived or where he was buried.

And of the victims who survived the wreck, their first-hand accounts and written recollections over some three-quarters of a century indicate that the Willowdale wreck was not something that was easily forgotten. It was, in fact, a haunting memory which most of those 400 individuals carried to their graves many years after they first cheated the *Grim Reaper* at Willowdale on a sunny morning in June, 1912.

Name Index

Topic Index

www.ingramcontent.com/pod-product-compliance
Lightning Source LLC
Chambersburg PA
CBHW060858120626
46553CB00001B/129